REIMAGINING THE NATION-S

REIMAGINING THE NATION-STATE
The Contested Terrains of Nation-building

Jim Mac Laughlin

Pluto Press

LONDON • STERLING, VIRGINIA

First published 2001 by Pluto Press
345 Archway Road, London N6 5AA
and 22883 Quicksilver Drive, Sterling, VA 20166-2012, USA
www.plutobooks.com

British Library Cataloguing in Publication Data
A catalogue record for this book is available from the British Library

Library of Congress Cataloging-in-Publication Data

Mac Laughlin, Jim.
  Reimagining the nation-state : the contested terrains of
nation-building / Jim Mac Laughlin.
       p. cm.
  ISBN 0-7453-1369-8 (hardback)
  1. Ireland—Politics and government—19th century. 2. National
characteristics, Irish—History—19th century. 3.
Nationalism—Ireland—History—19th century. 4. Irish question. I.
Title.
  DA950 .M19 2000
  941.5081—dc21

                                                    00-009418

ISBN   0 7453 1369 8 hardback
ISBN   0 7453 1364 7 paperback

10	09	08	07	06	05	04	03	02	01
10	9	8	7	6	5	4	3	2	1

Designed and produced for Pluto Press by
Chase Publishing Services, Fortescue, Sidmouth EX10 9QG
Typeset from disk by Gawcott Typesetting Services
Printed in the European Union by Antony Rowe, Chippenham   •

Contents

Acknowledgements

While researching and writing this book I have had to range far from the alienating world of the modern university. However, I have tried not to stray too far from the precious, and often anarchic, worlds of close friends and family members. Thus, while the university in Ireland today has become a far less critical, far more state-centred and colonised institution than it was even in the period described in this book, I literally still find enlightenment in the complex local, nationalist and international worlds of many old and new friends and acquaintances. These latter are far too numerous to mention. Many of them are – probably justifiably so – sceptical of writers and academics anyway to expect naming here. Nevertheless I thank, admire and respect all of you, and may you stay forever young.

As has been my custom over recent years, I offer this to the abiding memories of my sister, Evelyn, and my father, Paddy Mc Laughlin, and to the invincible spirit of my mother, Ellen Mac Callion.

Thanks also to Dr Willie Nolan of Geography Publications, Dublin, for permission to reprint as chapter ten a piece of work which I originally wrote for another volume.

Sincere thanks too to the Arts Faculty of University College, Cork, for financial support which helped defray costs incurred in writing this book. It has been appreciated.

Finally, if there is anything of worth here, I would like to dedicate it to Ethel Crowley, my cloud-lifter, who continues to bring light, wit and laughter into my life, and who brings not a little constructive criticism to all my work. Thanks.

Introduction

My father was a boy of ten at the start of the Great War and a married man in his early thirties at the beginning of the Second World War. I well remember him telling me how the teacher in the national school he attended, in a remote and very beautiful townland called Leckemy near the northern tip of Ireland, used to hammer out the shape of Ireland on the wooden floor of his classroom and would then get his pupils to draw around and copy this 'map' on to their jotters. He used the flat-headed brads with which blacksmiths fixed shoes to horses to literally nail Ireland to the floor of one classroom in the two-teacher school my father attended. There were no wallcharts and few maps in this school and the only decent map of the country would probably have hung on the wall of the local police barracks, some six miles away. Yet Master Kane's map left his pupils with an abiding image of Ireland which, in my father's case, could stay with them for almost 80 years.

Gramsci would have been a student at Turin University when my father was drawing away at maps in the 'fifth book', or fifth class, in this quiet country school. He coined the term 'organic intelligentsia' to describe men and women like those who taught my father and mother history, geography and the 'three Rs' – reading, writing and arithmetic – in between the start and the finish of the Great War. I have always respected the gentler among them for hammering maps into floorboards, instead of 'hammering' their pupils with anything that came to hand. Not all of them were gentle people, as I and many of those I grew up with in the 1960s and 1970s, can testify. Not more than a dozen families in the parish where my father grew up could afford to put a child through secondary school back then when he was a boy. Like the vast bulk of his generation he himself never went beyond the 'seventh book', or seventh class, in primary school. Yet, like many of his generation also, I never once remember him feeling in any way uneasy in the company of those whom he met later in life and who had far more formal education than he ever had. A builder and carpenter all his life, he was an avid reader of newspapers. He scarcely bothered with the local paper, however, and always considered the national paper superior to the local precisely because it carried world news and addressed national issues. He was also the possessor of one of the biggest books which we as children had ever seen, a dictionary of the English language and a doorstopper of a book of almost 1,500 pages. He bought it in Glasgow in the late 1930s and every time my parents 'flitted' house in the 1940s and 1950s, which was often in those days, that dictionary went with them. Like many new parents then, if not now, my father also owned an encyclopaedia, a ten-volume set of Harmsworth Encyclopaedia which had been published the year he was born and stayed in our family for the full duration of the twentieth century. These were the chief, and certainly the most valuable, books in our house right up until 'free education' was introduced in Ireland in the late 1960s. Our house was then flooded with books and comics, for ours was a large family in constant need of new, and secondhand, primary and secondary schoolbooks.

My father, at least at that time, had what might be called a tactile approach to books. The feel of a book, like the quality of the paper it was printed on, were as important to him as the knowledge contained between its covers. Even if he never got much of a chance at formal schooling himself, you see he had a nose for learning and a mind to go with it. Born into a large family on a small farm, he started working life as a stonemason and got less than four pounds per week in one of his first paid jobs – at the building of an ostentatious Catholic church 16 miles from where he lived. To this day my mother still remembers how priests then 'never paid anybody anything'. I learned from an early age that Catholic Ireland was built on the cheap by many men like my father. He left that job and set up as a 'jobbing builder' and his first son, Michael, joined him when he himself was still a young teenager. This was the norm for the time and together the two built dozens of fine houses, and repaired many more, all around the countryside where, as a result of their hard work, I was privileged to wander more freely and far more leisurely.

I recall these details here because this study insists that nations are socio-cultural and geographical constructs which literally have to be built from the ground up. That church which my father helped to build, that complicated map of nails on the floor of the school he attended, were far more influential than nationalist literature in stirring up images of the nation for his generation. Before nations can be built from the ground up they have to be lodged in the hearts and minds of people. Men like Master Kane clearly belonged to what Gramsci labelled the 'organic intelligentsia'. As elsewhere in nationalist Europe they were the unsung heroes of nation-building. They have been neglected almost as much as the men, like my father and oldest brother, who literally helped to build nations from the ground up and who peopled them with families.

The history of the past two centuries is adequate testimony that places have mattered as much to nationalists as they now do to critics of nationalism. The contested histories and geographies of Ireland have rendered this particularly the case in Ireland. To national separatists and unionist nationalists here places have always been 'debatable lands'. They were never simply the uncontested basis for the 'imagined community' of the nation. They were literally the contested terrains of nation-building. They were pawns in wider nation-building exercises, some of them going back to the seventeenth century. In Ireland as elsewhere in nation-building Europe small places nestled in symbolic landscapes of great antiquity. They were embedded in economic and geo-strategic landscapes that were part of much larger nation-building and empire-building projects. They literally were the homes of people, the homelands of what Gramsci, writing at the start of the twentieth century, referred to as 'people-nations' (Gramsci, 1971, p. 418). Not surprisingly nationalism in Ireland has been a banal force and an 'improving' ideology. To sceptical students of nationalism in more recent decades local places have literally been the starting points for politics. In Ireland they constituted the very elements of different versions of the nation. They are also keys to an understanding of interrupted nation-building exercises which, many believe, have yet to run their course. Whatever else they were, unionist nationalism and national separatism in Ireland have always been historically oriented, socially embodied ideologies. They literally had their own way of dealing with the land and its resources, and their own quite distinctive territorial imperatives.

Contrary to Gellner, Marxism was not the only social scientific tradition which contained within it 'an anticipation of the decline of nationalism' (Gellner, 1972, p.147). Students of nationalism, like postmodernists and globalisation theorists, have grown sceptical of the naturalisation of nationalism by nationalists, including nationalist social scientists. Chapter 1 shows how this intellectual rationalisation of nationalism accompanied its naturalisation. It had its origins in historiography and in ethnocentric accounts of the rise of the modern nation. It reached its climax in a powerful nineteenth-century defence of 'big-nation'/unionist nationalism –

not least in Unionist Ulster and Ireland (Mac Laughlin, 1986a, pp. 14–16). It condemned minority nationalisms as Balkanising forces for challenging the authenticity of a nation-centred modernity. Thus the authors of these accounts, whether in history books, political pamphlets, the provincial press, national newspapers or academic journals, insisted that nationalism was the prerogative of progressive peoples. It applied only to powerful – i.e. 'power-filled' – places. If today we have grown sceptical of the naturalness and limited universalism of nationalism, this is because we live in an age of postmodern scepticism. This is a world apart from the secular certainties and 'scientific' nationalisms of the nineteenth century. The rationalism of unionist nationalism then was so much taken for granted that few felt the need to challenge it. The fact that Irish nationalists did so is perhaps their most important achievement. It is also their most neglected, and problematic, contribution to the theory and practice of nation-building since the eighteenth century.

This study suggests that the imagined community of the nation in Ireland always possessed a logical contingency precisely because it was historically and geographically contingent. Yet historians and cultural nationalists have, until recently, generally taken the territorial integrity and historical inevitability of 'their' nation for granted. This naturalisation of nationalism was especially true of 'big nations' or unionist nations. As Ireland, Spain, Yugoslavia and Canada demonstrate, theorists of nation-building have for too long disregarded the rootedness of nationalism and political regionalisms in the ethnic geographies and divided communities of nation-building societies. Part of the reason for this was that hegemonic traditions in social philosophy in the nineteenth century looked upon minority nationalisms as political and regional anomalies. They regarded unionist nationalism as the natural attribute of progressive peoples. They treated the 'big nation' as the political and geopolitical norm. Scorned as 'Balkanising forces', minority nationalities all across Europe were expected to go gently in the dark night of unionist nations, and on terms laid down by the unionist state. Failing that they could, like the Irish, 'go it alone', reject 'big-nation' nationalist modernity, embrace a nineteenth-century version of 'small nation' post-modernity, and face an uphill struggle to establish the credentials and political legitimacy of the small ethno-nation.

This was a challenge which the ethnic intelligentsia in rural societies like Ireland had to accept more or less on their own. The ethnic intelligentsia of Europe's more powerful nations were literally arraigned against them. The latter were to the forefront of a quasi-scientific naturalisation of 'big-nation' nationalism. They defended the hegemony of the nation-building and imperialistic haute bourgeoisie. They functioned as scholar-politicians or scholarly nationalists who supported the projects of unionist nation-builders and empire builders alike. Never the friends of 'lesser peoples' or minority nations, they developed a whole range of racialised precepts that justified the marginalisation of ethnic minorities. It is not generally recognised that defences of small-nation nationalism then emanating from the peripheries of Europe, not least from Ireland, required colossal intellectual integrity. Those who defended the small nation went against the grain of unionist nationalism and imperial colonial aggrandisement in the nineteenth century. Academics then, not least state-centred 'ascendancy academics' throughout the United Kingdom of Great Britain and Ireland, were considered professionals precisely because they were skilled and proficient in knowledge sanctioned by academic disciplines and the sciences. They were professional in a wider sense also because they used their academic accomplishments to further the state-centred and colonial agendas of the nation-building bourgeoisie in the Darwinian half of the nineteenth century. In other words they viewed themselves, and were viewed by others, as state functionaries. They performed services for the public good, and in the national or nationalist interest. As Chapter 1 suggests, the institutionalisation and subsequent development of social science, political economy, eugenics, ethnography, geography and anthropology can partly be explained in terms of their 'scientific' legitimations of 'big-nation' nationalism and colonial expansion. Like the German geographer and social Darwinist Friedrich Ratzel, they believed that the struggle for survival literally involved a struggle for space (Ratzel, 1898, p. 356). To unionist nationalists everywhere, in Ireland, mainland Europe and North America, it also involved mastery of nature on a grand scale. Until the rise of the Irish Home Rule movement this resulted in the political incorporation of minority peoples within the folds of the powerful nation.

In challenging the prerogative of the Anglo-Irish aristocracy to own Irish resources and represent Irish people, the ethnic intelligentsia in Ireland were insisting that the Irish were as worthy of 'peoplehood' – and a homeland – as any other nationality. They transformed Irishmen and Irishwomen from mere 'serial numbers' in an Anglo-centric landscape into people in their own right. The

Irish now were a people who literally had a right to self-determination in their 'own land'. In so doing the Irish intelligentsia reacted against the 'hegemonism of possessing' that was such a distinctive feature of English rule from the seventeenth to the nineteenth century.

This study suggests that nations, whatever their scale, were historical 'happenings' and geographical constructs. They were rarely abstract 'imagined communities' as Anderson implies (Anderson, 1983, p. 15). They were never the 'natural' homelands of 'peoples' as nationalists insist. They entailed tremendous amounts of social and environmental engineering from a very early stage in the evolution of national modernities. They authenticated themselves, or more accurately had structures of authenticity imposed upon them. Thus unionist nationalists invented tradition, ethnicised historical records, claimed territory for the powerful nation, dismissed the demands of minority peoples and rival nationalities, and marginalised the interests of the socially subordinate. This study also suggests that nationalisms in Ireland were always expressions of practical politics. As such nationalism, whether in unionist or national separatist garb, was rooted in concrete socio-historical formations and in well-defined geographical milieux. That is why this study does not take the historical or geographical logic of Irish nationalists, unionist nationalists or Ulster Unionists for granted. It seeks to avoid the ethnic historicism of Anthony Smith (1986), the cultural reductionism of Benedict Anderson (1983) and Homi Bhabha (1990) and the economic reductionism of Hobsbawm (1962, 1988), Wallerstein (1974) and Nairn (1977). It recognises the inter-relatedness of intellectual, social, economic and political forces underlying the quite different and frequently contentious processes of nation-building that emerged in Ireland over the course of four centuries or more.

This study also emphasises the social class and ethnic origins of the organic intelligentsia. These 'organisational men' not only defended the historical legitimacy of the 'historic' nation on the one hand, or the 'Irish nation' on the other – they literally 'realised' their versions of the 'imagined community' in very concrete terms in the contested terrains of nation-building Ireland. They also fostered the political and cultural hegemony of the nation-building petty bourgeoisie. That is why this study devotes as much space to the structuring agencies of national consciousness as it does to the ideals of nation-builders, and to nationalist and unionist idealists.

In rejecting categorisations of the country as an 'English colony', this study views Ireland as a building block of the unionist nation from the seventeenth century onwards. Chapters 1 to 3 suggest that racist defences of nation-building here regularly constructed Ireland as a barbarous wilderness in need of taming by civilised 'planters'. Viewed thus seventeenth- and eighteenth-century Ireland was inhabited by 'good' settlers who were relentlessly 'stalked' by the 'barbaric' Irish. The latter, it was argued, were wilfully intent upon wrecking plantation projects for transforming Ireland into a 'home country' of the English nation. English visitors regularly painted Ireland as a country without history in any uplifting, ennobling or evolutionary sense. English settlers in Ireland placed England at the civilised centre of an otherwise disorderly world. They insisted that Ireland's proper place literally lay within an expansionist, nation-building Britain. They deemed themselves to be equipped with all the skills necessary for incorporating premodern Gaelic society into the modern English nation. They literally had mastery over the native Irish, and over Irish nature, and as such deserve to be ranked among the first lords of humankind. Chapter 2 suggests that modern demography as 'political arithmetic' had its roots in this Anglo-centric tradition of writing about Ireland and the Irish (Mac Laughlin, 1999d, p. 327). This tradition insisted that improvements in the 'common weal' could only be achieved when those guided by reason, rather than by custom or historical tradition, were granted land and entrusted with public office. Analysing the works of Hobsbawm, Gramsci, Anderson and Wallerstein, Chapters 3 and 4 show how nations were the building blocks of bourgeois society in the eighteenth and nineteenth centuries. This gave rise to a major paradox of nationalism, i.e. the most vociferous defenders of the rights of nations were themselves responsible for hostile constructs of minority nationalities as 'Balkanising forces'. They also reduced those living beyond the narrow metropolitan world of western Europe to the status of 'inferior peoples' and 'colonial subordinates'. They condemned Irish nationalism because it threatened the integrity of the 'historic' nation and challenged an English modernity in Ireland. The Irish had challenged a whole range of Enlightenment values in Ireland in the seventeenth and eighteenth centuries. In the nineteenth century they rejected 'big-nation' nationalism in Ireland and challenged the very structures of British modernity. Yet Hobsbawm is historically and geographically incorrect in arguing that claims to nationhood based upon such 'unfashionable traits' as ethnicity, religion, language and shared historical experiences were chiefly confined to the post-colonial half of the twentieth century (Hobsbawm, 1977, p. 5). Nationalism as national separatism in Ireland has a far more ancient history than that. It goes back at least to the eighteenth century when Irish nationalists staked their claims to nationhood precisely upon these distinctive traits. Similarly, Ulster Unionists revealed themselves as defenders of the 'historic' unionist nation in Ireland, and as successful separatists who wanted no part in the irredentism of Irish nationalism. As Chapter 8 shows, they based their defence of the Union on quasi-racial arguments regarding the 'inability' of 'lesser peoples' to govern themselves or rule 'successful people' like Ulster Protestants. They believed that nationalist Ireland could not go it alone in a new world order of powerful nations, colonised countries and peripheral minorities. Thus unionist nationalism in Ulster had its own rationale and a considerably longer pedigree which predated the rise of national separatism and Home Rule in the nineteenth century. It was rooted in a much deeper landscape of nation-building in Great Britain and Ireland and was saturated in a highly racialised tradition of state formation which, since the sixteenth and seventeenth centuries, insisted that Ireland's proper place was in the United Kingdom.

Chapters 7 to 10 show how the battle to win the plebeian sectors of Catholic Ireland to the cause of nation-building occupied most of Ireland's 'long nineteenth century'. It involved not only constitutional and revolutionary contestations with 'English rule' in Catholic Ireland. It also entailed a struggle for 'hearts and minds' by an organic intelligentsia who struggled to incorporate the subordinate poor into the nation-building world of their social class 'betters'. In the event the pragmatic 'new Ireland' of the late nineteenth century was radically different from more idealistic versions of Ireland and Irishness dreamed up by nationalist intellectuals. Despite the vigour of the cultural renaissance, the radicalism of plebeian politics, and the intellectual strengths of revolutionary thinkers, the country fell to men of property, not least to the substantial tenantry, owners of industry, the shopocracy and clergymen. They literally 'built' Catholic Ireland and Unionist Ulster. Catholic Ireland was a country constructed by and for hegemonic sectors in Irish society. Thus this study suggests that nationalism was not 'achieved' through a mass conversion of the subordinate poor to the state-centred agendas of their social superiors. It was achieved instead by priests, nuns, teachers, newspapermen and political propagandists who struggled relentlessly to convince the poor that their best interests lay in a nationalist Ireland under the leadership of 'natural leaders' drawn from the petty bourgeoisie. In this 'other Ireland' the pulpit and the national school forged citizens out of what remained of the Irish poor after famine, poverty, emigration and unemployment sapped their energies and depleted their ranks. In the event the Irish poor became citizens of the small Irish nation, subjects of a Catholic power that ranged well beyond the narrow ground of nationalist Ireland. Because the gospel of nationalism was preached from the same altars as the Christian gospels, the Catholic poor often found it difficult to know where the spiritual pronouncements of their religious superiors left off, and where their class preferences and political teachings took over.

1 The Naturalisation of Nation-building in the Nineteenth Century: The Anomalies of Minority Nations

Nationalism and the Modern Nation-state

One of the major paradoxes surrounding the study of nationalism is the fact that, despite the duration of the process in the metropolitan world at least, theories of nation-building and nationalism are of relatively recent origin (Blaut, 1987; Breully, 1982; Davis, 1978; Gellner, 1983; Hobsbawm, 1990; Hroch, 1985; Smith, 1981). This is all the more surprising in view of the fact that the nineteenth century was an age of nation-building which also witnessed the coming of age of the social and political sciences. For most of that century, however, the study of nationalism was imbued with nationalist and anti-nationalist sentiments inherited from highly charged racist, nationalist and anti-nationalist environments. The nineteenth was clearly also a century which, for the most part, frowned upon minority expressions of nationalism and ethno-nationalism. It was a time when everything was done to prevent Europe's ethnic and nationalist minorities from engaging in nation-building. On the other hand nationalism-as-national-unification was the nation-building norm for much of the nineteenth century. This expressed itself as Unionism in the contested terrains of nineteenth-century nation-building Ireland. It was equally evident in the powerful drives for national unification in Germany and Italy in the 1860s and 1870s (Clark, 1998; Rietbergen, 1998). This brand of nationalism had its origins in post-Revolutionary France in the late eighteenth century. It was especially important in class-divided industrial Britain in the nineteenth century. Indeed it was encouraged precisely because it contributed to a politics of national – if not nationalist – consensus while all the while fostering the growth of strong multi-national nation-states. As an expression of 'big-nation' nationalism this genre of nationalism was never meant to apply to minority nationalities – let alone minority nations – like for example the Irish, the Welsh, the Bretons or the Basques (Williams, 1984a, p. 114). From the start it cast serious doubt on the ability of these small nations, and other European ethnic minorities, to go it alone in a nineteenth-century world consisting of a handful of powerful nation-states lording it over myriad national minorities at home and a whole range of politically subordinate colonial societies abroad.

National separatism, especially minority expressions of nationalism – as in Irish nationalism and Basque nationalism – were to be resisted because they threatened the territorial integrity of some of western Europe's most powerful nation-states like late-nineteenth-century Britain and Spain (de Cortazar and Espinosa, 1994, p. 284; Heiberg, 1989). Minority nationalisms were also condemned because it was felt they could give bad example to struggling nationalities in central and eastern Europe and to colonial elites in countries as far apart as India and South Africa. Ethno-nationalist and national separatist movements were still being disparaged as 'Balkanising' forces as recently as the 1960s. They too were seen to threaten the breakup of highly centralised state systems and encourage the transformation of the late colonial world into innumerable nation-states. Elie Kedourie, a leading student of nationalism in the 1960s, rekindled this scepticism towards post-war expressions of nationalism when he suggested that this was an ideology that was invented in the nineteenth century but was now a redundant, even a retrogressive force in the brave new world of the 1950s and 1960s (Kedourie, 1960, 1971). Kedourie, writing of the nineteenth century, was clearly addressing a post-war western world that was witnessing the breakup of European empires. He insisted that nationalism was simply one of a whole series of Kantian Enlightenment doctrines which undermined world order and upset an old global political status quo. National liberation struggles, including the new anti-imperial nationalisms of the colonial world, were to be reviled because they threatened the destruction of this European world order which, some argued, had not yet reached its full developmental potential.

Hans Kohn, writing around the same time as Kedourie, was also extremely pessimistic about the future of nation-building and nationalism in the modern world. Writing between two world wars which saw Europe torn apart by international warfare, Kohn suggested that 'errors of judgement' regarding the centrality of nationalism in historical affairs contributed greatly to these global conflagrations (Kohn, 1955, p. 89). Bemoaning the lack of a

Rousseauian confidence in the goodness of individuals, he was even more sceptical than Kedourie about the ability of national collectivities to act as good and peaceful forces once the fetters imposed by colonialism and by traditional dynasties were once removed. Thus, writing from a clear Euro-centric perspective, Kohn insisted that the new nationalisms, particularly in the Middle East, Africa and Asia, could never hope to create the 'open society' which, he believed, classical nationalism had fostered in nine-teenth-century western Europe. Instead, he argued, post-war nation-building in the colonial world marked a trend towards collective and territorial self-assertions in global regions which the modern world, especially the west, could well do without. Nationalism, Kohn concluded, was a luxury which Third World countries could ill afford because it would result in escalating defence budgets and detach them from the overlordship of pater-nalistic metropolitan societies without whose help, so many anti-nationalists in the west believed, the Third World could not prosper.

Kedourie and Kohn were not alone in this disparagement of nationalism. Louis Snyder, another leading authority on this topic in the 1950s, labelled nationalism the 'great enigma' in an age otherwise characterised by a modern optimism (Snyder, 1954, p. 62). For Snyder indeed nationalism was an ideological relic from a more backward age. Harold Laski also regarded nationalism as an obsolete and destructive force in this modern world system (Laski, 1944, p. 7). Erich Fromm similarly excoriated nationalism as 'our incest, our idolatry, and our insanity' (Fromm, 1968, p. 19). Bertrand Russell encapsulated the western bourgeois Eurocentrism of all these writers, when he wrote:

> although everybody is agreed that the nationalism of other countries is absurd ... the nationalism of one's own country is noble and splendid and anyone who does not uphold it is a lily-livered cur. (Russell, 1965, p. 108)

More than any other modern political ideology nationalism, for a whole variety of reasons, has perplexed its students. Carleton Hayes, a leading analyst of nationalist movements in the 1930s, concluded that 'we really do not know what has given vogue to nationalism in modern times' (Hayes, 1953, p. 16). After a lifetime spent studying it, Hugh Seton-Watson, another leading authority on the nation-state, was driven to the conclusion that no 'scientific definition' of a nation can be devised. He went on to state:

All I can find to say is that a nation exists when a significant number of people in a community consider themselves to form a nation, or behave as if they formed one. It is not necessary that the whole of the population should so feel, or behave, and it is not possible to lay down dogmatically a minimum percentage of a population which must be so affected. When a significant group holds this belief, it possesses 'national consciousness'. Common sense suggests that if this group is exceedingly small, and does not possess great skill in propaganda, or a strong disciplined army to maintain it until it has been able to spread national consciousness down into much broader strata of the population, then the nationally conscious elite will not succeed in creating a nation, and is unlikely to be able to indefinitely remain in power on the basis of a fictitious nation. (Seton-Watson, 1977, p. 42)

As I have argued elsewhere, little is to be gained from this genre of criticism which suggests that nationalism in nineteenth-century Europe was an entirely natural and progressive force, whereas demands for national self-determination in the late colonial world of the mid-twentieth century were considered irrational at best, or worse still retrogressive (Mac Laughlin, 1986a, p. 313). We have to analyse the contextual settings of nation-building and nationalism, explain how nationalist ideology contributed to the development of bourgeois hegemony. We also have to relate the nation-centred social sciences which legitimised nation-building to the socio-economic and territorial environments within which they evolved. The sections that follow begin this general inquiry by critically examining the role of the intelligentsia, including professional academics, in the ethnicisation of politics in western Europe in the nineteenth century.

The Intellectual Origins of Modern Nationalism

The study of nationalism has been seriously hampered by the too close identification of the ideology with the nationalist intelligentsia, especially with cultural nationalists. Even today nationalism is regarded as a middle-class ideology imposed upon apolitical masses by an ethnic intelligentsia whose manifest destiny it is to convince the latter of the superiority of nation-centred goals over and above the narrow parochialism and sectionalist interests of the rural poor and working class. Discussing the nineteenth-century origins of Basque separatism Stanley Payne has argued that nationalism was born out of the 'intersection of traditionalism with modernity' (Payne, 1974,

p. 131). Like all modern ideologies, he added, it was a creation of the intelligentsia which was subsequently imposed upon the masses. Similarly Anthony Smith, one of the leading theorists of nation-building and nationalism today, has suggested that nationalism's primary function is 'the resolution of the crisis of the intelligentsia' (Smith, 1981, p. 15). Smith and his many followers interpret the resurgence of national separatism in western Europe since the 1960s, including the more recent upsurge of ethno-nationalisms in India and the Soviet Union in the 1970s and 1980s, as perfectly natural expressions of ethnic protest. Under the hegemony of a valiant ethnic intelligentsia, these new nationalist movements, it is argued, have been struggling against 'big-nation' nationalism, the over-centralisation of government, and the 'unnaturalness' of 'foreign' rule (Akbar, 1985, pp. 304–8; Chatterjee, 1986, pp. 18–25; Hiro, 1994, pp. 304–25; Huttenbach, 1990, pp. 1–7). The modern ethnic intelligentsia, Smith adds, not only comprises cultural nationalists and other idealists – it also includes 'hard-headed' technocrats intent on overcoming the 'political malaise induced by the bureaucratic apparatus of the modern state' (Smith, 1996b). He neglects to mention that many members of the nineteenth-century ethnic intelligentsia were equally 'hard headed'. They comprised what C. Wright Mills would have labelled 'organisational men', that is, local leaders who literally stitched local communities into the nation-state (Mills, 1963, pp. 23–34). Discussing the interplay between linguistic and ethnic factors on the one hand, with political and economic factors in nation-building on the other, Smith argues that most nationalist movements have been more concerned with cultural than with economic or political issues (Smith, 1996b). In so doing he fails to explain the relationship between the nationalism of language defence movements and cultural nationalists on the one hand and the political and economic objectives of powerful sectors in nation-building societies on the other. Many nationalist and separatist movements have begun life as coteries of cultural nationalists concerned more about language decline, folklore, traditional lifestyles and cultural imperialism than with state-centred political or economic issues. However, as the case of nineteenth-century Irish nationalism clearly shows, their transformation into full-blown national movements has often depended upon their linkages with more powerful sectors of society who had a far more materialist, and a far more state-centred political agenda than that of either cultural nationalists or language defence movements. A focus on the class origins of the ethnic intelligentsia and their relations with these powerful interest groups in capitalist, and now more recently in post-communist societies, can throw more light upon the reasons for nationalist successes and failures than an exclusive focus on the cultural and ideological underpinnings of modern nationalism.

The 'idealist' approach to nationalism which emphasises the role of the ethnic intelligentsia in the mobilisation of nationalist forces can be faulted on at least three grounds. First, it ignores the many transformations that can occur within nationalist movements between their moment of inception and their final victory. Historically speaking at least, nationalist movements which began as ethnic defence movements have had a habit of broadening out into much wider political blocs that served the disparate political and economic interests of whole sections of nation-building societies (Mac Laughlin, 1986a, p. 317). Second, most writers in the idealist mode of theorising tend to over-emphasise the role of subjective factors in the origins and success of nationalist movements. They tend to explain away their successes in terms of the cultural attributes, particularly the cultural authenticity, of ethnic populations in their struggle for self-determination (Smith, 1988, pp. 13–16). In so doing they reify ethnicity, transform it into an abstract theoretical category, and attribute historical agency to ethnicity itself rather than to the human agents of historical change. This is another way of saying that idealist interpretations of nation-building and nationalism attach more explanatory power to cultural and subjective factors – language, religion and ethnicity – than they do to objective forces and political and economic factors. At their most extreme they regard nationalism simply as an ideological expression of the intelligentsia whom they view as mere trajectories of underlying natural cultural forces. Finally, and perhaps most serious of all, idealist perspectives on nationalism are elitist in the extreme. They often ignore the capacity of subordinate social groups to oppose middle-class nationalist objectives, to reject the leadership of the nationalist intelligentsia, and to formulate their own socio-economic and cultural agendas inside and outside parameters set down by their nation-building 'betters'. This happened again and again in nineteenth-century western Europe, as the examples of Ireland, Spain, France, Italy and Germany clearly show. Workers and peasants here regularly rejected the nation-centred plans of conservative cultural nationalists and the nationalist middle class. They frequently gravitated instead towards socialism, syndicalism and even anarchism. As Hobsbawm has shown, they often tended to place internationalism and international class solidarity on a higher plane than inter-class solidarity and support for the narrow nationalisms of those who sought to tie them into the nation-state (Hobsbawm, 1982, pp. 75–85).

Quite often also the success of minority nationalist movements was predicated upon a widening of their cultural agenda to encompass the social and economic concerns of subordinate sectors like, for example, the working class and rural poor. This was the case not only with Irish nationalism in the nineteenth century but also with Plaid Cymru and a host of other smaller nationalist movements, in this century. As Gwynn A. Williams has shown, modern Welsh nationalism had its origins in a rural-based traditionalist nonconformist cultural pressure group concerned with the defence of the Welsh culture and the preservation of the Welsh language (Williams, 1985, pp. 280–5). Their narrowing of nationalism to a focus on purely cultural and linguistic issues, however, presented the leaders of Plaid Cymru with a whole range of problems in the formative years of the movement's growth. Emphasis on the language, for example, not only marked out the Welsh from the rest of Great Britain. As the geolinguist Colin Williams suggests, it also separated the Welsh-speaking Welsh from non-Welsh speakers and emphasised the gap between Welsh-speaking rural communities in the valleys and the industrial working class of south Wales (Williams, 1982, p. 12). The 1960s and 1970s witnessed the transformation of Plaid Cymru into a political party with a much wider regional, social and economic agenda, one that appealed across social classes to urban and rural communities alike.

Medhurst has shown how Basque nationalism in the late nineteenth and early twentieth centuries was firmly set in a socially conservative ultra-Catholic mould (Medhurst, 1982, pp. 37–42). Its principal ideologue, Sabino de Arana, sought to use nationalism to protect Basque culture, and the Basque country, from the forces of modernisation. While this seemed 'natural' in a region where rural fundamentalism and religious traditionalism were strong, middle-class supporters of the Partido Nacionalista Vasco (PNV) in the industrial heartland of the Basque country were not at all happy with the movement's clerical and rural leadership. This group split from the nationalist bloc in 1910 in order to form a breakaway party under the slogan of 'Fatherland and Liberty'. Their nationalism was more urban-based and far less identified with conservative Catholicism than the original founders of PNV were. Anti-clericalism at this stage, a powerful force in other parts of Spain, was not a major issue in Vizcaya, the heartland of national separatism and the most industrialised province of the Basque country. However, the steady growth of trade unionism clearly was. As Harrison has shown, the Basque middle class here gravitated towards nationalism partly because it thwarted class unity among the native working class and immigrants from the south of Spain (Harrison, 1977, pp. 371–6). Class differentiation in and around Bilbao had reached significant proportions in the early part of the twentieth century. Workers in the Bilbao region in particular often couched their demands for social change outside nationalist parameters. To remedy this situation bourgeois nationalists fostered the development of a nationalist trade union called Solidaridad de Trabajadores Vascos. This split the working class along ethnic and separatist lines and aroused the hostility of Spain's most powerful union, the socialist-led Union General de Trabajadores (UGT) which had branches all over Spain. The latter was deeply resentful of the nationalisation and ethnicisation of the Spanish working class and did all in its power to prevent further nationalist incursions into the arena of working-class politics.

Class and Bourgeois Hegemony in the Nineteenth Century

Hobsbawm has noted that nationalism in the nineteenth century rarely originated with the rural poor or the working class (Hobsbawm, 1982, p. 79). Instead, he argues, it usually developed outside the arena of subordinate class politics, while relying all the while upon these sectors for its success. Indeed Hobsbawm has argued that nations were building blocks of capitalism in the nineteenth century. Nationalism then also was crucial for the political success of the bourgeoisie and the petty bourgeoisie in western Europe and North America (Hobsbawm 1988, p. 105). International socialists and working-class radicals here often regarded nationalism as inimical to the interests of the working class. This was especially the case in Ireland by the late nineteenth and early twentieth centuries when nationalism frequently reflected the state-centred political objectives of a conservative Catholic bourgeoisie, including the petty bourgeoisie. Nationalist leaders here, as in other European countries, demanded that feminists, workers and small farmers should sink their class and gender differences with men of property in order to construct a unified and powerful Irish nation (Beresford Ellis, 1975). Insisting that Catholic workers should seek a nationalist, rather than a class-based or radical solution to their problems, they also contributed to the further alienation of the north-east's Protestant working class from rural Catholic, nation-building Ireland. In the event state-centred Unionism in Ulster became almost a Protestant mirror image of southern Catholic nationalism. Thus the rise of labour politics in the north and south of nation-building Ireland provoked rightist, and nationalist, responses among those most threatened by it. To deal with that threat Catholic men of wealth in the south, and Protestant landowners and industrial capitalists in the north-east, organised in regionally based ethnic alliances which transcended social class divisions. In so doing they aggravated, but did not create, the ethnic divisions that have since marked the political landscape of the island. This study will show that the replacement of a radical leadership by a conservative one drawn from the churches and the ethnic middle classes, at least outside the area of Unionist hegemony, had far reaching consequences for working-class unity in Ireland. In the north-east this fostered the development of a Unionist bloc wherein loyalism was as much a cross-class expression of political regionalism as a nation-centred political ideology. Here ethnic conservatism, tempered with a strong plebeian and sectarian tradition of rural and working-class activism, developed not so much at the expense of secular working-class radicalism but as a substitute for it. In the rest of the country a similar process of ethno-genesis was taking place among the rural Catholic population. The end result was a system of cultural and political apartheid which sought to immunise Catholic workers from radical influences emanating from Britain and the north-east of Ireland. Yet, as these and other examples also show, it was always hard to prevent working-class consciousness emerging in late nineteenth-century Ireland, even during periods of intense nationalist and national separatist patriotism.

Sam Clark and David Fitzpatrick have also emphasised the social class origins of Irish nationalism in nineteenth-century rural Ireland (Clark, 1978, pp. 23–39; Fitzpatrick, 1982, pp. 37–42). Far from simply being a primordial or cultural reaction against the forces of Anglicisation, nationalism here was a socio-economic and political construct that rarely presented a united front. Moreover, such unity as did exist did not signify much agreement on nationalist aims or nationalist strategies. Neither did it betoken undiluted enthusiasm for the cause of nationalism. In nationalist Ireland as in many other nation-building countries in central and eastern Europe, nationalist coteries saw themselves as unwilling witnesses to the demise of native cultures threatened by the forces of modernisation. Initially at least they avoided conspicuously political issues in case they might sever links between town and country, or otherwise disrupt the fragile cohesion that bound nation-building and class-structured societies together.

Fitzpatrick suggests that the risks and costs which different sectors of nineteenth-century Irish society were prepared to take for the cause of the nation were measured in terms of the benefits that they hoped to derive from it (Fitzpatrick, 1998, p. 113). That is why, as the present study argues, the success of nation-building here often depended upon the incorporation of the aims and objectives of dominant sectors in Irish society on to the agendas of cultural nationalists. This more than anything else transformed nationalism from a coterie of language defenders and Gaelic culture enthusiasts into a much broader-based political movement whose leadership derived from the Catholic church, the Catholic bourgeoisie, the petty bourgeoisie, the shopocracy and the professional middle classes. In their eagerness to harness every movement of rural and working-class activism to their state-centred projects, nationalist leaders here regularly resorted to the language of radicalism, if not political violence. This was particularly the case in underdeveloped regions along the west coast where national leaders often had great difficulty convincing local communities of the relevance of nationalism to their grassroots struggles. Elsewhere, especially in the agricultural heartlands of the south and south-east of the country, the language of rural radicalism gave way to cultural nationalism and rural conservatism. In this way nationalist parties were forged into national parties intent upon the upkeep of law and order, the defence of landed property, and the propagation of rural fundamentalism and conservatism.

Far from being epiphenomenal ideological abstractions unrelated to their socio-political and regional contexts, ethnic identities in late nineteenth and early twentieth century Ireland and France, as in other European countries, coloured many aspects of the lives of ordinary people (Fitzpatrick, 1998, pp. 35–47; Weber, 1977, pp. 234–46; Williams, 1985, pp. 1–43). They were never simply superficial characteristics of otherwise undivided societies. Thus, as this study suggests, the processes of ethno-genesis in Ireland as elsewhere could never be taken for granted. It always had to be carefully nurtured. Far from occurring in a regional, social vacuum, national separatism in the north-east of Ireland was in some respects a derivative political phenomenon, while in other respects it was sui generis. It was derivative in that it was partially a reaction against a 'one nation' nationalism that had its roots largely in the Catholic south of Ireland, particularly in the agricultural heartlands and prosperous provincial towns of the midlands and south-west of the country. However, it was also sui generis in that it reflected the socio-economic and cultural interests of Protestants in the north-east of Ireland at a particular stage in that region's social and economic development. The north-east was at once a place apart from rural Catholic nation-building Ireland and an integral part of the United Kingdom and the British empire. Ulster Unionism was also a confident expression of national separatism and an assertion of British nationalism which had its roots in the north-east of Ireland (Mac Laughlin, 1980, pp. 15–27). It differed in one important respect from contemporary manifestations of national separatism. Its objective was less the creation of an ethnic statelet than maintenance of the territorial integrity of the United Kingdom. Aside from Ireland, the Basque country and a number of other small nations in eastern and central Europe, national separatism for the most part has been a twentieth-century, not simply a nineteenth-century phenomenon (Williams, 1980). It generally rests its case on cultural distinctions and its watchwords are identity and regional autonomy as opposed to national conformity and cultural assimilation. Viewed thus Ulster Unionism was a reaction against the 'one nation' nationalism in Irish nationalism and a defence of 'big-nation' nationalism in British nationalism. It sought to maintain the integrity, not least the territorial integrity, of the United Kingdom of Great Britain and Ireland. Thus it was at once an expression of British nationalism and a manifestation of national separatism on nation-building Irish soil. It sought maintenance of the Union, while all the while seeking to separate the more industrialised north-east from Catholic nation-building rural Ireland. Its sheer success revealed the weakness of Irish nationalist assumptions that a country with clearly defined geographical boundaries should 'naturally' form a single nation.

The Ethnic Intelligentsia and the 'Naturalisation' of the Nation-state

Historians and cultural nationalists alike have, until recently, taken the territorial integrity and historical inevitability of the nation-state for granted. In so doing they have elevated nationalism above other ideologies and ignored the many socio-economic, political and indeed regional difficulties that often stood in the way of nation-building, both in nineteenth-century western Europe and in the Americas. As the history of Ireland, Spain, France,

Czechoslovakia, Yugoslavia and Canada (to name but a few) clearly demonstrate, most theorists of nation-building here have for too long disregarded the rootedness of political regionalism and ethnic differences in multi-national societies well into the twentieth century. Part of the reason for this was that dominant traditions in social philosophy and the social sciences in the nineteenth century treated nationalism as a natural attribute of progressive societies (Mac Laughlin, 1986b, pp. 14–17). This caused many, and not only nationalist elites, to look on nation-building as something which, to paraphrase the Irish nationalist leader Charles Stewart Parnell, not even 'the march of history' could stop.

J.D. Bernal has shown that nationalist historiography performed important propagandistic roles in nineteenth-century nation-building societies (Bernal, 1969, p. 1080). Following the French Revolution of 1792, and particularly after the national revolutions of the 1830s, leading historians throughout Europe revered 'volk' traditions (Hobsbawm, 1962, p. 164; Anderson, 1983, pp. 41–9). They recounted the heroic exploits of popular leaders, emphasised the importance of ethnic heritage to cultural survival, and provided strong historicist justifications for the nation-building objectives of the national bourgeoisie. As we shall presently see, the ethnic intelligentsia in Europe's more powerful nations were often to the forefront of this process of intellectual nationalisation. They regarded this as a prelude to the consolidation of nationalist hegemony and functioned as scholar-politicians who were often as not responsible for the institutionalisation of a whole range of academic disciplines in 'their' countries. These in turn served powerful nation-building interests at home and abroad. Indeed many of the intellectual projects that contributed to nation-building in the nineteenth century were raised to the status of academic disciplines and taught by professional academics in highly charged nationalistic environments. These nineteenth-century academics were considered professionals not simply because they were highly skilled, capable, proficient and accomplished in their disciplinary training, but also because they viewed themselves as public functionaries performing services in the public interest, for what they considered to be the public good. Thus the institutionalisation and subsequent development of new academic disciplines like social science, political economy, eugenics, ethnography, geography and anthropology can be analysed in terms of their contributions to nation-building projects in Europe between 1830 and 1914 (Anderson, 1986; Dijkink, 1996; Mac Laughlin, 1986a). Indeed the modern social sciences began as socially embedded intellectual activities which articulated and reflected the interests of European nation-builders at this time. Moreover, these disciplines did not simply operate within nation-alist milieus. They fostered the development of nation-building politics by advocating the political legitimacy of nationalism in 'their' home countries and defending racism and imperial expansion abroad. For many of these academics nation-building and imperial expansion were the twin bases for political and economic progress both in the colonies and in the nation-building metropolitan world of western Europe.

The state-centred role of universities and academies at this time was particularly evident during the unification of Germany and Italy in the 1870s (Hudson, 1979, pp. 32–7; Konvitz, 1987, p. 18). It was less evident, but no less effective, in a whole range of other European nations, ranging from industrial Britain in the west, to Imperial Russia in the east. Far from remaining aloof from the political and economic struggles of their day, leading academics here were themselves ardent nationalists who openly contributed to nation-building. As I have shown elsewhere, the demand for nationalist and nation-centred textbooks, like government demands for detailed social, statistical and cartographic data, played no small part in the institutionalisation and expansion of these academic disciplines in late nineteenth-century Europe (Mac Laughlin, 1986b, pp. 14–16). The professionalisation and national-isation of the physical as well as the social sciences also created divisions of labour in academia that mirrored both the division of labour in capitalist society in general and national divisions in European society. In this nation-centred scheme of things the social sciences performed three particularly important tasks. They amassed detailed social and geographical information about the nature and inner workings of 'their' societies. They supplied governments, military establishments, state bureaucracies, boards of education and the state-centred middle classes in general with national statistics and a whole range of other regional and social data needed by nation-building authorities. Finally, and most importantly, they formulated quasi-scientific defences of nation-building and colonial expansion which served the interests of nation-builders at home and empire builders abroad. Certainly the political geographer and social Darwinist Friedrich Ratzel justified the colonial domination of native peoples in Africa, the United States and Asia while simultaneously defending internal colonialism and the domination of minority peoples, not least the Celts, within Europe (Ratzel, 1898, pp. 34–41). For Ratzel the struggle for national development, both within Europe and at a global level, was literally a struggle for space. In a statement which had clear implications both for minority peoples in Europe and North America and for 'lesser races' elsewhere, he argued:

> Evolution needs room but finds the earth's surface limited. Everywhere old and new forms of life live side by side in deadly competition; but the later improved variety multiplies and spreads at the expense of less favoured types. The struggle for existence means a struggle for space.

In terms that could well have been used to justify the Cromwellian plantation of Ireland in the seventeenth century he went on to argue:

> A superior people, invading the territory of its weaker savage neighbours, robs them of their land, forces them back into corners too small for their support, and continues to encroach even upon this meagre possession, till the weaker finally loses the last remnants of its domain, is literally crowded off the earth ... The superiority of such expansionists consists primarily in their greater ability to appropriate, thoroughly utilise and populate territory. (Quoted in Semple, 1911, p. 97)

Ideas like these permeated nationalist ideology in North America, Britain and indeed all across western Europe in the latter – or Darwinian – half of the nineteenth century (Hofstadter, 1955, pp. 23–9). They particularly shaped popular attitudes towards minority peoples like the Irish, the Bretons, the Scots, the Welsh, as well as a whole host of other ethno-nationalities in eastern Europe.

Social scientists have long since recognised that statements like these were used to provide quasi-scientific justifications for the reign 'the lords of humankind' in the colonial world (Kiernan, 1972). Yet far less attention has been devoted to the role of such a dominant discourse in nineteenth-century political geography in legitimising the domination of Europe's indigenous minorities. Thus Hechter's analysis of internal colonialism in the Celtic fringe of the United Kingdom of Great Britain and Ireland does not even allude to the ideas of leading social Darwinists like Ratzel and Spencer whose work influenced popular attitudes towards minority nationalities in Britain and elsewhere (Hechter, 1975).

Thus, far from being autonomous agents of their own development, many of the founding fathers of the modern social sciences operated within, and greatly influenced the intellectual climate of the nation-building and colonial world in which they lived. They were not simply passive observers of a nineteenth-century world order. They acted as a socially embedded intelligentsia whose ideas played a crucial role in the construction of that new world order. The universities where they were employed were at once national, nationalist and nation-building institutions. Considering the political and geopolitical contexts within which they evolved, it is hardly surprising that many of them catered to the needs of the nation-builders and the interests of empire builders. To argue thus is not to support a structuralist view of academics as state functionaries, as 'lackeys' on the payroll of the powerful bourgeoisie, mere puppets in the hands of the nation-state (Lenin, 1966, pp. 78–81). It is to suggest instead that scientific, and especially social scientific literature and the research methodologies that supported it, did not evolve in any socio-historical or regional vacuums. They were embodied in very real people and developed in complex and intimate dialectical relationships with the nation-building societies that fostered them. As a result social scientific literature, not just nationalist mythology, nationalist history and the outpourings of cultural nationalists, was responsible for the cultivation of a well-developed sense of national identity in the intelligentsia of nineteenth-century western Europe. This literature was nationalistic and deeply racist. It borrowed heavily from an intellectual tradition dominated by social Darwinism and impregnated with evolutionary theories of social progress. It was imbued with biological categories borrowed from the natural sciences and transferred to the social sciences. Moreover, as Agnew and Duncan have shown, the transfer of ideas that resulted in this 'Darwinisation' of the social sciences was extremely uncritical (Agnew and Duncan, 1981, pp. 151–60). Scant attention was given to the compatibility between Darwinian concepts from biology and geology on the one hand, and the new political and highly nationalistic environments into which they were incorporated on the other. Concepts like territoriality, territorial imperative, natural selection and survival of the fittest, all of which were central to evolutionary biology, now penetrated to the heart of nationalist thought and social scientific thinking (Ardey, 1968). This resulted in the naturalisation of nation-building, at least in western Europe. The 'naturalness' of nationalism here was so taken for granted that the Spanish-born humanist philosopher George Santayana, writing in the 1930s, could argue that 'nationality is like our relations to women: too implicated in our moral nature to be changed honourably, and too accidental to be worth changing' (Santayana, 1905, p. 1032).

Statements like these literally litter the writings of cultural nationalists and nation-centred social scientists in the nineteenth century. With the exception of a marginalised group of anarchist thinkers under the influence of Peter Kropotkin and Elisee Reclus, few academics bothered, or were courageous enough, to challenge the 'naturalness' of nationalism and the inevitability of the nation-state's progress (Kropotkin, 1930, 1939; Reclus, 1876). Many more feared being castigated traitors if once they criticised the cause of nation-building. Thus was a legal category normally reserved for individuals found guilty of crimes against the public good applied to intellectual opponents of nation-building and the hegemony of the national, and nationalist, bourgeoisie. Henceforth the term 'traitor' could be applied derogatorily, and with great force, to a whole range of groups, from working-class socialists who supported internationalism, to advocates of multiculturalism and defenders of the rights of women (Viroli, 1997, p. 169). These latter, it was argued, were 'selling out' on the cause of progress because they were putting sectionalist and class interests above the national cause. Bertrand Russell has also suggested that the principle that nations, like individuals, had a right to be 'free' and not be ruled by either monarchs or foreigners, was the central doctrine of European liberalism (Russell, 1965, p. 132). It developed into the principle of nationality, i.e. the right of nations to self-determination, in Europe's most powerful countries in the 50 years that ended with the Great War. A minority nationality like the Irish had not only to fight an uphill battle against aristocratic privilege and British rule in 'their' country. They had to oppose a dominant western intellectual tradition which denied self-determination to 'lesser peoples' at home, and to 'lesser breeds' abroad. This was a tradition which defended 'big-nation' nationalism and regarded nation-building as the prerogative of expansionist capitalist societies alone. In the wake of the French Revolution, and especially following the commercial and industrial revolutions in Europe in the second half of the nineteenth century, nationalist principles were central to the struggles of the new middle class and men of wealth. The latter, operating in conjunction with the ethnic intelligentsia, sought to use nationalism to rid Europe of the last vestiges of seigniorial privilege, to end 'foreign rule', and to wipe away all traces of aristocratic privilege. Nationalist social scientists and cultural nationalists alike treated nationalism as a manifest and self-evident political principle upon which rational societies throughout the 'civilised' world at least could build their own futures. At best they regarded opponents of nationalism, especially anarchists and anarcho-communists who were also anti-statist, as deferential in their defence of communitarian values and the pre-nationalised moral economies of peasants and craft workers. At worst they viewed them as irrational and bigoted reactionaries. Opponents of nation-building, not least in Ireland, were seen as an artificial community dominated by aristocrats and bound together by sectionalism and quasi-feudal traditions that were considered best forgotten in an age of nationalist progress. Nationalists on the other hand were depicted as a natural community united by a justified fear of foreign domination and monarchical rule and led by a courageous, self-sacrificing leadership that exercised a rational claim to political and moral legitimacy.

Initially at least the intelligentsia in late eighteenth- and nineteenth-century Europe defended the Enlightenment as a European project. They sought to spread its moral and scientific values all across Europe, especially in western Europe. However, this general movement in favour of European revolution fragmented into national segments early in the first half of the nineteenth century (Hobsbawm, 1962, p. 164). Nationalists, and national leaders, acquired massive support in the wake of the new political revolutions that rocked post-Napoleonic Europe in the 1830s. The new revolutionaries thrown up by the latter demanded that liberation should literally begin at home. They insisted that 'enlightenment' should be a nationalist as opposed to a European project. It should, and could, only be delivered by the new organic intelligentsia that emerged from the industrial and commercial revolutions that swept western Europe in the course of the eighteenth and nineteenth centuries. This intelligentsia was to the forefront of nation-building political struggles all across Europe. Its members justified their concern for 'their' own nation by adopting the role of Messiah for all those whom they sought to lead. The new intellectuals, many of them academics, schoolteachers and local and national government officials, saw no contradiction between their demands for self-determination and those of other oppressed nations elsewhere in Europe. They even envisaged an international brotherhood of enlightened nationalist movements working to liberate Europe of the last vestiges of aristocratic rule and the last traces of ancient despotisms. However, this was a period which also brought its own modern darkness, a darkness that could only be partially assuaged through patriotism and a fervent belief in the internal national and external or international 'civilising' mission of one's own nation. In some countries indeed, not least in those where nationalism was closely identified with organised religion (Ireland, Italy, Spain, Poland and Hungary), the ideology of nationalism acquired the status of a state religion, just as many of its supporters literally became martyrs to the cause of nationalism. High priests of nationalism in these countries had such standing among their people that less educated and more plebeian nationalists found it difficult to know where religious doctrine left off and where political ideology took over.

At other levels of society it was the professional academics, intellectuals and newspapermen who were often to the forefront of 'big-nation' nation-building. Indeed it was through these sectors that the intelligentsia and national middle classes were often 'nationalised'. Academics in particular, not least those in disciplines like political economy, history, geography, ethnography, archaeology and politics, regarded the nation-state as the crucible of progress. Many of these were ardent nationalists first, and only afterwards considered themselves social scientists. They looked on the nation and nationalism as vehicles of political enlightenment. Divided along strict disciplinary lines, they were most united when defending the causes of nation-building at home and colonial expansion overseas. They considered the nation-state as eminently superior to the pre-capitalist parochialisms and political regionalisms that marked the political landscape of pre-nineteenth-century Europe. They defended a new nineteenth-century world order wherein self-determination, largely as a result of the influence of social Darwinism, was regarded the prerogative of strong nations and the White metropolitan world alone. As fervent defenders of 'big-nation' nationalism, they also favoured the assimilation of minority nationalities within larger European nations in much the same way as they defended the colonial domination of 'lesser breeds' inside and outside Europe.

Disciplines like history, ethnography, geography and anthropology also had their part to play in fostering nation-building and legitimising colonialism, whether this was an internal affair, as in the Celtic fringe of Britain, or external affair, as in Africa, Asia and the Middle East. These disciplines were the institutionalised embodiment of an increasingly nationalist intellectual tradition which, from the 1830s onwards, looked on the nation-state as an alternative to the 'idiocy of rural life' and a substitute for the banality of European provincial life. Thus they regarded a well-developed sense of national identity as superior to the parochial and regionalist identities of pre-modern and pre-industrial Europe. Locating national above class identities, they regarded patriotism as a progressive attribute of individuals because it bound class-divided communities together and helped overcome the ennui that characterised urban life in nineteenth-century Europe. To suggest that nationalism at this stage filled a vacuum created by the decline of religious orthodoxy, particularly among the new intelligentsia, is not to suggest that it superseded religion. Neither did it stem from the erosion of religious sensibilities or act, as Benedict Anderson sometimes suggests, as a substitute for religion in western Europe (Anderson, 1983, p. 85). In many European countries the rise of nationalism marked the coming of age of the ethnic intelligentsia and coincided with a decline in religious explanations for social phenomena, at least among the educated sectors of European society. Increasingly also nation-centred and enlightenment values formed the basis of bourgeois thought in modernising societies like Britain, France, the United States and Germany. The appeal of nationalism and the success of nation-building in these countries prompted even small nations like the Irish to imitate their success.

All of this was to have profound consequences for the geography of revolution in nineteenth-century western Europe. Prior to the 1830s Europe had only one great revolutionary role model, namely France, or more accurately Paris. Many also looked to England as the only truly industrial nation. As the century progressed, however, revolutionary ideals swept across large parts of western Europe. This led to the demise of Paris as the epicentre of revolution and rendered the nation the model for revolution for oppressed peoples in countries as far apart as Ireland and Poland. Henceforth nations, not cities, were to be the crucibles of modernity. With the exception of Paris during the 1870s, nations now also symbolised the 'risen people'. After that decade Paris, London, Vienna and Berlin were to be more famous for their urban culture, particularly their haute couture, than for their revolutionary cells. Moreover, when revolutionary ideals spread from the city to the nation, it proved all the more difficult for the forces of Europe's anciens régimes to contain them. By the middle of the nineteenth century the mantle of liberation had clearly fallen to national leaders and was firmly clutched by nationalist hands. It passed to groups like the Young Irelanders and the Young Turks of Europe, to the supporters of Young Italy, Young France and Young Germany (Hobsbawm, 1962, p. 164).

The nationalist intelligentsia were not alone in their struggle for self-determination. As we have already seen, many of them were linked through the educational establishment, the church, the press and local and national bureaucracies to metropolitan nation-building societies. Occupying socially strategic positions at national and local level, they were able to spread nationalism to society at large, not least to the subordinate social classes with which they were in regular contact. A political geography of nation-building was thus central to the cultural and political projects of these groups. As I have argued elsewhere, there was to be no room in these nation-building projects for a 'branching model' of development which would accommodate, or even tolerate, the separate existence of minority peoples within the borders of the modern nation (Mac Laughlin, 1999d, p. 135). As the example of British nation-building clearly demonstrated, neither was there to be much space for a cultural relativism which would validate the existence of a racialised and simianised minority like the Irish within the political and moral structures of the British nation. This was because the nation in Britain as elsewhere in western Europe and North America denoted a process of moral development. It implied the growth of a unique entity in response to a national sense of identity (Bowler, 1989, p. 49). It was widely believed that 'primitive peoples', including the 'wilde Irish', nomadic communities like European Gypsies, and many native American 'nations' in North America, indicated just how low national societies could sink if once they lost control over their social subordinates. It was felt that they could degenerate still further if they lost the gift of divine revelation or otherwise deviated from the paths of righteousness and national self-improvement.

Structuralist versus Hegelian Perspectives on the Nation-state

The study of nation-building has, until recently, been bedevilled by an over-emphasis on the objectives of cultural nationalists and on nationalist politics. Consequently it has tended to neglect the political regionalist and sectionalist differences within nation-building societies. To many indeed nationalism appeared so manifestly altruistic in its objectives that few were courageous enough to submit its quasi-sacred doctrines to social scientific or critical analysis. To do so would presumably have led to an exposure of the sexist, sectionalist and materialist interests of nation-builders. It would also point to the role of nationalist politics in quelling anti-capitalist and anti-statist struggles. The fact that some of the leading exponents of nationalist historiography and nationalist political thought in the nineteenth century were themselves strong advocates of national unification did little to alleviate this situation. These proponents of nation-building placed more emphasis upon the efficacy and historical legitimacy of nationalist struggles than on any critical examination of its role in consolidating the hegemony of the national bourgeoisie. Instead, as the case of nineteenth-century Ireland clearly shows, nationalist historiography was an integral and indispensable element in the cultural renaissances that typically preceded the establishment of nationalist hegemony all across western Europe at the end of the last century.

Ernest Gellner has suggested that lack of attention to nationalist political philosophy was due less to any scarcity of first-rate thinkers among the supporters of the cause of nationalism, than to the fact that the latter were simply viewed as dispensable (Gellner, 1983, p. 87). As he also suggests, if one or two fell by the wayside in the struggle for national independence, others were always there to fill their places. The quality of nationalist thought was hardly affected by the process of substitution. Nationalism had at least one other advantage over rival ideologies which advocated socialist revolution, class struggle and regional autonomy. It accorded well with the interests of dominant sectors of capitalist societies, and it was taught in national schools throughout western Europe. More often than not it was also preached from the pulpit. In view of the pervasiveness of state-centred and capitalist social thought, including its association with prestigious political leaders and national institutions, national liberation and the unification of the nation-state appeared to the public at large as the epitome of polit-ical endeavour, the panacea for all social and economic problems. At its most extreme this approach to nation-building considered nationalism in progressive evolutionary terms and regarded it as an autonomous social force with far more developmental potential than other political ideologies (Bowler, 1989, p. 37). It was said to be classless in origin and practice, altruistic in its intentions and 'untainted' by too close an association with the sectionalist inter-ests of any one social class. As such it was supposed to be over and above civil society, something whose causes could be ascribed to factors external to society itself, a phenomenon over and above both history and place. Coupled with the intelligentsia's faith in applied social science as the panacea for all sorts of problems that stood in the way of political progress, nationalist ideology was fused with institutionalised religion and became almost a state reli-gion. As we have already seen, it acquired doctrinal status in many European nation-building societies, not least in rural Catholic countries like Ireland, Italy, Spain and Portugal. It attained millen-nial proportions in the inner circles of cultural nationalists in these countries. This was especially true of rural Ireland and Catholic Poland where nationalist-minded priests and schoolteachers pursued their task of 'nationalising' and politicising their 'flocks' with near missionary zeal. Nationalist mythology has always been fundamental to the political projects of these 'local heroes' of nation-building (Branch, 1985; Clayton, 1982; Epstein, 1978; Isaacs, 1975). Indeed far from being redundant in this 'Darwinian' half of the nineteenth century, ancient myths and legends were carefully fostered and exploited by these nationalist groups, just as they were used to validate the construction of nationalist hege-mony at home and defend colonial expansion and cultural imperialism abroad. Nationalist mythology, together with nation-alist historiography, performed important communicative and educational functions in rural societies like Ireland and France still caught up in the process of state-centralisation under nationalist hegemony at the beginning of the twentieth century. Thus they not only constructed nations as imagined communities but helped mobilise mass popular support for the cause of nation-building. Indeed many of the social and political ideologies of the late nine-teenth century, not least nationalism, were so imbued with nationalist and racist mythology that they may be regarded as modern expressions of ancient myths. Like myths, they were by no means amoral or asocial. They functioned in such a way as to justify national unification and fostered a strong sense of place, and an equally strong sense of nationhood in ethnically mixed and regionally divided countries (Smith, 1984, p. 287).

Portrayed almost as a quasi-sacred doctrine, nationalism was often above criticism. It was an ideology that could be defined less in terms of the sectional and regional interests it sought to satisfy and more in terms of what it opposed. Formulated by a middle-class intelligentsia from an admixture of myth and historicist social philosophy, nationalist social philosophy, like nationalist economic thought, was shrouded in ambiguity from the start. Far from working to its disadvantage, the resulting vagueness actually promoted the nationalist cause by promising everything to everyone without specifying how the social contradictions of class-structured and regionally divided societies were to be resolved within the centralised nation-state. As the case of nineteenth-century Ireland also shows, the reformist nation-state, defined negatively in terms of what aristocratic and elitist privileges it sought to destroy, was depicted as an expurgated version of the paternalistic, landed aristocratic and seigniorial state from which 'Old Corruption', landed privilege and monarchical rule had been ousted. For many peoples in western Europe, not least for the nation-building Catholic Irish and the French, the degree to which privilege and aristocratic influence were to be curbed or abolished in the new nation-state became the defining criterion of benign nationhood. In many ways, the twentieth-century view of the modern state as a compassionate arbitrator in class-structured societies is a tradition that owes much to this ideology of liberal nationalism.

However, nationalism also accommodated the Hegelian view concerning the rationality and historical inevitability of the nation-state. Thus, far from being the 'executive wing' of a ruling class that it was in the writings of Marxist-Leninists, the nation-state was viewed by Hegelians, and especially by nationalists, as the incarnation of 'General Will' in the historical process (Lenin, 1966, p. 11). As such it was considered the pluralist institution par excellence, one which made the freedom of the individual possible, and through which freedom meant submission to the dictates of the national state. This was why Hegel considered the German 'nations' of the 1830s among the first to realise that freedom consisted in offering allegiance to state agencies as agents of the 'General Will' of the 'risen people'. Viewed thus the nation-state was the earthly manifestation of autonomous social forces that operated across space and throughout history. It represented the expansion of the consciousness of freedom, at least in the metropolitan world, just as it was said to be the epitome of national progress.

This Hegelian approach has initiated a tradition of abstract theorising about the modern nation-state that has served as the point of departure for neo-Hegelian autonomist models of nationalism since the 1970s (Mac Laughlin, 1987, pp. 5–7). This tradition has been elitist in its views of the role of the intelligentsia in historical social change, just as it has been metaphysical in its ontological origins. It regards universal phenomena as immutable and eternally separated from each other. In this nation-building model the causal roots of social and historical change are traced to external 'driving' forces, not to human agents or to social and physical phenomena. Morality, religions, political ideologies and the forms of social consciousness corresponding to these retain an appearance of independence and possess a history of rational evolutionary development of their own. This Hegelian and neo-Hegelian tradition is elitist in that it abstracts social and historical phenomena – like the nation-state and the nationalist intelligentsia – from the concrete socio-historical and regional settings that give them meaning. It also accords the categories 'nation' and 'nationalism' the highest values in its explanatory models of social and historical change. Thus modern neo-Hegelian and autonomist models may be regarded as theoretical elaborations on concepts and categories implicit in much nineteenth-century thinking on nation-building and nationalism. They have adopted, albeit often unconsciously, biological categories and ideas for progress from Darwinism and the natural sciences and adapted them to the study of nationalism and national separatism. In so doing they have often provided theoretical justifications for irredentist nationalism and national separatism. Through their defence of the politics of ethnicity they have detracted from international solidarities, not least international class struggles. They do this not least by stressing the 'naturalness' of ethnic over class identities and emphasising the alienating effects of class struggle in socially stratified, class-structured nation-states.

The study of nationalism has yet to escape its partisan origins. In recent decades 'ethnic revivals' in western Europe and ethnonationalism in eastern Europe and the Soviet Union since the 1980s have encouraged the re-emergence of autonomist models of nation-building (Smith, 1981). The revival of ethno-nationalisms in today's new world 'disorder' has encouraged the re-birth of neo-Hegelian autonomist explanations of nationalism and ethno-nationalism. Like its nineteenth-century predecessor, this mode of theorising generally fails to consider nationalism as an historical and geographical happening, one which binds people and place together in concrete social and political settings. It accords historical agency to the cultural and economic attributes of ethnic groups, rather than to social groups themselves. At its most extreme it regards the latter as mere trajectories of the former. Thus Lucio Colletti cautioned Marxists against the dangers inherent in this mode of theorising when he argued that it reduces the 'substance' of everything to 'logical categories' (Colletti, 1975, pp. 3–7). He hypothesised these abstractions into 'substances', retraced the steps that led to their emergence, and thereby presented concrete historical relationships as the objectification of abstract categories. This form of circular theorising is both ahistorical and aspatial. As such it is not helpful in studying an ideology as historically specific as nationalism clearly is, and as geographically rooted to specific locations as the nation-state. It is also inconsistent with the principles of historical materialism and the complex mode of historical analysis advocated by Marx himself.

This mode of theorising reached its most 'idealised' form in the abstract philosophical tradition of Althusserian Marxism. Here Marxism is a theoretical and political practice 'which gains nothing from its association with historical writing and historical research'. For Althusser, unlike Marx himself, and unlike other Marxist theorists like Antonio Gramsci, E.P. Thompson and Raymond Williams, the study of history is not only scientifically but also politically valueless (Althusser, 1977; Gramsci, 1971, 1977; Thompson, 1968, 1971, 1978). Paradoxically, Althusser's neo-Marxian mode of theorising is closer to Hegelian idealism and ideological abstractionism, the philosophical positions which Marx sought to demolish, than it is to cultural Marxism or historical materialism (Lovell, 1980, pp. 235–7). Criticising this 'idealisation' of Marxism, E.P. Thompson has shown how many of the most sophisticated and important categories of Marxian analysis – including the nation-state, social class, power, mode of production and political ideologies – are historical 'happenings' and historical geographical relationships that can only be fully comprehended by taking full account of the dialectical, socio-historical and regional contexts within which they evolved (Thompson, 1968, p. 9). No amount of abstract theorising or refined model building can dispense with the need to examine such phenomena in their regional and historical settings. Yet the neo-Marxian brand of Althusserian theorising parading as a sophisticated improvement upon the methodology of historical materialism and cultural Marxism reduces socio-historical and territorial categories like the nation-state to mere philosophical propositions. In so doing it threatens Marxian historical analysis with 'historical theoreticism', the very antithesis of Marxist, especially cultural Marxist, approaches to historical and geographical reality.

Abstract theorising, including secularised, neo-Hegelian views on the role of the state in capitalist societies, as in post-communist and socialist societies, has also penetrated to the very heart of much recent writing on ethno-nationalism and the modern ethnic nation. Borrowing too readily from disciplines that have been imbued with aspatial and ahistorical perspectives, these new theorists have ignored the historical and territorial contingency of nation-building and nationalism. In taking both for granted, they have failed to stress the historical and geographical contingency of nation-building and nationalism. Both these historical phenomena reached new heights in the second half of the nineteenth century, in the period which Hobsbawm aptly designates as the 'Age of Capital' (Hobsbawm, 1988). It would be difficult to envision functioning geographical nation-states and socially cohesive national societies emerging prior to the full maturing of nineteenth-century capitalism. Thus it is no coincidence that nationalism and the modern nation-state evolved alongside revolutionary changes which saw the western world acquiring mass education and mass markets. As later chapters in this study will show, the latter in turn laid the basis for nation-building in the nineteenth century and contributed to the growth of some of the most advanced centralised states in the modern world. Viewed thus the modern nineteenth-century nation-state emerged as an important building block of national and global capitalism. Then, as now, nationalism, including ethno-nationalism, was not a natural political ideology. Neither was it naturally inscribed on the hearts of men and women. It owed its origins to the joining together of a potent mix of ideological, social, economic and geopolitical forces to which very real people contributed in their efforts to construct the modern nation-state.

The writings of A.D. Smith, Ernest Gellner, Tom Nairn and Michael Hechter illustrate the fact that autonomist models which stress the 'naturalness' and primordial essence of nationalism are not to be confined to the nineteenth century. The revival of interest in nationalism now is partly due to the persistence of ethnicity and national separatist tendencies in some of the most centralised societies in the metropolitan world. In the more extreme cases, this persistence is regarded as proof of the 'naturalness' and primordial nature of nationalism compared to other 'man-made' ideologies. However, the form that a lot of this work has taken owes much to the survival of ahistorical and aspatial theoreticism over other approaches that link nation-building and nationalism to concrete social, geographical and intellectual contexts. Thus for example most recent theorists have been justifiably dissatisfied with modernisation theory as a basis for understanding the development of the modern states. Having inherited many of the methodological weaknesses and philosophical shortcomings that marked the Hegelian tradition of their intellectual ancestors, proponents of modernisation theory since the 1960s erroneously predicted the decline of ethnic allegiances and the growth of associational politics and regarded these as the essential hallmarks of modern political culture. The persistence of ethno-nationalism and the progressive fragmentation of multinational societies into separate nation-states are proof enough of the failure of modernisation to eliminate ethnic diversity.

According to Smith, a leading theorist in the autonomist, neo-Hegelian mould, the persistence of ethnic politics today also disproves the faith of liberals and Marxists in the imminent demise of ethnicity in the face of cosmopolitan assimilation (Smith, 1986). For Smith nationalism and ethno-nationalism are more 'natural' than socialism, fascism, communism and liberalism. In terms reminiscent of the optimism of nineteenth-century defenders of nation-building, Smith suggests that the failure of nationalism to develop any clear-cut eschatology has stood it in good stead. It means that nationalism, and now more recently ethno-nationalism, can be regarded as all things to all men, and all women, and that its benefits, somehow or other, will accrue to no particular sector in nation-building societies to the disadvantage of the rest. As Smith sees it, nationalism derives its power from the 'real feelings' of ethnically defined peoples 'rooted', not least through the 'anchoring' or 'territorialising' forces of nationalism, in the social landscape of the modern world and its values. He not only regards nationalism as a progressive social force – he exaggerates the degree of continuity between nineteenth-century nation-building and modern national separatism. To writers in the nineteenth-century nation-centred tradition it appeared axiomatic that states should both be nations, preferably under the hegemony of a powerful national bourgeoisie, but they were also supposed to have the political and economic potential to render them competent actors in the global arena. Eric Hobsbawm has shown how this meant that nation-building in the nineteenth century was the prerogative of powerful White capitalist societies in the metropolitan world (Hobsbawm, 1992, p. 73). It was argued that they, and they alone, were considered large enough to provide capitalists with national markets, while also allowing the national bourgeoisie to engage both in internal colonialism at home and colonial expansion abroad. Unlike today, nation-builders in the nineteenth century believed that these powerful nation-states were infinitely superior to smaller ethnically defined nations whose claims to statehood often as not were based on ethnic, not on political, economic or geopolitical considerations. This meant that ethnic minorities and minority nationalities were among the first to suffer the consequences of nation-building in the nineteenth-century 'Age of Capital'. Their historicist claims to autonomy, like their demands for self-determination, were considered retrogressive and irrational in an age of nation-building modernity. Defenders of the rights of small nations to self-determination were branded renegades who threatened to 'Balkanise' western Europe even before its larger nation-states had a chance to demonstrate their modernising capabilities. Smith has largely ignored this aspect of historical nation-building. Focusing on the prehistoric ethnic origins of nations, he often ignores considerations of size and growth potential inherent in most nationalist political thinking about the state and the nation in the nineteenth century. Lumping together nineteenth-century nationalism with modern day expressions of national separatism, he also fails to emphasise the fact that the former often sought separation out from crumbling, quasi-feudal, imperial structures – the Ottoman empire, the Holy Roman empire, the Hapsburg empire – or sought to unify fragmented social and territorial entities, while the latter threaten the breakup of powerful, well-established nation-states.

So far we have been discussing the intelligentsia as though they operated independently of other social classes in nation-building societies. We have also seen that this was clearly not the case. The section that follows outlines in more detail a much more useful cultural Marxist model of nation-building which recognises the inter-relatedness of ethnic and material interests in the emergence of the modern nation-state. More specifically it focuses on Gramsci's approach to class formation, especially his insights on the role of the intelligentsia in consolidating bourgeois hegemony in the nineteenth-century European nation-state. It is argued that this approach has far more merits than the reductionist models of Marxist-Leninists on the one hand, and the 'culturalist reductionism' of writers like Smith and Anderson on the other.

Towards a Gramscian Model of Nation-building and Nationalism

The Italian Marxist Antonio Gramsci was the first to outline a political, as opposed to an economic reductionist, account of nation-building within a materialist framework (Gramsci, 1966). In particular he insisted that crude materialist and economic reductionist approaches to state formation and socio-historical change were rarely up to the task of explaining socio-historical phenomena like nation-building and state formation. Returning to a pre-Leninist model of state formation wherein the intelligentsia were simply the executive wing of the ruling class, Gramsci also drew on non-Marxist social thought to construct a model of social change which recognised the role of human agency, particularly that of the ethnic intelligentsia, in the process of social and historical change (Gramsci, 1977, pp. 10–14; Joll, 1978, pp. 27–39). He argued that for any class to become dominant economically it must also achieve political and ideological pre-eminence. This meant that it must occupy all socially strategic or hegemonic positions in society. This in turn meant that it could then lead, or at least contain, subordinate social classes in nation-building societies. Gramsci also argued that the dialectic was something more than the blind clash of 'physical forces' as it was in crude materialist and Marxist-Leninist accounts. It was instead a movement to which real people contributed by entering the stage of history, by deliberately and of their own volition becoming an active force in the dialectical process (Joll, 1978, pp. 111–15). Thus with Gramsci human beings cease to be the more or less autonomous and free-acting agents that they are in voluntarist approaches to state-formation and nation-building. Neither are they totally determined agents, as in Marxist-Leninist, economic reductionist and determinist models of social change. Gramsci evaded both voluntarist and determinist approaches to nation-building and historical change by arguing in favour of a model which viewed human behaviour as both determined and determining (Mac Laughlin and Agnew, 1986, pp. 249–52). According to Lukes human behaviour was 'a web of possibilities for agents, whose nature is both active and structured, to make choices and pursue strategies within given limits, which in consequence expand and contract over time' (Lukes, quoted in Agnew, 1982, p. 275).

For Gramsci also the category hegemony was used to describe the cultural and economic modes of incorporation used by dominant sectors of class-structured and nation-building societies to establish, and legitimate, their control over subordinate classes and ultimately over state apparatuses. In contrast to Marx and Engels and most other philosophers of progress, Gramsci introduced peasants and small farmers into his analysis of social change. In France, Italy, Ireland and Spain these groups supplied a significant proportion of the intelligentsia and for that reason they often had a debilitating effect on urban working-class movements for radical and revolutionary change. Gramsci explained the anomaly of poor peasants and small farmers being led by a middle-class and petty middle-class intelligentsia comprising priests, religious leaders, teachers, clerks and other petty officials by showing that a major proportion of these were directly descended from peasants and small farmers who in turn regarded them in an ambivalent manner (Gramsci, 1971, pp. 22–3). On the one hand they looked up to them and accepted their spiritual and political leadership because of the fact that so many among this petty intelligentsia were their own flesh and blood. Thus for the peasantry, as for small farmers and rural working-class families in Ireland, having a member of the family elevated to the status of the intelligentsia gave the family standing and prestige in the local community and even caused it to have a disproportionate say in the political affairs of local communities. On the other hand, however, the rural poor and the working class in these class-structured societies often envied the intelligentsia their easy way of life and despised them at times for their identification with the interests of dominant sectors of society.

Gramsci extended this analysis of models of social and political incorporation to include other cultural, religious, educational and legal strategies adopted by ruling classes to prevent subordinate social classes from growing insubordinate. Gramsci's originality stems from his conception of the role of ideology, religion, the intelligentsia and human agency in the historical process. With Gramsci, therefore, we return to the idealist beginnings of Marxism, where the focus is less on the economic contradictions in class-structured societies than on political leadership and the role of human agency in the historical process. The concept of hegemony was central to this analysis. Thus Gramsci insisted that history was not made by 'great men' or political leaders and intellectuals separated out from the masses. History instead was made by an intelligentsia and by intellectual elites 'conscious of being organically linked to a national-popular mass' (Gramsci, quoted in Joll, 1978, p. 124). Gramsci called these the 'organic intelligentsia'. Viewed thus, hegemony implied cultural capital and political leadership, not just the economic power that ownership of the means of production conferred upon any one class. Being hegemonic meant that for any given historical period a social class or ethnic group could confine ethnic and class antagonisms to a terrain where its legitimacy was not seriously challenged. It also suggested that such ruling sectors were able to persuade others to accept their moral, political and cultural values as the sole legitimate values for the entire society. To the extent that a ruling class is successful in this mission it will exercise the minimum of physical force as the normal exercise of hegemonic power is characterised by a combination of consensus and force without force having to exceed persuasion and consensus in any regular manner. In periods of crises – such as those that follow economic collapse, war and exposure to new political and economic stresses – the apparatus of hegemony often breaks down and parties long accustomed to monopolistic control over state apparatuses can split apart in the face of new challenges to hegemonic power. Thus situations can arise that are ripe for a shift of power and the creation of a new apparatus of hegemony and a new basis for political consensus.

As used by Gramsci hegemony is not synonymous with ideology. Neither is it a superstructural phenomenon or a secondary experience. It is lived at such depth and 'saturates ... society to such an extent; even constitutes the substance and limits of common sense for most people under its sway that it corresponds to the social reality of social experience very much more clearly than any notions derived from the formula of base and superstructure' (Williams, 1980, p. 37). If hegemony were merely an abstract set of ideological propositions about reality imposed from above by intellectual or political elites, if socio-political or cultural ideas were merely the result of ideological manipulation, then societies and political structures would be much easier to transform than they have proved to be in practice. As Williams and Thompson have also shown, hegemony is neither static nor singular. Instead it is dynamic and pluralist – its internal structures have constantly to be renewed, revived and defended because they can be continually challenged from below and subjected to revolutionary stresses that can rip apart the status quo (Williams, 1980; Thompson, 1978). Thompson in particular has argued that 'hegemony does not entail any acceptance by the poor of the gentry's paternalism upon the gentry's own terms or in their approved self-image. The poor might be willing to award their deference to the gentry, but only for a price' (1978, p. 97). Viewed thus, ruling class hegemony in socially stratified and ethnically divided societies – although it may permeate all aspects of society – rarely envelops the lives of subordinate social groups to the extent of preventing them from defending their own view of the just life, and their own ideas about the moral economy. Indeed ruling class hegemony regularly runs the risk of being pushed too far which causes dominant social groups to lapse into state violence in order to maintain the status quo. Hegemony therefore offers only 'the bare architectural structure of relations of domination and subordination, but within that architectural form many different scenes could be set and different drama enacted' (Thompson, 1978, p. 163). Though the hegemony of the ruling sectors of class-structured and ethnically divided societies often defines the limits of what is seen to be possible, although it limits the growth of alternative worldviews, there is nothing permanent, absolute, determined or inevitable in all of this. Hegemony is always sustained with great skill, through the proper, and often surreptitious use of moral and physical force on the one hand, and political persuasion, diplomacy, discrimination and patience on the other. Although it may impose blinkers that prevent subordinate social classes and ethnic minorities from uniting across social class, religious and ethic lines to overthrow ruling elites and establish an alternative hegemony, hegemony rarely involves a total blindfolding of subordinate groups to the extent that they never attain consciousness of their independent political, cultural and economic potential. Supporting this view Genovese has shown that a paternalism or hegemony that is accepted by both the dominant and subordinate affords a fragile bridge across otherwise intolerable social contradictions that mark the most oppressive of societies (Genovese, 1976, p. 5). Wherever paternalism exists, whether in late nineteenth-century Ireland, or in the southern slave-holding states of eighteenth-century America, it undermined solidarity among the oppressed by linking them as individuals, and more especially as members of social and political networks, to their oppressors. But paternalism's insistence upon mutual obligations that are binding upon both the dominant and the dominated in nation-building societies implicitly recognises the political potentialities of the latter to alter any ruling class hegemony, just as it compels the former to consider their own weaknesses when considering the limits of their political power.

Gramsci, writing in an Italian context where deep social divisions also manifested themselves regionally on the political and economic landscape of the nation-state, recognised that hegemony had clear geographical dimensions also. He was particularly interested in the way in which nation-building strategies were used to link the peasant south with the far more industrialised north of the country in the late nineteenth century (Gramsci, 1957, 1971). Recognising that the state was one of the chief regulators of political and economic life in the nation, he showed how state policies also had regional effects. He also showed how the southern intelligentsia attained local and regional dominance by siding with northern politicians in exchange for a share of public finance which they often used for their own gain. In so doing they helped maintain the territorial unity of the nation-state, fostered the development of clientalist politics and political corruption in the south, and did little to alleviate the region's dire social and economic inequalities. Instead the peasant south was used as a rural conservative force which could be called upon, almost at will, to counteract working-class radicalism in Italy's industrial heartlands. The net result was that the conservative rural south was used to consolidate capitalist hegemony in the industrial and radical north. This in turn meant that the hegemony of northern capitalists could be extended to the country as a whole. Their political and moral concerns became those of the Italian state. Divisions between north and south, including the rigid divisions between southern peasants and northern workers, rendered this hegemony all the more indomitable, although this did not mean that it was not contested.

In the late-nineteenth-century Irish context also regional and ethnic divisions were manipulated chiefly, but never exclusively, in the interests of dominant social groups, in such a way as to maintain two separate hegemonies, one in the north-east, the other in the south of Ireland. Thus this study will show how in the north-east a pro-Unionist regional hegemony was constructed using the fragile ties that bound Protestant small farmers and the Protestant working class to the region's political-economic Protestant elite. As a result the nationalist minority here found themselves excluded from Catholic nation-building Ireland, just as they found themselves socially entrapped within a regional hegemonic structure which was not of their making, and to which they could offer no allegiance. In the south of Ireland on the other hand the rural poor and substantial tenant farmers were united under the hegemony of the more substantial Catholic bourgeoisie in the late nineteenth and early twentieth centuries. This in turn ensured the hegemony of the Catholic church and the rural bourgeoisie throughout the country, and not just its agricultural heartlands, where Catholic power and rural conservatism were at their strongest. Thus in the south and west of Ireland, as in southern Italy, the ties that bound the rural poor to the Catholic church and the petty bourgeoisie made it all the more unlikely that unity would be achieved between small farmers on the one hand and the urban working class on the other. In the event all of Ireland outside the Protestant north-east fell under the hegemony of substantial Catholic farmers and the Catholic intelligentsia. Thus Gaelic nationalism fused with rural fundamentalism to become a prominent feature of the hegemony of the bourgeoisie in Catholic nation-building Ireland. Both forces were regularly mobilised to resist the power of the organised working class and to counteract urban influences whenever and wherever Catholic power groups found cause to do so.

2 English Nation-building and Seventeenth-century Ireland: The 'Fabulous Geographies' of Nation-building

So far we have seen that nationalism historically was widely considered a welcome ideological development because it fostered territorial unification and helped cultivate a politics of national consensus, at least in nineteenth-century western Europe. Viewed thus it was an ideology which appeared to transcend political regionalisms and overcome class divisions, especially in this metropolitan world and in North America. When rooted in territorially unified and urbanising societies it was regarded as an ideology for fostering the development of powerful nation-states, themselves welcome alternatives to the banality of pre-industrial society and the 'idiocy' of rural life. We have also seen that most defenders of nation-building in western Europe in the eighteenth and nineteenth centuries scarcely considered disentangling themselves sufficiently from the nation-building project to develop a critical political geography of nationalism and its state-centred ideology. Many indeed, especially the English, perceived ethno-nationalisms and minority expressions of nationalism as potentially dangerous 'Balkanising' forces which could shatter the political landscape of western Europe before modern nations here even got off the ground. Nationalism then, unlike nationalism today, was a unifying force. Bourgeois nation-builders were more concerned with the economic viability and geopolitical standing of large nations, than with the cultural authenticity and nationalist credentials of small nations or ethnic minorities. Within Britain small nationalities like the Irish, the Scots and the Welsh were seen both as potential threats to the territorial integrity of the British nation and as building blocks of a larger British state-system centred on England. At best they were wards of a greater Britain, peoples whose interests, it was argued, would be better catered for within a united kingdom of Great Britain and Ireland than in a fragmented and disunited British kingdom or in a parochial and regionally divided Ireland.

Finally we have seen that the new academic disciplines which were institutionalised at the height of this nation-building era articulated the territorial imperatives of nation-builders and legitimised western colonial expansion. In particular they defended the rights of powerful progressive societies to rule themselves, and racial and ethnic minorities, both at home and abroad. The practitioners of these disciplines were often as not ardent social Darwinists who subscribed to the nation-building project in their own countries and defended frontier expansion out to the colonial world. They also insisted that it was entirely natural for peripheral nationalities within Europe to be led towards progress and modernity under the guidance of strong European states that had already shown their capacity to reap the harvest of progress by engaging in colonial expansion. These states, and these alone, it was argued, were to become nation-states. They had markets and resource bases large enough to foster capitalism at home and to bring progress and modernity not only to 'lesser peoples' in the colonial world, but also to minority peoples and underdeveloped regions around the peripheries of Europe and North America. Thus there was a forceful political geography underlying the modern nation-state which, from the seventeenth and eighteenth centuries onwards, insisted that powerful modern nations, not disorganised minority peoples, were to be the natural geopolitical units of the new modern world system. This indeed was a geography which, backed up by race theory, evolutionary biology and ethnography, acquired political significance and scientific respectability because it literally was a highly politicised and deeply acquisitive 'earth science'.

'Fabulous Geographies' of Ireland in the Seventeenth Century

Political geography at this stage also attracted considerable support from nation-builders and empire builders, just as it was patronised by military leaders and statesmen (Mac Laughlin, 1986b, p. 15). As O'Tuathail suggests, this was because it facilitated the 'subjugation and management of space conceptualised as a territorial container [and] requiring effective occupation by a central state apparatus' (O'Tuathail, 1996, p. 3). Ireland, whether we consider it as 'England's first colony' (Strauss, 1951), or as a 'New England' and one of that country's 'home countries', provides abundant evidence that the subjugation and management of space transformed the island of Ireland into a container of English state-power and commercial influence. It also allowed Ireland's new administrators to literally 'make' – or more accurately 're-make' – the country. Thus these new rulers rendered Ireland 'the site of an English Renaissance self-fashioning, a negative mirror of an emerging English self-image, a locational projection of negations of "Englishness"' (O'Tuathail, 1996, p. 6). Writing of Elizabethan Ireland in particular, David Barker has demonstrated how the country first came into being as a 'nation' when 'those who administered it marched across it, wrote about it, and, generally speaking, produced and assembled a physical domain which, for them at least, was coextensive with the space of their own discourse' (Barker, 1993, p. 81). The country which resulted from their nation-building labours was as much as anything else, a figure of Elizabethan speech.

Not everyone was happy to let English administrators make Ireland over in a paler image of the neighbouring island. Sir John Davis, Solicitor-General of Ireland in 1609, described how the inhabitants of the 'north parts' of Ulster, in their efforts to resist incursions of English power into their territories, 'tooke off' the head of one of the geographers sent to draw up a 'trew and perfet mapp' of this isolated corner of Ireland. They did this, Davis records, so that 'they would not have their cuntry discovered' (Davis, quoted in O'Tuathail, 1996, p. 1). Long before the nine-teenth-century age of nation-building then, Ireland had been submitted to the 'English gaze' and was considered one of nation-building England's natural 'home countries'. The state-centred ideologies and race-thinking which justified its incorporation into an expansionist English state system in the seventeenth century have received far less attention than 'colonialism' in Ireland in the nineteenth century. Granted to Henry II in the middle of the twelfth century, administered from England in the mid-sixteenth century, Ireland was extensively planted with communities of settlers and merchant capitalists in the course of the sixteenth and seventeenth centuries. As such it bears two characteristics worth mentioning because they tend to be overlooked in most recent post-colonial, and indeed post-nationalist, theorising about Ireland. First, Ireland was an internal periphery of England whose culture was geographically of western Europe while in part still subject to what Lloyd terms 'a dissimulated colonialism' (Lloyd, 1993). Second, Ireland was one of Europe's oldest settler societies in that it had a history of settler plantation even longer than that of Spanish Latin America (Strauss, 1951). This is why it is all the more surprising to find it excluded from most accounts of post-colonialism. This exclusion, I would argue, is only partly explained in terms of the serious neglect of Ireland and most things Irish in the British leftist tradition of scholarship. It stems also from the fact that in many accounts, with the notable exceptions of the works of Tom Nairn, Michael Hechter and a small number of other scholars, seventeenth-century colonialism has been regarded as an external, not an internal phenomenon. Thus 'colonies' have been seen more as extensions of the expansionist nation than as components or building blocks of modern nation-states like Britain and France. With a number of notable exceptions also – e.g. Said, Eagleton, Kiberd and Lloyd – most post-colonial theorists today fail to take seriously Ireland's claim to colonial status. They look instead to the amorphous Third World and rarely look to Ireland, or the peripheries of Europe, for examples of the post-colonial syndrome. What makes this all the more remarkable is the fact that ethnic minorities such as the Bretons, the Basques, the Catalans, the Welsh, the Scots and the Flemish, have always been treated by nineteenth-century nation-builders not so much as ethnically distinctive people in their own right, but rather as building blocks of larger, more powerful, and far more state-centred nations. Even within contemporary Ireland it is as if the country's recently acquired status as a 'Celtic Tiger', and its geographical location relative to Europe, have clouded the fact that for much of their history the Irish were considered part of a wider geopolitical world order that stretched all the way from the doorstep of metropolitan Britain to the hill stations of colonial India. Indeed Ireland has long been perceived as a country which belonged somewhere else. Today that 'somewhere' is the European Union. In the sixteenth and seventeenth centuries it was assumed, rightly or wrongly, to constitute a 'natural' part of an expansionist Britain. As such it was also said to belong 'rightfully' and 'naturally' to Great Britain.

Certainly many seventeenth-century English statesmen believed that Ireland should be refashioned as a 'New England'. In arguing thus they suggested that Ireland's geography – its relative position, its island location, its small size and its compact geographical make-up – and English mercantilism predestined it to become a settler 'home country' of England. This is particularly evident from early modern English writing about Ireland and the origins of 'English rule' here. There is certainly abundant evidence in the travelogues, what may be termed 'fabulous geographies', of Ireland in the sixteenth and seventeenth centuries to suggest that the country was likened to a maiden awaiting the sexual attentions of a domineering overlord to bring it out of a prolonged childhood into a mature state of nationhood. In his *Discourse on Ireland* in 1620 Luke Gernon wrote:

This nymph of Ireland is at all points like a young wench that hath the green sickness for want of occupying. She is very fair of visage and hath a smooth skin of tender grass. Indeed, she is somewhat freckled (as the Irish are) – some parts darker than others. Her flesh is of a soft and delicate mold of earth, and her blue veins trailing through every part of her like rivulets. She hath one master vein called the Shannon, which passeth quite through her … . Her bones are of polished marble, the gray marble, the black, the red, and the speckled, so fair for building that their houses show like colleges … Her breasts are round hillocks of milk-yielding grass, and that so fertile that they contend with the valleys. And betwixt her legs (for Ireland is full of havens) she hath an open harbor, but not much frequented … Neither is she frozen-hearted: the last frost was not so extreme here as it was reported to be in England. (Gernon, 1620, pp. 42–4)

Gernon began his Irish career as Second Justice of Munster in 1619 and assumed the judgeship of Limerick some time around 1620. He was by no means a dispassionate observer of planter society in the Ireland of his day. He was certainly among the first to develop a geography of appropriation and a nationalist rhetoric of possession which claimed Ireland for the overlordship of England. In so doing he inadvertently – and exuberantly – delineated some of the infrequently acknowledged dimensions of English nation-building in an early modern European setting. In a statement which ironically equated settler good husbandry here with sexual possession through rape, Gernon suggested that this 'nymph of Ireland wants a husband … she is not embraced … she is not hedged and ditched … there is no quickset put into her' (Gernon, quoted in Falkiner, 1909, p. 34).

Several other seventeenth-century commentators referred to England's nation-building and civilising mission in 'barbarous' Ireland. They did this in terms which suggested that the country would be far better off if it were incorporated into nation-building Britain than left to perish in the political isolation of Atlantic western Europe. Thus William Brereton, who visited Ireland in 1635 after touring in Holland the previous year, was surprised to find that the Irish were 'not ashamed of their religion, nor desire to conceal themselves' (Brereton, quoted in Calder, 1981, p. 67). This surprised Brereton as it did William Petty. Petty, writing of the Irish in the 1670s, stated: 'there is much superstition among them, but formerly much more than is now; forasmuch as by the conversation of Protestants, they become ashamed of their ridiculous practices, which are not de fide' (Petty, quoted in Harrington, 1991, p. 125). Indeed Petty found that the religious adherence of poor people here was less to God than to their traditional leaders, namely grandees, Old English landlords and the heads of their native septs and clans. He went on to state:

> When these were under the clouds, transported into Spain and transplanted into Connaught, and disabled to serve them as formerly about the year 1656, when adventurers and soldiers appeared to be their landlords and patrons, they were observed to have been forward enough to relax the stiffness of their pertinacity to the Pope, and his impositions. (Petty, quoted in Harrington, 1991, p. 126)

William Brereton was also shocked to find that 'most Irish women were bare-necked and wear a crucifix, tied in a black necklace, hanging between their breasts'. Irish houses he described as 'the poorest cabins I have seen, erected in the middle of fields and grounds, which they farm and rent'. For Brereton indeed Ireland was 'a wild country, not inhabited, planted, nor enclosed, yet it would be good corn if it were husbanded' (Brereton, quoted in Harrington, 1991, p. 114).

Following the 1641 rebellion which saw Catholics rise up against the new settlers we also find English commentators here calling for the garrisoning and re-subjugation of Ireland and the Irish. Thus Gerald Boate, in an account of Ireland's Natural History published in 1652, described Ireland under the Cromwellian plantation as 'a fruitful and domesticated land'. In particular he distinguished between the 'naturall inhabitants', or 'wilde Irish', who, he argued, mismanaged the land, and the more civilised outsiders who tamed it. He went on to suggest:

> Before this 'bloody rebellion' the whole land, in all the parts where the English did dwell, or had anything to doe, was filled with goodly beasts, both Cowes and Sheep, as any in England, Holland or other the best countries of Europe: the greater part whereof hath been destroyed by those barbarians, the naturall inhabitants of Ireland, who not content with to have murthered or expelled their Englishe neighbours … endeavoured quite to extinguish the memory of them, and all their civility and good things by them introduced into that wild Nation; and consequently in most places they did not only demolish the houses built by the English, the Gardens and Enclosures made by them, the Orchards and Hedges by them planted, but destroyed whole droves and flocks at once of English Cowes and Sheep, for they were not able with all their gluttony to devour one tenth part thereof, but let the rest lye rotting and stinking in the fields. (Boate, 1652, p. 67)

Like other seventeenth-century writers, Boate recommended a radical deforestation of Ireland as the only way to root out the country's rebellious human 'weeds'. For Boate indeed the woods of Ireland were the abode of 'Theeves and Rogues'. As such they literally were dangerous places because English law did not prevail there. They had to be 'taken' and 'tamed' by improving settlers from mainland Britain if ever they were to be redeemed from their lack of civility. Thus, in a classic statement on environmental engineering as a prelude for a whole range of projects for bringing about 'civilising' social change in Ireland, Boate argued:

> The trees being cut down, the roots stubbed up, and the land used and tilled according to exigency, the Woods in most parts of Ireland may be reduced not only to very good pastures, but also excellent Arable and Meddow. (Boate, 1652, p. 45)

Boate not only looked on the 'natural inhabitants' of Ireland as 'barbaric nomads'. He literally attributed that barbarism to their ethnic constitution, just as he traced the underdeveloped state of Irish agriculture to environmental mismanagement by an 'inferior people', to racial and ethnic causes, and not simply to natural causes. In so doing he traced the roots of 'barbarism' in Ireland to its 'natural inhabitants'. In his eyes Ireland was underdeveloped because its inhabitants literally were a 'vile' and 'lazy' race, a veritable race of 'bogmen'. He defended the transplantation of English settlers to Ireland as the only solution to what he perceived as an Irish lack of civility and civilisation. In so doing he, like Edmund Spenser, Luke Gernon, William Brereton, Edmund Campion and Fynes Moryson, was among the earliest defenders of English national frontier expansion into Gaelic Ireland. All of these writers saw this as a strategy for ensuring that the resources of Britain's less developed peripheries would fall to the tutelage of those who knew best how to utilise them, rather than to native 'barbarians' and the 'natural inhabitants' who inhabited these 'wild' regions. The bogs of Ireland, Boate argued, owed their infertile state 'not by any naturall property, or primitive constitution, but through the superfluous moisture that in length of time hath been gathered therein'. Castigating the Irish for not applying themselves to drainage schemes that would 'improve' them, he went on to state:

> it may easily be comprehended, that who so could drain the water, and for the future prevent the gathering thereof, might reduce most of the bogs of Ireland to firm land, and prefer them in that condition. But this

hath never been known to the Irish, or if it was, they never went about it, but to the contrarie let daily more and more of their good land grow boggy through their carelessness, whereby also most of the Bogs at first were caused. (Boate, 1652, p. 56)

Similarly, he argued, the woods of Ireland were always 'reckoned among the barren lands', and the reasons for this once again were traced to the 'naturallness' of the Irish and underdeveloped nature of the Irish psyche. Thus Boate states that:

although the land which the Woods doe take up, is in it self very good in most places, and apt to bear Corn and Grass plentifully, yet as long as the Woods remain standing, it is unfit not only to be made either Meadow or Arable, but even for Pasture, by reason of the overmuch moisture, the roots of the trees staying the rainwater, so as it hath not the liberty to pass away. (Boate, 1652, p. 34)

Finally, describing an incident when the 'wilde Irish' attacked 'poor English and Dutch workmen', laying waste the mine at which they worked, he wrote:

not content to lay waste the Mine, and to demolish all the works thereto belonging, [they] did accompany their barbarousness with bloody cruelty against the poor workmen ... the which some of them being English and the rest Dutch (*because the Irish having no skill at all in any of these things, had never been imployed in this Mine otherwise than to digg it, and to doo other labours*) were all put to the sword by them, except for a very few who by flight escaped their hands. (Boate, 1652, p. 33; emphasis added)

What is remarkable about this account is that it describes an incident in seventeenth-century Ireland in much the same way as Hollywood movies would later describe 'savage Redskins' attacking 'settlers' on the frontier white Anglo-Saxon America in the eighteenth and nineteenth centuries. Ireland certainly was regarded both as a country that was underdeveloped and as one that had great developmental potential. It could only become developed, it was argued, as a result of enlightened intervention, when it would literally come under new management. Thus Fynes Moryson, secretary to the Lord Deputy of Ireland in the opening years of the seventeenth century, concurred with his peers in his denigration of native society and the nomadic practices of Gaelic agriculturists. Like his predecessors he was afraid that intermarriage between the 'naturally lazy' Irish and the industrious English stock would end in a state of degeneracy. Moryson, justifying intervention in Ireland on the grounds that the Irish were a naturally slothful race who were disrespectful of private property, stated:

> *The land of Ireland is uneven, mountainous, soft, watery, woody, and open to winds and floods of rain, and so fenny, as it hath bogs upon the very tops of mountains, not bearing beast or man, but dangerous to pass, and such bogs are frequent all over Ireland ... The air of Ireland is unapt to ripen seeds, yet the earth is luxurious in yielding fair and sweet herbs ... The fields are not only most apt to feed cattle, but yield also great increase of corn ... .* [The] best sorts of flowers and fruits are much rarer in Ireland than in England, which notwithstanding is more to be attributed to the inhabitants than to the air. For Ireland being oft troubled with rebellions, and *the rebels not only being idle themselves, but in natural malice destroying the labours of other men, and cutting up trees of fruit for the same cause, or lese to burn them.* For these reasons the inhabitants *take less pleasure to till their grounds, or plant trees, content to live for the day in continual fear of like mischiefs.* (Moryson, quoted in Harrington, 1991, p. 93; emphasis added)

These writers, like Elizabethan visitors before them, regularly described Ireland as a wilderness. They placed England firmly at the civilised centre of an otherwise disorderly and barbaric world. They portrayed Britain as an illustrious player on a world stage, a country dedicated to the task of bringing its nearest neighbour – Ireland – in from the periphery by claiming it for the great British nation. They particularly sought to make Ireland part of the commonwealth by peopling it with Protestant settlers. When they portrayed the native Irish at all, they painted them in colours so dark that they appeared to be 'savage participants in bizarre tribal rites and darkly superstitious religion' (Harrington, 1991, p. 14).

Edmund Spenser, writing at the dusk of the sixteenth century, described Ireland as 'untamed' and likened it to other 'untamed' landscapes in far-off North America. Those who lived there, he believed, belonged to 'the vile and brutish part of mankind and bore many of the marks of an alien race' (Spenser, quoted in Morgan, 1975, p. 325). Thus English visitors who came to Ireland constantly complained of the food, the weather and the customs of the people. Although they agreed that it could never quite be a pristine Arcadia, they nevertheless suggested that Ireland could certainly be a finer and better place if it were 'dis-inhabited' or cleared of the Wilde Irish. These men did not travel to Ireland to broaden their minds or understand native ways. They came here 'for gain, either monetary, political or spiritual, and they returned home firmly convinced of their own superiority'. William Parry, one such traveller, found the Irish to be not unlike the 'barbaric Turks'. They too were 'beyond all measure a most insolent super-bous and insulting people ... . They sit at their meat (which is served to them upon the ground) as Tailors sit upon their stall, cross-leg'd [and] passed the day "banqueting and carrowsing"'. Travelling in the Middle East at the close of the sixteenth century Parry made direct comparisons between the anti-social behaviour of the Kurds and that of the Irish. The Kurds, he stated, 'were not unlike the Wilde Irish' and were 'altogether addicted to theaving' (Parry, quoted in Cormack, 1997, p. 49).

Race-thinking and the English Mission Civilatrice in Seventeenth-century Ireland

The 'fabulous geographies' compiled by these visitors to sixteenth- and seventeenth-century Ireland suggest that the roots of anti-Irish racism run much deeper than the nineteenth century. What made the 'barbarism' of the Irish and 'darkness' of the Irish countryside all the more frightening was the fact that, in the eyes of visiting Englishmen, these were the defining features of a people, and a country, located on England's doorstep, and at the heart of a nation-building metropolitan world. Yet in the seventeenth century the Irish were more likely to be located alongside 'inferior races' in the colonial world than with the urban and rural 'masses' in England. Like Native American Indians and Australian Aborigines they were deemed an inferior people who mismanaged the natural environment because they lacked civility.

Unlike the native Irish, new English settlers to the 'New England' in Ireland possessed many of the mathematical skills and knowledge of estate management which enabled them to control the country's natives and its natural landscapes. Because they understood the language of estate management and were adept at land surveying, these new inhabitants of 'barbarous Ireland' were considered superior to its 'natural inhabitants'. They literally had mastery over the Irish and Irish nature, and possessed managerial skills which the 'wilde Irish' lacked. The 'mere Irish' were said not to appreciate the land they lived in. Inasmuch as many of them still practised a form of transhumance – known in Ireland as 'booleying' – they were likened to barbarians and Gypsies. As such they were deemed unfit for self-government because they belonged to the 'inferior races'. Thus Boate once again, describing the Irish as vagrants, said: 'the people that live thus ... grow thereby the more barbarous and live more licentiously than they could in towns, using what means they list, and practising what mischiefs and villainies they will, either against the government there by their combinations, or against private men, whom they malign by stealing their goods and murdering themselves'. To Edmund Spenser these 'wilde Irish' were 'half exempted from law and obedience, and having once tasted freedom do, like a steer that hath been long out of his yoke, grudge and repine ever after to come under rule again'. The 'English-Irish' were no better, he argued, since they had 'degenerated and grown almost mere Irish, yea and more malicious to the English than the Irish themselves' (Harrington, 1991, p. 63).

In his *History of Ireland* in 1571 Edmund Campion also stressed the dangers of intermarriage and cultural miscegenation. He constantly warned against 'the creeping debasement of the English settlers in Elizabethan Ireland'. He continually insisted that new settlers here must resist 'assimilation into barbaric Irish society'. He even expressed a fear that the English visitor to Ireland might 'become degenerate in short space [of time]' if he were to be over-exposed to Irish nature and Gaelic barbarism. Referring to the more aristocratic among the Gaels, he believed that even these were unfit to rule over any civilised nation because, he added: 'Without either precepts or observation of congruity they speak Latin like a vulgar language'. In describing the more aristocratic among them as a social group 'unfit for leadership' and lacking in good manners, he wrote: 'I have seen them ... grovelling upon couches of straw, their books at their noses, themselves lying flat prostrate, and so to chant out their lessons by piecemeal, being the most part lusty fellows of twenty years and upwards'. Irish 'ladies', Boate contended, were 'tall, round and fat ... [and] trimmed rather with massy jewels than with garish apparel'. Their infants, especially those of the 'meaner sort' were, he said, 'neither swaddled or lapped in linen, but folded up stark naked in a blanket till they can go, and then if they get a piece of rug to cover them they are well sped' (Campion, 1633, quoted in Calder, 1981, p. 65).

Discussing these 'fabulous geographies' written in the seventeenth and eighteenth centuries, Anne McClintock has argued that the territorial expansion of the British state at this time cannot be fully understood without a proper theory of power relations. This would suggest that the gender and power relations expressed in the descriptions of Ireland we have been discussing so far were never simply 'the superficial patina of empire' (McClintock, 1995, pp.

6–7). Neither were they an ephemeral gloss over the more decisive mechanics of class or race operating in seventeenth-century Ireland. They were instead fundamental to the securing and main-tenance of a nation-building enterprise here because they sought to incorporate Gaelic Ireland within the borders of an expanding English nation-state system. Thus in the minds of English nation-builders and planter communities alike, the military conquest and plantation of Ireland with 'improving' English and Scottish settlers found both their shaping metaphors and political sanction in the prior subordination of nature as feminine and women as a category of nature. Viewed thus both the far-flung 'colony', and in this case the neighbouring 'home country' of Ireland, were often considered as 'peripheral' or 'feminised political space'.

Yet McClintock's argument, especially as applied to Ireland, would suggest that frontier development and settler plantation here were as much products of a crisis of identity in the Englishman as settler-planter and nation-builder, as products of political or economic expansion. The chief merit of this feminist anthropological approach to seventeenth-century English expan-sionism is that it supplements more conventional approaches to English rule and plantation society Ireland. However, it should not substitute for, or replace, other explanations of state expansion in seventeenth-century Ireland. Neither should it diminish our understanding of other aspects of relationships between Ireland and Britain during that century. To categorise the conquest of Ireland as 'rape', for example, is to suggest that it was a 'one-off' affair, an act of aggression inflicted on a vulnerable victim by a powerful male 'other'. The plantations of Ireland in the sixteenth and seventeenth centuries were not like that. They were certainly not spontaneous events. Neither were they passively accepted by 'feminised' and 'taciturn' natives. They were meticulously planned, long drawn out and violently resisted affairs. They were much more akin to forced marriages than spontaneous acts of rape.

Anti-Irish racism also extended to descriptions of native agricul-tural practices and settlement patterns. The Irish were described as a 'debased people' because they were said to lack any really signif-icant urban centres. They lived instead in 'clachans' or nucleated settlements which had neither church nor stately manor. These could therefore not be compared to orderly English villages either in terms of social and economic functions or architectural form. Indeed because the Irish were said to mismanage the land and waste the resources of the country, their removal from the land-scape was justified on the grounds that new settlers could literally 'husband' the land better than the native Irish ever could. That new settlers were brought here in very large numbers is clear from Petty's estimates of Ireland's population in the late seventeenth century. He estimated that just under one-third of the country's inhabitants in 1672 were immigrants or of immigrant origin. Through a highly original and careful use of poll tax returns for 1660, Smyth was able to map the settler population of Ireland at this time. He suggests that one-fifth of all immigrants were in Munster, under one-third were in Leinster, almost one-half were in Ulster and less than 5 per cent were in Connaught. He also suggests that 'no other west European country was to witness such a flood of in-migrants at this time' (Smyth, 1992). Unlike migrant workers in Europe today, these 'in-migrants' were by no means 'marginal men' – they spearheaded the economic transformation of the country, thus refashioning this 'New England' in a fair imitation of the larger 'home country'. As Smyth shows, they were put to work in woodland clearance and the timber trade. They were also employed as artisans, in housebuilding, in glassworks, in mining, in ironworks and in a whole range of occupations that cropped up with the introduction of new towns to the country. Referring to the upheavals in landownership following the Cromwellian conquest, he stated that Gaelic lords here were literally felled in the same way that the country's last vestiges of forest were levelled (Smyth, 1992). All of this brought about huge changes on the face of the country. Finally, in discussing one of these plantations Smyth describes how:

> the metropolitan state ... moved to formally and literally put in place a more carefully planned and mature plantation which would see the full panoply of settlers – from lords to artisans – brought in to run and build the towns, seignories, bawns, mills and ironworks. Attempts at village concentration of farmers and artisans yielded to both existing territorial arrangements and a pastoral economy. Thus the rural immigrant settlement pattern became embedded in ancient townlands. A very complicated amalgam of both old and new worlds was thus grafted onto one of the oldest corners of Europe. (Smyth, 1992)

Two points are worth emphasising at this stage because of their bearing on my argument about the role of plantations in a wider nation-building exercise. First, these plantation schemes certainly complicated settlement patterns in Ireland as Smyth very properly suggests. However, they did not leave any doubt in the minds of either native or newcomer as to who the lords of the land and humankind in Ireland really were. Second, given the scale of settler immigration, and given also its 'rounded' social composition and geographical distribution, it seems safe to suggest that plantations here were intended as a nation-building demographic remapping exercise carried out almost on a national scale. Certainly given the scale of immigration, given the degree of social engineering it entailed, it is more likely that plantations were part of a nation-building arsenal than simply exercises in colonial exploitation.

Military conquest in Ireland, like the military conquest of Spanish America a century and a half before this, involved the conquest of nature and the domestication of the land as well as 'its people'. It meant the acquisition of the land and natural resources of Ireland, and the simultaneous subordination of the country's Gaelic overlords to the overlordship of planter rule. Reducing the woods of Ireland allowed English and Scots-English planters here to literally 'settle' the land and to simultaneously make way for more loyal and civilised subjects who could in turn settle the 'wilde Irish'. Thus plantations in Ireland had a profound structuring effect not only on Irish society but also upon Irish nature and on the Irish landscape. Discussing the cultural and economic processes underlying the plantation project, another writer has argued that Ireland's regional economic structure, including the territorial organisation of its national landscape, were 'induced by the nature of the colonial relationship with England' (Duffy, 1985, p. 35). Irish landscapes, in other words, were more the products of mental processes and nation-building projects, than outcomes of mere natural processes.

The whole notion of 'civilisation' underlying these 'fabulous geographies' confidently expressed England's elevated sense of self-consciousness in relation to what it perceived as a 'savage' and underdeveloped Irish countryside. Norbert Elias has suggested that the whole notion of civilisation in the seventeenth century perceived this as a process rather than a 'state of being'. As he saw it, the civilising process summed up:

> ... everything in which Western society of the last two or three centuries believes itself superior to earlier societies or more 'primitive' contemporary ones. By this term Western society seeks to describe what constitutes its special character and what it is proud of: the level of its technology, the nature of its manners, the development of its scientific knowledge or view of the world, and much more. (Elias, 1978, pp. 3–4)

Elias also showed how the curve of the civilising process could be observed, especially over the longue duree, across a whole range of social behaviour. Thus it could be traced through changes in attitudes towards private and communal property, including attitudes towards work, leisure and idleness. It was equally traceable to changing attitudes towards settled life and nomadism, towards dress and personal hygiene, towards good manners, filth, aggression, cruelty and suffering. This was also the case in plantation Ireland where English frontier expansion had created far more space for 'planter' communities, and for the Reformed church and planter civilisation, than it did for the native 'wilde Irish'.

Raymond Gillespie has similarly argued that the seventeenth century saw dramatic changes in the structures of everyday life in Ireland, not least in the remoter regions of the country that had hitherto managed to avoid the grasp of centralising state institutions and bureaucratic control (Gillespie, 1997). 'There was', he states, 'a shift from a lineage dominated lordship society imbued with a traditional catholicism to a world governed by the rules of common law'. In a statement which testifies to the unifying role of plantation geography in the wider context of the British Isles, he goes on to suggest that common law, Tridentine Catholicism and the new Protestantism formed the ideological cement which held together a rapidly commercialising economy dependent on markets and contracts (Gillespie, 1993, p. 114).

Ireland, although it had a long history of commercial and cultural contact with Britain, the Mediterranean, Scandinavia and Atlantic Europe, now entered into a new core–periphery relationship with England. Its new trading relationships also involved power relationship in that the native Irish were subjected to new forms of domination, both by the core state in England and by its new social classes in Ireland. In addition to being subject to the harsh laws of nature, they were increasingly also subject to English laws. They became victims of property take-overs, a people who saw their lands and natural resources literally passing into new hands. This meant that they were more and more subject to the vagaries of commodity markets and political authority in England. Their mental worlds also were invaded by forms of consciousness which were evolved at the centre and applied in the periphery (Peet, 1986, p. 195). All this meant that the twin exercises of 'civilising' Ireland and introducing Protestantism from England greatly reduced the area under pre-settler legal and religious practices. This in turn overturned traditional property relations in Ireland, greatly diminished the area under Gaelic control, and transformed both the direction and the very nature of linkages that once bound Catholic Ireland to mainland Europe. From the late seventeenth century onwards this was, to a limited extent at least, to lead to an identification of Catholicism with the national cause, albeit chiefly only among the more well-off in Gaelic and Catholic Ireland. Indeed Catholicism in Ireland at this time, like Protestantism in the Dutch Republic, enhanced, and was enhanced by, an early sense of national identity, at least among the upper echelons of native Irish society (Elliot, 1982, p. 302). In both countries affiliation to a supranational religious community was often as not also instrumental in securing international assistance for local causes, especially during periods of international conflict (Geyl, 1932, pp. 89–94). In sixteenth- and seventeenth-century Ireland, as in the Dutch Republic and Poland in the latter century, the native religion drew new strength from its identification with a national cause. Thus, as Wallerstein has noted, even though Irish society was far less sophisticated than that of the Dutch Republic, 'its struggle against English domination was characterised by many of the same features as the Dutch struggle against the domination of Spain' (Wallerstein, 1974, p. 207). Catholicism here was, in Lewis Namier's apt phrase, 'a sixteenth century word for nationalism' (Namier, quoted in Hill, 1967, p. 23). It was a sort of social cement which bound together a native society under attack from the superior forces of Protestant expansionism. Yet we should not confuse nation and nationalism here. As a mass sentiment, nationalism at best involves 'acceptance of the members of the state as members of a status group, as citizen, with all the requirements of collective solidarity that implies' (Wallerstein, 1974, p. 145). It would be difficult indeed to apply this definition of nationalism to Catholic Ireland in the sixteenth and seventeenth centuries, a time when the Protestant nation was in the ascendancy and when Catholicism was associated with all that was backward and medieval. Indeed, in the late seventeenth and early eighteenth centuries Protestant nationalism here was fuelled by the framework of mercantilism. It found its leading advocates not so much in Gaelic society as among the Protestant bourgeoisie. The idea that society here should be integrated within one culture, under one state, that people should have the right to self-determination, belonged far more to Protestant settlers and nation-builders in Ireland than it did to the beleaguered Irish.

Yet the abiding link between Catholicism and the wider world was particularly important in Ireland's case. Right down to the beginning of the twentieth century, for example, identification with a wider world centred upon Catholic France, Italy, Spain and Portugal, meant that the Irish, including perhaps even the plebeian

Irish, were as much part of a Euro-centred Catholic world as inhabitants of an appendage of England. This is a neglected dimension
of the wider historic meaning of unionism in Irish politics. It
suggests that, unlike Unionist Ulster which was far more single-
mindedly centred upon Britain and the Empire in the nineteenth
and early twentieth centuries, the south of Ireland has long been
part of a wider world. It was, and increasingly still is, much more
focused upon Europe and the global economy than upon England
and Great Britain, the chief focus of Unionist politics, and, until
recently, of the 'Unionist economy' of north-eastern Ireland.

Certainly plantation and English rule in Ireland from the
sixteenth century onwards meant that the country was brought
under a whole variety of new forms of political tutelage. It also
brought the country into a much closer relationship with state-
centred bureaucracies and absolute monarchy in England. Thus
Ireland, and the Irish, now came under the control of newly
emerging social classes in England, particularly merchant capitalists, landowners and new commercial elites. It also experienced
different forms of institutionalised political and economic control
as new farming practices, new forms of 'husbandry', new methods
of estate management and new geometries of power and resource
exploitation were quite literally superimposed upon the land. Here,
as in eighteenth-century North America, Australia and Spanish
South America, plantation involved a growing concentration of
land in the hands of a few hundred very powerful estate owners
who were surrounded by the dispossessed native population. The
plantation of Munster, for example, created estates ranging from
4,000 to 12,000 acres. Sir Walter Scott alone acquired approximately 40,000 acres of prime land in this plantation scheme. The
proportion of land held by Catholics in Ireland declined from 59
per cent in 1641 to less than 14 per cent in 1703 (Regan, 1980, p.
5). A century and a half later 2,000 estate owners, each holding
2,000 acres or more, accounted for no less than two-thirds of the
country's land surface (Hoppen, 1984, p. 87). By then the pattern
of land ownership in Ireland was not that different to the situation
prevailing in Central America today. As in contemporary El
Salvador, Nicaragua, Honduras and Colombia, for example, a
powerful ruling oligarchy controlled the bulk of the country's agricultural land. Thus an estimated 800 individuals owned half the
land of Ireland in the 1870s. This sector also enjoyed a gross
annual rental of 10 million pounds, no small income indeed at a
time when total UK expenditure on civil government amounted to
approximately 6.6 million pounds (Vaughan, 1977, p. 187). By

1870 only 3 per cent of the Irish population actually owned land. Moreover, the majority of the landless in Ireland were not urban dwellers, as they were in Britain, but propertyless rural dwellers paying high rentals to a very small group of powerful estate owners (Slater and McDonough, 1994).

Thus plantation and military conquest, particularly as they impacted upon the remoter interiors and 'backward places' of the country, involved a radical and qualitative break with traditional systems of resource utilisation, including traditional methods of ruling and farming the Irish countryside. In areas under English hegemony, it was not only that settlers now set about 'tilling the land in English style'. The landholding patterns, including patterns of land utilisation, in these areas changed out of all recognition. Crucially also the whole idea of 'nature' in Ireland at this time was radically transformed. Nature in this Anglicising and 'settler Ireland' was not only increasingly 'domesticated' – it was differently regulated and 'consumed' by 'newcomers', rather than by the native elites who had ruled the country in pre-plantation times. Land use patterns also changed dramatically in the eighteenth century as potato cultivation and intensive flax production created entirely new human landscapes. This was particularly obvious in the case of marginal lands along the Atlantic fringe, but it was also true of the small holding landscape of the intensely farmed north-east of the country. Even in the seventeenth century Ireland was transformed from a country in its own right into an experiment in plantation as it became a blueprint for the subsequent plantation of Virginia. That which was tried and tested in the plantations of Ireland was later on often transposed to new environments in North America.

Thus the 'civilising process' in Ireland also involved, and may even have been motivated by, the extension of new forms of environmental management, new geopolitical considerations, and new systems of land utilisation and social administration. Certainly, as I have already suggested, the mission civilatrice of settler society here greatly prioritised the husbandry of the newcomer over the traditional farming and commercial practices of the native. Like the entire neo-liberal modernising project in the contemporary Third World, it also prioritised the experience, and expertise, of the 'outsiders' over those of the more parochially minded native 'insiders'. In particular it placed a new emphasis on such modernising projects as urban development, social engineering, forest clearance, environmental management, horticulture, landscaping, village development and the growth of large estates and estate management. Thus the seventeenth-century plantation of

Ulster has been cited as 'the first reasonably successful attempt at regional planning in Ireland'. It certainly transformed the province from 'a stronghold of pastoral non-urban Gaelic traditions' into a 'bastion of peoples whose speech, habits, traditions, unwavering loyalties and resolute Protestantism differed totally from native ways' (Quinn, 1967).

Describing the plantation of Ulster thus is to ignore the power politics underlying the plantation scheme and its devastating consequences for native society and the pre-plantation or 'native' environment. In this plantation scheme of things, the new planned towns and villages of Ireland, including in Ulster, were, in the words of one contemporary, 'her palaces' (Gernon, 1620). As Smyth recently put it, the new ruling elites in Irish society henceforth 'took most of the glittering prizes and lived out their dream of ascendancy as ... agents of the wider British state' (Smyth, 1997, p. 421). In Ulster also industrial enterprise and the commercialisation of agriculture resulted in the total transformation of the natural and human landscapes, especially in the east of the province. New uses and new commercial outlets were found for native resources such as linen and timber, just as new and more exploitative man–land relationships emerged in areas densely settled by newcomers. The very categories 'plantation' and 'transplantation' implied this.

Thus frontier expansion through plantation in seventeenth- and eighteenth-century Ireland was unifying and integrative in a dual sense. As the view from England suggested, it was an Enlightened attempt at constructing an ideal nation-centred society, and an ideal commercial system in a country now referred to as 'New England'. To the Gaelic overlords of an older Ireland it was a catastrophe which contributed to the shrinking of their world and drove underground, but by no means extinguished, the culture of the plebeian Irish. It gradually also shifted the focus of Irish trade away from continental Europe and far more firmly towards Britain. By shifting the axis of market dependency away from continental Europe, with which Ireland had long and intimate relations since well before the fifteenth century, plantation also contributed to a deeper integration of Ireland into a narrow power geometry where power and privilege resided either in England, or in the English Pale in and around Dublin. Equally significant, English plantations in Ireland were a unifying force in a regionally divided political landscape. Until then, and despite intermittent attempts to do so, no Gaelic overlordship was ever powerful enough to transform the country from a fragmented world of political regionalisms into a modern national polity. It took plantation and English rule to turn the fragmented world of Gaelic Ireland into a far more unified political space. This more than anything else laid the foundations for the centralisation of political authority in Ireland. It turned the country into a functioning, albeit subordinate, entity in a new system of core–periphery relationships which linked Ireland with Britain and the British Empire. Plantation policy, and English rule thereafter, placed new values on people, places and resources in seventeenth-century Ireland and forced the country into a new geo-strategic system that was under English hegemony. Smyth suggests that the gaps separating the landscapes and environments of Ireland in the early sixteenth century from those of the early 1800s were vast indeed. By the latter date, he insists, 'the plough and the spade had colonised more arable land than ever before or since in Irish history'. By this stage also, he argues, 'the openness of the sixteenth century landscape had also disappeared'. Henceforth Ireland was covered with a widespread network of privatised farms and 'civilised demesnes'. Indeed it possessed 'one of the densest road networks in the whole of Europe, linking even the remotest rural communities to the now almost ubiquitous market and fair towns' (Smyth, 1997, p. 421).

All this meant that Ireland did not just come under a new and different economic order – it experienced different forms of political surveillance than those which prevailed in the pre-plantation era. Plantation created the basis for a permanent state bureaucracy in Ireland, just as it also laid the basis for a single market and contributed to the consolidation of a unified field of communication here which ultimately linked English-speaking Ireland to the United Kingdom. English rule also fostered a new codified legal system and laid the basis for new and far more centralised systems of local and national government (Regan, 1980, p. 10). Thus plantation and the territorial expansion of English power here greatly contributed to the gentrification and Anglicisation of the country's physical and human landscapes. Ireland was 'garrisoned', 'ordered', surveyed and 'tamed', just as its landscapes were 'possessed' and 'raped' by new settlers.

Finally the racist ideas that permeated English nationalist ideology in Ireland in the seventeenth century shaped European attitudes towards other minority peoples like the Bretons in France, the Basques and Catalans in Spain, and a whole host of ethno-nationalities in the Balkans and central Europe. Social scientists have long recognised that racism provided quasi-scientific justifications for the reign 'The Lords of Humankind' in the colonial world of the nineteenth century (Peet, 1985; Stoddart, 1986; Kiernan, 1972). Far less attention has been devoted to the role of race-thinking in legitimising the domination of indigenous minorities in Britain and Europe in the sixteenth and seventeenth centuries. Yet a political geography of nation-building was central to many of these early forms of racial discourse. As we have already noted, this was a discourse which literally left no room for a 'branching' or alternative model of development within Great Britain and Ireland, one of Europe's earliest and most strongly unified nation-states. Indeed the case of seventeenth-century Ireland shows that there was no place at all within this British national model of development for a cultural relativism which would even validate the existence of the Gaelic Irish in a country which increasingly was not 'their homeland'. This was because the nation in Britain, as elsewhere in Enlightened Europe, not only expressed itself as opposed to absolutism and what it considered as medieval superstition. It also denoted a process of moral development and political awakening. Thus it literally was a step ahead of the kingdoms and petty fiefdoms into which the British Isles, not least Ireland, had been divided prior to the sixteenth century. It also implied the growth of a unique socio-economic and geographical entity in response to a much wider, more national sense of place and sense of identity under the strict tutelage of the Protestant nation in Ireland.

'Pollution' through Miscegenation: Fear of the Native in Colonial Ireland

That planter communities here frequently feared corruption or racial pollution through contamination with the 'wilde Irish' is evident from much writing about Ireland in the seventeenth century. This is particularly clear from the following petition of English soldiers demanding the full implementation of the 'transplantation' system in the mid-seventeenth century. The soldiers in question stated that one reason for the 'transplanting of the Irish' was to prevent those of 'natural principles becoming one with the Irish, as many thousands did who came over in Queen Elizabeth's time'. Quoting scripture to support their case, they went on to state:

> Would not the lord be angry with us till he consume us, having said The land which ye possess is an unclean land, because of the filthiness of the

people that dwell therein. Ye shall not therefore give your sons to their daughters, nor take their daughters to your sons ... . Nay, ye shall root them out before you, lest they cause you to forsake the Lord your God. (Petition of Soldiers, 1655)

Viewed thus, 'destroying the enemies of the Faith' was simply a prelude to a civilising project which invited 'honest men to come and live' in this new Ireland. Lest their superiors might oppose a 'transplantation' which was in fact a form of cultural apartheid backed up by a seventeenth-century expression of ethnic cleansing, these same petitioners went on to state:

You may thereby free many from being murdered by those whose rela- tions were killed ... they [i.e. the 'wilde Irish'] *being a people of such inveterate malice as to continue and labour to revenge themselves twenty or thirty years after an injury received* – which they cannot do when separated – neither can they take such advantages to surprise your garrisons, or engage your soldiers in every design against us, as they can by living among us. (Petition of Soldiers, 1655; emphasis added)

As statements like these and others testify, the planter in seven- teenth-century Ireland was literally suspended between 'home' and 'away'. He was equally suspended between rape and emasculation, between the fantasy of conquest and the dread of subsequent engulfment in a strange and alluring land. Moreover, the constant and harsh gendering of Ireland as both naked and passive, as simultaneously violent and cannibalistic, also represents the abju- ration of an English male identity displaced on to a 'feminized' space called Hibernia. Ireland as a feminised space inhabited by a 'wilde' people was consequently denied a self-governing role in the modern sense of that term. It became instead a part of the British nation where the act of 'discovery' often involved a male baptism by fire and exile in a 'foreign' land. In both rituals men took possession of, or elected themselves into a sacred space. They publicly disavowed the creative agency of others, in this case the native Irish and their allies from among the 'contaminated', and hence 'degenerate, Old English who settled here well before the seventeenth century'. In so doing the new planter communities arrogated to themselves the power of origins and denied agency to the 'wilde Irish', their religious and ethnic enemies. This is why McClintock equates the imperial act of discovery with a surrogate birthing ritual (McClintock, 1995, p. 29). However, as we have already seen, in using 'colony' as a 'metaphor' for woman, feminist geographers and anthropologists risk reducing these simply to metaphors. As the case of seventeenth-century Ireland shows, 'plantation' was a substantial reality indeed for whole sections of the native population. It was not a figment of an imperial imagination or a fragment of virtual reality. It was certainly much more than a metaphor for 'woman' and femininity. Indeed, in Ireland's case, it is possible to go even further than this and to suggest that 'discovery' and 'good husbandry' here literally allowed English planters, both large and small, to give birth to the country. Through discovery and subsequent good husbandry powerful planters could literally take possession of the country, both as geographical reality and as a cartographic construct. This allowed them to fetishise and domesticate Irish land and Irish natural resources. It also permitted them to mark the country as an English possession, not least in the aptly titled early maps of the United Kingdom of Great Britain and Ireland. Writing of another such project of environmental conquest in the late nineteenth century, one writer described how an 'empire of agriculture' was carved by the United States from the 'jealous and resentful jungles' of Central America (Adams, 1914, p. 122). As in seventeenth-century Ireland, this allowed for a new commerce between the Old and New World which led to a 'crusade' against 'raw nature' in the latter. This in turn resulted in a 'peaceful Conquest of the Tropics' on the one hand, and the violent subjugation of society and nature in Ireland on the other.

The 'fabulous geographies' of plantation which we have been discussing so far also point to Ireland as the location of one of the earliest overseas expressions of environmental engineering, and one of the first places where ethnic cleansing was attempted. This, as we have seen, was because plantation here involved a 'crusade' against nature, and a mission civilatrice that had as its objective a literal gentrification of the human landscapes of the country. As we have also seen, the authors of these plantation schemes were among the earliest defenders of an organic territorial theory of the modern nation-state which justified the extension of English rule to Ireland as the only chance of that country ever becoming 'tamed' and civilised. They insisted that developing nations like England, unlike underdeveloped pastoral and regionally fragmented polities like Ireland, were living organisms that needed space in order to grow. In so doing they insisted that English history should be the sovereign over the histories of the 'lesser breeds' – like the Irish – who inhabited the Celtic fringes of Britain. They finally suggested that the acquisition of land and power in Ireland would help deflect internal conflicts in English society on to an Irish terrain. Plantations in Ireland, it was argued, would satisfy the twin lusts of English nation-builders for power, just as it would feed the appetites of English yeomen and noblemen for land. Thus behind what appeared an illogical extension of English power to Ireland lay a highly articulate political ideology which justified English frontier expansion on the grounds that it brought the country, and its 'natural inhabitants', within the realms of a modern Anglicising civility.

Certainly these seventeenth-century writers reflected the concerns of English nation-builders as much as they represented the interests of landed elites. They even justified England's mission civilatrice here by raising the ideology of plantation to new heights and recruiting Enlightenment ideals to the service of nation-building through internal colonial expansion in Ireland. This literature, together with the political pamphleteering to which it gave rise, had the effect of spawning heroic images of English and Scots-English settlers in the darkest corners of barbarous Ireland. Planters were depicted as pioneers on the frontiers of the then known civilised world. They were altruistic administrators who cherished notions of the superiority and civilised nature of planter rule in Ireland. Not surprisingly planters and other newcomers to Ireland grew accustomed to their own superiority and were convinced that they were literally born to rule over all things Irish. They made the code of the civilised settler synonymous with that of English nation-building and Anglo-Irish rule in Ireland. Later still in the eighteenth and nineteenth centuries, English officialdom, through the medium of learned societies of gentlemen, merchants, antiquarians and artists, fostered an image of British rule here as an advanced intellectual project. As in far-off Egypt and the Orient, this type of territorial and state expansion fitted in with an English addiction to rule so-called underdeveloped societies, and to tame the wild landscapes that harboured them. It fitted in also with an obsession for colonial inquiry and intellectual control over new territories and newly discovered peoples. Geography and geographical imagery provided the cartographic underpinnings for this type of knowledge about Ireland. To quote Said, it allowed military conquerors to 'dignify simple conquest with an idea, to turn the appetite for more geographical space into a theory about the special relationship between geography on the one hand, and civilized and uncivilized peoples on the other' (Said, 1991, p. 216).

Indeed, geographical thinking and theorising about Ireland was so far advanced in the expanding 'imagined community' of seventeenth-century England that speculation about remedies for Irish 'barbarism' were almost a national pastime. The study of geography in this early modern England was not only essential to the creation of an ideology of imperialism – it underpinned English nation-building. Thus those who studied the subject found in it 'a set of attitudes and assumptions that encouraged them to view the English as separate from and superior to the rest of the world' (Cormack, 1997, p. 1). Large numbers of young men who studied geography at the time were searching for a national identity of themselves as superior and separate from Roman Catholics, not least Roman Catholics in Ireland. Their new nation-building ideology was clearly articulated in the fabulous geographies we have been discussing in this chapter. Theirs was a geography which claimed both the supremacy of the English nation and its right to seize land, and resources, in Gaelic Ireland. According to this view, God was on the side of the expansionist English nation, particularly during times of military conquest, when he intervened through the medium of sword-wielding Cromwellian soldiers to protect English civility in Ireland and extirpate Irish barbarism.

Not surprisingly as a result of all this, Ireland and the Irish acquired 'negative values'. The Irish people were seen as 'disrupters' of English civility in Ireland, and ultimately as 'obstacles' to the creation of the Protestant British nation. The native Irishman was also seen as a seventeenth-century 'stalker' of the English settler in Ireland. In the space created by the shadow that stretched between the native stalker on the one hand, and the stalked immigrant on the other, were placed all the latent distrusts, prejudices and racial hatreds that the settler felt for the 'low Irish'.

In Ireland's case also this allowed the defenders of plantation to tutor public opinion in England into an acceptance of anti-Irish racism as an integral element in English nation-building through frontier expansion. Indeed the underlying geography of civility in this discourse suggested that the world outside the narrow ground of the English pale in Ireland was in a state of timelessness, and in an advanced state of physical and moral decay. Viewed thus Gaelic Ireland was a world crammed full of violent and barbaric incidents and practices. It was a world hushed into silence by its own mysteries, incapable of self-expression except through its colonial overlords. Because of their capacity to 'tame' the landscape, because of their propensity to live together in towns, to control trade, and to engage in new forms of economic activity, the new settlers in this new Ireland not only perceived themselves as different from the native Irish – they also saw themselves as fundamentally superior to them.

Thus plantation not only created new human landscapes in Ireland – as along the frontier of nineteenth-century colonial North America, and in modern Israel – it also created new men, and new women, communities capable of doing battle against natives and nature in the foreigner corners of the world. It also involved the superimposition of new landscapes upon much older Gaelic ones, thereby creating novel geometries of power wherein the native, and native economic practices, were, as we have already seen, always subordinate to those of the newcomer. The power differentials which separated the latter out from the native Irish did not simply stem from a monopolistic control over the means of production or means of exchange. They were due also to the high degree of social cohesion which gave members of the new settled communities a fixed claim on, if not always a fixed residency in, the new Ireland. Fixity of tenure conferred on newcomers the status of loyal subjects of the Crown. It had the effect of separating out newcomers from the native Irish. This also contributed to a radical disavowal of the Irish as a pathologically disloyal and socially inferior people who could only be redeemed within the political and moral structures of an expanding British nation. For that very reason, and not simply for any narrow economic reasons, the 'mere Irish' were always denied fixity of tenure in plantation Ireland.

Absentee landowners, like visiting English magistrates, had higher ranking than the native nobility in this new social hierarchy. Indeed absenteeism was attacked, albeit for different reasons, both by the defenders of plantation schemes in the sixteenth and seventeenth centuries, and by Irish nationalists and Catholic tenant farmers in the nineteenth century. That visiting magistrates in the sixteenth century, like absentee landowners three centuries later, could be chided for their lack of commitment to Ireland is clear from the following statement criticising some English officials for not staying in Ireland long enough to do the country good. Thus Fynes Moryson, writing of Ireland in 1617, likened magistrates to 'hungry flies' who sucked the blood from the body politic of the country. He particularly castigated them for not being 'much bent on reform of the commonwealth', accusing them instead of being ever 'vigilant to enrich themselves and their followers'. Such officials, because they possessed at best only a few years experience of Irish affairs, could never hope to govern a 'crafty and subtle nation' like seventeenth-century Ireland (quoted in Foster, 1988, p. 22). Those who did stay in Ireland literally set about claiming the country by reclaiming it from nature and local control. They did this while all the while constructing social and physical barriers for keeping the Irish at bay, for literally keeping them at the edge of civilised settled society. That is why, as Smyth has argued: 'Cromwellian conquest and settlement was to see a radical revolution in the character of the larger towns ... . Cromwellian strategy was not only to debar Catholics from membership of civil government and from juries but also set about expelling the old merchant families from within the walls. The Cromwellians, therefore, set about reconstructing both the social and political components of port-city and county towns rather than create new corporations' (Smyth, 1997, p. 26).

Their residency in Ireland, their greater potential for social cohesion, and the activation of this cohesion into strategies for social control and social action also gave planter communities a high degree of monopolistic control over nature, and over the native Irish. They used this power to represent their interests, and to marginalise those of the native and propertyless Irish poor. What made this all the easier was the fact that many English visitors to Ireland had commented on what they perceived as the downright mis-management of Irish lands and the under-utilisation of the country's resources. As we have already seen, they particularly pointed to the fact that nomadism still was a prominent feature of rural life in Gaelic Ireland and used this as an indicator of Irish backwardness. They also stressed the fact that Ireland's rich fishing industry was practically under the control of foreigners from Norway and Spain. They pointed out that the bogs of Ireland were undrained due to Irish 'carelessness'. They pointed out that the 'royal' deer and abundant wildfowl were not hunted here to the same degree as they were in 'civilised' England. Because so many of the rural poor were forced into vagrancy after the plantations, they too were seen as lacking in the social cohesion necessary for the construction of a modern civilised society in Ireland. For many of the native Irish plantation may have resulted in vagrancy. It probably also involved significant internal migration to the marginal lands of the west and north-west of the country. The issue of vagrancy, regularly raised against the native Irish, was used again and again to label the Irish an 'inferior race'. As we shall see, the issue of nomadism would be raised with renewed vigour against Irish Travellers in the nineteenth century, especially after the Famine, when large numbers of the rural poor had literally 'taken to the road' in order simply to survive.

3 'Political Arithmetic' and the Early Origins of Ethnic Minorities

Race, Political Arithmetic and the Irish

Modern demography as 'political arithmetic' had many of its roots in this seventeenth-century nation-centred, intellectual tradition of writing about Ireland and its people. It was argued that 'improvement in the public weal' and in the very constitution of society could only occur where and when those guided by clear, rational and scientific principles were entrusted with public office. This was considered especially important in underdeveloped societies like Ireland, and in the colonial world of the seventeenth and eighteenth centuries (Craske, 1997, p. 91).

This line of thinking reached maturity in nation-building Britain, France and Germany in the course of the nineteenth century at a time when the national bourgeoisie were in the political and intellectual ascendancy. However, it had its origins in the political demography of Hobbes and reached its fullest and indeed earliest expression in William Petty's *Political Arithmetic* and *The Political Anatomy of Ireland* published in 1672 and 1691 respectively. Petty was responsible for surveying Irish land in the late 1650s and used this socially strategic position to vigorously defend land transfers to Protestant settlers as the only means of saving Ireland from its lack of civility. Students of demography in Ireland after Petty did not so much collect information about the country's population – they warned of the putative consequences of untrammelled population growth in Ireland. They particularly focused upon the social class, religious and racial composition of the country's population. In so doing they transformed the category 'population' from the 'natural' entity that it was in the pre-plantation era, to a pseudo-scientific and ideological construct in the seventeenth and eighteenth centuries.

Viewed thus, the Irish 'population' was literally constructed by English demographers and political economists. From the start

Ireland's 'population problem' was widely used in 'civilised' circles in Ireland, particularly among the landed elites, to discuss, in highly alarmist terms, the threat posed by the 'lower orders' to English civilisation in Ireland. Ireland's population thus became a 'spectre' hovering over an Enlightenment nation-building project which sought to make 'barbarous' Ireland one corner of a wider metropolitan world under the hegemony of a nation-centred English aristocracy. Indeed the transition from general reasoning about numerical data about population derived from local sources in Ireland, to their subsequent mathematical treatment in modern demography meant that population statistics in Ireland, as elsewhere in the west, became the 'new Latin' of modern political science (Duden, 1992, pp. 73–5). As a result the term 'population', especially in Ireland, lost all links with actual people and was increasingly used to refer to the reproductive capacities of the native Irish compared to those of settler communities. Thus Irish population growth was said to endanger future prospects for nation-building and economic progress in Ireland. It was also said to undermine the country's carrying capacity, thereby upsetting the fragile relations between an emergent nation-centred settler population on the one hand, and the amorphous and 'underdeveloped' world of the 'wilde' Irish on the other. When the national 'mix' of Irish population was upset, as it appeared to be when the 'native' population seriously outstripped 'civilised' society, or when the profligate poor took to land subdivision in order to survive, settler elites called for more state institutions (such as prisons and other *penal* institutions) in order to reform the Irish poor. Indeed they deemed 'reform of the poor' more acceptable than agrarian reform as a solution to the problems besetting English settler society in Ireland. Rudyard Kipling later reminded these upper echelons of settler society that they had demographic responsibilities which they could neglect at their peril. What is important to note here is that well before Kipling, Britishers in seventeenth-century Ireland argued that their conquest of virgin nature and heathen races here was a peaceful crusade for bringing the Irish into the British nation, and for helping them to raise themselves a little higher on the hierarchy of racial classification. Kipling, like the nineteenth-century German historian Treitschke, argued that 'all great nations in the fullness of their strength have desired to set their mark upon barbarian lands'. Kipling put this same idea in more poetic form when he called on powerful nations to:

> Take up the white man's burden
> Send forth the best ye breed –
> Go bind your sons to exile
> To serve your captive's need;
> To wait in heavy harness
> On fluttered folk and wild –
> Your new-caught, sullen peoples,
> Half devil and half child.
> (Kipling, quoted in Weber, 1972, p. 334)

What is crucial to note here is that arguments like these, although couched in somewhat different terms, were rife in the 'fabulous geographies' of Ireland, Scotland and Wales, written in the sixteenth and seventeenth centuries. As early as 1540 English observers in Wales were worried about the preference of the native for livestock farming rather than cultivation. As one writer wrote, the native Welsh 'did study more to pasturage then tylling, as favours their consuete idilness'. All pastoralists, in other words, were 'idle', while only English farmers were 'industrious'. By the early sixteenth century we similarly find visitors deploring the aversion of Highlanders to 'honest industry'. Phillip Sidney also accused the Gaels of Ireland for choosing 'rather all filthiness than any law' (quoted in Quinn, 1966, p. 56). Sidney's fellow poet Edmund Spenser went into frenzies of prurient aversion over the dress of Irishmen and Irishwomen. He declaimed that the mantle worn by the wandering loose Irishwoman was only 'half a wardrobe'. He added:

> In summer you shall find her arrayed commonly but in smock and mantle, to be more ready for her light services; in winter, and in her travail, it is her cloak and her safeguard, and also a covering for her lewd exercise; yea, and when her bastard is born it serves instead of swaddling clouts. (Spenser, quoted in Calder, 1981, p. 36)

Written well before Britain became a 'great nation' in the nineteenth century, these descriptions of the Irish insisted that Protestant 'settlers' in Ireland at this time also had a responsibility to 'wait in heavy harness on fluttered folk and wild' in order that they too could make a contribution to the early forging of an English nation in the seventeenth century. Kipling argued that the White rich were obliged to produce 'good stock' in order to compensate for the poor quality of the 'lower orders' in their midst. English visitors to seventeenth-century Ireland developed similar arguments in relation to settler society here. They argued that 'settlers' should breed only with 'settlers' in order to raise up a population that would be superior to the 'low Irish'. They also insisted that 'settlers' here had to take great care lest cultural miscegenation or intermarriage might lead to the socio-political degeneration of a nation-building planter society.

Before the construction of a new settler society here in the sixteenth and seventeenth centuries Ireland was a very different country indeed. Even as recently as the late fifteenth century land and cattle in the remoter swathes of Gaelic Ireland were held as much for the status and prestige they conferred upon their owners as for their market value. For that reason Ireland was a country which belonged as much to the slow moving world of the medieval interior of Europe, as to the outward-looking maritime fringe of Atlantic Europe. Indeed, despite its small size, it straddled both these worlds and its socio-economic structures contained elements from the nation-building mercantile world of Atlantic Europe as well as some from a far more secluded and medieval world. Thus in the pre-plantation interior of the country, especially in the west of Ulster and in isolated parts of Connaught and Munster, long-distance commerce was far less common than conspicuous consumption of agricultural surpluses and short-distance trade in local produce engaged in by petty merchants. Plantation, land confiscations and a growing commercialisation of rural life in the seventeenth century in particular would rapidly draw these areas away from 'the idiocy' of rural life, including the 'idiocy' of medieval life, and integrate them into an evolving world system tied together by settler merchant capital and English maritime trade.

Even before the plantations, however, many of the port towns and coastal regions of Ireland were noted for their independence and political pretensions (Foster, 1988, p. 17). The more powerful inhabitants of these towns may even have emphasised their 'civility' and 'Englishness' in order to set themselves apart from subordinate sectors of Gaelic rural society. Prior to the plantations also towns and rural communities in Ireland could be divided into two very broad categories. The first included the many inland towns and rural localities that were built upon pre-existing foundations going back for several centuries. Towns and regions belonging to the second category included those located in or near maritime inlets, or those situated inland and away from the estuaries of the larger Irish rivers. Regions attached to the former category of towns tended to live politically and economically within their agricultural limits. They traded locally in basic agricultural commodities and had little contact with long-distance trading networks. Towns and regions in the latter category partici- pated in, and developed alongside, the growing commerce in agricultural exports and luxury goods that brought products from as far away as the Mediterranean, Scandinavia and continental Europe all the way to the rural and maritime Ireland. Indeed many of the larger towns belonging to this category in Ireland had the right to self-government granted to them by the king, or by some powerful lord, centuries even before the plantations of the sixteenth and seventeenth centuries. Some even possessed their own courts and held great fairs or markets which attracted merchants from regions as far away as northern Africa and Scandinavia. The right of these chartered towns to manage their own affairs was a vital factor in their development as trading centres. Their legislative rights enabled them to make by-laws regu- lating commercial activity to the advantage of the more powerful of their citizenry.

Thus while many towns along the maritime fringe of Ireland were little more than villages, others had 'paved and occasionally lighted streets, shops and tradesmen of all sorts [and] even running water'. As Lydon has noted, Galway in the fifteenth century 'even went so far ... as to replace the common law with "the law of the Emperor" called civil law' (Lydon, 1984, p. 15). The use of Roman law here reflected that city's far-flung trading links with conti- nental Europe where Roman law was respected. As we have already seen, towns like these, and to a lesser extent their hinterlands, often had as close links with the port cities of continental Europe and the east coast of nation-building England as they did with remoter regions in the interior of Ireland. They also saw them- selves, and were seen by others, as continental, even distinctively 'English' in outlook (Foster, 1988, p. 17). Like much of the country in general they operated in a quite fragmented world. They never really matured into an integrated field of national communication, or developed into a national urban system. Attached instead to local hinterlands, they looked to the expanding British nation for sustenance and commercial outlets. This in turn meant that new plantation towns and cities here were probably closer to the urban ways of mainland Britain, than to the rural ways of Gaelic Ireland. They engaged in long-distance trade with the former and in short- distance trade with their own limited hinterlands. More noted for their independence and meagre displays of urban ostentation than for their 'Gaelicness', these towns in turn also emphasised their 'continental' outlook for political effect. Thus they were part of a world wherein urbanisation and commerce were equated with advancement, civility and good manners. In the late nineteenth and early twentieth centuries those who lived in towns like these would, significantly, be labelled 'West Britons'. The 'true Irish' were said to live elsewhere, in a 'Hidden Ireland' of rural valleys and secluded upland regions well outside the pale of a modernising, nation-building English civility.

As elsewhere in Europe, frontier expansion in Ireland also marked the slow and final transition from medievalism to modernity. In the other land-locked countries that had far more extensive interiors, including France, Spain, Germany and Poland, this hastened the demise of the closed world of medievalism and the beginnings of modern nation-building (Fox, 1975). It also contributed to the emergence of a modern world system wherein powerful nations, not absolute monarchies, would rule the global economy. The transition from medievalism to modernity in large parts of western Europe, including Ireland, contributed to the unification of some countries and the geographical extension or expansion of others. Equally important it replaced the 'idiocy' of medieval life with the centralised rule of a landed aristocracy ruling in association with 'enlightened' monarchs and an improving nobility. In England's case frontier expansion into Ireland provided the basis for a subsequent 'great lunge forward' across the Atlantic to the colonisation of North America. Thus it is important to note that the end of the Middle Ages in England was marked as much by contraction and reorientation as by territorial expansion. On the one hand England progressively withdrew from continental Europe, ceased dreaming of conquest in France and focused instead upon its Celtic fringe and what Wallerstein refers to as 'its border-lands within' (Wallerstein, 1974, p. 57). On the other hand defenders of England's territorial expansion justified the plantation of Ireland on the grounds that it provided a 'vigorous English outreach' in this turbulent and comparatively underdeveloped periphery of Britain (Meinig, 1986, p. 30).

Writing some three centuries later, the English nationalist historian A.L. Rowse suggested that 'enlightened intervention' in Ireland was an entirely natural development, one that made England a fitter and better nation while simultaneously bringing the seeds of progress to the 'wilde Irish'. He showed how the very people who were most deeply involved in the early plantations of the south of Ireland – Walter Raleigh, Humphrey Gilbert, Richard Grenville – later on took the lead in planting the first colonies in Virginia (Rowse, 1957, p. 315). Indeed in Rowse's nation-centred and imperial history the unification of Britain and Ireland under English hegemony was something that was ordained by nature and sanctioned by a sixteenth-century equivalent of the doctrine of manifest destiny. Ireland, he averred, was literally 'on the way to America'. As he proudly pointed out, it was a group of West Country settlers with hard-won experience in the plantations of Ireland who later carried forth the colonisation and plantation of North America. Finally, Rowse implied, it was England's political responsibility, its manifest destiny and mission civilatrice, to bring progress to the Irish and to make Ireland part of the great British nation. At best this was a view which suggested that it was Ireland's destiny to end up in the United Kingdom. At worst it suggested that Ireland was forevermore to function, not so much a country in its own right, as a mere stepping stone to the more formal and far larger transatlantic world of the Americas.

Ireland: English Colony or 'Home Country' of England?

Although denied political autonomy by monarchical authority in the sixteenth and seventeenth centuries, Ireland did have an important, albeit subordinate role to play in a territorially unified and increasingly powerful nation-building Britain that was about to launch into imperial expansion across the Atlantic. Whether or not it did so as a colony or as an English 'home country' may now seem academic but is nevertheless a moot point. Harry Magdoff has suggested that the essential aims of colonial policy, in the modern world at least, always aimed 'to create a self-sufficient empire, producing as much as possible of the raw materials and food needs of the mother country and providing exclusive markets for its manufactures' (Magdoff, 1978, p. 103). The problem with this definition is that it applies less to a 'home country' or 'internal colony' like Ireland in the sixteenth and seventeenth centuries, than to colonial possessions of advanced capitalist states in the nineteenth century. It was then that the term 'colony' acquired popular meaning and political significance. Whatever the accuracy of this description of English policy in the nineteenth century, it did not describe relations between Ireland and Britain in the sixteenth or seventeenth centuries. Initially at least, Ireland was not ruled like a colony – it was an integral part of an expanding English nation-state. Prototypes of modern colonial rule scarcely existed then upon which 'colonial policy' in Ireland could be modelled. Instead Ireland acted partly as a 'home country' and partly as a prototype for colonial rule elsewhere. Initially at least also it was ruled as a part of Britain, and as a place that was clearly considered apart from England.

Nevertheless, chief among the most immediate effects of incorporation into Britain were the termination of native rule in Gaelic Ireland, the transformation of social relations with the land in many parts of the country, and a heightened commercialisation of social relations of production throughout the country. Equally significantly it also involved at least a partial disengagement of Ireland from the cultural and economic life of continental Catholic Europe and its incorporation into a world that was sometimes as wide as Britain's imperial reach and more often than not was as narrow as the kingdom of Great Britain and Ireland. Thus, and this is the crucial point here, the plantation of Ireland was simultaneously an exercise in frontier expansion and an early expression of 'big-nation' nation-building in Ireland.

Certainly anti-Irish racism at this stage was as much an expression of English nationalist prejudice as an assertion of colonial superiority. As we have already seen, England's geographical expansion into the Celtic peripheries facilitated transatlantic expansion in the seventeenth and eighteenth centuries. However, in England as well as in continental Europe frontier expansion was an internal affair long before it became a global or colonial affair. Viewed thus it was a step towards nation-building which subsequently facilitated colonial expansion elsewhere. The motivations for this expansionism were not simply ideological or geopolitical. They were also influenced by strong territorial and environmental considerations. Thus for example, expansionism in Britain was the means whereby England could literally close its own frontiers while simultaneously defining the western frontiers of Protestant Europe. Viewed thus also territorial expansion saw England engage in the conquest and pacification of Ireland as a land beyond the pale of English civility. This also allowed royal bureaucracies in England to draw fiscal sustenance from maritime regions and towns in Ireland, including those that had long-established trading links with continental Europe.

That towns were not a major characteristic of Ireland's Gaelic lordships in the sixteenth century is borne out by the fact that two-thirds of the 117-odd municipal corporations in Ireland in 1692 had been established after 1603 (Foster, 1988, p. 17). Yet towns did litter the maritime fringe of Ireland long before the setting up of plantation towns in the sixteenth and seventeenth centuries. Coastal towns like Limerick, Galway, Cork, Youghal and even tiny

Dingle had a long record of trade with Europe and England for centuries before the plantations. Waterford then was Ireland's gateway to Europe, and trading vessels with tonnages up to 300 could penetrate right up to the city centre. These towns belonged as much to the commercial world of Atlantic Europe as to the world of Gaelic rural Ireland. Located around the maritime fringe of Ireland, they were more extrovert and outward looking than the interior of the country. They had especially strong links with the port cities of France, Spain, Portugal, England and Scotland. Prior to the plantations, the interior of Ireland probably had far fewer towns than the maritime fringe. Plantation in these areas not only spelt the demise of Gaelic power – it marked the beginnings of modernisation and urbanisation of early modern Ireland.

Ireland was not unique in this respect. As Archibald Lewis has shown, many other countries in western Europe 'followed an almost classical frontier development from the eleventh to the thirteenth century' (Lewis, 1958, p. 475). For sixteenth-century England the most important frontier was not that separating the English from the Celts but 'an internal one of forest, swamp, marsh, moor, and fen' (Lewis, 1958, p. 476). Certainly at this stage England looked upon Ireland in much the same way that it looked upon Scotland and Wales – an internal peripheral possession of considerable geo-strategic and economic significance, and a place which, after a period of frontier expansion, would take its rightful place within the great British nation. To the English monarchy, as indeed to the military establishment, the yeomanry, and the land-holding nobility, Ireland was as much a 'home country' as part of any 'colonial' world. The cultural and political relationships of those transplanted here to their own 'home country' could never really be compared to the far more tenuous ties that bound the colonial communities of North America to Great Britain. Ireland's proximity to mainland Britain, the fact that it was an integral part of a common market for labour and property, meant that by the seventeenth century it was regarded as much an appendage of the British nation as an overseas colony. It owed its dual status as a 'home country' on the one hand, and Britain's 'first colony' on the other, to the fact that it had for so long been part of a northern White European world wherein Britain was a major nation-state (Strauss, 1951). As the very name even suggests, and as we have already seen, the 'plantation of Ireland' involved a high degree of environmental imperialism, just as it implied a strong element of state penetration into Irish affairs. Consequently land and natural resources here were not just 'raped' or spontaneously 'possessed', either 'once-off' or on a regular basis, simply for the sake of it. As we have already seen they were appropriated outright, after much forethought and detailed planning, for a whole range of socio-economic and geopolitical purposes. Similarly also the woods, bogs and fisheries of Ireland were 'consumed' or 'used' quite differently by the new settlers than they were by native chiefs and their social subordinates.

Woods in particular were 'consumed' in vast quantities at this stage. In 1600 an estimated 15 per cent of the land surface of Ireland was under woods. By 1700 these had virtually all disappeared. Woods as haunts of resistance were not only removed as part of military strategy for pacifying the countryside. They were of course also cleared for sound economic reasons. Timber from Ireland was used in a whole range of English industries at this time, including the tanning of leather, iron smelting, shipbuilding and the manufacture of barrels (Mitchell, 1976, p. 192). Irish land in particular acquired new significance at this time as new definitions of property, and indeed territory, began to operate which had the effect of outlawing Gaelic notions of property and territory that had prevailed in pre-plantation times. Land now became territory in the classical and literal meaning of the term – i.e. as 'terra torium' it became 'land belonging to' settlers. Land now also ceased to act as the basis of social existence and political prestige that it was in Gaelic Ireland. It became a marketable commodity whose variable productivity and value from one part of the country to another laid the basis for uneven development right through to the eighteenth and into the nineteenth and twentieth centuries.

Certainly the thirst of English nobles and yeomen for land was partly assuaged in Ireland. Coupled with the general turbulence of the Celtic fringe, this made the incorporation of Ireland into Britain an attractive proposition from a very early stage in the evolution of a British nation-state. State-assisted land acquisitions in Ireland were also part of a wider strategy whereby the loyalty of at least one section of the English nobility was assured. This helped maintain and extend the political authority of new social classes in the English state throughout the seventeenth and eighteenth centuries. As in most exercises in frontier expansion, the merchant adventurers and planters who came to Ireland, especially Ulster, at this time were investing in land both as an economic resource and as a marketable commodity. Unlike the old native ascendancy, or even the Old English who settled here before the sixteenth century, they looked on land as a speculative resource which could be rented or profitably disposed on a seventeenth-century equivalent of the modern 'futures' market. They at once sought to recreate, even rejuvenate, themselves on England's frontier lands in Ireland, and to literally transform the land that they wrested from native overlordship at the same time.

The amount of land held by the new settler population increased dramatically at this time. One estimate suggests that seven million acres of land passed from native into 'settler' hands between 1640 and 1688 alone. By the latter date English and Scottish Protestants held more than three-quarters of all the land in the country. They held almost all of Ulster, acquired four-fifths of Leinster and Munster and owned about half of the poorer province of Connaught (Regan, 1980, p. 4). The Catholic share of good agricultural land in Ireland declined still further in the late seventeenth and early eighteenth centuries. By 1688 Catholic landowners held only 22 per cent of Irish land, much of this in poorer parts of the country. Less than a century later that figure had dropped to approximately 5 per cent. Henceforth plantation meant the marginalisation of native interests and the relegation of Gaelic society to some of the most marginal lands in the country. Plantation also contributed to a Manichaean construction of Ireland as a country inhabited by 'civilised' settlers and 'avenging natives'. Indeed in the mid-seventeenth century the English Pale around Dublin was often regarded as a country embanked against marauders. Edmund Campion, writing about this 'English toehold' in Gaelic Ireland in 1571, noted that it had 'the fattest soil, [was] most defensible ... and most open to receive help from England'. He went on to add: 'Hereupon it was termed their pale, and whereout they durst not peep. But now both within this pale, uncivil Irish and some rebels do dwell, and without it, countries and cities English are well governed' (Campion, quoted in Harrington, 1991, p. 35).

Forcing many of the native Irish to live in conditions of extreme poverty and moving them on to marginal lands also placed them at the centre of settler objections to Gaelic culture. These new settlers regularly complained even of the Gaelic presence in a modernising Ireland. Not surprisingly this gave rise to a new genre of anti-Irish racism which consolidated the Manichaean view of Ireland as a country inhabited by 'good' and industrious settlers on the one hand, and the 'evil', 'lazy', or 'wilde' Irish on the other. If the life of the former was said to be governed by civility and rationality, the life of the latter was said to be a life which marauded on civilised settlers and their private property alike.

Describing the dietary habits of the 'wilde Irish' just before the Ulster Plantation, Fynes Moryson stated:

> *Many of these wild Irish eat no flesh but that which dies of disease or other-wise of itself.* Neither can it escape them for stinking. They desire no broth, not have they any use of a spoon. They can neither seeth arti-chokes nor eat them when they are sodden. It is strange and ridiculous, but most true, that some of our carriage horses, falling under their hands, when the found soap and starch, carried for the use of our laun-dresses, *they, thinking them to be some dainty meats, did eat them greedily ... They feed most on whitemeats, and esteem for a great dainty sour curds ... These wild Irish never set any candles upon tables. What do I speak of tables? Since indeed they have no tables, but set their meat upon a bundle of grass and use the same grass for napkins to wipe their hands ... To conclude, ... these wild Irish are not much unlike to wild beasts, in whose caves a beast passing that way might perhaps find meat, but not without danger to be ill enter-tained, perhaps even devoured by his insatiable host.* (Moryson, quoted in Harrington, 1991, p. 100; emphasis added)

Viewed thus, the life of the native Irish not only suggested that they showed disregard for public laws, civility and good manners. Natives, it was said, lived a life worse than that of the beasts, because beasts at least were seen to be guided by wholesome instinct. At its most extreme, therefore, this genre of anti-native racism suggested that the Irish were without both the ennobling intellect of the civilised settlers and the steadying instinct of animals. Views such as these also implied a rigid policing of the boundaries between 'settlers' and 'outcasts'. Thus the settlers often now called for the removal of the Irish from new towns and villages in plantation Ireland, and a strict separation out of civilised landscape of the settler from the natural and 'savage' land-scapes of decaying Gaelic Ireland.

The entire layout of the plantation schemes imposed on Ireland at this time, together with the high level of anti-Irish sentiment in plantation thinking, made it extremely difficult for the native Irish to develop any meaningful political response to their socio-economic marginalisation. Yet, because they mimicked neither settler yeomen, farm worker nor nobleman, the native Irish were also victimised and criminalised by practically every sector of settled society here. Their presence in Ireland at all was often liter-ally a source of 'astonishment' or 'shock' to the enlightened thinkers who defended Irish plantation schemes. It 'intimidated' their sensibilities, not least because so much in the life of the Gaelic poor, not least their nomadism and 'ribald' manners, resembled more the habits and customs of the wild inhabitants of mountainous Europe than those of a people living at England's back door. This was partially because history in England from the seventeenth century onwards was an increasingly 'fixed' affair. It was something that settled into concrete, albeit discrete, dramas that were enacted between civilising 'society' on the one hand, and wild Irish 'nature' on the other. Until then, the native Irish, although they lived within the British Isles, were perceived as social 'pariahs', as 'parasites' who 'marauded' on settled communities all across planted Ireland. As such they were considered even lower than the barbaric 'savages' who, at the birth of European civilisation, regularly plundered the heartlands of Europe from their impregnable fastnesses in the east (Mac Laughlin, 1999b).

Having constructed the native Irish as a savage subject, it was only a matter of time before settler communities in Ireland would depict that subject as 'expendable' and socially 'dispensable'. Like the nomadic Highlanders in Walter Scott's narratives, they were seen as historical subjects. They were from a different place and an earlier epoch in the evolution of civilised society, a people who literally had to be consumed, 'spent' or otherwise 'used up' if the narrative of modern English history in Ireland was to proceed apace. Indeed it was as if it was their destiny to be so 'expended', or dispensed with, so that nation-building history itself could 'continue' (Richards, 1994, p. 134). This view of Ireland and the Irish also suggested a geography of savagery. It marked out those furthest from the centres of English civilisation as the most savage of all the inhabitants of 'the British Isles'. The 'wilde Irish' were said to occupy the lowest rungs of this seventeenth-century racial hierarchy. Despite their close geographical proximity to England, they were considered miles apart socially from the English and had not managed to borrow either their 'good manners' or the trappings of an elevating English nation-building civility. Indeed they were often considered as savage as the peripheral landscapes that harboured them. They were deemed all the more 'backward' because they had so long inhabited places where nobody went 'unless they lost their way' (Rehfisch, 1975, p. 85).

Representations of Ireland and the Irish in Colonial Art and History

The Irish and Ireland were clearly symbols of disorder in a Britain where national order was of increasing concern. This is brought out in representations of Ireland in English art from the sixteenth century onwards. The series of woodcuts used to illustrate John Derricke's poem, 'The Image of Irelande' contain some of the earliest representations of the native Irish in English art. They depict the Irish as both opposite and inferior to the English in everything from eating habits, table manners, toilet training and bowel movements. D.B. Quinn has suggested that these woodcuts were 'intended as a satire on Irish residual primitiveness' (Quinn, 1967, p. 76). Catholic Celts in Ireland epitomised an immoral and disruptive force. As such they were considered a blemish on the face of the 'Faerie Queen' and for that reason they had to be eliminated entirely from the peaceful Anglican Commonwealth. Similarly, when English artists later represented Irish landscapes, they contrasted the orderliness of the Anglicised countryside with the chaos and confusion of native and natural landscapes. As Cullen suggests, what needs to be emphasised about this artistic tradition 'is not that the empirical fact of the production of visual records of carefully maintained estates, but the fact that ... parts of Ireland ... were being physically transformed into "little replicas of England"' (Cullen, 1997, p. 45). Later in the eighteenth century English artists here privileged Ireland's Anglicised – hence 'civilised' – landscapes. They depicted the country as a rural Arcadia filled 'with peaceful walks through well cared for estates'. The image of Ireland they sought to convey was one of 'serene environments boasting a richness in natural beauty' that would attract more settlers to invest in the country. They suggested that Ireland rightly belonged within the Anglican commonwealth and that it should never be allowed to revert back to nature, barbarism or the 'wilde Irish'.

As Ann Stoler has suggested, strong parallels were also made between the immoral lives of the British underclass and the Irish poor and 'primitive Africans' (Stoler, 1995, p. 125). However, most writers have ignored the sixteenth- and seventeenth-century *indigenous* origins of racism in Europe, including in this case, anti-Irish racism in England. They have preferred instead to see modern racism as a late eighteenth-century phenomenon which crescendoed in the development of social Darwinism and 'scientific' race theory in the nineteenth century. Kiernan has similarly argued that racial hatred of the 'other' in colonial societies, including Ireland, had its roots in fear of the nineteenth-century urban and rural masses living in the metropolitan, and 'brutish', world of industrial capitalism. Discontented natives in the colonies, he argued, were lumped together with the poor at home and viewed as 'the same serpent in alternate disguise'. As Kiernan has argued, talk of 'barbarism' and 'darkness' in the nineteenth century was thus little more than a 'transformed fear of the masses at home' (Kiernan, 1972, p. 316). This was not the case in the seventeenth and eighteenth centuries when 'barbarism' and 'darkness' resided on the Celtic peripheries, while civility and righteousness clung to the Anglo-Saxon core of an English nation-state system.

Richards has suggested that the European world, by the sixteenth century at least, had already been divided along an immutable axis of binary and self-excluding differences (Richards, 1994, p. 56). These were centred around the ascendant versus the descendant, the human versus the animal, the bodily versus the spiritual, the settled versus the vagrant and nomadic, the civilised versus the 'wilde'. In Ireland these same differences also centred around the 'civilised' and 'settled' English on the one hand, and the 'wilde' or semi-nomadic Irish on the other. British art then, like British literature and much of its political commentary, was part and parcel of a much wider English nation-building and Enlightenment project which was concerned with appropriating and 'taming the savage' in Gaelic 'backward' Ireland. In planted areas this was a project that also sought to placate the 'baser' native instincts and tame the natural landscape of the country. Thus writing and painting, like the very acts of planting and landscaping the 'wilde' Irish countryside, were as much civilised, nationalistic and patriotic endeavours as they were inspirational acts. They glorified all that was settled, dignified and noble in British national civilisation, while simultaneously denigrating as savage and uncouth the native Irish and their rugged habitats.

Within the genres of painting established by the art theorists of Italy in the sixteenth century, landscape painting, portraiture and still life were of less importance than history painting. The latter was considered morally and intellectually 'elevating' precisely because it depicted groups of people whose actions and interactions 'told a story which was uplifting to the beholder' (Baddeley and Fraser, 1992, p. 10). Thus painting from this genre selected subjects from a glorious and distant past, particularly from classical Greek history and ancient mythology, in order to edify the actions of modern-day state-builders. Landscape painting as we know it was considered an inferior form of artistic representation at this time. It did not depict people doing anything of interest, i.e. anything that would attract the attention, or improve the mind of the spectator. Artistic representations of planted landscapes in Ireland and colonial societies abroad proved an exception to this general rule. Indeed landscape painting here, particularly when it focused on newly settled landscapes, on towns, estates and urban space, and on the subjects of urbanism, was an integral part of an English nation-building mission civilatrice in Ireland. As such it depicted landed elites and planter communities 'taming' the landscape and appropriating it for a modern, preferably urban, civility.

Visiting artists, including a small number of resident Anglo-Irish painters, depicted settled landscapes and urban scenes here as outposts of modernity in a sea of rural Irish medieval backwardness. Much in the same way that revolutionary artists in Mexico in the twentieth century painted the people caught up in great nationalist endeavours to clear the land and make it fit for new citizens, this eighteenth-century artistic tradition in Ireland depicted uplifting scenes showing 'improving' landholders and settler communities clearing the land and making it fit for *civilised settlers*. This was a self-referential inward-looking artistic tradition which was clearly rooted in the new power relations that bound Ireland to England. It had its roots in the military extension of English power to Ireland and carved out precise and meaningful landscapes from the 'wilde' Irish countryside. In so doing it largely ignored the harsher realities of colonial dispossession as experienced by native elites and the rural poor. If the native Irish were painted at all by these artists they were depicted as drifting in and out of sight of the visiting artist in Ireland. Sometimes they were captured as stage props for urban scenes, as relics from a less progressive, barbarous past who acted as useful contrasts to improving settlers in the present. Thus Irish subjects in these paintings often sit hunched and alone. They are separated out from the newcomers, and literally 'litter' the genteel landscapes of civility with their uncouth presence. 'Improving artists', like 'improving landlords' in the eighteenth and nineteenth centuries, made such scenes of rural and urban improvement the centre-pieces of their concern.

The full flowering of portraiture in the eighteenth and early nineteenth centuries also coincided with a marginalisation of the Irish in British high culture. This coincided with the development of a deeply nationalistic school of history painting which denigrated the Irish and glorified the heroic deeds and national and settled qualities of British people. As Richards states:

> The rise of portraiture is intimately connected to a sense of a uniquely national contribution to the arts and the recording of the beautiful nobility of the English face amounts to a patriotic duty no less than the historical record of the nation's achievements. (Richards, 1994, p. 114)

If the 'savage' Irishman entered this scene at all he did so as a darker alter ego of the civilised, usually urban, Englishman. At best he was 'a romantic shadow', a mysterious and secretive anti-self who not only lived along the peripheries of the metropolitan world but was also filled with the secret allure of the peripheral. Suppression of the 'wilde Irish' by such Apollonian tendencies in British culture during the Romantic period could sometimes give rise to a curiosity about the 'noble savages' who lived in these peripheral places. This occasionally took the form of a return to basics, a reaction against what Freud later termed 'the excesses of civilisation'. However, for most cultural nationalists in eighteenth- and nineteenth-century Britain, imitation of foreign ways, especially those of French polite society, was said to make British people shallow and artificial. Insisting that all that was true in British civilisation must arise from native English roots, from the life of the common people, not from the cosmopolitan and denatured life of the Francophile upper classes, it is hardly surprising that Romantic poets and artists never considered rooting British identity in an Irish soil. Aside from a very occasional eulogisation of the Irishman as the 'noble savage', and the Irish woman as 'distressful damsel', most British artists looked upon Irish history and Irish culture as something debased and debasing. For many indeed the Irish were said not to have a history, at least not a history that was meaningful in any evolutionary sense. Instead they were treated as though they were still living through an endless repetition of hardship and poverty which lacked its own narrative and narrators. For many Enlightenment thinkers the very presence of the 'wilde Irish' so close to Britain at all was literally a source of shock and astonishment. They 'intimidated' the sensibilities of polite society, not least because so much in Irish behaviour, including their 'disrespect' for the rule of law and order, their 'ribaldry', their approach to husbandry, the practice of transhumance, the 'idiocy' of Irish rural life and their other quite nomadic ways resembled more the behaviour and manners of those living in the mountains of India and jungles of Africa than those living at Britain's back door. This, as we have already seen, was a period when history in Britain was a more or less 'settled' drama which had already gone through four separate and quite distinctive acts. The first stage, the savage epoch, had hunting and gathering as its dominant mode of subsistence. As social parasites and primitive rebels who attacked outposts of English civilisation in planted Ireland, the 'wilde Irish' were still considered to belong to this stage. The second, or 'barbaric' stage was at once unsettled and unsettling, and was intimately bound up with pastoralism and semi-nomadic practices. This was the stage which the Irish had attained just prior to the plantations of the sixteenth and seventeenth centuries. The third or agricultural stage saw people settling down and 'taking roots' in places. The fourth stage, which saw the commencement of civilisation proper, was dominated by industry and commerce. English settlers in Ireland were said to belong to the latter stages and for that reason were located beyond the native Irish in terms of social development.

This stageist theory of social evolution was based on the conviction that all societies developed according to the regulated principles of history. It also insisted that a British 'past' could sometimes be seen in the lives of contemporary primitives living in a 'previous' epoch around the wilder peripheries of the British Isles. Travel to these communities involved not only a geographical journey – it also involved a journey backwards in time to an earlier phase of human evolution. Having constructed the Irish as inferior subjects of settled society, it was only a matter of time before social thinkers would depict that subject as expendable. Like the nomadic Highlanders in Walter Scott's historical narratives, the Irish peasantry were considered as historical subjects from another epoch. They literally had to be consumed, or 'spent', by the narrative of modern history before that history could continue (Richards, 1994, p. 134). Thus the writings of Scott and others also suggest a geography of savagery which argued that those located furthest from the centres of British civilisation were the most savage of all. In eighteenth- and early nineteenth-century colonial Ireland the Irish poor were perceived as savage and 'untamed' as the peripheral landscapes that harboured them.

When visiting artists or resident Anglo-Irish aristocrats painted Ireland at this time at all they also focused upon urban and rural scenes in such a way as to unite the two countries in a common canvas of progress and civilisation. Theirs was a patriotic and 'improving' art. It was never simply a product of artistic inspiration. Maire de Paor has argued that depictions of Ireland and the Irish in the seventeenth and eighteenth centuries were inseparable from their military subjugation. Thus these painters painted Ireland as a land devoid of native peoples, a country filled with Druidic remains and smouldering ruins. She also suggests that the art of visitors to Ireland at this time had two aspects: it contained representations of themselves and their world; and it 'discovered' and literally *contained* the world they had conquered (De Paor, 1993, p. 120). Thus in eighteenth-century Ireland, as in the

American colonies, the 'wilde natives' discerned by earlier conquerors were painted, after their subjugation, as noble savages, as rural idiots and simple peasants. This was an artistic tradition which otherwise silenced Irish achievements. Where these artists did include the native Irish in their streetscapes and cityscapes, they did so in order to contrast their raggedness and poverty with the wealth and grandeur of English architecture in Ireland. For the most part, however, they painted towns, streets and landscapes as orderly and gentrified places largely devoid of Irish people. In this tradition church towers, particularly those of the Reformed Church, vie with secular buildings and houses of the new improving merchant class.

Much of this elitist art in the south of Ireland at least sought to define and 'fix' 'planted' Ireland as a haven of upper-class nation-building civility awash in a sea of plebeian Gaelic backwardness. Kevin O'Neill has remarked that this genre of 'settler' painting was part of wider, but no less elitist, intellectual activity that was deeply at odds with an energetic and popular Irish culture (O'Neill, 1993, p. 56). Throughout the seventeenth and eighteenth centuries this latter tradition deployed 'a "plastic" or "organic" idea of community' that was more suited to the interests of the native Irish. For that reason hostility to popular culture in Ireland stems from the fact that this was a local-based cultural tradition that underlay, and was often at odds with, the national orientation of elitist high culture. Indeed the very fact that popular Irish culture at this stage was regionally based and focused on the local and the community, meant that settler elites here could brand it as inferior and literally castigate it as an 'unelevating' exercise. As O'Neill also remarks, 'the urban elite view of popular culture, which saw "rustics" as at best rough clay, or at worst irremediable primitives, was confirmed by juxtaposing the rural culture produced by communal enterprise with its own ideologically constructed notion of the individual artist interacting with "culture" without mediation by a collective community' (O'Neill, 1993, p. 56). Given this scenario, Irish folk art was simply considered an act of replication, while 'settler' art was an act of creation.

However, as this chapter has argued, settler art and architecture were also fundamental to England's civilising mission in Ireland. As two strategies for 'rescuing' Ireland from what settler communities here perceived as 'the idiocy' of Gaelic life and the barbarism of Irish nature, they were also an integral part of a much wider intellectual project. Thus in many seventeenth- and eighteenth-century paintings of Ireland, loyal 'civilised' and 'Anglicised' subjects live in the city and the countryside is depicted as rife with rebels and 'heathenish practices'. Thus Francis Place's cityscapes of Dublin painted in the late seventeenth century not only portray the city as part of a modernising world spreading out from its medieval core. He also paints Dublin as a city whose very bridges even then were beginning to link the developing and more privileged north side of the city with the more medieval and far poorer southside (Gillespie, 1993, p. 110). In so doing Place sought to locate Dublin in the wider metropolitan world of English modernity. He treated it as a centre of European civility, and in so doing heightened its cultural and administrative significance in Gaelic 'backward' Ireland. Dublin, a provincial, timber-built town of less than 20,000 people harboured about 1 per cent of the country's inhabitants in 1600. By the early eighteenth century it was well on its way to becoming a citadel of urban civility and nation-building gentility. This was in stark contrast to earlier representations of the country's largest city. Luke Gernon, writing around the 1620s, likened Dublin to Bristol, but, significantly, he felt that it 'falleth short' of its provincial English counterpart. He also suggested that the 'ravaged settlements' of the native Irish were more like 'the remnants of unfinished meals' than true towns. By the 1690s old medieval Dublin was transformed out of all recognition. New churches were built and older ones repaired. Viewed thus, English-built bridges and new roadworks rescued the city from medieval oblivion and transformed it into a modern, functioning, organic urban space.

Coffee-houses flourished here from the 1680s onwards and were not only centres of entertainment but places where business was conducted and foreign news and good manners were disseminated. A Philosophical Society was founded in 1683 that was modelled on the Royal Society in London. Fashionable townhouses, public parks, a bowling green and new suburbs were added to make the city 'a smart centre of sociability for the upper classes'. In a telling remark which summed up the ethnocentrism of the commentator and the rate of progress in seventeenth-century Dublin, one visitor, writing in the 1680s, compared the city to London and added that 'men live alike in these two cities' (Gillespie, 1993, p. 104). Another observer placed Dublin at this time among the top twelve European cities. Sir William Petty, writing in 1687, avowed that the city had outgrown its provincial status to become a European city in the same league as Paris, London, Amsterdam and Venice. Its architecture not only housed new settlers and accommodated new arrivals to the city, something which could be done by renting,

rather than constructing new buildings. It also gave these communities prestige and standing and made the city a vital urban
outreach in Gaelic Ireland. Here, as in colonial Egypt and India,
new towns, suburbs and aristocratic buildings had significance
beyond their size and expense. This was an architecture which
literally 'embodied' an English nation-building presence in Ireland.
Indeed settler architecture and estate management were the twin
forms through which English nation-building ambitions and
national identities were made physically apparent in Ireland. As
such, English architecture in Ireland articulated an ideological
space. It forged actual locations for planter civility in an
'uncivilised' Gaelic Ireland. In time, it was hoped, these new buildings might even help to 'replace force with civility and
governability' (Crinson, 1996, p. 3). Thus English-planned towns
and villages in Ireland were not simply accompaniments to English
rule – they mapped out a common social and political horizon in
such a way as to make Ireland a 'natural' part of a larger and
civilised kingdom of Great Britain and Ireland.

4 Theorising the Nation: 'Peoplehood' and Nationhood as 'Historical Happenings'

Nation as Construct

This chapter adopts a quite different approach to nation-building than that taken in most historical accounts, including those written at the height of two divergent and uneven strategies for nation-building in late nineteenth-century Ireland. The latter present students of nationalism with more problems than they do solutions. One way of regarding these generic histories of nationalism and Unionism is to see them as the ideological components of much wider literary and cultural renaissances then sweeping through the south, and north, of Ireland (Kiberd, 1995, pp. 263–85; Lloyd, 1993, pp. 19–26; Stewart, 1967, pp. 32–42). As integral elements in two quite distinctive cultural 'awakenings', they were instrumental in creating – or more accurately bringing to fruition – organic expressions of popular nationalism and Unionism where none previously existed. Thus they either justified Irish nationalism and condemned Ulster Unionism, or they defended the latter and vilified the former. As elsewhere in nation-building Europe, including Britain, they 'invented tradition', 'created' national culture, and constructed national identities from a rich admixture of folk history and historical myths (Hobsbawm and Ranger, 1996, pp. 1–14, 263–83). As Gellner suggests, such 'awakenings', while presenting themselves in this light, generally 'created' nations where none previously existed (Gellner, 1983, p. 48). Thus the nationalism and Unionism found in histories and political pamphlets written at the height of nation-building represented 'the crystallisation of new units' suitable for conditions then prevailing in different parts of Ireland and used 'as their raw material the cultural, historical, and other inheritances from the pre-nationalist world' (Gellner, 1983, p. 49). To the extent that this chapter does focus on nation-centred generic histories of nation-building it does so in order to show how they popularised and promoted the cause of 'their' nation, often, as we have already seen, by disparaging that of their opponents, including their Unionist nationalist opponents.

This chapter treats Irish nationalism and Ulster Unionism as rational expressions of political regionalism and suggests that they were much more than simply 'political ideologies'. As programmes for constructing a nationalist Ireland or a Unionist Ulster, they literally penetrated into every corner of nation-building Ireland. As momentous 'historical happenings' they influenced the way individuals, social groups and ethnic collectivities related to each other and to the land that they literally inhabited. In his *Making of the English Working Class*, a classic study of the origins of working-class consciousness, E.P. Thompson classified class as a major 'historical happening' (Thompson, 1968, p. 9). Like 'nation' it was never simply a structural component of a wider social or international system. As such class formation, like nation-building, always owed as much to agency and agents as to conditioning structures. Thus for example Thompson insists that the English working class 'did not rise like the sun at an appointed time – it was instead present at its own making'. So also with nation-building and the 'making' of national consciousness in nineteenth-century Ireland. Here 'big-nation' nationalism as in Ulster Unionism, and 'small-nation' national separatism as in Irish nationalism, did not simply separate out 'coloniser' from 'colonised' at this late stage in the development of Irish and Unionist modernities. Expressions of national consciousness here had a fluency which, like class, can evade analysis if we attempt to stop them dead at any given moment and anatomise their structure.

This chapter is divided into four parts. Section one discusses Anderson's anthropological definition of the nation as an 'imagined community' and examines some of the major paradoxes of nationalism in the nineteenth century as these relate to Ireland (Anderson, 1983, p. 15). The second section examines the anomaly of Irish nationalism and the rationality of Ulster Unionism in a nineteenth-century world where 'big-nation' unionist nation-building was the accepted norm, and where separatism was widely ridiculed. This section critically analyses the writings of Eric Hobsbawm, one of the strongest defenders of 'big-nation' nationalism on the left. This section contains a debate on his views on 'historic' nations in the nineteenth century and, to a lesser extent, in the contemporary world (Hobsbawm, 1988, p. 107). It outlines his views on the political and economic criterion of nationhood in the nineteenth century. This includes a discussion of the pitfalls, again as Hobsbawm perceives them, of nationalism and national separatism in an ethnically divided society like Ireland. Section three introduces Wallerstein's concept of 'peoplehood' to the discussion of Irish nation-building and critically adapts the logic of Thompson's analysis of 'class' to that of 'nation' and nation-building in Ireland in the late nineteenth and early twentieth centuries (Balibar and Wallerstein, 1991, pp. 73–84). In so doing it seeks not so much to evade but rather to confront the essential commonalities and distinctions between 'class', 'nation' and 'peoplehood' in late nineteenth-century Catholic Ireland and Unionist Ulster. Thus I agree with Thompson, and to a lesser extent with Hobsbawm, when these writers suggest that class consciousness, unlike national consciousness, is largely determined by the productive relations into which men are born – or enter voluntarily (Hobsbawm, 1982, p. 79; Thompson, 1968, p. 10). However, as the final section shows, class consciousness in Ireland as in other nation-building European countries, was also intimately linked to national consciousness and to historic constructions of 'peoplehood'. This meant that in the contested terrains of nineteenth-century nation-building Ireland, class consciousness was never a 'pure' class experience and was always much more than the sum of its parts. Here, for example, the class consciousness of workers and small farmers was intimately bound up also with two very different and diametrically opposed views on nation-building and the nation. This meant that class consciousness in Ireland was not forged on an abstract plane. Like national consciousness it was forged on the anvil of nation-building and was articulated in a plurality of social class and regional contexts. National consciousness in Ireland was probably more nation-centred than in already existing nations elsewhere in Europe, including Britain. Whether in the north or south of Ireland it expressed the material and cultural interests of groups who were intent on realising the political potential of 'peoplehood' and nationhood in nation-state and national form. This again was quite unlike the situation in 'really-existing' nations like England, France and Germany. Here the class consciousness of workers and rural sectors of society generally did not threaten the territorial integrity of the nation-state. In Ireland the quest for 'peoplehood' united different social classes across broad cultural fields in two different parts of the country. Yet it did not stop at that. Constructions of 'peoplehood' here gave rise to quite new social relationships between different social groups. It also forged new organic relationships with territory and resulted in the formation of social blocs whose leaders insisted that 'the people' had a right to their own nationhood and their own nation-state. That is why the 'nation' in Ireland always entailed notions of historical and territorial relations. However, unlike in more powerful European nations, statehood in Ireland has involved something more than an organic relationship with the territory of the nation. It also involved territorial contestations which resulted in acceptance or rejection of geopolitical and geo-ethnic relationships with the United Kingdom and the Empire. Thus nation-building and nationalism in Ireland existed at two levels. One of these, as we have seen, was a 'small-nation' nationalism which was essentially separatist in that it sought the 'breakup' of nineteenth-century Britain. The other was a 'big-nation' nationalism which was essentially unionist and nationalist in outlook. Both were expressions of national consciousness that were literally rooted in real places in different provinces of nation-building Ireland. They were also embodied in very real people, in people who by their actions and political behaviour showed that they were willing to fight for the right of 'their nation' to survive. Finally, it will be argued, these different expressions of 'peoplehood' or 'nationhood' were the regionalised institutional constructs of an historical capitalism which reflected not only the uneven development of capitalism but also, and much more significantly, the uneven development of national separatism in Ireland. First, however, we must look at Anderson's rather abstract model of the nation as an 'imagined community' in order to appreciate the role of print capitalism and the ethnic intelligentsia in something as concrete as Irish nation-building. Therefore the section that follows provides the broad theoretical context for understanding rival approaches to nation-building in Ireland in the nineteenth century.

Anderson's Nation: An 'Imagined Community'?

Anderson has pointed to three paradoxes which, he argues, have perplexed theorists of nationalism in this century. The first stems from the contradictions between nationalist assertions regarding the antiquity of nationalism on the one hand, and evidence from historians, social scientists and historical geographers pointing to the historical and spatial contingency of nation-building and nationalism on the other (Anderson, 1983, pp. 13–15). As Smith and others have demonstrated, this means that we have at least two schools of thought on nation-building and nationalism. To one belong the nationalists, and what he terms the 'primordialists', those who insist upon the 'naturalness' of the nation as a territorial unit, including those who stress the 'naturalness' of nationalism as a political ideology. To the other school of thought belong the modernists and non-nationalists, those who look upon the nation as a social and territorial construct, which emerged, in the western world at least, chiefly in the course of the nineteenth century (Smith, 1986, p. 7). This latter school of thought also stresses the historical and spatial contingency of plebeian and 'banal' nationalism. Like Anderson, and others belonging to the constructionist/modernist school, it emphasises the role of print capitalism and mass education in nurturing 'the imagined community' of the nation as a prelude to the formation of the nation-state. Whereas 'primordialists' emphasise the altruism, and indeed the spirituality of nationalism, elevating it to the status of a state religion, the scepticism of modernists has caused them to stress what Billig refers to as the banality of nationalism in this century, as well as in the last one (Billig, 1995). Thus, despite the claims of nationalists and social Darwinists to the contrary, modernists insist that nation-building never was the product of primordial forces. Neither was it inspired by pure altruism, or the product of autonomous social forces operating independently of time and place (Agnew, 1987, pp. 167–93; Mac Laughlin, 1987, pp. 1–17). It was instead the outcome of a whole range of socio-economic and political forces operating across space and within quite specific socio-historical and spatial contexts. So much for the first set of paradoxes of nationalism discussed by Anderson.

As he sees it, the second paradox of nationalism stems from what he calls the 'formal universality' of nationality as a socio-cultural concept, versus the 'particularity' of its concrete manifestations both historically and today. Thus nationalism today exists in a whole variety of forms and contexts in many, but – as Rwanda, East Timor and Kosovo have recently demonstrated – in no means all parts of the world. In the nineteenth century in particular, nationalism was by no means a ubiquitous ideology, even within continental Europe. This was a century which saw the world, including the European world, clearly divided between powerful self-governing nation-states on the one hand, and colonial societies and peripheral small nations ruled from the real centres of national power on the other hand. However, for most of this century we have taken it for granted that everyone should have a 'nationality', and indeed a national homeland. As the examples just referred to demonstrate, this clearly is not the case. So also in the nineteenth century it was powerful societies, especially those organically linked to historic homelands, with sufficient human and natural resources to sustain nation-states and dominate 'mini-nations' at home and carve out colonies abroad, who were deemed to have the first claim to national self-determination. The manner in which they articulated their nationalism, and indeed their national colonialism, was what gave the nineteenth-century world political map such diversity and cultural mix. If that diversity has since then been eroded through the homogenising forces of globalisation this should not blind us to the cultural – even the ecological – richness of that world, including that which stemmed from the plurality of nationalisms that ranged across a metropolitan world then consisting chiefly of Europe and North America. The appeal of nationalism to Europe's minority nationalities, including Ireland, at that time can be partially attributed to a belief in nationalism as the Angel of History and harbinger of progress. It was not only Herder who believed that each ethnically defined people, in western Europe at least, had something special to bring to the construction of a 'civilised' and multicultural Europe. Many struggling nationalities also believed this, including small nations within bigger nations. Prominent among the latter were Catholic nationalists in nineteenth-century Britain, the Scots in the United Kingdom, the Basque people and Catalans in Spain, and the Quebecois in contemporary Canada.

For Anderson the third great paradox of nationalism, historically as well as today, has been its power to mobilise people in large numbers, versus its philosophical poverty as a political ideology. Thus, he argues, unlike others 'isms', nationalism has never produced its great thinkers. It has produced instead bands of followers led by passionate leaders without any clear-cut social or political philosophy beyond that of 'national liberation'. Thus nationalism has produced no Marxes, no Hobbes, no Tocquevilles or no Webers. Instead the relative 'emptiness' or shallowness of its ideology has caused Nairn to argue that nationalism has been 'the pathology of modern developmental history' (Nairn, 1977, pp. 329–34). Rooted in dilemmas of helplessness and modernity, in the nineteenth century as also today, it possessed almost the same capacity for mass descent into dementia as neurosis does in individuals. That is why to its sceptical opponents at least it appears at once an irrational, irreversible and 'incurable' social force (Ignatieff, 1998).

To resolve these paradoxes Anderson suggests that we treat nationalism less as a political ideology comparable to other ideolo-

gies. We must equate it instead with much deeper and more integrative belief systems. We must treat it, in other words, as a form
of national 'kinship' which has its own belief systems or 'religion'.
Historically at least nationalism was never simply an ideology in
the way that Liberalism, Socialism or even Conservatism were
ideologies. It was always much deeper than these. It was something
akin to a state-centred creed which had as its goal the construction,
or defence, of something as sacred as the nation-state. This meant
that nineteenth-century nation-builders recognised the significance of territory not only in symbolic terms, but also as a national
and ideological resource. They saw nation-building as a way of
interpreting, exploiting and reorganising social space (Williams
and Smith, 1983, pp. 502–8). They interpreted nationalism as an
ideology which in the widest possible sense was more akin to a religion than a state ideology.

Rather than treat nationalism, and indeed the nation, as givens,
as things to be spelt with a big 'N', Anderson proposes both an
alternative approach to nation-building, and an alternative definition to 'the nation'. For him the nation is 'an imagined political
community', which is imagined as both inherently limited and
sovereign. It is an imagined community because the members of
even the smallest nation can never hope to meet, or even hear of,
all their fellow members. Yet in the mind of each citizen resides an
image of the national community tied together usually by a
common history, a shared geography or national territory, a
common culture, common religion and common language
(Anderson, 1983, pp. 14–16). The nation is imagined as inherently
limited because even the large nations of the nineteenth century,
and unlike the empires which they spawned, set clear limits to the
extent of the nation. Even the largest nation had finite – albeit
elastic – boundaries beyond which lay other nations. Despite their
hunger for colonial possessions, nations in nineteenth-century
Europe never 'imagined' themselves as coterminous with
humankind, even though many considered themselves the 'Lords
of Humankind'. Finally the nation, according to Anderson, is
imagined as 'sovereign' because it developed in the aftermath of
the French Revolution and during the course of the industrial and
commercial revolutions that transformed the political and
economic life of a large part of Europe in the nineteenth century.
Gellner has suggested that this was not so much a century which
saw the awakening of nations to self-consciousness – it was instead
a period which saw the invention of nations where none previously existed. That is not to suggest that nationalism promised

what it could not deliver. Neither did it always masquerade under false pretences. Nations were historical and geographical creations whose 'imagining' was conditioned by the historical and geographical circumstances in which they evolved. This was because, as Anderson suggests, rational secularism in the eighteenth and early nineteenth centuries brought with it its own modern darkness for which nationalism acted as an antidote (Anderson, 1983, pp. 17–21). In particular the ebbing of certainties, especially those of a political and religious nature – belief in the divine rights of monarchy, teachings on the origins of life and the nature of moral order – left in their wake a whole array of doubts and sufferings that once were assuaged by religion but could now be soothed by belief in the nation and in nationalism. Anderson, however, is very careful not to suggest that nationalism was not somehow or other 'produced' by the erosion of religious sensibilities which somehow or other 'superseded' religion. In order to throw new light on the historic appeal and mobilising force of nationalism he simply suggests that we align it, not so much with other ideologies – Liberalism, Conservatism or even Socialism – than with larger cultural and belief systems like Christianity, Islam and Confucianism. Viewed thus, nationalism in the nineteenth century was a veritable new Angel of history. Nairn has described it as a 'Janus-like' and 'hydra-headed' creature, one that was capable of looking forward as well as backward (Nairn, 1977).

As Anderson sees it, the possibility of imagining the nation arose when, and where, three fundamental cultural conceptions underlying western life since well before the Middle Ages lost their appeal. The first was the idea that sacred script languages offered privileged access to deep ontological truths because they were inseparable from them. The second was the belief that societies are naturally organised around divinely ordained monarchies and dynasties which implied that human loyalties were always, and everywhere, necessarily hierarchical and centripetal in character. Anderson's third cultural conception suggested that history and cosmology were indistinguishable because the origins of the world and of men were essentially identical. When these conceptions of spirituality and temporality began to break down and lose their appeal human lives had a tendency to go into a spin and lose their rootedness. The old everyday certainties of pre-modern life – belief in an afterlife, acceptance of loss of freedom, belief in the rights of monarchies and landed elites – became meaningless. The new scepticism that grew out of the dusk of traditional modes of thought was spread chiefly through the secular channels of newspapers and the other products of print capitalism. These in turn made possible a new form of 'imagined community', the nation. They did this by fostering nationalism and elevating it almost to the status of a state religion that gave new meaning to life and rooted people in the meaningful landscape of the nation-state. Viewed thus, I shall argue, nationalism in countries like Ireland, Spain and Poland prolonged the political power of the Catholic church. Here also it gave many people a new lease of the spiritual, by simultaneously giving them a political future and mission civilatrice, both in their quasi-sacred homelands at home and in their colonial possession abroad. As a result nations were never simply countries. They literally were the Fatherlands and Motherlands of peoples, at least in Europe and in the wilder outliers of White settler society in the colonial world.

It has been suggested that the true value of Anderson's perspective on nations lies only partially in its emphasis on the nation as an 'imaginative construction' (Cubitt, 1998, p. 56). It also resides in the whole area of articulation of national identity, especially in the creative elaboration and reinforcement of different senses of community at local regional and national levels. These were the levels at which the imaginative power of nation-building agents were exerted in the contested terrains of nineteenth-century Ireland. This suggests that the 'Irish nation', and 'Unionist Ulster', were as much socio-geographical realities as 'mental' or 'imaginative' constructs. More than that, the imagined power of nation-building in both parts of Ireland was fostered and sustained through the labour and discursive habits of a whole range of actors, institutions and social groups, including, not least the press and the political establishment.

Anderson's phenomenological and constructionist approach to nationalism is also a modernist one. It suggests that nations 'happen' when and where people-as-creators of the nation can imagine themselves as part of a nation, and as part of a national collectivity. Anderson suggests that this happened initially in western Europe, specifically in France, Germany, Britain and Italy, in the period between the dusk of the eighteenth century and the dawn of the twentieth century. It was no coincidence that it coincided with the emergence of the national bourgeoisie in these European countries. After the French Revolution, and especially after the English industrial revolution, a whole range of important infrastructural and structural shifts occurred in western Europe which literally reconstructed countries here as regionally united territories. As Harvey has shown, these 'happened' at different national scales and included the cultural, political and economic transformation that accompanied the spread of modernity (Harvey, 1982, pp. 34–45; Harvey, 1992, pp. 10–38). Equally important were the spatial transformations which turned many European countries into functioning geographic units. These facilitated the development of the new 'imagined communities' of nations by allowing the inhabitants of Europe's 'new' countries – 'new' in the sense of being recently unified, or recreated through the forces of modernisation – to now think of themselves as 'a people' and play around with different abstract ideas of themselves as constituting a nation. The French Revolution showed that popular revolution was not only possible but that it had to be contained if it were not to jeopardise the interests of the national bourgeoisie. The industrial revolution, accompanied as it was by processes of industrialisation, a heightened commercialisation of agriculture, and the spread of bourgeois and petty bourgeois values, provided the developing societies of western Europe with a blueprint for the successful nation. Hence nations were not just 'imagined communities', each with its own distinctive styles of living and thinking. They were also the building blocks of modernity and the territorial expressions of national capitalism. As such they were to be strictly confined to the metropolitan world and were not for replication anywhere in the colonial world, in small, peripheralised nations like the Basque country, Catalonia, Brittany, Ireland, Scotland and Wales. Anderson plays down these particular aspects of nation-building. He also ignores the marginalisation of Europe's ethno-nationalities, including the Irish, as a result of 'big-nation' nation-building in the nineteenth century. In filling in these gaps in Anderson's argument Eric Hobsbawm and Immanuel Wallerstein point us in the direction of a more rounded, cultural, historical materialist theory of nation-building and nationalism.

To summarise Anderson's highly generalised account of the origins of national consciousness. Operating as it does at a supra-national European level, and at the level of the post-colonial Third World, his model of nation-building is highly generalised indeed. Its universal 'truths' are arrived at not so much through careful analysis of the specificities of nation-building in concrete social and spatial settings as by broad-ranging and highly insightful historical arguments. For that reason his analysis of the emergence and spread of national consciousness largely ignores the specificities of nation-building in 'actually-existing' countries. More to the point, it does not contain anything like a regional geography or social class analysis of nation-building in either the nineteenth or the twentieth century. With these comments in mind it is still useful to summarise Anderson's highly influential (if not very detailed) account of the origins of national consciousness. Thus as he sees it the convergence of capitalism with print technology, particularly in the peculiar conditions of the eighteenth and early nineteenth centuries, gave birth to print capitalism both as an industry and as a mass medium. This in turn created the possibility of a new form of imagined community which was radically different, both in its morphology and in its political loyalties, from the great global communities of the past, like for example Christendom, the Islamic Ummah, and China's Middle Kingdom. Each of the latter had its own sacred rites and languages, as well as clearly defined rules about membership and admission. The basic morphology of the 'imagined community' of the nation mapped out, albeit in the very roughest of terms, the terrain upon which the modern nation-state was constructed. The national print languages of these new imagined communities were of political, geographical and ideological importance. Thus for example they were often, but by no means exclusively, responsible for the shattering of older dynastic realms into territories that were, vernacularly at least, relatively homogeneous. Equally important, they united hitherto disunited societies, especially those, like Ireland and Spain, marked by high levels of rural parochialism and a fragmented regionalism. After the French Revolution the 'nation' was something to which other societies, including the Irish, could consciously aspire. For others, particularly those in ethnically divided class-structured societies, nation-building had a 'Balkanising' effect and fear of the 'risen people' ran deep into the established institutions of power and privilege. Here the nation was often as not imposed from above in order to contain plebeian protest from below. As the section that follows suggests, this was not the way nationalism had evolved in Ireland, or Ulster, by the late nineteenth century.

Hobsbawm's Nation and the Nation in Ireland

Hobsbawm's most comprehensive analysis of nation-building and nationalism is to be found in *Nations and Nationalism since 1780*. Published in 1990 under the subtitle 'Programme, Myth, Reality', this work is of interest to students of nationalism in general, but it is of particular interest to students of nationalism and Unionism in Ireland. Thus for example it testifies to the fact that Hobsbawm, like most nineteenth-century defenders of nation-building, still is more sceptical of 'small-nation' nationalism than he is of 'big-nation' nation-building. It also points to the fact that he belongs to the modernist school which traces modern expressions of nationalism to the late eighteenth and nineteenth centuries. Hobsbawm sees nations as dynamic constructs of historical capitalism. However, the juxtaposition of 'myth' and 'reality' in the subtitle suggests that he now believes nationalism to be well 'past its peak'. Certainly he is extremely sceptical of 'small-nation' nationalism, both in the nineteenth century and also today. This scepticism stems from his doubts about it progressive credentials but it does not extend to a critique of 'big-nation' or 'unionist nationalism' in the nineteenth century. Indeed Hobsbawm betrays a high level of Euro-centrism, and Anglo-centrism, when he insists that powerful, unified and 'moderately large' nation-states are the suitable units for modern capitalist society. This argument suggests that ethno-nations and minority nations were expected to accept their lot as part of, and not set themselves apart from, these dominant nations. Hobsbawm generally accepts the legitimacy of this approach to nation-building. He rarely misses an opportunity to stress the divisive effects of small-nation nationalism on the territorial integrity of powerful nations. He is particularly scathing in his comments on the emptiness of national separatism as a political programme for the working class in the nineteenth century.

Nations and Nationalism's intellectual origins are also significant. The work is a condensation of many years studying nation-building and nationalism, but its more immediate origins were a series of lectures delivered at the Queen's University of Belfast in 1985. As Hobsbawm himself states, the location of these lectures 'suggested the topic'. He chose Belfast, the provincial capital of one of the oldest and most contested terrains of separatist and unionist nationalisms as a place to deliver his thoughts on two topics which have engaged him throughout a long and extremely rich intellectual career.

Hobsbawm's other writings on nationalism are scattered throughout his histories of European modernity and the triumph of industrial capitalism. These begin with *The Age of Revolution, 1789–1848* (Hobsbawm, 1962). Herein nationalism is described, rather ominously, as the force which split the general movement in favour of European revolution after the French Revolution into national, and ultimately into nationalist camps. In western Europe at least, but not in Ireland, it was, he insists, a middle-class ideology. Thus for Hobsbawm, as also for Benedict Anderson and

Anthony Smith, the progress of nationalism was intimately bound up with the emergence of a secularised middle-class intelligentsia. By and large, he argues, its progress was marked also by that of print capitalism, specifically by the output of textbooks and newspapers preaching the gospel of nationalism and written, usually, in standardised vernaculars. These vernaculars subsequently became the official national languages of European nations. Aside from the problematic example of the Irish 'national movement' under Daniel O'Connell, Hobsbawm suggests that the great proponents of nation-building in Europe were 'the lower and middle professional, administrative and intellectual strata, in other words the educated strata' (Hobsbawm, 1962, p. 170). Although he does not say as much, these nationalist leaders contributed to the modernisation of their nation-states, and to a secularisation of political ideologies.

There were a number of exceptions to this general rule. Significantly, most of these were relatively small, non-industrial nations on the peripheries of Europe. They included Ireland, Poland, the Basque country and Czechoslovakia. Here the hegemonic power of a rural-based Catholic church, coupled with low levels of industrialisation and urbanisation, meant that nationalism was a force for controlling the pace of modernisation which allowed new hegemonic groups to control levels of exposure to secularism and modernity (Larkin, 1972, pp. 625–34). This in turn meant that in Catholic nation-building Ireland, as also in the Basque country and Poland, nationalism was an introvertive force which impeded the process of secularisation. Indeed Basque nationalism was not so much a product of linguistic distinctiveness as a strategy which allowed the Partido Nacionalista Vasco to resist modernity and oppose direct rule from Madrid from the late nineteenth century down to the mid-1960s (Heiberg and Escudero, 1977, pp. 47–55). Similarly also in Catholic Ireland national separatism, especially in the latter half of the nineteenth century, was a strategy for controlling the pace of modernisation by attuning it to the interests of the middling tenantry rather than those of a beleaguered Anglo-Irish ascendancy. In focusing almost exclusively on the secular liberalism of 'big-nation' nationalism, however, Hobsbawm gives a distorted image of the specificities of nation-building in a rural society like Ireland. He particularly misreads the material and ideological significance of nationalism in small nations like Ireland which did not have a powerful national industrial middle class or a well-organised industrial proletariat. Here advances in nationalism were measured by the progress of church-building, the spread of elementary education, the success of the provincial press, and by improvements in any means of communication which could bring ordinary people out of their parochial worlds and lead them on to the 'institutional' or 'procedural landscape' of the modern nation-state.

Hobsbawm suggests that pre-Famine Ireland presented 'the only Western national movement organised in a coherent form before 1848' that was 'genuinely based on the masses' (Hobsbawm, 1962, pp. 170–1). Yet he implies that this was a non-progressive movement because it was controlled by traditional forces and under the influence of the Catholic church. Thus, he argues, the national movement here 'enjoyed the immense advantage of identification with the strongest carrier of tradition, the Church'. Like other students of modern nation-building, Hobsbawm finds it difficult to decide whether this national movement was a proactive articulation of native nationalism or reactive expression of peasant traditionalism. When discussing such national movements, he sometimes opts for the former, but at other times he opts for the latter interpretation. In the case of Ireland he wisely stops short of labelling O'Connell's 'national movement' a nationalist movement. Instead he sees it simply as a 'mass movement of agrarian revolt' organised in 'secret terrorist societies which themselves helped to break down the parochialism of Irish life'. However, despite his expertise in the whole area of 'primitive rebels' and 'social banditry', Hobsbawm fails to appreciate the extent to which the plebeian leaders of agrarian revolt in Ireland at this time had more in common with 'social bandits' than they did with modern nationalists (Hobsbawm, 1958). In his pioneering study of social banditry published several years after *The Age of Revolution*, Hobsbawm describes social bandits as 'peasant outlaws whom the lord and the state regard as criminals, but who remain within peasant society'. As such they are 'considered by their people as heroes, as champions, avengers, fighters for justice, perhaps even leaders of liberation, and in any case as men to be admired, helped and supported' (Hobsbawm, 1969, p. 17).

'Primitive rebels' and 'social bandits' made up the rank and file of Irish secret societies in the late eighteenth and early nineteenth centuries. They were by no means unique to Ireland at this time. We find them all across Europe in the fifteenth and sixteenth centuries. We also find them in the colonial world of the nineteenth and early twentieth centuries, including in countries where their activities could not be construed as 'nationalistic' or 'state-centred' in any modern sense. They are marginalised people who refuse to submit to state-centred controls. As a result they stand out from their fellows and in so doing often 'find themselves excluded [from mainstream society] and therefore forced into outlawry and "crime"' (Hobsbawm, 1969, p. 24). Those who flocked to their secret societies were peasant activists and radicalised craftworkers. They were not the prophets or social theorists of a modernising and nation-building Ireland. By and large, in other words, they were not individuals from whom novel political visions or national plans for the social and political reorganisation of Ireland as a nation-state could be expected.

Social banditry of the sort we have been discussing, while common throughout history, tended to thrive in 'transitional societies' across Europe from the sixteenth through to the eighteenth centuries. It was especially common in societies, like late eighteenth- and early nineteenth-century Ireland, caught up in the transition from tribal and kinship systems of social organisation to variants of capitalist modes of production, whether in agriculture or in industry. Indeed, in Ireland's case as elsewhere in the peripheries of Europe, agrarian unrest and social banditry were most widespread during the transitional phase linking the disintegration of kinship societies to the emergence of free labour markets and agrarian capitalism. Moreover, it was capitalist modernisation, not just failure of their paramilitary tactics or any supposed lack of political acumen, that ultimately contributed to their demise. They were literally out-dated in their own lifetimes and bypassed by history. This was clearly the case in Ireland, but it was also true of other European countries like Italy and Spain (Macfarlane, 1833). Here economic development, particularly when accompanied by improvements in communications and growth in the apparatus of the state, deprived secret societies and other pre-modern expressions of social banditry, of the very conditions they required in order to survive. They did not simply decline through take-over by, or incorporation within, wider nationalist political movements, as nationalists themselves imply. They disappeared also underneath the barrage of social and infrastructural change that created a new Ireland in the middle decades of the nineteenth century.

Interestingly, however, and despite the appropriateness of such a categorisation to agrarian unrest in pre-Famine Ireland, Hobsbawm never really applies it to the leaders of Irish secret societies. Yet it could be argued that those engaged in this form of rural agitation were more like social bandits than modern-day nationalists or nation-builders. This is another way of saying that they probably were more reactive than proactive in their political outlook. They certainly played a highly ambiguous role in the transformation of Irish society in the late eighteenth and early nineteenth centuries. This was because they were, like Hobsbawm's social bandits, 'not so much political or social rebels, let alone revolutionaries, as peasants who refused to submit, and in so doing stood out from their fellows' (Hobsbawm, 1969, p. 17). As a group they were little more than symptoms of crisis and tension in Irish society. As such they shared another characteristic of the classic social bandit – i.e. they did not possess a programme for national social change, preferring instead to follow the leadership of their social and political 'betters', in this case Daniel O'Connell. The latter is described by Hobsbawm not so much as a nationalist as 'a moderate middle class autonomist'. He is lavishly also described as a 'golden-voiced lawyer demagogue of peasant stock' who was 'the first ... of those charismatic popular leaders who mark the awakening of political consciousness in hitherto backward masses' (Hobsbawm, 1962, pp. 169–70). Although he uses the term 'charisma' here Hobsbawm never really defines it. For that reason he misses the true nature of relationships between 'leader' and 'led' in the pre-Famine national movements of Ireland. Weber understood this term to mean 'an unstable amalgam of extraordinary personal leadership and emotionally grounded followership in structurally contingent and historically uncertain situations'. He went on to argue that 'the charisma of a person can be converted into the charisma of office (e.g. priest, pope, president), but in either case it is subject to the probability of routinisation and the constraints of everyday life, especially if problems of securing material resources and leadership succession push the nonrational basis of charisma into a more rational and bureaucratic direction' (Weber, 1978, pp. 1381–469). Gramsci, like Weber, also used 'charisma' in a very explanatory fashion, and in a whole range of very specific regional and historical contexts. He clearly attached great importance to the role of charismatic leadership during a period of historical transition such as that experienced in Ireland in the late eighteenth and early nineteenth centuries. He defined 'charisma' as any quality which causes a leader to be followed in spite of his lack of legitimate or institutional authority (Gramsci, 1971, pp. 210–11). The historical preconditions conducive to charismatic authority exist when critical awareness replaces naturalistic spontaneity in periods of deep-seated historical change. It is then that the artful or charismatic leader can lead subordinate masses to overthrow an old 'naturalistic' schema and build a new one. As one such leader, O'Connell achieved the former but never realised the latter. He acquired 'charisma' through active and conscious co-participation and 'compassionability' with subordinate social groups in Irish society. He particularly cultivated close links with the great masses of the discontented Irish Catholic poor. In so doing he developed what Gramsci called a 'living philology', which literally allowed him to almost read their minds. This more than any of his notorious other more personal qualities transformed O'Connell into a Gramscian 'collective man'. The Cork-born Irish writer and novelist Sean O'Faolain captured the essence of O'Connell's leadership skills very well when he aptly labelled him 'the king of the beggars' (O'Faolain, 1980). Yet in a letter to his friend P.V. Fitzpatrick written in May 1839, O'Connell inadvertently revealed his almost quasi-racial dislike of those whom he led. In it he states: 'I never will get half credit enough for carrying [Catholic] Emancipation, because posterity never can believe the species of animals with which I had to carry on my warfare with the common enemy. It is crawling slaves like them that prevent our being a nation' (quoted in O'Faolain, 1980, p. 10). Here, interestingly, O'Connell inadvertently also offers his own quasi-racial explanation as to why he thought Ireland could not become a modern nation like other European nations in his time – i.e. the bulk of the Irish were like a 'species of animal' and were not 'fit' for nationhood. Indeed what makes this statement all the more remarkable is the fact that it accorded well with European Enlightenment thinking on who should and, more especially, who should not aspire to nationhood and acquire statehood in the nineteenth century.

Looking back on the obstacles to nation-building early in the nineteenth century, and comparing this to the situation confronting the Young Irelanders in the 1840s, Charles Gavan Duffy, one of O'Connell's staunchest critics, also alluded to the social inadequacies of the Irish poor as an impediment to nationhood in the first half of the century. Thus he stated:

> Marvellous as were O'Connell's energy and resources, they were not sufficient to move the mass of prejudice and dumb indifference which confronted him. The bulk of the people were gifted with a generosity which shrank from no sacrifice, but they were ill-equipped ... The majority could not read or write. They had got a political training, which in some degree compensated for their want of culture or self-knowledge – they had learned concert, self-reliance, the necessity of making mutual concessions, and the lesson invaluable to a suffering people, the secret of their own power, but they had been taught for the most part as men are taught before the invention of writing. Their

courage was not fortified by knowledge, or that pride of place which feeds the self-respect of nations. (Boyce, 1991, p. 150)

This statement is uncannily close to the ethnic constructs of nationhood in the writings of Benedict Anderson and Anthony Smith. Like them, Duffy stresses the importance of reading, writing and print capitalism in the construction of the 'imagined community' of the nation in Ireland. To appreciate the full import of this statement, however, and to understand the difference between O'Connell and the Young Irelanders, we have to realise that below O'Connell were social bandits, men organised in regionally based, parochial, self-help organisations. In Hobsbawm's eyes, these men were deemed to have 'no ideas other than those of the peasantry'. They were 'primitive rebels' or pre-modern political activists, not ideologists or prophets of nation-building. As Hobsbawm suggests, and as O'Connell and Gavan Duffy also imply, they were not of the stuff from which nations were made. Neither, as we have seen, were they men from whom 'novel visions or plans of social and political organisation were to be expected'. Left to their own devices indeed, it could be argued that their political actions would not have added up to a social movement, let alone a nationalist movement. But for the leadership of O'Connell, they would simply have acted as a surrogate for a social movement.

Hobsbawm shows how O'Connell himself entered the Irish historical stage not as a nation-builder but as a charismatic leader of peasants, craftworkers and other marginalised groups who were witnessing the demise of one moral economy and the birth of a new, and much more laissez faire political economy of the landed aristocracy and the middling tenantry. This was a period when older customary and organisational forms of politics based on deference and respect for Anglo-Irish authority were being swept away by the twin forces of modernisation and rural capitalist commercialisation in Ireland. The latter benefited the emergent middling tenantry more than they did the rural and urban poor. O'Connell emerged out of this period of socio-economic and moral confusion when traditional leaders in petty bourgeois society and the landed ascendancy – e.g. landlords, middlemen, church leaders, strong farmers, merchants and the professional class – were becoming more and more detached from subordinate groups in urban and rural Ireland. The latter included not only the peasants but also poor tenant farmers, craft workers, the urban poor, and the proto-industrial working class of town and country alike. Gramsci notes that it is with these groups, and at precisely such periods of crisis, that traditional political conventions fail and new political strategies emerge. In the case of pre-Famine Ireland the crisis of authority brought on by the early modernisation of Irish society meant that the field was literally opened for the adoption of violent solutions and the operation of 'unknown forces' by what Gramsci terms 'charismatic men of destiny' (Gramsci, 1971, p. 429). O'Connell's charisma must be measured with this conflict between the 'represented' and the 'representatives' clearly in mind. In particular it derived from his ability to impress and steer 'social bandits' – i.e. lesser 'men of destiny' – away from 'violent solutions' and 'unknown forces' into a grudging acceptance of the emerging hegemony of their 'natural' and national 'social superiors' among Catholic church leaders, the urban and rural lower middle classes, the more substantial bourgeoisie and the new class of Catholic professionals.

As we have already seen, the hegemonic ascent of this broad Catholic bloc was made all the easier when famine and emigration decimated the ranks of the subordinate but radicalised poor. Yet it was the radical poor, as well as the bottom layers of the petty bourgeoisie who, in O'Connell's time, provided the grassroots support for great 'mass meetings' organised in support of Catholic Emancipation and Repeal of the Union. These, significantly, were organised with the help of priests, teachers, farmers and a whole range of other Catholic activists. These groups also had their own political agendas, they were the very people who, later in the century, were to the forefront of nation-building all across the south and west of Ireland. They were particularly opposed to the Act of Union because it made Ireland an integral part of a unionist nation and seemed to heighten their status as second-class citizens in a land which they increasingly looked upon as 'their own'. They were just then beginning to appreciate the potential of national separatism to resolve their social and political problems, not least the problem of political leadership. When the pre-Famine 'underclasses' whom they claimed to represent disappeared from Irish society through famine and emigration, the way was quite literally clear for proto-nationalist and national movements to undergo the transition to become fully-fledged modern state-centred nationalist movements. Thus, by the second half of the nineteenth century, new social and political leaders and new social movements emerged to articulate the interests of tenant farmers and the urban middle class.

In many parts of the rural south and west of Ireland all this not only contributed to a consolidation of the spiritual and political power of the Catholic church. It also marked a geographical extension and social deepening of the political power of the Catholic church, particularly in disadvantaged rural areas (Larkin, 1972; O'Shea, 1983). In such places, as we shall see, secular leaders and the intelligentsia were so thin on the ground that the poor were led chiefly, and often only, by 'their' priests and religious leaders. In such areas, as in the contemporary Islamic world, religious leaders often acted as what C. Wright Mills termed 'organisational men' (Rahnema, 1994). They also led the poor into a grudging acceptance of their hegemony as something that was in the interest of the poor as well as in the interests of the struggling middle classes in town and country alike. This meant that they did not so much represent the 'pure' class interests of the landless poor or the lumpenproletariat, two groups who were anyway regularly excluded from the moral and political structures of the nation-state everywhere in Europe. Instead they used their hegemony to prioritise the interests of the social classes from which they derived, namely the Catholic middling tenantry, the shopocracy, the merchant class, the urban and rural petty bourgeoisie, and the professional class. From then onwards Ireland's 'men of no property' were well on the way to being represented, almost exclusively, by substantial men of property. The latter, as we have seen, sought to make the Irish nation a cradle for petty bourgeois Catholic respectability. They did this by marginalising the interests of the indigenous poor and dismantling the faltering hegemony of an Anglo-Irish ascendancy.

Hobsbawm's appraisal of the Irish national movement under O'Connell, together with his assessment of agrarian revolt in pre-Famine Ireland, are of interest to students of Irish nationalism for a number of reasons. In the first place he describes Ireland as a 'backward' and 'mass' society. In so doing he displays a poor understanding of the nature of agrarian revolt and social change in a country that was already fragmenting into distinctive social classes and ethnic collectivities, and into distinctive national and nation-building regions. Indeed Hobsbawm seems more at home describing class formation and social change in industrial societies in mainland Europe, and especially Britain, than in a peripheral and rural society like Ireland. Second, he shows little understanding of the complexities of the political geography of nation-building in Ireland at a time of great social and economic transformation in the late eighteenth and early nineteenth centuries. In particular he ignores the fact that the agricultural heartlands of Catholic Ireland were already caught up in twin processes of capitalist modernisation and class formation in the first half of the nineteenth century (Lee, 1981, pp. 9–11). This added to the power of the middling tenantry and the Catholic church while simultaneously strengthening the power of the Catholic intelligentsia, the merchant class, the professions, and the urban Catholic middle class. Even at this stage these groups were articulating a nationalist agenda for Catholic Ireland. They were certainly acquiring more say in the political and economic affairs of the country than Hobsbawm's plebeian leaders or 'social bandits'. It was from these groups, not the rural poor, that the leaders of national and nationalist movements in rural Ireland, as elsewhere in mainland Europe, were to derive later in the century.

Hobsbawm's next major comments on nationalism come, significantly, in a chapter called 'Building Nations' in *The Age of Capital, 1848–1875*, first published in 1975. This is significant precisely because he, like others, now sees nations as the major building blocks of European capitalism, the cradles of its bourgeois societies. He defines the period as the 'springtime of peoples'. Yet it also saw the emergence of international tensions between nation-states, growing territorial claims on the colonial world, an intensification of rivalries between big nations like Britain, France and Germany, and the incorporation of minority nations into the large 'core' nations of nation-building Europe. Yet criteria of nationhood at this time, he argues, gradually shifted away from ethnic factors like religion and language towards their economic potential and military capacity. In this work, and later on in a *New Left Review* paper on the breakup of modern Britain, he gives a clear impression of being opposed to separatist nationalism per se. In his description of the specificities of nation-building in the late nineteenth century he argues that:

> a strong case can be and was made ... for a certain type of 'nation-state', though it has little to do with nationalism in the current sense ... such nations were the building blocks of world capitalism during a lengthy period of its development, and with it of bourgeois society in the 'developed' world ... They represented that crucial element – the creation of internal conditions (e.g. a 'national market') and the external conditions for the development of the 'national economy' through state organisation and action. The case for such nation-states was not nationalist in the current sense, inasmuch as it did not envisage a world of nation-states irrespective of size and resources, but only one of 'viable' states of medium to large size, which consequently 1. excluded a large number of 'national' groups from statehood, and 2. de facto abandoned the national homogeneity of most accepted 'nation-states'. (Hobsbawm, 1977, p. 4)

For Hobsbawm, therefore, the criterion of what he terms 'historic' nationhood was 'the decisive importance of the institutions and culture of the ruling classes or the educated elites' (Hobsbawm, 1988, p. 107). The basis of this sense of nationhood, in other words, was economic and political, and not necessarily 'ethnic'. He goes on to imply that small nations like the Irish were 'unhistorical' or 'semi-historical'. This was because, like other champions of the 'big nation', Hobsbawm assumed that the nation must not only be national – it must also be 'progressive'. Aside from rural Catholic Ireland and a small number of other peripheral societies in northern and eastern Europe, the objective of this 'historic' nation-building was 'unification', not just the desire for 'independence'. Faced with the national aspirations of small nations, Hobsbawm suggests that the defenders of this genre of nation-building had three choices: 'they could deny their legitimacy or their existence altogether, they could reduce them to movements for regional autonomy, and they could accept them as undeniable but unmanageable facts'.

When discussing national separatisms supported by 'Nationalist-Marxism' in this century and discussed in Nairn's *The Break-up of Britain*, he also points to three contradictions in the twinning of nationalism with Marxism. The first lies in the irreversibility of the national separatism once it has succeeded in Balkanising the unionist nation. The second has to do with the 'weakening' effect of separatism on the dismembered body politic of the once united working class. As he sees it, the real problem for left-wing supporters of nationalism – historically as well as today – is the fact that 'there is no way of turning the formation of "national communities" … into an historic engine for generating socialism either to replace or to supplement the Marxian historic mechanism'. The third contradiction of separatism, he contends, is that there is no way of using the general argument in favour of Balkanisation 'as a specific argument for the independence of any one putative "nation"'. This, he adds, is a problem for nationalists as well as the left. Thus he states:

> To assume that the multiplication of independent states has an end is to assume that 1. the world can be subdivided into a finite number of homogenous potential 'nation-states' immune to further subdivision – i.e. 2. that these can be specified in advance. (Hobsbawm, 1977, p. 12)

Later on in this argument Hobsbawm comes close to attacking all manifestations of nationalism as a betrayal of Enlightenment values. Thus he states, the real danger for all those who have the interests of workers at heart is:

> the temptation to welcome nationalism as an ideology and programme rather than realistically to accept it as a fact, a condition of their struggle as socialists ... . Quite apart from implying the abandonment of the values of the Enlightenment, of reason and science, such a conversion also implies a withdrawal from realistic analysis of the world situation, Marxist or otherwise. (Hobsbawm, 1977, p. 15)

Given these attitudes to small-nation nationalism and 'mini-nations', it is not surprising that Hobsbawm holds Giuseppe Mazzini, the ultimate unionist nationalist, in such high regard. Mazzini fought for Italian unity and independence throughout his life and as a consequence spent most of it in exile. He was deeply involved in revolutionary nationalism in the 1850s, at a time incidentally, when mass nationalism already was a force to be reckoned with in rural Ireland. In 1861 he was bitterly disappointed at the establishment of a unified Italian kingdom rather than a Republic. In his outline of 'Europe of Nations', first published in 1858, he envisaged a Europe comprising no more than eleven or so states, all of which were essentially multi-ethnic in character. Given the ethnic diversity of Europe at the time, it was inevitable that the majority of European nations, including Ireland, were not so much national as multi-national or multi-ethnic societies. Yet Mazzini, like Cavour, found it difficult to fit into his scheme the Irish, the most obvious upholders of popular nationalism in his day. This was because as a defender of 'big-nation' nationalism, Mazzini was less interested in national independence than in the viability of nation-states. As a unionist nationalist he was opposed to the separatism in Irish nationalism, just as he was opposed to the pulverisation of strong states and the creation of 'mini-states' in their wake. Hobsbawm concurs with Mazzini when he condemns mini-nations and is in favour of unified nation-states. Defending the latter as the 'natural units' of bourgeois society, he insists that, even among nineteenth-century nationalists, the prejudice against the pulverisation of states and the rise of mini-nations was 'deeply ingrained, at least in Europe'.

In his later writings, particularly in *The Age of Empire*, Hobsbawm identifies the period between 1880 and 1914 as a new phase in the evolution of modern nationalism (Hobsbawm, 1992, pp. 142–51). This 'post-Mazzini phase' of nationalism differed in three respects from the 'historic' nation-building we have been discussing so far. First, it abandoned the 'threshold' principle, arguing that any body of people, provided they considered themselves a nation, could now claim the right to self-determination. Second, language, ethnicity or religion now became the decisive criteria of potential nationhood in late nineteenth-century western Europe, including Ireland. Third, there was what he terms a sharp shift to 'the political rights' of the nation in the closing decade of the nineteenth century. This found expression in the right to have one's own flag, to have one's own national anthem, and to have a separate and separatist ethnic identity.

Hobsbawm insisted that nationalism in the 'historic' nations also implied a hegemony of the institutions and culture of the ruling classes or educated elites, assuming these were also supported by the common people. Aside from these 'historic' nations most other nations in Europe, including the Irish, were deemed 'unhistorical' or non-progressive because they were considered too small a nation to go it alone, or too poor to stand alone. Ireland presented these nation-builders with an even greater dilemma – it was home to a small-nation nationalism or national separatism which existed side by side, and in opposition to, a 'big-nation' unionist nationalism concentrated in the north-east but with outliers existing elsewhere in the country. Thus it harboured Ulster Unionists, the defenders of the 'historic' nation', and Irish nationalists who were supported by the majority of the Irish nation. Whereas Unionists were affiliated to the 'historic nation' of Britain, the Irish belonged to what Hobsbawm and other opponents of national separatism refer to as the 'unhistoric' nation of Ireland. This is what made Ireland such a contested terrain of nation-building. On one side were Ulster Unionists who saw themselves on the side of progress and industry. On the other were Irish nationalists who saw themselves as the defenders of tradition from the full frontal attacks of an Anglicised modernity. While the former paraded themselves – and were paraded – as loyal defenders of a unionist nationalism, the latter saw themselves as champions of the small nations in a lesser peripheral Europe carved out among less powerful nations. For that reason Unionists in the north-east also considered themselves racially superior and more progressive than Catholic nationalists. In defending the Union, they argued, they were defending what they regarded as the moral economy of a Protestant people in a 'non-progressive' Catholic island society. In protecting the territorial integrity of the 'historic' nation in their corner of an 'unhistoric' Irish nation, Protestants of course were also condemning the nationalist minority in their midst to a permanent state of powerlessness. Reprehensible though this was, Unionist treatment of the nationalist minority here was not that different to the treatment accorded to minority groups in Europe's other powerful nations, including Francoist Spain and early twentieth-century France. Nineteenth-century nation-building regularly involved the coercive absorption or incorporation of minorities. Ulster Protestants looked to unionist nationalism as a way of keeping themselves within the fold of the progressive 'historic nation', while simultaneously banishing Catholic nationalists in their midst to a sectarian world of capitalist competition and religious intolerance. It was not, as Henry Patterson suggests, that the bourgeoisie in Ulster were able 'to mobilise the other classes in the Protestant community because they could plausibly present a victory for [Catholic] nationalism as leading to economic regression'. It was because Protestant unionist nationalism here was far stronger than Catholic national separatism. As he sees it bourgeois hegemony in the north-east of Ireland was:

> based on a strategy of articulating Ulster's distinctive social and political history. This strategy was successful because, as in its economic positions, it reflected a particular reality: the existence of a distinct Ulster Protestant nation whose democratic right to self-determination was threatened by a nationalist movement which consistently refused to recognise that Ulster Protestants were not part of the Irish nation ... The threat to their material position and Catholic nationalism's disregard for their distinct political and ideological traditions made their [i.e. Protestant working-class] conflicts of interest with the bourgeoisie of secondary significance in relation to their shared interests in mobilising against the nationalist enemy. (Patterson, 1980, p. 145)

To argue thus, I have suggested, is to deny historical agency to Protestant workers and small farmers and reduce Ulster Unionism to the status of a Home Rule 'wrecking machine' under the control of the Protestant bourgeoisie (Mac Laughlin, 1980, pp. 15–27). Patterson is wrong also in interpreting Protestant resistance to national separatism in Ulster simply as proof of the existence of a distinct 'Protestant nation' here. Indeed the logic of his argument would imply that Ulster Unionism was an historical and political anomaly, and that it contained a level of ethnic isolationism which it never had, at this time at least. However, Unionist behaviour at this time was far from anomalous. Indeed it appeared so chiefly only to Irish nationalists, and in the specific contexts of nineteenth-century Irish nation-building. Viewed from the wider European perspective, it was a rational expression of political regionalism which sought to keep Ulster Protestants as part of, not apart from, that most 'historic' nation, the United Kingdom. Yet, according to Patterson, 'Unionist mobilisations' in the Protestant north-east and in outliers elsewhere in Ireland were one and the same thing. They must be seen 'as in part an element ... in the struggle of an important section of the national ruling class against [Irish] Home Rule' (Patterson, 1980, pp. 147–9). Because he fails to see in Protestant opposition to Irish nationalism in the north-east an expression of 'big-nation' nationalism, he suggests that Protestant workers and small farmers here were motivated more by class interests than by nationalist interests. To suggest this is to miss the connections between class and national consciousness in late nineteenth-century Ireland, and Ulster. This also ignores the political geography of nation-building here in the late nineteenth and early twentieth centuries. According to Patterson, the integration of 'the economy of the north-east' with that of the UK 'went beyond movements of capital, labour and commodities'. Instead it:

> provided the basis for an identification with a developing British labour movement and a theory of history which relegated nationalist demands to a past stage of historical development, thus denying its current legitimacy. (Patterson, 1980, p. 148)

In arguing thus, Patterson underestimates the wider context of plebeian Unionist working-class opposition to national separatism in Ireland. Like Hobsbawm, he seems to suggest the class consciousness of Ulster's Protestant working class was somehow or other formulated separately – even independently – from their unionist nationalist consciousness. Like Hobsbawm, he suggests that 'nationalism' in Ireland had 'nothing to offer' Protestant workers because it was narrowly interpreted as an Irish Catholic affair, something that had more to do with defence of Gaelic culture and protection of traditional values, than with economic advancement and political development. Thus his problematic contention that nationalism had 'no appeal for Protestant workers' because it belonged to 'a past stage of historical development'.

Patterson's arguments share a number of features with Hobsbawm's discussion on the naturalness of class consciousness and the divisive nature of national consciousness in ethnically divided societies. Both writers fail to identify different versions of nationalism and different scales of nation-building in nineteenth-century Ireland. They generally also fail to locate these conflicting nationalisms, in Ireland as well as Unionist Ulster, in their wider

British and European contexts. Patterson, like Hobsbawm, also fails to explain why Unionists in Britain and indeed the empire were so anxious to retain the north-east of Ireland as an integral part of the United Kingdom. Both writers conveniently also explain away the complex political geography of Ulster Unionism. In particular they suggest that all of Ulster did not come under Unionist rule primarily because Ulster Unionists were not interested in the underdeveloped west and south-west of the province. More signif icantly still, they fail to account for Catholic nationalist hegemony in these areas of Ulster, which as we shall see, dates from at least the 1880s.

Hobsbawm's comments on national versus class consciousness are more general but no less confusing than those of Patterson, especially when applied to the contested terrains of Ireland. They are also far less scattered than his extremely rich commentaries on the dialectics of nation-building and capitalism in nineteenth-century Europe. His comments on class versus national consciousness are largely confined to his well-known *New Left Review* paper on the threat of 'Balkanisation' to Britain published in 1977. This offered a highly stimulating and sustained critique of the consequences of the 'breakup' of nations by 'Balkanising' force in today's world. The paper was sparked by Nairn's neo-Marxist speculations on national separatism in Britain published in the same year. Hobsbawm used the *New Left Review* paper to express a strong traditional socialist opposition to ethno-nationalism in general. He saw this as a way of defending working-class unity and protecting the precious territorial integrity of 'big nations' in the contemporary world.

However, in a little-discussed essay on 'Working Classes and Nations' published, significantly, in the journal of the Irish Labour History Society in 1982, he also makes a strong historical case for resisting small-nation nationalism and national separatism in the core economies of nineteenth-century Europe (Hobsbawm, 1982, pp. 75–85). In this paper he makes a number of distinctions between class consciousness and national consciousness which merit critical attention here. In the first place this essay, like the *New Review* paper, reveals Hobsbawm as a powerful defender of 'big-nation' unionist nationalism. In the paper 'Working Classes and Nations' he constantly insists that the class consciousness of Irish workers was impeded by divisions brought about through the rise of the nationalist bourgeoisie and the emergence of national differences. Second, like other traditional leftists, he regards the class consciousness of workers as more authentic and less divisive than

national consciousness. Third, he completely ignores class formation in rural society and neglects the links between urban and rural
interests in late nineteenth-century nation-building societies.
Indeed Hobsbawm's analysis of class and national consciousness is
weakest of all when dealing with the class interests of rural society
and the relationship between rural and urban social classes. Like
Patterson, he avoids any serious discussion of class interests in rural
Ireland at a time when the combined population of the three largest
cities was still well below one million at the opening of the twentieth century. Despite the existence of strong links between
rural-based nation-builders and rural social classes, and notwith-
standing the cultural and political consequences of nation-building
for the urban working class, Hobsbawm focuses exclusively on the
'class question' as it related to the latter, not the former.

Written during a period of heightened political violence in
Northern Ireland, Hobsbawm's reflections on the breakup of Britain
is not so much an analysis of sectarianism and ethno-nationalism.
It is nothing less than a history lesson which seeks to illustrate the
'errors' that Protestant and Catholic workers made when they fell
under the influence of sectarian nationalist or Unionist leaders.
Thus Hobsbawm implies that 'nationalism' was either an 'Irish
affair', something confined to the Catholic south and west of
Ireland, or it was a product of sectarian rivalry that erupted in the
north-east of Ireland in the late nineteenth century. In either case
it was essentially conservative, an ideology concocted by the forces
of tradition in order to weaken working-class unity. Referring
obliquely, and very awkwardly, to 'southern Ireland' he suggests
that the historic appeal of nationalism there was effective because
'nationalist agitation … building on memories of a former political
state or autonomy, or organisations embodying the separateness of
a nationality (e.g. the Catholicism of the dependent people as
against the Protestantism or Orthodoxy of the ruling state) were in
existence before an industrial working class developed'
(Hobsbawm, 1982, p. 82). This, he argues, was also the case in
Poland and Czechoslovakia in the nineteenth century. Having
explained the historic appeal of nationalism in these terms he next
proceeds to condemn patriotism as a divisive force that is always
inimical to working-class interests. In nineteenth-century Ireland,
he suggests, national sentiment became an 'explosive' force which
destroyed the cross-national unity of the working class because it
was 'intertwined with issues directly affecting the state and its institutions'. Hobsbawm does not explain why class consciousness can
take 'second place' to national consciousness either in the south of

Ireland or in Protestant Ulster. This failure is all the more striking in the context of late nineteenth-century Ireland.

Here, as I have argued elsewhere, national consciousness was not only intertwined with the class consciousness of workers – it expressed itself in two separate oppositional forms, one of which was separatist while the other was unionist. Separatist nationalism had the support of Catholic workers, small farmers, the shopocracy, the middle class, the petty bourgeoisie and the intelligentsia. While this genre of nationalism also had the support of the Catholic minority in the north-east, the real heartlands of Catholic nationalism lay outside this very distinctive region. The unionist nationalism of Ulster Protestants on the other hand reflected the interests not just of large landowners and industrialists – it also had the wholehearted support of Protestant workers, the middle classes, and the urban and rural poor. Here working-class consciousness was not secondary to the national consciousness of Protestant workers. It was inseparable from it. The class consciousness of workers in Ireland's case did not grow out of any primordial 'religious divide' – still less from a 'tribal divide' – in Irish society. As elsewhere in Europe and North America it constituted one part of much wider and often conflicting expressions of social identity. However, what made Ireland 'special', to some extent at least, was the fact that class consciousness here also evolved alongside two opposing and territorially based strategies of nation-building in the late nineteenth and early twentieth centuries. Yet even here Ireland was not an exceptional case, as the history of class consciousness in countries as diverse and as apart as Canada and the Basque country clearly testify. In ethnically and regionally divided contexts of nation-building Ireland, class consciousness was clearly forged on the anvil of national consciousness. Because it was embodied in 'real people' and was not simply an abstract 'category', class consciousness could not, and rarely intended to, transcend the national contexts within which it evolved. In the event it grew up behind the ethnic, religious and quasi-racial barriers separating an older established Protestant working class from Irish small farmers and a weakly developed Catholic working class at crucial stages of nation-building in Ireland and the UK. Often indeed the class consciousness of workers, including agricultural workers and small farmers, did not come into conflict with their religious, ethnic or racial consciousness. At other times, however, it did. Here as elsewhere in nation-building Europe and North America it was so intertwined with national and racial consciousness as to be inseparable from it. More than that, it was so central to the lives of ordinary people, so inextricably linked to their daily lives in very 'real' places – e.g. the north-east, the midlands and south of Ireland, the 'west' – that it became a crucial force in the struggle for nationalist and Unionist hegemony in the contested terrains of this fragmented nation-building Ireland (Fitzpatrick, 1998).

Hobsbawm's analysis of class and national consciousness is of interest to the student of Irish nation-building for a number of other reasons. In the first place it ignores the political geography of nation-building and nationalism in late nineteenth-century Ireland. This is particularly remarkable when one considers just what a patchwork of Orange and Green (including all shades in between these two colours) late nineteenth-century Ulster – and Belfast – actually was. It is all the more remarkable when one also considers the rootedness of two diametrically opposed expressions of national consciousness – one national separatist the other unionist – in different parts of Ulster and the rest of Ireland at this time. Thus Hobsbawm discusses class consciousness in Ireland in highly abstract terms when he portrays it simply as a 'product' of the 'proletarian condition'. As such, he suggests, it was assumed to be more 'logical' than national consciousness. For Hobsbawm also nationalist movements were to be condemned not only because they:

> naturally accentuated the linguistic, religious and physical distinctions between 'their' sector of a heterogeneous working class and the rest, but also because their objects were by definition at odds with those of class consciousness. They sought to substitute the dividing line between 'the nation' (including both its exploiters and exploited) and 'the foreigners' (including all workers classifiable as such) for class lines. (Hobsbawm, 1982, p. 79)

In a follow-up statement which comes close to suggesting that working-class consciousness is 'natural' while national conscious-ness is 'irrational' and 'divisive', he argues that it has always 'proved difficult to prevent class consciousness, since it arises natu-rally and logically out of the proletarian condition, at least in the elementary form of trade unions' consciousness, that is to say in recognition that workers as such need to organise collectively against employers in order to defend and improve their conditions as hired hands'.

In portraying working-class consciousness in such abstract and generalised terms, Hobsbawm, unlike Thompson, ignores the regional and national attachments of workers, the strong sense of place, and sense of community, that tied workers to 'their' place and 'their' nation. Thus the identification of Protestant workers with Loyalist Ulster, and with the ready-made nation of the United Kingdom, and Catholic workers with a nation-in-the-making like rural Ireland. For that reason two different varieties of cultural homogeneity emerged in Ireland. Both were products of objective relations of production, but they were also products of two different approaches to nation-building, and two very different images of the imagined community of the nation in Ireland. Throughout this period of 'turbulent readjustment' the political and cultural boundaries of Ulster were modified so as to satisfy a modern unionist territorial imperative which was now making itself felt for the first time. As Gellner suggests, the transitional period in nation-formation in Ireland, as elsewhere in ethnically divided societies in mainland Europe, was 'bound to be violent and conflict-ridden'. This was especially the case in the north-east where Catholics and Protestants were locked in an unequal contest to establish nationalist and Unionist hegemony. Here 'rival cultures' and rival conceptions of 'peoplehood' coexisted as nationalists on both sides literally sought to capture 'the souls of men'. To do this they had to construct rival centres of political authority and capture territory for Catholic nationalist Ireland on the one hand, and for Protestant Unionist Ulster and the United Kingdom of Great Britain and Ireland on the other.

Wallerstein's 'Peoplehood' and Historical Constructs of Ulster and Ireland in the Nineteenth Century

In this chapter, and in much of the remainder of this work, I shall seek to overcome the dualities of 'class' and 'national' conscious-ness in Hobsbawm's analysis of nationalism. However, I now wish to suggest that one way this can be achieved is to combine Wallerstein's category 'peoplehood' with E.P. Thompson's histor-ical approach to the 'making' of social classes in the eighteenth and nineteenth centuries. For Wallerstein, as for Hobsbawm, classes are 'objective' analytic categories which, under certain circumstances, realise themselves and thereby become classes 'fur sich', as opposed to classes 'an sich' (Balibar and Wallerstein, 1991, p. 84). Viewed thus, however, classes are not simply or always products of the social relations of production. As statements about contradictions in an historical system, they are also quite unlike

'races', 'nations', 'ethnic groups' and 'peoples'. These are also terri-
torialised descriptions of social communities, not simply
sociological constructs or analytic categories.

Thus as Wallerstein put it, 'the concept of "race" is related to
the "axial division of labour in the world economy". The concept
of "nation" is related to the political superstructure of this historical system, the sovereign states that derive from the interstate
system'. As used in the Darwinian half of the nineteenth century
these categories of 'race' and 'nation' tended to be applied more to
powerful ethnic groups than to weaker ones (Mac Laughlin, 1998,
pp. 1014–15). They were especially applied to those organised
within existing nation-states which selected their own cultural
markers in such a way as to exclude 'the other', including other
national minorities. Thus, unlike popular usages of race in Europe
today, 'nation' and ethno-nationality in late nineteenth-century
Ireland were used to self-consciously forge identities from within
rather than have these imposed from above by hostile 'others'. The
category 'race' was linked to social progress in Ulster in such a way
as to inform bourgeois thinking about the limits of social and
political change. This suggested that 'Honest Ulstermen', particularly those under the hegemony of the industrial bourgeoisie,
would have unlimited cultural and development potentialities
within the United Kingdom. Ulster's new ruling classes then not
only saw themselves as lords of all they surveyed within this
corner of the United Kingdom – they also saw themselves as
belonging with the lords of humankind in general (Mackenzie,
1986; Springhall, 1986). Race thinking coloured their perception
of themselves as a chosen people, a people with a mission civilatrice in backward Catholic Ireland. It also influenced perceptions
of themselves as a people steeped in history and rooted in a
progressive metropolitan domain. Because Catholics were viewed
as 'a people without history', and because they were perceived to
literally lack industry, they were excluded from this corner of the
'historic' nation in Ireland (Wolf, 1985). Like other European
elites, especially their White Anglo-Saxon counterparts in North
America, Ulster Unionists were impregnated with the ethos of
change and social progress. They invested Industry, Trade and
Commerce with the same divine authority that monarchy
formerly claimed (Kiernan, 1972). Adam Smith called the Europe
of these elites the magna virum mater, the mighty mother of men.
The combination of unionist nationalism and anti-Irish racism in
Ulster made this a powerful nation-centred and patriarchal place.
As Unionists saw it, this bred great character in the 'honest'

menfolk of Protestant Ulster and rendered them uniquely capable of great designs (Smith, 1972).

Because 'race' and 'nation' are so intertwined in many historical accounts of nation-building, it could be argued that Wallerstein suggests a too rigid division between these two categories in the contested terrains of a nation-building country like Ireland. Writing from a world system perspective, he suggests that 'race' arose primarily as 'a mode of expressing and sustaining core–periphery antinomy'. 'National categorisation' arose originally 'as a mode of expressing competition between states' in an international system. He adds that race and racism 'unify intrazonally the core zones and the peripheral zones in their battles with each other'. 'Nation' and nationalism on the other hand 'divide core zones and peripheral zones intrazonally' (Balibar and Wallerstein, 1991, p. 79). The latter process operates in a complex intrazonal and interzonal competition for rank order whereby 'core nations' are considered more powerful than peripheral nations. That is why, for example, even apart from locational factors, a 'core nation' like Britain could be accorded much higher status than a peripheral nation like Ireland (Mac Laughlin, 1999e, pp. 53–66). This meant that Ulster Unionists always considered themselves to have the political advantage over Catholic nationalists. The European interstate system in general, not just Britain, usually respected the rights of powerful nations more than it did those of small nations like rural Catholic Ireland.

Yet Wallerstein, unlike Hobsbawm, recognises a place for small nations in this nineteenth-century world order. Thus he argues that 'any group who sees advantage in using the state's legal powers to advance its interests ... in any sub-region of the state has an interest in promoting nationalist sentiment as a legitimisation of its claims' (Balibar and Wallerstein, 1991, p. 82). The nationalism of 'sub groups' acts as a sort of social cement, tying urban and rural classes together in a quest for statehood, while simultaneously binding them to the history and territory of 'their' nation. These 'sub groups' in turn use their 'pastness' as 'a central element in the socialisation of individuals, in the maintenance of group solidarity, in the establishment of or challenge to social legitimisation'. Their 'pastness', as we shall see, is pre-eminently a moral and political phenomenon. It can be defined in terms of attachment of territory, and in terms of historical association and socio-political groupings. Viewed thus, unionist nationalists and national separatists in Ireland used their own distinctive brands of 'pastness' to promote state-level uniformities. However, their nationalisms were also the consequences of these same uniformities as realised in the socio-political and economic landscapes of late nineteenth-century Ireland. Both expressions of nationalism were mobilised to claim 'national' territory, and to defend, or reinforce, the cultural and ethnic homogeneity of 'their people'. This meant that ethnic intolerance and religious bigotry, on both sides of the nation-building divide, were not primordial attributes of 'warring tribes' in Ireland. They developed out of the longing which each ethnic sub group had for oneness, uniqueness and cultural purity. The Irish experience of nation-building was not unique in this respect. As elsewhere in Europe the 'nation' at this time signified unity and purification. In Ulster's case this translated into 'a Protestant parliament for a Protestant people'. In the Republic of Ireland it meant a Catholic constitution for a Catholic people.

While recognising the role of race-thinking in dividing the colonised from the colonisers and legitimising the hegemony of powerful nations in a global arena, Wallerstein underestimates the part played by racism in the legitimisation of ethnic supremacy within nations. In nineteenth-century Europe, for example, 'race' was frequently used for 'expressing and sustaining core–periphery antimony' within nations. But it did not just express conflicts of interest between nations and their 'colonial possession'. In Unionist Ulster, as in Anglo-Irish Ireland, 'nation' and 'race' were so intertwined in anti-Catholic discourse that it was impossible to distinguish one from the other. Catholics in general were attributed with 'racial' and 'national' characteristics which made them 'unfit' for self-government. Those in the north-east were considered especially 'unfit' to have any say governing a 'progressive' and 'prosperous' province like Ulster. For that reason they were literally placed below Protestants, the 'chosen people' of God in an otherwise 'superstitious' island society. Thus the 'nation' was fused with 'race' to justify an axial division of labour within Ulster, one wherein Catholics held down low-status jobs, and often inhabited quite different worlds, to those of Protestants.

Wallerstein stresses that ethnic groups as socio-historical constructs can correlate heavily with objective social classes, particularly when the latter literally 'realise' themselves as classes *fur sich*. Unlike Hobsbawm, he does not portray classes in abstract terms. Neither does he insist that they are more 'natural' than ethnic or nationalist constructs of peoplehood. For Wallerstein, class consciousness is first and foremost 'people-based'. Class associations, including trade unions, employers' groups, workers' organisations, farmers' grouping, the intelligentsia, and coalitions of professional workers, are never simply social abstractions. They also have implicit, and de facto, 'people bases'. Like 'nations' and 'ethnic groups', they are what E.P. Thompson, in his discussion of class formation, called 'active processes'. Similarly also 'nations', 'classes' and 'ethnic groups' did not develop independently of each other. They did 'rise like the sun at an appointed time'. They were historical and geo-ethnic happenings, in the sense that very real people were 'present' at their making. As Wallerstein puts it, 'peoples have names, familiar names ... and they seem to have long histories' (Balibar and Wallerstein, 1991, p. 172). This was especially the case in Ireland where Unionism literally 'named' Ulster as a place apart from Catholic nationalist Ireland, and 'named' Protestants as loyal defenders of the Crown in Ireland. National separatism on the other hand 'named' the Catholic Irish as a nation distinct from the United Kingdom.

Finally Hobsbawm, like other traditional leftists, all too often bemoans the fact that workers in Ireland, especially in Ulster, have organised themselves in 'people forms'. Wallerstein on the other hand sees this as a perfectly natural and unavoidable historical development. For him, it is impossible to have class activity that is entirely divorced from 'people-based political activity'. We have seen this in national liberation movements all across the colonial world in the 1960s and 1970s. We see it also during the 'spring-times of peoples' in Europe, including Ireland, in the latter half of the nineteenth century. This was a period when the nation-building processes which fostered the construction of 'peoplehood' were inextricably bound up with class formation and the growth of class consciousness in concrete regional settings. 'Pure workers' organisations then were as rare as 'pure rural organisations' were, simply because both were so deeply embroiled in the whole process of 'people formation'. In this period, as also in the 'Third World' since the 1960s, class struggles 'were also national liberation struggles, and class-based political activity' was often 'extremely nation-centred'. Unlike Hobsbawm, Wallerstein puts as much emphasis on 'peoplehood' as on 'class consciousness' in his analysis of these institutional constructs of historical capitalism. More than that – he insists that 'peoplehood' has been 'an essential pillar' of historical capitalism. 'Peoplehood', he argues, has kept pace with ethnic geography of individual nations on the one hand, and that of the new world order on the other. Thus we have become more, not less, attached to 'peoplehood', this in part is because it has been an important expression of *Gemeinschaften* in the nation-building world of the nineteenth century and in the globalised contemporary world. Thus, unlike Hobsbawm, his analysis allows for different political geographies of nation-building and nationalism, just as it allows for different scales of nation-building in the nineteenth century and today.

Wallerstein also points to the links between nationalism and the consolidation of industrial capitalism in the nineteenth century. Like Hobsbawm he argues that nation-states historically were essential pillars in the evolution of a European world system under the hegemony of the national bourgeoisie. Focusing on the cultural aspects of nation-building he insists that the whole idea that a society should be integrated, that it should 'have one language, one culture, one race', that it should have the right to self-determination, was a product of nineteenth-century western political thought. Showing a greater appreciation of the specificities of nation-building in a small peripheral nation like Ireland, he also asserted that 'the creation of strong states within a world-system was a historical prerequisite to the rise of nationalism, both within the strong states and in the periphery'. This, he argues, was because nationalism conferred citizenship upon members of the state while simultaneously transforming them into collective social and ethnic solidarities. In rural Catholic Ireland these solidarities emerged, in modern form at least, in the course of the nineteenth century. They emerged partially as a reaction against 'big-nation' nationalism in Ireland, and partially because of the rise of a native Catholic bourgeoisie who felt that they too had a right to self-determination. In Catholic Ireland these social groups looked on nationalism as a cultural defence – a hedge against the untrammelled forces of modernisation or 'Anglicisation' – and as a strategy for developing Ireland's peripheral capitalism.

To conclude this discussion of 'peoplehood' and nation-building as it applied to nineteenth-century Ireland. It is suggested that Unionist and nationalist 'peoplehoods' emerged in Ireland chiefly during the latter half of the nineteenth century. This was a period when 'as a result of common experience, inherited or shaped', people articulated the identity of their interests as between themselves and other people (Thompson, 1968, p. 9). At this historical conjuncture Catholic nationalists in the south and Protestant Unionists in the north-east articulated their interests 'as against other men and women whose interests were different, and usually opposed to theirs'. A sense of 'peoplehood' here was linked through a whole range of socialising agencies and class mechanisms to two different scales, as opposed to two different types of national consciousness. This was what gave rural and urban communities throughout the north and south of Ireland such a heightened sense of place, a sense of themselves belonging either to an Irish nation-in-the-making, or to the already-existing and unionist British nation. This in turn literally raised the whole contentious issue of territorial attachments in an island economy marked by strong regional and cultural differences. Yet Irish nationalism and Ulster Unionism were much more than ideological constructs or forms of 'imagining' that could be imposed from above on an ethnically divided society by its hegemonic bourgeoisie. They embodied the essence of 'common sense' for many ordinary people who lived out their lives, not in an abstract plane of 'social relations of production' but in the very real, and very different, regional contexts of Ireland in the late nineteenth and early twentieth centuries. They informed whole aspects of life, including attitudes towards politics, progress, community, religion, work, land, history and identity. That is why national separatism and 'small-nation' nationalism as in Irish nationalism, perhaps even more so than the 'big nation' of Ulster Unionists, was also socially constructed as an ensemble of sensibilities that were projected across a wide range of social, cultural and territorial fields.

The sections that follow look at locational aspects of nation-building and nationalism in general and then in Ireland in particular. The anomalous state of nation-building here presented nationalists, national separatists and contemporary theorists of nationalism with many classic examples of the difficulties involved in building nations from the ground up. They also emphasise just how difficult it is to theorise, and generalise, about nation-building in the late nineteenth and early twentieth centuries.

Despite the plethora of descriptive and highly partisan accounts of nationalism and Unionism in Ireland in the nineteenth century, critical theoretical accounts that seek to explain, rather than simply describe, legitimise or condemn these ideologies have been few and far between. Then, and to a lesser extent now, most Irish nationalists took the naturalness of 'the nation' in Ireland for granted. They either condemned Unionism as a conspiracy to wreck Irish Home Rule through bigotry or malice, or insisted upon the congruence of the nation-state with the 'national' territory. In so doing they maintained that the island of Ireland was the natural basis of a 'united Ireland' and mobilised nationalist ideology to lay claim to the 'national' territory. In tracing Unionist power to the Tory heartlands of the United Kingdom, they underestimated the strength of plebeian Unionism in the enclave economy of the politically distinct north-east of Ireland. They ignored the rootedness of plebeian Unionism in this part of Ireland where conflicting, but no less legitimate, claims to nationhood were being articulated by Protestant Ulstermen. In literally claiming space as their own and for their own, Irish nationalists and Ulster Unionists clearly renounced the geographies of Irish nationalism and Unionism in the different regional contexts of nineteenth-century Ireland. In taking the logic of 'their' respective nation for granted nationalists and Unionists alike failed to see the 'Irish nation' and 'Unionist Ulster' for what they were, namely geographical constructs and political aspirations which were products of concrete historical transformations, the outcome of regional and historical 'happenings'. What these historians failed to stress was that their respective 'nations' were never 'natural'. They had to be invented. They were not simply products of geography or history. Thus others since then have shown that the nation in Ireland as elsewhere in Europe had to be mediated through a whole variety of historical agents, and agencies, that were rooted in particular places or countries. In nineteenth-century Ireland, as also in France, Germany, Italy and Poland, the nation-building agents included the church, the national bourgeoisie, the provincial press and the educational establishment, as well as infrastructural networks of roads, railways and canals.

As we have already seen, most nation-centred historians in nineteenth-century Europe not only described but strongly defended nation-building processes at work in 'their countries'. This was particularly the case in powerful nations where, as a result of the influence of social Darwinism, nationalist historians regarded it as inevitable that strong nations would prevail over colonial societies abroad and weaker nations at home. In Ireland's case Catholic nationalists Anglicised the causes of the country's social and economic problems and nationalised their solutions. Their defence of nationalism was not only a separatist and nation-centred vindication of Ireland's right to self-determination. This was one of the earliest, and most forceful demands for the 'breakup of Britain' ever to have been articulated. The Irish were not only calling for the 'Balkanisation' of Britain – from their nation-building outpost on the margins of Europe they were calling for the creation of a new world order which would accord small nations the same rights that large nations had garnished to themselves through the Balkanisation of dynastic empires in the seventeenth and eighteenth centuries. It would be wrong to suggest that it is only modern-day expressions of ethno-nationalism that can contribute to regional instability in countries as far

apart as former Yugoslavia and Indonesia. Small-nation nationalism in late nineteenth-century Ireland also threatened the
regional stability of the United Kingdom. It was widely recognised
that the success of nation-building here could have serious reper-
cussions for the regional stability of Britain's imperial possessions.

The other tradition in writing about nationalism in Ireland
championed what was considered the much more 'respectable'
cause of Irish Unionism. In Ulster at least this genre of nationalism
defended the territorial integrity of the United Kingdom of Great
Britain and Ireland. Those supporting this tradition insisted that
Ireland's future was best left in the hands of British Unionists, the
widely recognised 'Lords of Humankind'. As a 'superior people' in a
'troublesome' land, Ulster Unionists were proudly proclaiming their
membership in the United Kingdom, both because they were
already commercially united with it and because Britain anyway was
considered the model nation which other struggling nationalities,
apart from the Irish, sought to emulate. In so doing Ulster Unionists
recognised the existence of two expressions of nation-building in
nineteenth-century Ireland, but insisted that their's was the more
legitimate because it had the sanction of history and race theory.

Nation, Place and Class in Nineteenth-century Ireland

Anderson, Hobsbawm and Wallerstein all point to one of the
persistent paradoxes of nineteenth-century nation-building – the
fact each nation proudly proclaimed its own distinctiveness, yet, in
western Europe at least, all were the product of more or less similar
nation-building processes. This was also the case in nation-
building Ireland. The latter included the nation-building agents
and agencies we have already been discussing, print capitalism, the
popular press, the provincial press, the bureaucratisation of society
under the hegemony of the bourgeoisie, national education and
elaborate networks of road and rail communication which reduced
the relative costs of travel within Ireland and Britain. Taken
together, all of these made social interaction and inter-regional
communication at a 'national' level both possible and imperative.
They certainly made it easier for large sections of the population to
think of themselves as a modern 'nation'. Thus more and more
members of society now had what Anderson calls a 'vertical and
horizontal sense of comradeship' with people they had never met,
or even seen before. Equally important, they could also 'imagine'
their country as a national homeland, a compound of territory,

society, environment and politics. At this stage in its evolution the 'nation' referred to much more than the possibility of becoming a nation. It designated instead a concrete reality, that amalgam of language, religion, economy, way of life, territory, history and politics that formed the basis of the nineteenth-century nation-state. It was what one writer recently labelled a 'unit of analysis with a holistic undertow' (Jordanova, 1998, p. 199). As such it gave meaning to life, precisely because citizens of the nation found shelter from the storms of modernity, from its ennui, its facelessness, its rootlessness and its meaninglessness. As members of the nation were forged into an organic community they also developed deep, often spiritual, attachments to the country they inhabited. They began to develop a sense of identity, a sense of place and a Herderian sense of mission. So there developed a collective memory, a collective vision of the future, as citizens of the nation developed a capacity to project themselves forward as a people of distinction, and with a distinct contribution to make to the wider world of nation-building.

Central to the imaginative construction of any nation, not least in nineteenth-century Ireland, was the assumed existence of national collectivities and the very real existence of agents and agencies capable of transforming the country into a nation. As we have already seen, this coincided in Europe with the rise of the bourgeoisie, including the petty bourgeoisie, the emergence of the popular press, the growth of national education and the spread of other 'nationalising' agencies associated with the development of the modern administrative state. It 'happened' especially with the imaginative conversion of 'national' culture, and the 'national' territory, into a compound of community, economy, environment and mentality (Cubitt, 1998, p. 16). This in fact is what we mean when we talk of the nineteenth-century nation as 'organic community', as opposed to the transient assemblies of citizens and non-citizens in pre-modern and pre-nationalist societies. In Ireland as elsewhere in Europe this organic community of the nation had to be constructed through a careful nurturing of inter-class and inter-regional alliances. This was achieved through the cultivation of a common sense of identity and the teaching of shared myths and common history. This encouraged citizens of the nation to invest, culturally and psychologically, and not just materially and politically, in the national territory as a 'national homeland'. Given the multi-ethnic and multi-national character of most societies in nineteenth-century Europe, including Ireland, nation-building regularly involved the coercive absorption or incorporation of minorities into the nation of the dominant majority. We have already seen that nation-building even on the Irish scale had profound implications for Irish Travellers and also resulted in the marginalisation of workers, women, the rural poor and religious minorities. Ireland's absorption into the United Kingdom is of course a classic example of ethno-nationalist incorporation at a higher and much more extensive scale. That small ethno-nations like Ireland were expected to assimilate into the nation of the dominant majority, in this case Britain, is clear from the writings of liberal unionists like John Stuart Mill. His *Considerations on Representative Government*, published in 1861, contains one of the strongest, and highly racist, defences of this process to be found anywhere in the writings of nineteenth-century political theorists. Mill contended that:

> Experience proves that it is possible for one nationality to merge and be absorbed by another; and when it was originally an inferior and more backward portion of the human race, the absorption is greatly to its advantage. Nobody can suppose it is not more beneficial to a Breton, or a Basque of the French Navarre, to be brought into the current of the ideas and feelings of a highly civilised and cultivated people – to be members of the French nationality ... than to sulk on its own rocks, the half savage relic of past times, revolving in his own little mental orbit, without participation or interest in the movement of the world. The same remark applies to the Welshman or the Scottish Highlanders, as members of the British nation. (Mill, 1946, p. 65)

Although he does not name Ireland here, elsewhere Mill staunchly defended its absorption into Britain. In defending 'big-nation' nationalism, liberals like Mill clearly questioned the rationality of ethno-nationalist minorities like the Irish, the Scots, the Welsh and others who chose 'to sulk on [their] own rocks'. As we have already seen, the process of absorption and integration was particularly lengthy and tortuous in the case of Ireland. What matters here is that it was greatly intensified in the latter half of the nineteenth century when 'big-nation' British nationalism led to renewed efforts on the part of Unionists to make Ireland part of the United Kingdom by attempting to 'kill Irish Home Rule with kindness'. It was then in particular that renewed efforts were made to bring the Irish, 'the half savage relics of past times ... into the current of the ideas and feelings of a highly civilised and cultivated people' like the British. More importantly still, however, this was happening just as it became possible for the Irish to imagine themselves a nation in the modern sense of the term.

Catholic Ireland then was only one example of an attempted assimilation of an ethno-nationalist minority into the nationhood of the majority. In Spain, France and Germany, as also in the countries of Scandinavia, ethno-national minorities were incorporated into the nation-state of the dominant majority. As these cases show, minority nations were regularly expected to accept as rational the democracy of majority, even if it did not serve the interests of minorities. Nationalist parties representing the latter were considered sectionalist or 'regional parties'. For that very reason they were expected to assimilate to the mores of the dominant majority and accept as democratic the decisions of democratic majorities. This was because, being sectionalist and regionalist, ethno-nationalist minorities were also considered non-progressive. Because they were not 'emblematic' of the nation as a whole they were expected to accept absorption in the majority nation on its terms. Thus marginalisation of minorities was often considered justified on the grounds that minority interests ran counter to 'national interests', including the need to literally hold the nation together and prevent falling apart. If, as in the case of nationalist Ireland, they threatened the territorial integrity of the dominant nation, they had to be coerced or, as was later the case, forcibly partitioned.

All this suggests that the process of marginalisation which resulted from nation-building also had clear spatial implications. In nineteenth-century Ireland, as in post-independence Africa, some regions were considered too valuable to be lost to rival nations. Some had more symbolic significance than others. Some places were considered dispensable, while others were regarded as indispensable to the nation-building drive. Yet underlying all of the spatial implications of nation-building was the desire to link the 'imagined community' of the 'nation' to the 'national' territory. This was how the nation literally was constructed. Moreover, in the nineteenth century at least, it was constructed as an organism linked to a national territory with sufficient social and economic potential to hold its own in a world then dominated by powerful nations. Thus, in order to qualify as nation-states, nineteenth-century nations had to command a national homeland, just as they had to be inhabited by citizens with sufficient developmental potential to place their nation alongside the progressive nations of the world.

This, as we shall presently see, was considered problematic in the case of Catholic nation-building Ireland. In supporting unity with Great Britain, Ulster Unionists not only believed themselves to be more rational but 'better' nationalists than Catholics. The latter were considered irrational because they sought secession from a united kingdom in the process of becoming a united nation under a national bourgeoisie. The 'irrationality' of the Irish was stressed at a meeting of some 300 Unionists in Donegal in the remote north-west of the country in March 1886 when one speaker declared that:

> It seemed remarkable at this period of the nineteenth century, when minor states were asking for the protection of greater states, that a section of the Irish should ask to have the country launched forth as an independent entity – a speck in the ocean. (*Donegal Independent*, 27 March 1886; quoted in Anderson, 1989, p. 154)

Much in the same manner that the United States during the Reagan administration constructed El Salvador and Nicaragua as threats to its internal security, Ulster Unionists and the Conservative party constructed Irish Home Rule as a threat to the integrity of the British Empire and the death-knell of landlordism. The *Donegal Independent* of 17 July 1886 predicted that Home Rule would lead to the 'dismemberment of Empire'. Three months earlier the *Coleraine Constitution* said it would lead to 'the loss of India'. The fiercely pro-Union *Londonderry Sentinel* believed it had 'incited the Indians to agitate', adding that, if passed, this Bill would 'stir up the natives in every country over which the British flag waves'. It pointed out that:

> a revolution so complete as to turn a whole class accustomed to rule for centuries from their seats of power, and to place over their heads another class long accustomed to obey, is a dangerous policy. (Quoted in Anderson, 1989, p. 153)

In their efforts to construct their organic nation, Irish nationalists had literally to scramble for territory, including symbolic territory, anywhere they could get it. As these statements show, they were unlikely to find such territory in the staunchly nationalist–unionist north-east. Nineteenth-century Irish nation-building contained strong elements of geographical exclusion and inclusion. In the industrialised north-east it lost out to Protestant Unionists, while elsewhere in the country it entailed inclusion of underdeveloped, yet culturally vital regions like the barren western seaboard. Nation-building here also subordinated urban interests in Ireland to the interests of the rural Catholic bourgeoisie. This meant that the agricultural heartlands of the country always had higher priority than urban centres and the underdeveloped peripheries. The fact that the north-east chose to stay within the United Kingdom also inadvertently contributed to the social disintegration of communities throughout Catholic nation-building Ireland well into the twentieth century. In losing the country's most industrialised province to the unionist nation of Great Britain, rural Ireland continued to lose large numbers of young adults to emigration, not least emigration to mainland Britain and the United States, as migration to the industrial heartlands of Ulster never was an option for these 'surplus' sons and daughters of nation-building Ireland. Indeed the peripheralisation of rural Ireland during the first thirty or forty years of the state was not unconnected to processes of core-formation which caused this part of the country to be linked with mainland Britain, and not with nation-building Ireland. While Ireland was integrated into the world economy through the commodification and internationalisation of Irish labour, Unionist Ulster remained an integral part of the UK economy. In the event Marx's fatalistic prediction that Ireland's people would be 'banished by sheep and ox', had largely come true, not least because they did not have access to the industrial labour markets of Unionist Ulster.

This 'scramble' for territory, which was all-important for a small nation like Ireland, was no less evident, even if it was not so extreme, in Unionist Ulster. Here, as a later chapter will show, impoverished counties like Donegal, Cavan and Monaghan, all of them part of the historic province of Ulster, could be set apart from Unionist Ulster without too many, at least in the Unionist heartlands, lamenting their loss. They could be dispensed with because they were considered of no great symbolic significance, and of still less political or economic significance, to 'Protestant Ulster' as it fought to maintain its position as an enclave economy within the United Kingdom. It was not just that inclusion of these counties would have stretched the boundaries of Protestant Ulster beyond the bounds of Unionist control. The post-Famine relic landscapes of west Ulster in particular were considered by Unionists as 'backward' and 'tradition-bound'. For that reason they were literally considered to have no place in a commercially 'advanced' and 'successful' community like 'loyalist Ulster'. In the event these western counties fell under the hegemony of a Catholic nationalist petty bourgeoisie which often had only very tentative links with nation-builders and powerholders elsewhere in the country.

5   Nationalising People, Places and Historical Records in Nineteenth-century Ireland

Nationalist Myths and the Nationalisation of the Past

Despite more than half a century of professional historiography, nationalism still influences popular images of the past in Ireland as in most European countries. However, this is particularly the case with images of Ireland under 'English rule' in the seventeenth and eighteenth centuries. According to nationalists, and nationalist historians, government in Ireland then was so bad that it could not be worse if the English 'went to Hell for their principles, and to Bedlam for men to administer them'. In describing this Ireland, one noted nationalist historian wrote:

> The gentry were gay, gallant, enjoying Patricians, who had a pride in the free parliament which they ruled, but a fear and detestation of the people. There is not a crime recorded in Irish history which was not represented by a great estate or great position. The brutal soldier, who had murdered and plundered a territory, the scheming courtier, who gave sly counsel how to circumvent the natives, was represented by a noble; the untrustworthy servant who sold his master's blood, or the convenient Judas who was a spy on his neighbours for officials in Dublin, by a substantial squire; and they could neither forget their origin, nor escape its consequences. Ireland, in that day, was like a slave ship; a jolly crew held a carouse in the cabin, while a multitude of their fellow creatures were starved and stifled in the hold. (Duffy, 1882, p. 196)

According to such accounts, the rural Catholic population of Ireland fought valiantly, and continuously, to oppose the oppression it had long suffered at the hands of heartless, and mostly absentee, landlords. This was a struggle that was said to have lasted from before the plantation of Ulster right up to the late nineteenth century. In a pioneering analysis of the social class origins of agrarian conflict in nineteenth-century Ireland, Sam Clark has criticised this interpretation for focusing almost exclusively on the ethnic origins of conflict (Clark, 1979). According to this view the contests waged were always nationalist ones, supposedly waged by different people in different places, and at different periods throughout the eighteenth and nineteenth centuries. However, they were always considered, by nationalists and by nationalist historians alike, as essentially the same seamless struggle for land and self-determination. As such this was a struggle waged by the dispossessed Irish, especially Catholic peasants, to regain land lost through English confiscations since before the seventeenth century. Discussing the nineteenth century in particular, Clark has also shown that this interpretation of Irish history suggested that the battle was fought in the early nineteenth century by violent secret societies. By the latter half of the century it was a struggle repre- sented by the Land League. In the 1880s this 'culminated' in a great Land War when the 'oppressors' of the 'Irish people' were finally, and deservedly, 'vanquished', as tenant farmers subsequently came into their rightful ownership of the land they had lost to landlords and an ascendancy church (Clark, 1978, pp. 23–39).

So many of these nationalist histories were written at the height of the Irish nation-building drive that a separate volume would be required for their proper analysis. Yet, to get some slight flavour of their content, it might be useful to briefly examine one, namely Sir Charles Gavan Duffy's 'enlarged and carefully revised' *Bird's-Eye View of Irish History* published by James Duffy and Sons in London in 1882. Writing from Nice in May 1882, Duffy dedicated this volume to the Right Reverend James Donnelly, Bishop of Clogher, whose 'fruitful life and labours [were] devoted to the well-remem- bered places where I first studied Irish History, and gathered the traditions and memories which interpret the past better than the historian' (Duffy, 1882, p. v). Further on in the Preface he proudly proclaimed that 'a Paris publisher' reproduced this work as *Histoire d'Irlande à Vol d'Oiseau* in translation form by Marie Wilson Cowley. That this was also amateur history is clear from the proud assertion that he had stated nothing herein which he had not 'ascertained to rest on solid grounds' after studying Irish history 'from boyhood'. This history was written 'within such limits that it may be conveniently read in a single evening' to 'encourage young men to enquire for themselves', and to 'serve them as a primer and skeleton map for such studies' (Duffy, 1882, p. vii). However, it was also intended for 'strangers anxious to shed some light on the question which they find so perplexing, why Ireland, with all her natural resources and native vigour is so perpetually poor and discontented'. Finally, in launching into his 'bird eye's view of Irish history' the author asserts:

> Many men refrain from reading Irish history as sensitive and selfish persons refrain from witnessing human suffering. But it is a branch of knowledge as indispensable to the statesman or publicist as morbid anatomy [is] to the surgeon. To prescribe remedies without ascertaining the seat of the disease, and the habits of the patient, is empiricism and quackery. *For Irishmen there is no portion of the annals of mankind so profitable a study. It will teach them to understand themselves and their country; a knowledge essential to national prosperity, but which is far from being common amongst us. It will teach them how much we have often to unlearn; for writers of great authority have ignorantly or wilfully caricatured our history, till there is scarcely a transaction concerning which it is more necessary to enquire what are the facts which may be accepted and relied upon, than what is the skilful and current misrepresentation of them which ought to be rejected.* (Duffy, 1882, pp. 1–2; emphasis added)

This is nineteenth-century Irish nationalist history at its purest. Untarnished by 'empiricism or quackery', it portrays Ireland as the victim of historical misrepresentation and English 'misrule'. It lifts the 'native race' to heights unprecedented in histories of Ireland written before this and urges young Irishmen to 'unlearn' the 'caricatures' of the Irish past that proceed from 'writers of great authority' in the past. This is also 'boyish' history and history as adventure. It provides a patriarchal bourgeois view on the past and sets out the framework for 'a political economy and a political morality for the special use of Ireland'. Thus it elevated successful Catholic businessmen, farmers and the professional classes to positions of 'natural leadership' in nationalist Ireland. It insisted that 'a great change' had taken place among 'middle class Catholics' in the mid-nineteenth century in that:

> A generation had reached manhood who knew the penal laws only by tradition. *Their fathers had grown rich in trade or the professions, had purchased land, and shared the excitement of a great political contest*, and the sons educated for the most part in English or foreign colleges, or in Dublin University, laughed at the pretensions of Protestant ascendancy. (Duffy, 1882, p. 273; emphasis added)

Written and popularised in political pamphlets and the provincial press by a Catholic intelligentsia at the close of the nineteenth century, this genre of history writing clearly romanticised the Irish past, condemned English rule in Ireland, and ethnicised its historical records. It also historicised the causes of Irish social ills and nationalised the solutions to many of Ireland's political and economic problems. In so doing it gave an ancient and deeply nationalist lineage to what were essentially modern defences of nation-building in the latter half of the nineteenth century. More accurately still, these popular histories 'Catholicised' – even 'Gaelicised' – the Irish past and literally sanctified the Irish countryside. Thus Duffy had no doubt that the Catholic church here was a nationalist church and the defender of the poor. This is how he encapsulates the history of Irish Catholicism in the eighteenth century:

> In the monasteries and houses established for Irish students on the Continent, a succession of priests of Irish birth or blood were trained to face the savage rigours of the Penal Code. *They found their way to Ireland in disguise, and lived the lives, wore the dress, and endured the privations of peasants, to keep alive the faith of the nation.* The persecuted race loved God, acknowledged the mercy of his chastening hand, and clung closer to the creed for which they had made so many cheerful sacrifices. The prayer and incense ascending from a thousand altars in the great Cathedrals of Christendom, did not, to my thinking, furnish a spectacle so sublime and touching as the Mass solemnized under the dripping roof of a cave, among a crowd of rugged peasants – the unconquerable remnants of a brave and pious nation – by a priest who served God at the constant peril of his life. (Duffy, 1882, pp. 162–3; emphasis added)

Here again we have all the ingredients that went into the making of popular nationalist history in Ireland in the late nineteenth century. These included a victimised clergy enduring the privations of peasants, a persecuted Irish race who were the remnants of a pious nation, and a prayerful people more worthy of God's love than those attending mass at the great cathedrals of France or Germany. Finally, Duffy argues, the Penal Law prevented Ireland becoming a nation by depriving it of its 'natural leaders', the rural and urban middle classes.

Far from analysing history from a social class or regional perspective, such interpretations of the Irish past viewed it instead through green-tinted ethnic lenses. That is why Connolly's brief study, *Labour in Irish History*, was so unique in its day. Here was a pioneering interpretation of Irish history, written amid a furore of nationalist agitation, which viewed history from a class perspective. It criticised the ideology of national capitalism while simultaneously attacking the iniquities of class rule, not just English rule, in nation-building Ireland (Connolly, 1971). Like Lenin's polemic on imperialism and monopoly capitalism written

at the height of the Great War, it sought to refute hegemonic interpretations of history which ignored the role of class in historical
social change (Lenin, 1966).

Those who wrote, and especially those who popularised, these
nationalist histories of Ireland in the late nineteenth and early
twentieth centuries, were clearly operating from within what one
historian has described as 'a history-saturated' environment
(Hudson, 1979, p. 3). They powerfully conditioned, just as they
were conditioned by, the national, and indeed international, environments of nation-building within which they wrote. With the
exception of Connolly and a small number of other writers, they
wrote history simply from a strong nationalist perspective, hoping
that in so doing they could give added strength to the cause of
nation-building, and improve their standing as scholars in 'their
nation'. The more conservative among them adopted Catholicism
as a nation-building dogma, regarding it as an 'anchoring' or 'territorialising' ideology, and as an historically oriented ideology which
suited the interests of nation-building power groups. The ultimate
intellectual exemplar of this historico-religious view of the Irish
past was the London-born and Oxford-educated Catholic theolo-
gian, John Henry Newman. Newman ceaselessly challenged
caricaturisations of Catholic Ireland as merely the home of 'the low
Irish'. He particularly attacked those who talked of 'the wretched
fecundity of Popish Ireland' as a threat which spread 'ignorance
and superstition over the empire' and threatened the 'moral fibre
of the Protestant nation by endangering the integrity of all [its]
national institutions'. Indeed, from this angle, Ireland was a
'damnable country' precisely because it was so 'damnably' Catholic
and Irish. As O'Farrell has remarked:

> Newman discerned in the English an almost instinctive hostile reaction
> to all things Catholic stemming from the equation of Catholicism with
> spiritual and political absolutism, and the belief that the Pope remained
> a dangerous enemy of England, ambitious to possess her ... The imagery
> of which Newman complained had much of its derivation from encoun-
> ters with Catholic Ireland. It was injected with particular vigour by the
> coincidence of the Catholic revival in England – emancipation, the
> Oxford Movement, spectacular conversions and the restoration of the
> hierarchy – with efforts to meet Irish Catholic grievances and with the
> influx of Irish Catholic immigrants ... *So, the condition of Ireland and the
> Irish proved the inferiority and depravity of their religion, whose nature was ...
> the main reason for that debased condition. All of this was direct threat not
> only to British religion, but to British prosperity.* (O'Farrell, 1975, p. 83;
> emphasis added)

Thus, many of Newman's philosophical torments, including those concerning Ireland and Irish Catholic society, were almost exclusively historical ones. They were induced by what he regarded as the evils of secularism and the growing political power of a purely secularised intelligentsia. They were literally aggravated by the inclusion of Ireland in the 'enemy territory' of the British nation, i.e. by its position within a United Kingdom where Protestantism, the state religion, was hostile both to Catholicism and to its adherents. At another level they were about the competing claims of Rome and English Protestant rule in a predominantly rural Catholic nation-building Ireland located at the edge of an increasingly industrialised Europe. Viewed thus, Newman's 'agonies', like those of many Irish Catholic bishops of his day, were quite literally also arguments about the place of the Christian nation in a new world order. His Catholic nationalism, including that of many Irish bishops and religious leaders influenced by his writings, was an intellectualised and historically oriented ideology. It justified some of the most cherished beliefs of Catholic nationalists – e.g. the legitimacy of religious authority, the doctrinally legitimising role of tradition, the location of truth and error in a secular age – largely through recourse to historical tradition and historical precedent, rather than relying solely on metaphysical arguments to make their case (Hudson, 1979, p. 4).

Men like Newman, and the many Irish church leaders and priests influenced by him, were not simply religious leaders. They literally were 'statesmen' and classic examples of C. Wright Mills' 'organisational man' (Mills, 1963). Eagleton has branded them 'fixers and brokers, unofficial lawyers and political organisers, social workers and financial counsellors, policemen, school governors and electoral managers, amateur physicians and intercessors with authority' (Eagleton, 1995, p. 78). I have described them elsewhere as the prime 'movers and shakers' in Irish society, the ultimate controllers of social and personal morality (Mac Laughlin, 1995b, p. 611). Describing the political roles of priests and bishops in county Tipperary in the mid-nineteenth century, O'Shea has remarked:

> their farming background and the outlook of farmers were of fundamental importance, while the power of the bishops to control clerical political activity cannot be ignored either. It seems reasonable to suggest that while social background was essentially the formative, and political opinion the motive, force which dictated their political path, theology was a guiding influence within the broad confines of that path. The

bishop's influence was essentially preventive, although rarely used in this manner. (O'Shea, 1983, pp. 232–3)

Of course not all priests, and certainly not all bishops, could be considered nationalists – even if many of those who were not can be considered nation-builders in the wider sense of the term. Many indeed believed that Catholic Ireland would be better off within the United kingdom than taking a separatist route out of it. Eagleton has suggested that the church's position for much of the first half of the nineteenth century was somewhat analogous to that of a modern trade union movement – both organizations

> sought to promote their own power by convincing the ruling system of their own respectability, while simultaneously guarding their backs from the disgruntlement this is likely to breed in their own ranks. Like a trade union, the Church was forced to collude with an authority it took a dim view of, for the purpose of advancing its own interests; but by the same token it could be led to defy it, not least when pressed from below by a militancy it needed to placate ... To preserve credibility with the people, the hierarchy had to put some daylight between itself and Dublin Castle, but to condone political agitation was to risk forfeiting its own credibility with the sate, as well as to countenance a rejection of authority which might finally rebound on itself. (Eagleton, 1995, p. 79)

However, with the upsurge of radical nationalism and Fenianism in the 1860s, many priests and bishops felt it necessary to record their own conservative nationalist sentiments, 'thereby hoping to refute any suggestion that they were less patriotic than the Fenians' (O'Shea, 1983, p. 237). By the close of the century the political outlook of many priests certainly coincided with that of their conservative middle-class kinsfolk. This in itself was 'unmistakable evidence of their educational training, plus Episcopal influence, which made them such sharp catalysts' in nation-building Catholic Ireland (O'Shea, 1983, p. 239).

In addition to playing a very strong role in organising nation-building Ireland priests, and more especially their superiors, often also championed the international rights of Irish people as Catholics. This was particularly true of priests and bishops making political pronouncements at the end of the nineteenth and beginning of the twentieth centuries. Thus they never ceased asking themselves, and prominent members of Irish Catholic society, whether Ireland should remain within the Protestant United Kingdom, or whether it should go it alone as an exemplary Catholic nation in secularised western Europe (Newman, 1851). In so doing they were inadvertently also raising the issue whether this small nation could go it alone in a Catholic world centred on Mediterranean Europe, rather than remain an integral part of a more powerful one centred on Great Britain, the empire, and north-western Europe.

In categorising the English and the Anglo-Irish aristocracy as 'alien oppressors' of the Catholic Irish, most popular accounts of Irish history written at the end of the nineteenth century took the focus off the class divisions in native Irish Catholic society. Neglecting the structural roots and indigenous origins of many of Ireland's social problems, they focused instead on the exogenous and ethnic sources of the country's national grievances. This, as we have seen, was partly because historians and political polemicists in the late nineteenth century required little justification for inter- preting the past – and looking to the future – from anything other than a nationalist perspective. As Sheehy has argued:

> People in nineteenth century Ireland looked more and more to the past: they looked at the church and plate jewellery which had survived from the Early Christian period, they examined the not inconsiderable archi- tectural remains scattered around the country, and most of all they studied ancient manuscripts for information about Irish history and civilization. They realised that vestiges of this ancient culture remained in the music, storytelling and customs of the Irish-speaking population, and began to study those too. Such interests were already apparent in the late eighteenth century, and they gained momentum in the nine- teenth. They began among scholars – historians and antiquarians – who were essentially the middle class, but then gradually filtered through the whole country, so that a people who had been told for years that they were savages, with a barbarous language and no evidence of civilization, were persuaded that this was not so. (Sheehy, 1980, p. 7)

Ireland was in no way exceptional in this regard. Like other nine- teenth-century nation-building countries, including much more powerful nations like Britain, France and Germany, it was simply constructing a national identity from a rich mixture of historicist argument, ethnic folk custom, religious faith, nationalist mythology and complimentary images of themselves from a heroic, and largely prehistoric, Golden Age. Thus Irish historians, artists and social scientists, many of whom were also clergymen, mobilised history and religion in order to construct a national society and to forge a strong nationalist identity. They resorted to the past to recreate the present. They used national 'style' to bolster the ethnic credentials and political legitimacy of their nation-building objectives. In defending Irish nation-building through the 'breakup' of Britain, they also mobilised and 'nationalised' folk culture in Ireland. More importantly still, they insisted that the growth of the Irish nation was a moral evolution as spontaneous, and uncontrollable, as the evolution of the human organism. This idea was clearly in tune with Parnell's dictum that no man could 'halt the march of a nation'. What has been less frequently commented upon is the fact that it also oozed the ethos of late nineteenth-century social Darwinism. It was based on two social Darwinian premises in particular. First, it postulated that the modern nation-state was a perfectly 'natural development', and that national identity, unlike social class identity, was both natural and perfectly desirable. Second, it assumed that the nation-state, especially the unified and powerful nation-state, was the optimum geopolitical unit of social power in a new world order divided into self-governing nations presiding over far-flung colonial dominions. Irish nationalists clearly felt that their country belonged more to the world of the former than to that of the latter. Like nineteenth-century Catholic nationalists and national separatists elsewhere in Europe, they claimed autonomy not just on economic grounds, but also on the basis of distinctive religious and cultural traits. For that reason they were branded a retrogressive force, not least because they threatened the territorial integrity of Britain, one of the most powerful nation-states in this nineteenth-century world order.

As elsewhere in Europe also myth and myth-making were mixed in equal proportions in these nationalist histories which legitimised the state-centred agendas of Irish nation-building (Leerssen, 1996; O'Giollain, 2000; Wilson, 1976). Myths, especially mythical histories, allowed the Irish to 'reclaim' Ireland and 'repossess' their own history. This caused those who had been downtrodden in – as well as by – history to literally take Ireland back from the Anglo-Irish ascendancy and its historical tradition of 'misrepresentation' of the Irish. It also gave the Irish bourgeoisie, not least the Catholic church, a new mission civilatrice which called on all sectors of Irish society to construct a new Ireland for a new century (Gwynn, 1924). Thus, far from 'disproving' myth or 'dispensing with' tradition, cultural nationalists nourished the political imagination of this modern Ireland with mythical histories and quasi-racial folk beliefs. In so doing they introduced strong elements of fabricated tradition into the political consciousness of nineteenth-century Irish society. Thus myths and folk beliefs often supplemented, and sometimes even substituted for, rational explanations of historical change. In addition, they served the useful purpose of giving the rural poor, if not the urban working class, a new sense of place in Catholic nation-building Ireland, including a sense of pride and an elevated sense of what it meant to be Irish both in the modern world and in the new Ireland. As a result the categories 'Ireland' and 'Irishness' gradually lost many of the associations of inferiority that they possessed in nineteenth-century race-thinking, and in the popular press of late Victorian Britain (Curtis, 1971, pp. 29–58; Mac Laughlin, 1999f, pp. 50–76). The 'native', including native iconography and Irish 'local heroes', now belonged to Ireland. They also acquired a lofty and symbolic significance in modern Irish consciousness and in the Irish landscape.

These nationalist histories suffer a number of defects which nevertheless point to their social and ideological functions in nation-building Ireland. First, they Romanticised the historic role of the Irish Catholic church as a defender of the faith and protector of the oppressed. In particular they portrayed the clergy as the unremitting defenders of the rural poor against the ravages of the 'Saxon foe'. Second, they ignored the modernity of popular-based Catholic nationalist agitation in Ireland and greatly exaggerated the antiquity of popular expressions of nationalism by locating them in pre-eighteenth-century Ireland. Third, as we have already seen, they over-emphasised the ethnic basis, and clouded over social class issues underlying Irish nation-building. Thus for example they forged simplistic and strong links between the political actions of late eighteenth-century agrarian secret societies on the one hand, and twentieth-century Irish nation-builders on the other.

Given the popular appeal and mythical nature of much nationalist historiography, we clearly need to uphold more recent 'de-mythologisations' of the Irish past (Dunne, 1992; Eagleton, 1995; Kiberd, 1995; Leerssen, 1996; Lloyd, 1997; O'Ceallaigh, 1994). We particularly need to continue the 'de-romanticisation' of the Catholic church as a church built with the pennies of the poor, and of the clergy as the perennial defenders of the marginalised in Irish society (Whelan, 1996, 1998). This will involve a more thoroughly critical focus not only on the role of the church in Irish society, but more particularly its central nation-building roles. It also means that we have to extend the historical class analysis adopted by Clark and others in order to understand the nation-building roles of the Catholic church in the ethnically divided society of Ireland in the eighteenth and nineteenth centuries (Clark, 1979; Clark and Donnelly, 1983; Vaughan, 1984). We especially need to support recent efforts to trace the emergence of a substantial Catholic collectivity of Catholic middlemen, middling tenants, professionals, Catholic gentry, Catholic landholders, shopkeepers and merchant class from the late eighteenth century onwards (Connolly, 1982, 1995; O'Shea, 1983; Whelan, 1985, 1996). These were the groups which filled the ranks of the Catholic intelligentsia, including the church, and formed a distinctively Irish and distinctively Catholic social and cultural identity in nine-teenth-century Ireland (Mac Laughlin, 1995b). They were also responsible for literally remodelling Ireland in their image, and for creating new socio-economic and regional linkages that under-pinned Irish nation-building from the late nineteenth century onwards.

Penal Laws and Nationalist History

The late eighteenth and nineteenth centuries were the crucial period in the formation of the social groups which forged the social collectivities that provided the backbone of the Irish nation-building movement. Far from being a socially homogeneous and impoverished population, Irish Catholic society in the late eigh-teenth century had its own complex social structure. At its apex were a scattering of aristocratic families, including Gaelic poets and survivors of the plantation schemes of the sixteenth and seven-teenth centuries. Next came the Catholic middlemen who often sublet or rented lands to tenants below them. Next to these came the expanding urban middle classes consisting chiefly of merchants, professionals, industrialists, urban property owners and other representatives of a modernising Ireland. Below them lay the substantial tenant farmers, a complex social group which dominated the Irish political arena for most of the nineteenth century. Further down the social hierarchy came the proto-indus-trial working class and craftworkers. Last of all came Ireland's 'labouring poor', the landed labourers, landless labourers, cottiers and the 'men of no property' (Andrews, 1982). In stressing the role of the penal laws as barriers to Catholic advancement, nationalist histories have generally ignored the existence of these social class and status differentials in Irish society. They also portray eigh-teenth-century Catholic Ireland as a country without history in any evolutionary sense of the term. Indeed, viewed thus, the eigh-teenth is the lost century of Irish history. Progress was said to have been totally retarded by penal legislation which caused Catholics to suffer under a version of apartheid not that different to that which prevailed, until recently, in South Africa. Singling out the uniquely Irish features of the Penal Laws, they condemned this legislation as anti-Catholic and anti-nationalist. In so doing they reduced 'penal legislation' to a British conspiracy for preventing the advancement of the indigenous Irish towards nationhood.

To argue thus is to ignore the fact that penal legislation existed not just in Ireland but elsewhere in Europe, and that it was not primarily a strategy for preventing the march towards nationhood. Yet in Ireland 'penal' legislation has generally been explained away by nationalists as a venal and oppressive institution devised for the purpose of hindering the development of the Irish nation. As such it represented only the interests of a settler ascendancy in a country where Catholics, the numerical majority, were presumed not to exist. Thus Charles Gavan Duffy insisted that the mass of the Irish people 'were left poor and uneducated' by the Penal Laws, their country 'hampered by laws of shameful unfairness'. For Duffy indeed:

> The Penal Code had left nearly four millions of them unable to read or write, and nearly a million and a half more who could read but not write. The island no longer possessed national trade, manufacture, or local industries; they had all once existed and been destroyed by the jealousy of the stronger nation; the facilities which nature had bestowed on it for a foreign commerce, were rendered nugatory by the same influence. The produce of the soil, which alone remained to furnish the population with the necessaries of civilised life, was squandered in a prodigious and wasting subsidy. It was estimated that half a million sterling was remitted to England monthly, in rent. (Duffy, 1882, pp. 273–4)

Quite clearly this interpretation of the Penal Laws suffers from a high degree of 'national exceptionalism'. It ignores the fact that elsewhere in western Europe, not least in France, penal legislation was an anti-Jacobin strategy. It was used to restrain the influence of the Catholic church and to curb the political power of religious and ethnic minorities (Boyce, 1991, p. 97). Nationalists in Ireland have always insisted that these laws were enacted against the entire social spectrum of a nation-building society. Historical reality, however, appears to suggest otherwise. Laws were neither consistently nor uniformly enforced. When enforced, they appear to have been most strictly executed when, and where, fears of Jacobin invasion ran high. They were rigidly enacted when and where the Catholic church was perceived as a 'fifth column' with Jacobite sympathies subversive to the maintenance of good order and the rule of law in Ireland. Historical evidence also suggests that Catholics regularly slipped through the many loopholes in penal legislation. By the mid-eighteenth century they were amassing considerable wealth through commerce, trade and in the professions, even if they could not so easily accumulate wealth through outright ownership of good agricultural land. Indeed the central thrust of penal legislation was aimed at Catholic ownership of land and the acquisition of political power. However, this did not halt social progress or prevent the emergence of new social classes in Catholic Ireland, even at the height of penal legislation in the eighteenth century. Even here legislation could be lax. Thus for example many leases, particularly those that were sanctioned before 1704, were not subject to discovery proceedings by legal authorities. Whelan has shown how this allowed prominent Catholic families to retain a sub-gentry status for much of the eighteenth century (Whelan, 1996, p. 34).

It is also possible to argue that penal legislation was more reactive than proactive. Laws were reactive in the sense that they sought to prevent the return to, or an increase in, Catholic political power in Ireland, a country then regarded as an integral part of the Protestant nation of Britain. Moreover, and contrary to nationalists, 'penal laws' were not the only impediment to the progress of nation-building in Catholic Ireland before the nineteenth century. From the sixteenth century onwards the 'core' state of England was always able to exploit the advantages which market capitalism and a strong administrative system had bestowed upon it. It used these advantages to expand into Ireland and to make that country a more integral part of one of the most progressive nation-states then in existence. As Hechter and Nairn have shown, this expansionist state had also been exploiting other ethnic hinterlands of Britain, and not just Ireland. Hence, as early as the eighteenth century, Britain was transformed from a loosely bound, multi-ethnic polity into a strongly unified, highly centralised nation-state that had 'outliers' in the 'home countries' of Ireland, Scotland and Wales. It is against this much wider nation-building context that the Penal Laws in Ireland can be examined. They were enacted not so much to prevent the 'breakup' of Britain by Irish nationalists, as the logic of nationalist interpretations implies. They aimed instead to create conditions that would allow the Protestant nation to flourish not only in mainland Britain, but more especially in the 'home country' of Ireland. Far from being motivated by anti-nationalist prejudice, they were a crucial element in the political arsenal of an English state intent on making Ireland a more integral part of an expansionist British nation-state. Thus they were enacted not so much to extinguish 'popery' for the sake of it, but rather to consolidate the Protestant nation in Ireland.

Protestantism then was certainly considered an infinitely more progressive and rewarding doctrine than Catholicism. The latter was equated with 'popery', with Rome, with the medieval, with the peripheral, with treason, poverty, papal servitude and religious superstition. It was not until much later in the nineteenth century that the Catholic intelligentsia would systematically refute the contention that 'things were very wrong with Catholics in general, but most of all with the Catholics in Ireland' (O'Riordan, 1905, p. v). In so doing they insisted that the direct purpose of the Catholic church and that of the secular world were at odds with each other. Thus Newman argued that:

> The world believes in the world's ends as the greatest good; it wishes society to be governed simply and entirely for the sake of this world. Provided it could gain one little islet in the ocean, one foot upon the coast, if it could cheapen by sixpence a pound, or make the flag respected among the Esquimaux or the Otaheitans, at the cost of a hundred lives and a hundred souls, it would think it a very good bargain. (Newman, quoted in O'Riordan, 1905, p. 57)

The Catholic church, on the other hand:

> considers the action of this world and the action of the soul as simply incommensurate, viewed in their respective spheres; she would rather save the soul of one single wild bandit of Calabria, or whining beggar of Palermo, than draw a hundred lines of railroad through the length and breadth of Italy, or carry out a sanitary reform, in its fullest details, in every city of Sicily, except in so far as these great national works tended to some spiritual good beyond them ... If she encourages secular enter-prises, studies or pursuits ... it is either from their indirect bearing upon her great object ... or from the spontaneous energy which great ideas, such as hers, exert, and the ... influence ... they exercise ... in matters and in provinces not really their own. (O'Riordan, 1905, p. 58)

According to this view the Penal Code made the Irish a better people by making them the most fervent Catholics in all of Europe, inspiring them to 'great fervour' in the defence of 'their faith'. As such, indeed, it was even praised by Catholic nationalists in the late nineteenth century precisely because it made the Irish more attached to their Catholic faith.

Certainly there is no denying the effects of penal legislation on the socio-economic standing of Catholics in Ireland. By its very nature, however, this legislation was aimed more at the upper echelons of Gaelic landed Ireland, than at the plebeian sectors of urban and rural society. The combined effects of land confiscation and penal legislation on the former, reduced Catholic ownership from about 60 per cent of all land in 1641 to less than 15 per cent in 1703. By 1776 it was estimated that Catholics owned only 5 per cent of Irish land (Regan, 1980, pp. 4–13). Yet, alongside this decline in Catholic ownership of prime agricultural land we can discern the slow but inexorable growth of a substantial middle class whose wealth derived from commerce, industry and the professions. For much of the eighteenth century this group was beyond the orbit of penal legislation.

From the mid-eighteenth century onwards their ranks were probably augmented as any force that the Penal Laws still possessed was by then greatly relaxed. Indeed, after Culloden and the devastating defeat of the Scots in the 1740s, Catholic clergy in Ireland were gradually considered a moderating, not a subversive, force. By the last quarter of the century when anti-colonialism was at its height in North America and revolutionary changes were sweeping through France, priests and bishops here were valued as promoters of good order. In a letter to his clergy in 1778, the bishop of Ossary welcomed government leniency in the applica- tion of penal legislation and reminded his priests of their obligation to 'give unto Caesar that which belongeth to Caesar, and unto God that which belongeth to God'. He urged a 'cheerful compliance' with the law, believing this to be particularly requisite:

> in these days of discord and calamity, when our fellow American subjects, seduced by the specious notions of liberty and other illusive expectations of sovereignty, disclaim any dependence on Great Britain, and endeavour by force of arms to distress their mother country which has cherished and protected them. (Boyce, 1991, p. 124)

His letter ended with an offer of 'fervent prayers' for 'the spiritual and temporal happiness of his most Gracious lord and Sovereign King George the third'. With Irish bishops urging Catholic priests to share these sentiments in a period of national revolutionary change in both Europe and North America, it is little wonder that the Protestant state in Ireland spent less effort in interfering in their ministries. Indeed the loyalty of these new Catholic leaders ultimately pushed the English government closer to supporting the civil and religious rights of the emergent Catholic middle classes. Thus by the 1780s, relief legislation was passed which mitigated some of the worst effects of penal legislation on this new Catholic Ireland. Henceforth Catholic leaders increasingly expressed their pleasure at being 'allowed to have a home in our native land'. By then also laws requiring the registration of Catholic priests were finally repealed. More significantly still, new laws were enacted which allowed those taking an oath of allegiance to actually purchase land, or at least bequeath it on more or less the same terms as those of their Protestant counterparts. This not only brought about a fundamental shift in the relationships between Catholics and Protestants in Ireland. It also altered the relationship of substantial tenant farmers, and other Catholic owners of wealth, to the land and resources of Ireland. It meant, for example, that better-off sectors could now gradually shed feelings of social inferiority and look on Ireland as their 'homeland' in the modern sense of that term. What made this all the more significant was the fact that Catholic Ireland now also was a far more 'rounded' and ethnically conscious society. As it entered the nation-building nineteenth century this then was a society which also appreciated the centrality of nationalism to the socio-economic and cultural survival of the Irish as 'a people'. It comprised new, modernising and ethnically alert groups drawn from all across the social spectrum, not just from the subordinate poor.

Ireland then was never simply a country inhabited by the rural and urban poor, presided over by an Anglo-Irish aristocracy, as Irish nationalists insist. From this stage onwards Catholic property-owners, not least Catholic middlemen and businessmen, had a strong organic relationship with the land of Ireland and with an evolving modern Irish society. Eagleton caught the wider implications of this new relationship with the land among the rural poor and Irish landlords when he wrote: 'Sowing potatoes is not the kind of material relation to the landlord that reaping his harvest is, and this economic infrastructure serves to undermine political hegemony' (Eagleton, 1995, p. 55).

What needs emphasising here, however, is that the middling sectors of Irish Catholic society, especially those in the country's richer agricultural heartlands, also developed new organic relationships to the territory of Ireland as the homeland of the 'Irish race'. They certainly had deeper roots in the land, a quite different political relationship with it, and with the rural and urban economy of Ireland, than either their seventeenth- and eighteenth-century predecessors, or their nineteenth-century social subordinates ever had. By the nineteenth century indeed they had a more national, and nationalist, attachment to Ireland as a country and as a homeland. This was especially the case after the repeal of penal legislation coincided with the extension of property rights to some of the wealthier elements in Catholic society here. As a result of these and other changes many dropped their Jacobite allegiances to become what later were known as 'castle Catholics' or 'West Brits' (Inglis, 1962). These 'castle Catholics' were obedient subjects of English rule in Ireland. By and large they functioned as a socially conservative force in a country caught up in the full force of rural modernisation, and hence riddled with 'agrarian unrest' and political 'outrage'. In more than one sense they literally had roots in the land and a firm footing in its emerging new social and political structures. Describing this group in the eighteenth century Whelan has labelled them 'an underground gentry' (Whelan, 1996, p. 36). Even in the opening decades of the eighteenth century they exercised a considerable degree of hereditary authority over their property and other material possessions. Their petty dynastic families possessed no small amount of local, regional, and provincial influence. By the early nineteenth century many of these were clearly emerging from their provincial underground to become instead a national force, at least in rural Catholic Ireland, if not in the Protestant and far more industrialised north-east.

What is crucial to note here is that these 'half-mounted Catholic gentlemen' were in many ways growing apart from their social subordinates in Catholic society. As arrivistes they did what all arriviste social groups do when they arrive on the scene – they loudly proclaimed their new presence on the landscape with ostentatious displays of bourgeois, and petty bourgeois, wealth. They built new houses and churches, patronised the arts, supported Irish craftwork, adopted styles of dress commensurate with their status, and were generally responsible for a Hibernisation of the cultural artefacts of nineteenth-century Ireland. Yet it was in the applied arts and crafts, rather than in 'high art', that Irish national symbolism was used in the most exuberant fashion. As Sheehy points out, 'stonecarvers, stuccodores, makers of furniture and souvenirs in bog oak, jewellers producing reproductions of Celtic ornaments, were much less inhibited than their brethren in the Academies' (Sheehy, 1980, p. 71). Those engaged in these crafts literally created and built the macro and micro environments that were the embodiment of an increasingly nationalist Ireland. Their work created such an upsurge of national sentiment that it lasted into the beginning of the twentieth century. By the middle of the nineteenth century Irish motifs and symbols – gaudy as they were in this age which saw the rise of artist Antonio Gaudi – had become pervasive, at least outside the Protestant north-east of Ireland. They quite literally plastered the architectural face of Catholic Ireland.

To a great extent also the arriviste Catholics 'aped' the manners, if not the mannerisms, of their peers in Protestant society in Ireland and Britain. Yet we should not exaggerate the role of the arrivistes in fostering a confidently Irish identity in the arts and crafts. Thus Sheehy, writing about the Celtic revival in art and artefacts in the hundred years after 1830, suggests that:

> Anyone who shares the hopes and ambitions of the artists themselves can hardly avoid a sense of disappointment in the fact that a national style failed to materialize clearly. On the other hand, if one stands back from the period and looks at it dispassionately as part of a wider phenomenon, the Irish experience assumes a new dimension. For Ireland was by no means alone; elsewhere in Europe there were small nations struggling for independence and in that struggle trying to express their identity through the imagination. The progress of art in Norway, Sweden and Denmark offers remarkable parallels to that in Ireland: there too the mid-nineteenth century saw a vigorous interest in early medieval history; later in the century, this interest led to the adoption of authentic stylistic features in decoration and building; and, to complete the parallel, there too the literary figures produced by the movement (Ibsen, Strindberg, Bjornson) must be admitted to have outshone the painters and designers. Hungary is another example; there the search for a national style led one architect to design in the manner of Moorish India, on the theory that the Magyars originated in India ... Finally, at the opposite end of Europe, the artists of Catalonia, whose past was if anything more heterogeneous than that of Ireland, Scandinavia or Hungary, created a fantastically individual style made up of Moorish and Gothic elements plus an evocation of the Catalan mountain landscape. Here architecture was the dominant 'nation' art form. These parallels should enable us to see Ireland in a richer context and to assess it in different terms to those of simple success or failure. In a sense, all these nationalist movements failed, because national styles are not created by acts of will. In another, they all succeeded, for they expressed the nation's sense of continuity with its past. (Sheehy, 1980, pp. 190–3)

Meanwhile back in the Irish countryside the social distance between arriviste Catholics and the rural poor was growing apace. Yet the distance between the cabins of the poor and the dwellings of wealthy Catholics was never over-extended. What kept the two groups locked together in an uneasy relationship of unequals was the fact that the latter could wrap the former in an ethnic blanket of common identity. In so doing they proclaimed their common 'Irishness' to counterbalance their quite different class backgrounds, and equally different political agendas. In town as well as in the country, 'new' Catholics were now occupying substantial dwellings and living in a modern world that was in many ways a world apart from that of Irish poor. In the countryside Catholic middlemen, including the substantial tenantry, began to build sturdy two-storied slated farmhouses, the mark of social distinction and Catholic success in any eighteenth-century modernising landscape. Where once Catholicism was associated with poverty and subversion, it was gradually now linked with respectability, success and social order. These 'new Catholics', in other words, were behaving just like 'good Protestants'. Whelan described this sector better than most when he suggested that their houses mimicked more the formal fashions in rural living elsewhere in Britain, than they did those of the Irish poor. Their 'arrival' on the Irish landscape was literally signalled by a whole array of appendages of wealth that typically accompanied bourgeois lifestyles elsewhere in nation-building Europe. In Ireland this included the addition of orchards and gardens to the family farm, the construction of avenues and pillared gateways to the entrance of farms, the building and maintenance of sturdy stone wallsteads to indicate the limits of farms, and all the other trappings of social advancement that typically accompanied newly acquired property.

In the towns new symbols of personal wealth among Catholics was indicated by cultural capital, notably by the addition of the parlour, or drawing room, to the family home, and the possession of such items as pianos, good furniture, 'special' china and even 'delftware'. As Whelan again suggests, these new social pretensions could sometimes symbolise the emergence of yawning chasms between the urban rich and the sprawling urban poor. They were reflected in a heightened Anglicisation of the language and manners of the former, and the persistence of 'ribald' conduct among the latter. In diet, leisure patterns, lifestyles, fashions, even in the matter of table manners, these substantial Catholics resembled more their Protestant peers than they did the Catholic poor. Caomhin O'Danacher (1978, p. 87) has graphically defined the rural component of this new Irish society as those privileged enough to 'bull' their own cows. Whelan has described them as those who were likely to have a 'priest in the parish, a pump in the yard and a piano in the parlour' (Whelan, 1996, p. 26). In poorer parts of the country the teacher or petty official would suffice as the human status symbol of a successful Catholic family. Having a nun in the family might sometimes even substitute for a priest as an indicator of a family's social standing. Yet for all their class differences, those inhabiting the 'people-nation' of Catholic Ireland were locked together by a common sense of 'peoplehood' which marked them out from the Protestant nation of Great Britain and Ireland.

By the late nineteenth century Catholics belonging to these new social groups lived in a world infinitely more cluttered with personal possessions than that of their predecessors of even one generation earlier. To borrow a very apt phrase from Henry James, they had created little 'empires of things' – and they were prepared to protect their new petty bourgeois world-in-the-making. They also constituted an 'historical bloc'. Gramsci used this term to refer to the coming together of material and ideological forces in such a way that one influences the other. Thus he argued, material forces are literally unthinkable without some sort of historical form, just as ideologies are inconceivable without material bases and social forces – e.g. newspapers, history books, political pamphlets, cate-chisms, schools and colleges, churches etc. Viewed thus, 'ideologies' helped to 'organise' and mobilise human masses, not least in nation-building Catholic Ireland, and in Unionist Ulster. As such they created the terrain on which people here moved, acquired consciousness, marked out their positions, and literally struggled to act in history. Crucially also Gramsci insisted that an historical bloc was a moment in history, 'when the economic struc-ture of the older structure is collapsing but when there also are people with the will, determination, and historical insight to take advantage of this' (Joll, 1977, p. 114).

He seems to have thought of it as something of great psycho-logical importance in the development of the character of the individual and the 'nation-people'. It was of central political importance to the development of national society. Thus he insisted that men created their own personality and that of their nation by giving specific and concrete national direction to their own will and that of the 'nation-people'. They did this by identi-fying the means whereby they could make their will concrete and specific and not simply ephemeral, arbitrary or capricious. They built schools, published newspapers, founded political parties and policed the social and political morals of 'their society'. In so doing they modified 'the ensemble of concrete conditions' for realising their will to act in a rational and national manner. This more than anything else helped them become hegemonic. They maintained this hegemony through control of consensus-creating institutions like schools, colleges, newspapers, universities, churches, political parties and even public meetings. To arrive at this position and to create a 'popular national bloc' great care is taken to ensure that leaders do not lose touch with the masses and that their ideas are subjected to the test of common sense by the common people (Joll, 1977, p. 131). Thus Gramsci insisted history and politics cannot be made without passion, without some sort of emotional bond between the intelligentsia and their 'people-nation'. In the absence of such a bond, he argued, relations between leaders and led are reduced to contacts of a purely bureaucratic and formal kind. In such circumstances the intelligentsia, like those associated with English rule in nineteenth-century Ireland, become a caste removed from, but nevertheless still presiding over, society at large.

Once this organic relationship between the intelligentsia and the 'people-nation' is forged, however, then and only then can relationships of representation occur. Only then can 'there take place an exchange of individual elements between the rulers and the ruled, leaders and led, and can the shared life be realised which alone is a social force – with the creation of the "historical bloc"' (Gramsci, 1971, p. 418). This occurred in Ireland in the course of the 'long nineteenth century', i.e. towards the end of the eighteenth and right through the nineteenth century. Given the famines, and famine-induced emigrations, that this period witnessed it was inevitable that the creation of both the 'people-nation' and the historical bloc here was a long, drawn-out and strongly contested process. Thus there was nothing inevitable about the hegemonic rise of the nation-building classes in nineteenth-century Ireland. However, famine and emigration – not just conventional political manoeuvrings of different social classes – greatly facilitated the establishment of this hegemony. This greatly altered the ideological perspectives of Irish people, not least attitudes towards Irish nation-building and English rule in Ireland. At a more material level famine and emigration literally changed the economic landscape of Ireland. They depleted the ranks of the rural poor and removed whole sections of Irish society who could have altered the shape of Ireland's political landscape.

Thus the new social groups which emerged in Catholic Ireland from the eighteenth century onwards were never simply a social class in the strict Marxist or socio-economic meaning of that term. They were deeply rooted in, and organically linked to, the 'people-nation' that Irish society was fast becoming. Their 'obsession' was 'self-government', social cohesion and consensus, and the politico-territorial unity of the country. Even in the pre-Famine period they constituted a social collectivity which had outgrown class boundaries. Later on they showed that they could challenge the Protestant nation in Ireland more energetically than their plebeian predecessors belonging to secret societies here in the early nineteenth century. They constituted a far more effective opposition to English rule in Ireland than their Gaelic ancestors ever thought possible. In the event they sought to lead the former and to forget the ways of the latter. They believed that the Irish poor could not govern their own affairs, let alone those of a nation-state. They insisted that the Protestant nation and ascendancy rule had outlived their usefulness in a Catholic nation which, in their eyes at least, was rapidly coming of age.

Plebeian Rebels: The Limits of Popular Protest in Nation-building Ireland

The period between 1770 and 1830 undoubtedly witnessed the beginnings of massive changes in the social and economic landscape of Ireland. We have already seen how this later facilitated the nation-building drive of the substantial Catholic middle classes. This period also witnessed great changes in relations both between Britain and Ireland on the one hand, and between the maritime fringes and agricultural heartlands of Ireland on the other. The new power blocs in Catholic Ireland sought to forge the country into a unified territorial entity. As the century progressed Catholic Ireland was also part of a new world order firmly bent on nation-building. Thus this period saw the beginnings of a profound commercialisation of Irish agriculture, particularly in the rural heartlands of Ireland. Large-scale land enclosures here nurtured the seeds of an emerging new Catholic hegemony, just as they contributed to the destruction of the moral economy of peasants and small farmers. This period finally witnessed a growth in sustained demand for primary products produced in Ireland, the production of which further enhanced the position of these new classes and whetted their appetites for land and resources.

These groups now began to change the very face of rural Ireland and transformed it into a functioning geopolitical unit of ethno-nationalist power. The agricultural heartlands and maritime fringes of Ireland had already been integrated into an expanding colonial trading system in the seventeenth and eighteenth centuries. However, massive developments in infrastructure in the nineteenth century helped to further reduce the parochialism of rural Ireland. They had transformed even the remotest corners of the country into functioning communities with linkages to a wider national and indeed global economy. All of this not only coincided with, but actually instigated a huge upsurge of popular protest by secret societies and other regionally based grassroots movements opposed to the destruction of traditional ways of life in urban and rural Ireland. These groups were opposed to the further extension throughout the land of a free enterprise system of rural capitalism based on laissez faire principles, not on the dictates of historical tradition or social custom. However, far from being united with the secret societies, or sharing in their political outlook, the newly emergent Catholic middle classes that we have been discussing were opposed to their methods and objectives. Like their Protestant overlords they had sought to harness rather than oppose capitalist modernisation. In some parts of the country, popular protest and political violence was directed almost as much against the substantial Catholics as against the 'Protestant landlords' in nationalist accounts of the period. Both groups were perceived by subordinate sectors in Irish society to be implicated in the material and social destruction of the moral economy of the poor, including the 'respectable poor'.

As the Catholic middle classes grew progressively more distant from, and refused to sanction the defence of the moral economy of the latter, secret societies emerged to the forefront of popular protest. They challenged the fragile hegemony of Catholic power-holders and fought to resist the spread of the commercialised system of production and distribution that even then was beginning to benefit Catholic middlemen and strong farmers. Thus the period between 1770 and the 1830s saw the rural poor entering the historical stage not so much for the cause of Ireland, as nationalists imply, but in order to violently oppose new social orders, comprising Catholics as well as Protestants, which were intent on sweeping rural custom and the rural poor aside so as to make room for a new Ireland under the hegemonic control of privileged sectors in Irish society.

Although not strictly nationalist in the modern sense of the term, the violence of secret societies was deeply political and far from being 'instinctual' or 'unstructured'. It certainly was extremely widespread, especially in the country's rich agricultural heartlands in the midlands, north Munster and much of Leinster (Beames, 1982, pp. 128–44). This suggests that opposition was strongest precisely in areas exposed to the full force of capitalist modernisation and rural restructuring. It was here that social class stratification, not just ethnic differentiation, was proceeding most rapidly.

Secret societies were in many respects the Irish equivalent of the 'crowd' in eighteenth-century English and French history. To some extent they have recently been accorded, and certainly deserve, the complex historical treatment here that the 'crowd' and the 'mob' have received in the work of writers like Barrington Moore (1966), Hobsbawm (1958), Tilly (1975, 1978), Thompson (1971, 1975), Rude (1964, 1980), Wolf (1973, 1985), Margadant (1979), Scott (1976) and Landsberger (1974). Thompson has suggested that their entry on to the historical arena has given rise to a misplaced 'spasmodic' view of popular history. According to this the 'people', more accurately the 'risen people' and 'common people', can scarcely be considered historical agents in their own right anytime before the French Revolution. Prior to this they were assumed to intrude only occasionally, and spasmodically, upon the historical scene. Their 'intrusions' moreover were portrayed as compulsive acts of the 'mob' or the 'crowd', rather than the arbitrary actions of self-conscious, political protest movements. Aside from nationalist historians who recruited them uncritically, to the cause of nation-building, their actions were widely regarded, until recently, as mere responses to socio-economic stimuli. Only rarely were they considered for what they were, namely structured political defences of moral social orders which gave meaning to the lives of ordinary people. They fought relentlessly, not so much for the cause of nationalism but to defend themselves against the forces of rural restructuring and capitalist modernisation. In England, France and Ireland these uprisings were led by what Hobsbawm (1958) has labelled 'primitive rebels' and not political parties or 'political leaders' in the modern sense of these terms. To their enemies, including in this case unsympathetic historians, they were simply 'rebellions of the belly'. As such they were assumed to be 'elementary', 'instinctive', pre-modern struggles motivated only by hunger and lack of the material necessities of life.

The 'spasmodic' nature of popular protest in Ireland as elsewhere in Europe has been harnessed by nationalist historians in order to write the revolting poor into nation-building history. Both views – i.e. the 'spasmodic' and the nationalist – reduce the complexities of social unrest to simple causes. In the case of the former, 'riotous behaviour' is reduced to economic causes, thereby painting the main actors in popular protest as 'economic men'. In the case of the latter it is assumed that all those engaged in popular protest were motivated by nationalism. There is little denying that the late eighteenth and early nineteenth centuries were a transitional period in the emergence of an historical bloc in Ireland. It is equally clear that this was a period when the Irish poor, in town as well as country, sought to have some input into the type of Ireland that was then being constructed before their very eyes. However, it is much more problematic to postulate – as some historians and many nationalists have done – that this therefore was the age of plebeian nationalism, a period when the 'risen people' were up in arms in defence of the modern Irish nation. Certainly there is little doubt also about the levels, and prevalence, of political violence in the Irish landscape at this time. Enemies of primitive rebels, including again unsympathetic historians, constantly talked of the Irish peasants' 'propensity to violence' and their cruel and 'bloodthirsty behaviour'. More important still, they painted Ireland as a country where agrarian unrest was 'endemic', a country replenished with 'loathsome outrage', 'civil warres, and domesticall discentions'. In terms reminiscent of present-day portrayals of the Irish Republican movement, Captain H.B.C. Pollard, in his study, *The Secret Societies of Ireland*, in 1923 wrote:

> The problem of the Irish secret societies raises a vital question for solution by statesmen rather than by politicians. So long as there exists a powerful criminal organisation rooted in the United States, as well as in Ireland, and with ramifications all over the globe, whose avowed object is the establishment of an independent Irish Republic by methods of political assassination and secret murder, then how long will any settlement of 'The Irish Question' endure? (Pollard, 1923, p. ix–x)

For Pollard, secret societies in Ireland in the early part of the nineteenth century were analogous to revolutionary cells of 'Carbonari' operating in France and Italy. He also believed that 'a combination of German and Jewish interests' was behind later expressions of political violence in Ireland. The motives of both were 'far less love of Ireland than a searing hate of Britain ... a hatred which the British will never recognise and can never comprehend' (Pollard, 1923, p. 54).

Describing the 'anti-pathous instinct of the Irish race', he went on to quote from a letter by Lord Hugh Cecil, MP to *The Times* where it was stated that:

> the true sine qua non of murders in Ireland is not a political grievance, but a widespread *moral depravity. The Sinn Fein movement and its abominable crimes are only the last of a long series, certainly going back to the days*

of the Whiteboys, 160 years ago. The evil is a moral one, and the remedies must be moral. The two great remedies are law and religion. (Quoted in Pollard, 1923, p. xi; emphasis added)

Ernest Hamilton, MP for the rural constituency of North Tyrone from 1885 to 1892, explained the link between the morally depraved Irish and 'agrarian outrages' in purely racial and ethno-nationalist terms when he bluntly stated:

> agrarian outrages, the foremost stock weapons employed for regaining Ireland for the Irish, have always been exclusively associated with Nationalist or native tactics. The Protestants are not built that way. (Hamilton, 1917, pp. 157–8)

For Hamilton indeed the English or Scottish 'settler' in Ireland was always 'a farmer, or a trader, and his ways [were] for the most part for peace'. He went on to argue:

> The curse of Ireland is, and always has been, lack of moral courage. The native Celt will do anything rather than incur the unpopularity of his fellows, and so, from inability to say no, he is dragged into a [nationalist] conspiracy which he loathes. His ineradicable desire to be on good terms with all parties leads him, for a time, to attempt the complicated manoeuvre of running with the hare and hunting with the hounds, till in the end he finds the double role an impossibility, forsakes the conspiracy and becomes an informer, ... not out of any deliberate treachery, but rather from the promptings of an over-charged conscience. The first cause of his trouble is moral weakness which prevents him standing up to the insinuating overtures of the bad man; the second cause of trouble is the potheen ... Every horrid act in the long red list of Irish atrocities has been perpetrated under the influence of this fiery stimulant. And as long as potheen is distilled, or as long as cheap fusil-oil whisky can be bought, the march of events in Ireland will be largely shaped out of its fumes. (Hamilton, 1917, pp. 150–1)

Like many in the early nineteenth century, Hamilton and Pollard clearly viewed the 'revolting poor' in nation-building Ireland as a threat to social progress. As such they were a source of moral contagion and a fundamental challenge to the political hegemony of the Protestant United Kingdom. Yet in the increasingly commercial, sanitised and bourgeois society of nineteenth-century Ireland, the poor were also considered, both by well-off Irish nationalists and by Ulster Unionists, as inferior to propertied sectors of society because they literally had no territorial stake in the land. Thus the new Ireland was being constructed by, and for, hegemonic groups in Irish society, not for the subordinate, 'backward' and 'low Irish'. Later in the nineteenth century, social Darwinists on both sides of the Irish Sea would justify the marginalisation of the urban and rural poor on socio-biological and racial terms.

Long before this, however, defenders of progress in Ireland branded the poor a 'dirty' and 'rightless people', a people who had no right to be included within the material and moral structures of a progressive Irish society. Like Gypsies in continental Europe, the rural poor here were prone to the lowering of thresholds of tolerance that separated them out from modernising sectors in Irish society. As the sensibilities of the latter became more bourgeois and refined, their tolerance of the poor, like their tolerance of the stench and filth which they associated with the poor, was similarly lowered (Corbin, 1986; Elias, 1978). Their very presence, particularly their 'revolting' activities, in this modernising Ireland sometimes even took the new middle classes by surprise. The poor intimidated their sensibilities, not least because so much in their behaviour, their vagrancy, their lack of respect for church or state, their disrespect for the new laws of the land, suggested that the poor here were more like 'savages' and 'aborigines' than fit citizens of a modern nation-state (Mac Laughlin, 1999b, pp. 129–51).

If the 'food riots' of the latter were highly complex forms of popular protest, so also were their 'agrarian outrages'. As we have already seen, both were essentially organised defences of the moral economy of a quite different Ireland that was under attack from internal and external modernising influences. Behind the hunger of the poor for land and work lay the larger hunger for social respect, including respect for time-honoured rural and urban traditions that were now in danger of extinction. However, far from being uniformly nationalistic or state-centred, most rural unrest in Ireland at this time was retroactive and defensive, not proactive and offensive. Whelan has described one such group, the Defenders, as follows:

> [they] wished not to repudiate but embrace history. They saw Catholics as the authentic, aboriginal inhabitants of the island ... the Defenders wished to flex time, to bend it back to a pre-plantation idyll, to suture the earlier lesions inflicted on the Irish body politic. Their potent sense of dispossession expressed itself in hopes of avenging their seventeenth century setbacks. Their solution to Ireland's ills was to reverse their seventeenth century setbacks by overturning the church establishment, the land settlement and the social hierarchy which rested on their defeats. Thus they were fundamentally historicists who looked to the

past for explanations of their traditional grievances – tithes, taxes, rents, labour and living conditions. (Whelan, 1996, p. 40)

Yet despite their many differences, some secret societies at least could be proactive in political outlook. Their politics represented plebeian attempts by radicalised Catholics 'to prise open a sealed political system of the self-proclaimed Protestant aristocracy'. At another level they were about 'the interaction of radicals and catholics with an informal non-elite culture, represented in one of its aspects by the secret society tradition' (Smyth, 1992, p. 23). Thus the more 'advanced' in these societies had links with the non-elite, and with the 'high politics' of the country, including those of the United Irishmen. As Whelan again shows, they were often 'linked to volunteering and electioneering disputes, and to national politics, especially the resurgence of the Catholic question on the active political agenda' (Whelan, 1996, p. 87). The right to bear arms, not simply the right to vote, constituted the fundamental badge of citizenship in this pre-democratic Ireland. The bearing of arms, indeed, was a pivotal political issue for many members of grassroots social movements in Ireland at this time. This was because, in asserting their right to bear arms, plebeian members of Irish secret societies were asserting their right to participate in, and to mould the character of the political nation in Ireland. Viewed thus, secret societies could be reactive and proactive. They were never always the Green, or Orange, nationalists that partisan historians have painted them. They were hydra-headed organisations which looked to the past as well as the future. Not only did they hark back, like cultural nationalists later in the century, to a pre-plantation idyll which never existed. They also sought to establish new rental arrangements, a new system of tithes, and new contractual arrangements that would be legally binding on tenant farmers, peasants, craftworkers, small property owners, middlemen and landlords in the new Ireland. In a wider sense, therefore, they were more anarchists than nationalists. By their actions they sought to defend an archaic, anarchic and highly regionalised landscape from disappearing under the centralised structures that new men of wealth, and new ideologies of power, were foisting on the Irish landscape and on Irish society.

Viewed thus, the period between 1770 and 1830 may even be considered an age when the peasantry and urban poor were opposed to state-formation. They were especially opposed to state-centralisation, and to the new men of wealth who considered themselves their 'betters' and who did not recognise traditional customary rights. They fought strongest of all when their world was being turned upside down, whether by the new forces of a Catholic commercialism or by Protestant landholders and other representatives of the Anglo-Irish ascendancy. They regarded the wider social and economic agendas of the former in much the same light as they did the political agendas of the latter. They saw both as inimical to their class interests and politically destructive of their traditional lifeworlds. Contrary to nationalist historians, the grievances of the poor did not always stem from ethnic sources. Neither were they always traceable to the greed of 'rack-renting' landlords. Far from deriving from ancient sources – e.g. 'confiscations' of Irish land in the fifteenth and sixteenth centuries – they had their origins in the present, in rising prices, in new legislation and new practices of law enforcement, in the progressive encroachment of central authority and the ethos of commerce into the world of the rural and urban poor. Those in the countryside insisted that the new practices of pasturage being encouraged by commercial farmers were actually creating land hunger and militating against tillage farming practices with its complex patterns of crop rotation and land redistribution upon which so many of the peasantry depended. Thus, besides seeking to regain traditional rights to work and farm the land, including the right to an equitable share in taxes and tithes, secret societies also targeted the stewards, tax collectors, tithe collectors, placemen, and the new tenantry that landholders, both Protestant and Catholic alike, were responsible for introducing. The composition of these societies points to the fact that they often comprised marginal men and women who were being pushed aside by the dictates of 'progress' in rural and urban Ireland. They included poor labourers as well as small farmers and cottiers. They also included craft workers and artisans fighting to resist pauperisation and proletarianisation, men and women whose crafts depended upon access to a plot of land for subsistence in order to supplement meagre earnings from the sale of craft goods or personal services. Societies like these cropped up especially in the rich grazing lands and agricultural zone centred upon south Tipperary, north Cork, the Golden Vale, and parts of Waterford. As roaming bands of armed and discontent peasants and craftworkers, Whiteboys, for example, like most other secret societies in Ireland at the time, had immediate and quite specific social and political grievances. They were opposed to the tithe system not simply because it upheld a Protestant church and aristocratic privilege in a supposedly poor Catholic society, but because the tithe collector in Ireland, like his counterpart in France and elsewhere in Europe, could make a profit out of the poor by imposing excessive tithes (Beames, 1982, pp. 128–42; Donnelly, 1978, pp. 23–35). In other words their objections were not simply with tithes as a system, but with the inequities in its operation. Viewed thus, these poor people's movements were self-protection organisations out to defend the poor from the abuses of land-lordism and agricultural change in Ireland. They were never simply about the abolition of landlordism. They were intent on ensuring that the market in land would not lead to the demise of their way of life, and their customary values, to the benefit of new nation-building classes in town and country alike. In other words their conflicts were about the relative weights given to custom and contract in the new social scheme of things emerging in early nine-teenth-century Ireland. Aside from the 'Orange outrages' of the north-east, they were rarely if ever simply ethnic or religious conflicts.

6 Social and Ethnic Collectivities in Nation-building Ireland

'Pirating' the Nation

It could be argued that the period before, and especially the decades after the Great Hunger, was the great era of emergent nationalism, including Romantic nationalism, in Ireland. This was also the case in Europe where nationalism often as not expressed itself as Romantic nationalism, and where nationalist movements had strong roots in town and country alike. Culturally this was the age of vernacular languages, a period when the languages of Europe's native masses regularly became the national language of the modern nation-state. Geographically it was a period which witnessed the discovery of the home country as the place where 'the people' were nurtured and born. Henceforth the term 'native', in Europe at least, began to lose many of its negative connotations to become instead a positive category in the arsenal of nation-builders. Increasingly now the terms 'native' referred to those subjected to monarchical authority or 'alien' rule, people who were capable of, and were now aspiring to, national self-determination. Most crucial of all, however, this was not so much an era of resurgent nationalism as a period which witnessed the birth of modern nationalism. Gellner argues that nationalism at this time was not so much the awakening of nations to self-consciousness. It was an ideology – more accurately a powerful political movement – which invented nations where they did not exist (Gellner, 1983, p. 49). This was clearly the case in Ireland in the aftermath of the Great Hunger.

Phillip Bull has shown how farmers, rather than landlords, now became 'the focus of parliament's attention and an ever-increasing pre-occupation of government in administering the affairs of Ireland' (Bull, 1996, p. 2). These legislative developments in turn altered Irish perceptions as to where legitimacy lay in the endemic conflicts between Anglo-Irish landlords on the one hand, and Catholic tenant farmers and other groups in Irish society on the other. They also reinforced the attractions of nationalist myths about the land and its rightful occupiers. Henceforth there was a 'continuing identification of Irish nationalism with the ethos and ideas engendered through the land agitation and through contin- uing cultural and other influences attributable to the long-standing nexus between national identity and the interests of the small farmer' (Bull, 1996, p. 3). By the last quarter of the century it was widely acknowledged, by English as well as Irish commentators, that landlordism in Ireland was not sanctioned by history in the manner that it was in England – nor, indeed, in most other European societies. Instead it was viewed as an institution which had been implanted by conquest and could no longer be defended in a modern nation-building society. The Land Act of 1870, like the Irish Church Act of the preceding year, struck at the heart of British conceptions of the state. As Bull has suggested:

> The changes now being made in the Irish land law not only introduced a new principle of differential legislation between different parts of the UK, but also offended many of the most cherished values of traditional society, especially as they were understood by the ruling elites ... The Union of Britain and Ireland had also been carried through simultane- ously with the laissez faire revolution in economic philosophy, and to a degree was influenced by it. The idea of a single market, a political unit which could operate as a cohering and potent economic force, was an important part of the evolving concept of the state, and clear, simple and uniform principles of property-ownership were essential to it. Irish land reform in 1870 struck a significant blow to it, and was as such a very large concession by parliament to Irish pressures. (Bull, 1996, p. 55)

If the period between 1850 and 1870 marked the growing nation- building strength of substantial tenant farmers, we have already seen that the earlier decades of the century broke the back of peasant resistance and witnessed the decline of more traditional expressions of popular resistance, especially those associated with secret societies and the proto-working class in Irish towns and cities. Here therefore, as elsewhere in Europe, this period saw the rise of national, and increasingly also nationalist, organisations which were more proactive and state-centred than their late eigh- teenth- and early nineteenth-century predecessors. The leaders of these new movements derived not so much from the peasantry or the rural poor, but from the petty bourgeoisie and the urban and rural middling classes. Discussing the role of collective action in redrawing the political map of western Europe in the first half of the nineteenth century, Charles Tilly has suggested that collective action then differed from earlier political struggles in three principal ways (Tilly, 1978, pp. 143–78). In the first place it was more national and less local in character. Second, it was less reactive or defensive of customary rights and practices, and it was far more proactive and assertive in its political claims and objectives. Finally, it was less communal and more associational in organisational form and structure.

All of these changes can be observed in the political landscape of Ireland in the transitional phase between the rise of secret societies in the late eighteenth century, and the emergence of middle-class nationalist movements later in the nineteenth century. Ireland was in no way exceptional in this regard. Thus the political changes that took place during this period in Ireland were part and parcel of political developments occurring elsewhere in mainland Europe. As part of the United Kingdom of Great Britain and Ireland, indeed middle-class Catholic Ireland increasingly now looked for political inspiration from the moderately liberal revolutionary movements emerging across Europe in the aftermath of the French Revolution (Elliot, 1982, pp. 35–50). Unlike the revolutions of the late eighteenth century, however, those that punctuated this post-Napoleonic period, whether in Ireland or on the continent, were 'intended', even 'planned' affairs. Indeed Hobsbawm suggests that the most formidable legacy of the French Revolution was 'the set of models and patterns of political upheaval which it established for the general use of rebels anywhere' (Hobsbawm, 1962, pp. 141–2). By the second decade of the nineteenth century there were three such models of revolutionary change. These included the moderate liberal, the radical democratic and the socialist model. All of them reflected the internationalism, not simply the nationalism, of the period. Hobsbawm also suggests that the inspiration for the first was the Revolution of 1789–91 and its political ideal was the quasi-British, constitutional monarchy with the type of property qualified parliamentary systems introduced into France, Britain and Belgium after 1830. The inspiration for the second was the Jacobean Revolution of 1792. Its political ideal was a democratic republic with 'a bias towards a "welfare state" and some animus against the rich'. The inspiration for the third were the far more radical post-Thermidorian uprisings of the 1790s, especially Babeuf's radical 'Conspiracy of Equals', that were led by extreme Jacobins and early communists. These were the child of radical Sansculottism and the rural poor. The sansculottes were economically reactionary in that they stood for a small-owners' society where the proletariat would be kept in check but where capitalists and aristocrats would also be excluded (Soboul, 1964, pp. 78–84). As radical democrats they were opposed to monarchical authority and state-centralisation. They were far less amenable to middle-class control than the other two models of revolutionary change thrown up in the course of the French Revolution. For that reason their ideals were far less likely to be adopted by the European middle class in the opening decades of the nineteenth century.

Certainly after the French Revolution the 'nation' in Ireland as elsewhere became 'something capable of being consciously aspired to from early on, rather than a slowly sharpening frame of vision' (Anderson, 1983, p. 78). The nation now could not only be 'pirated' from mainland Europe. The manner in which it was 'pirated' suggested that new nation-builders now followed bourgeois standards of nation-building laid down in the wake of the French Revolution in order to avoid the risk of plebeian social revolution from below. In mainland Europe it was generally the secular intelligentsia who were to the forefront of these nationalist movements. Ireland was to some extent different, however, in that here it was not the progress of the secular state but the power of the Catholic church and the expanding influence of the national schools, not the university or the university-educated elites, that measured the progress of nationalism. Thus Hobsbawm's dictum that 'the progress of schools and universities measures that of nationalism, just as schools and especially universities became its most conspicuous champions' is only partially correct in the case of nineteenth-century Ireland (Hobsbawm, 1962, p. 71). In many other European countries also, particularly Catholic societies like Poland and small nations beyond the pale of industrial capitalism and large-scale agriculture, this dictum scarcely applied.

Irish Nationalism and the Fragmentation of European Revolutionary Tradition

Even at this stage, however, opposition to absolute monarchy in Europe, like opposition to Anglo-Irish ascendancy in Ireland, was not yet divided into distinctive social, ethnic or even national groupings. Those opposed to anciens régimes here, as in continental Europe, 'regarded themselves, with some justification, as small elites of the emancipated and progressive operating among, and for the eventual benefit of, a vast and inert mass of the ignorant and misled common people, which would no doubt welcome liberation when it came, but could not be expected to take much part in preparing for it' (Hobsbawm, 1962, pp. 143–4). As Hobsbawm has shown, all of these saw themselves fighting against a single enemy, i.e. monarchical or ascendancy absolutism. All of them therefore conceived of revolution as unified and indivisible; it was to be a single European phenomenon, rather than a 'local affair, or an aggregate of national or local liberations'. However, in the aftermath of restorationist attempts to revive monarchy and protect aristocratic privilege in the anti-revolutionary decades of the 1830s and 1840s, this general movement in favour of revolution in Europe split along national and ethno-nationalist lines. One important product of this split was the emergence of self-conscious nationalist movements – in Ireland and elsewhere in Europe – under the leadership of the ethnic, and usually secular, intelligentsia. The latter were anxious to defend their cultural worlds from extinction in an era of global capitalism, while all the time defending the establishment of national capitalism under their hegemony. Not surprisingly nationalism to these social groups was as much a secularised religion as a political ideology.

The new nationalism that emerged in Ireland in the course of the long nineteenth century was quite different from the well-established and official nationalisms of Britain and Europe's other dynastic regimes. Anderson suggests that the latter were polyglot formations which were already centuries old by the nineteenth century (Anderson, 1983, pp. 21–7). As an unwilling partner to one such polyglot formation – i.e. the United Kingdom of Great Britain and Ireland – nationalism in Ireland may best be described as national separatism. It sought the breakup of Britain and the creation of a self-governing Irish nation. Thus nationalism here probably was a force that was more recent than most nationalists care to admit. Far from being 'sui generis' or purely imitative of French revolutionary nationalism, it was forged in opposition to 'big-nation' British nationalism in the course of the nineteenth century. It owed its existence in part to the integration of Ireland into the United Kingdom, and to the way English rule had for centuries aspired to create, and intimately control, a human landscape of perfect visibility in Ireland. One condition of the creation of this 'visibility' was the fact that everyone and everything 'Irish' had been coded and classified for centuries. Thus, as we have already seen, the style of 'imagining' the nation in Ireland was a product of technologies of navigation, astronomy, horology, surveying, photography and print that had been operating here since at least the sixteenth century. This meant that Irish nationalism may have borrowed a lot from the new nationalisms that emerged in continental Europe after the French Revolution, but it also derived from the deep driving power of a native capitalism in nineteenth-century Ireland. It owed a lot to the fact that, ever since the eighteenth century, English maps of Ireland, and official 'head counts' of Irish people, had long 'shaped the grammar' which literally made 'Ireland' and 'the Irish' possible in the nineteenth century (Anderson, 1983, p. 185). This meant that the 'concretisations' of the possibilities of 'Ireland' and 'the Irish' derived as much from indigenous social forces, as from the English state's peculiar way of imagining 'Ireland' and controlling 'the Irish' from the sixteenth century onwards.

The movements which best symbolised these new developments in nationalism on the continent were the 'youth' movements inspired by Giuseppe Mazzini after the revolutions of 1830 (Clark, 1998, pp. 78–81). However, as Hobsbawm suggests, these organisations – Young Italy, Young Poland, Young Ireland, Young Germany, Young Switzerland – in themselves were of no great importance. Generally speaking they failed miserably in their objectives, until, that is, they attracted the attention of more powerful forces, especially the middle classes, which then were emerging into political consciousness (Hobsbawm, 1962, pp. 163–4). Weber shows that in France the most significant of these new forces were the lesser landholders and petty gentry. They also included the new middle and lower classes whose spokesmen were the professional intelligentsia, a group who were increasingly now defined in ethnic as well as social class terms (Weber, 1977, pp. 33–45). In Britain they included men of industry, and businessmen, as well as the professions and 'improving' farmers. The most significant new social forces in Catholic Ireland at this time were the Catholic church, the merchant class, the shopocracy, the substantial tenantry and the Catholic – and Protestant – ethnic intelligentsia. The latter were the chief proponents of nation-building and nationalism throughout western Europe. They were not distinct from the business class, or from the commercial and industrial sectors of nation-building societies. They were instead an integral element in the new social blocs emerging all across western Europe, including Ireland, from the mid-nineteenth century onwards. The organic intelligentsia that derived from these new social groups articulated the moderate demands of 'their' people at this crucial juncture separating pre-modern Ireland from modern capitalist Ireland.

Symbolically therefore, the 'youth movements' which took their inspiration from Giuseppe Mazzini in the 1830s and 1840s were of extreme importance. They signified a growing awareness of the differences in revolutionary prospects in a variety of European countries, including Ireland. They shattered the unified internationalism to which some European revolutionaries had aspired in the first 30 years of the nineteenth century. They marked a decentralisation of a European revolutionary movement by giving birth to national movements whose social and political objectives were more pragmatic, less utopian and more realistic than those inspired by the radicalism of the sansculottes in the French Revolution. When France refused, or was prevented, from acting the role of liberator for all of Europe, nationalist movements of liberation, not least those with strong links with men of property and the political right, were quick to fill the gap. In so doing they copper-fastened the disintegration of a European revolutionary movement into national and nationalist movements. This marked the birth of the modern nation-state for many nation-builders. As Hobsbawm has noted, each of these movements had much the same political programme – the construction of the nation-state under bourgeois, or at least petty bourgeois, hegemony. They generally shared the same tactics and political strategies. Adopting the role of Messiah for all, their primary concern was their own nation, and its place in a new world order of powerful nation-states and disempowered colonial outliers. Indeed, as we have already seen, the nationalisms that sprang up in western Europe in the course of the nineteenth century were able to work from a visible model of nation-building provided by the French Revolution (Hobsbawm, 1962, pp. 163–79).

As Anderson also shows, the new national solidarities that emerged at this time also were different from the pre-bourgeois solidarities that marked Europe's anciens régimes (Anderson, 1983, pp. 20–9). The latter generally generated social solidarities above – and sometimes even below – the level of the nation, and well outside the realms of national languages and national culture. The solidarities of pre-nineteenth-century Ireland on the other hand, like those operating in a number of other European countries (e.g. Poland, Spain and Italy), as often as not were formulated at the level of the region, or reflected in international influences. They were rarely, or simply, national solidarities in the modern meaning of the term. As products of kinship, clientship or other localised forms of personal loyalty, they gave rise to pre-modern expressions of social solidarity. With the emergence of the bourgeoisie, including in Ireland's case the middling tenantry and lower middle classes in town and country alike, all this would change. Here, as Anderson points out, were classes that came into being as so many replications of each other (Anderson, 1983, pp. 75–7). Far from being mere abstractions or 'imagined communities', as Anderson implies, however, these social classes were literally powerful forces in the land. They forged the powerful regional and national networks – schools, churches and local government institutions – that formed the hegemonic basis of the modern nation-state. It was through their control of these hegemonising institutions that power-holders in mid-nineteenth-century Ireland first exerted control over their subordinates and brought them within the nation-building project.

This, of course, was a long, drawn-out process which probably commenced in the modernising heartlands of east Leinster, north Munster and the south-east in the first half of the nineteenth century. Later on it was spread, especially by priests and schoolteachers, but also through a class alliance with small to medium sized farmers, into the core areas of subsistence farming and to peasant communities along the west and north-west coast. Certainly after the Great Hunger substantial tenant farmers, especially the Catholic clergy, strong farmers and businessmen, were exerting hegemonic control over their social subordinates, at least outside the north-east of the country. More importantly still they were challenging the political and economic dominance of the landed aristocracy in a wide variety of ways ranging from a stronger Catholic presence in regional Poor Law Boards of Guardians and other local institutions, through to greater Catholic control over local rates, education and cultural life. By the mid-1880s effective control of half the Poor Law Boards had passed into the hands of these strong tenant farmers and their social class allies. By then also the political power of the landed aristocracy was severely curtailed as nationalist candidates swept to power in practically every constituency outside Protestant-controlled Ulster. Even in Ulster Catholic candidates in that year captured 16 seats, one short of a majority (Boyce, 1991, p. 297).

This meant that the substantial tenantry and Catholic power-holders were not only coming to dominate resource bases in the countryside – they were hegemonic also in the one organisation, namely the church, which, aside from the constabulary, had a nation-wide network of power, influence and patronage. By the last quarter of the nineteenth century the sons, and to a much lesser extent the daughters, of these same social groups were holding down hegemonic or socially strategic positions – as shop-keepers, publicans, petty officials and schoolteachers – in towns and villages throughout the length and breadth of Catholic

Ireland. This meant that the urban and small town kinsmen of the better-off tenantry played a crucial role in articulating the political and class interests of the middling tenantry. It was these groups who were primarily responsible for carving out an Irish nation from the older polyglot multi-national formation of the United Kingdom of Great Britain and Ireland. Indeed, it was in this critical interaction between town and country, between the middling tenantry and the Catholic church, between shopkeepers, local newspapermen, the professions and small businessmen, that the regional vehicles for demolishing the landlord system in Ireland were forged. These social groups reinforced their capacity to survive and prosper by literally sinking deep roots into the very soil of Catholic Ireland. They forged a national and regionally specific historical consciousness which stressed the importance of the family farm, and the centrality of private property, both to the survival of Catholic society and to the future of the nation-state in Ireland.

Irish Nationalism: A Territorialising Force?

All of this meant that the Irish nation was not only constructed by these social classes – it was chiefly constructed for them also (Lloyd, 1993, pp. 6–10). Their views on nationalism and nation-building, like their views on state-formation, were far from exceptional. Instead they concurred with those of some of the leading political theorists of the late nineteenth century, not least with those of social Darwinists. One such Darwinist was Friedrich Ratzel, the founding father of German political geography, who would have well understood the territorial strategies of Irish nation-builders in the run up to the establishment of the Irish nation-state. Born in 1844, Ratzel died in 1904 and he lived through one of the most significant eras of nation-building and colonial expansion in the history of western Europe. Ratzel's ideas were widely adopted, both by nation-builders and by supporters of empire in the late nineteenth century, and, more notoriously, by supporters of the Third Reich in the 1930s (Taylor, 1993, p. 50). This was because his evolutionary theories of social development particularly justified the territorial aggrandisement of the nation-state through internal and external expansion (Mac Laughlin, 1986b, pp. 20–3; 1998, pp. 419–20; O'Tuathail, 1996, pp. 36–8). Petty bourgeois defenders of nation-building in Ireland would also have agreed with Ratzel when he insisted that the state was an organism linked to the land, an organism which required *leben-sraum*, or 'breathing space', in order to grow. For Ratzel, as for Catholic Irish nation-builders, the state was defined as much in geographical terms, as in social or political terms. Like Irish nation-alists, and indeed Ulster Unionists, he held that the struggle for existence literally involved a struggle for space and resources (Semple, 1911, pp. 56–96).

Like all true social Darwinists, including nineteenth-century Irish nation-builders, Ratzel also stressed the territorial imperatives of state formation which insisted that the transition from lower to higher stages of social development was predicated upon two prem-ises; the enlargement of the territorial domain and natural resource base of the nation; and increasing the numerical and political strength of hegemonic groups within it. Therefore, he argued, progressive societies, like progressive ethnic groups and social classes within the nation-state, always encroached upon the territo-ries of less powerful neighbours, both at home – hence internal colonialism – and abroad – hence imperialism. Indeed they maximised their control over other social groups and their habitat at national, local and international levels by developing a more exploitative relationship with the lands they inhabited. Viewed thus, 'civilised' societies, especially their most 'civilised' sectors, had a moral responsibility to expand socially as well as geographically. In taking over 'debatable lands', including the lands of their less powerful neighbours (in Ireland's case these would have included the landed estates of the Protestant aristocracy and the abandoned tenancies of those who fled the country after the Great Hunger), they carved out their own spheres of influence. In so doing they confirmed their right to nationhood, and to statehood. Finally, Ratzel would certainly have agreed with a nationalist leader like Charles Stewart Parnell when, in a famous statement in Cork City in 1885, he cautioned 'no man could assign a ne plus ultra to the march of a nation'. This usefully vague concept later became the catch cry of the Irish Home Rule movement and is inscribed on a statue of Parnell still standing in Dublin's O'Connell street.

Ratzel also saw the boundary of the nation as something that was constantly in a state of flux. He likened it to the outer layer of skin on plants and animals, it nurtured and protected the organism it covered. Equally important, it expanded with it and gave the nation-state room on the world stage. For Ratzel, as for nineteenth-century Irish nation-builders, boundary lines were never fixed lines on a political map. They were always in a state of flux because boundaries defined the vitality as well as movement or expansion of nations and races. For that reason they were contested terrains and debatable lands, zones where the limits of state power were tested, places which pointed either to the expansion, or contraction, of nations and empires (Mac Laughlin, 1998, pp. 419–21). The substantial tenantry and strong farmers of Catholic Ireland were certainly becoming more and more rooted to the economic landscape and the land of Ireland in the decades after the Famine. This was especially true of those living in the agricultural heartlands of the midlands and south of the country. In one study of farm ownership in Tipperary in the 1970s it was found that 30 per cent of farmers could trace their farms, and their farm boundaries, back to the mid-nineteenth century. Using land valuation records for 1851 this same survey revealed that 46 per cent of families could trace their family names back to at least the 1840s (Smyth, 1988). This showed that, just when the landless poor and the cottier class were being decimated by Famine, not least by post-Famine readjustment, the Catholic middling tenantry and strong farmers were going from strength to strength. By hitting at the lower echelons of Irish society far more than it did these sectors of Catholic Ireland, the Famine facilitated the expansion of the substantial farmers by clearing away the uneconomic holdings of small tenant farmers and removing many of the landless poor and the cottier class. This, together with the bankruptcy of many in the landed aristocracy, literally left more and more of the land of Ireland in the hands of a sturdier, more thrifty, and far more puritanical rural Catholic bourgeoisie, including the petty bourgeoisie. These sectors, as we have seen, provided the backbone of the Home Rule movement and were the most forceful and conservative nation-building groups in late nineteenth-century Ireland. In the richer agricultural heartlands they were clearly separated out from the poor farmers and the landless poor from as early as the first half of the nineteenth century. After the Famine this process of 'kulakisation' speeded up and the hegemony of the rural middle class became more nation-wide as emigration of the surplus poor was knitted into the very fabric of Irish rural society.

We have also seen that the propertied elements in Catholic Ireland did not mourn the death of 'traditional' Ireland through the twin forces of capitalist modernisation and mass emigration. Indeed, during and after the Famine they had practised their own crude version of rate-capping and sought to ensure that Poor Law legislation passed in Britain would not pose an obstacle to rural development under bourgeois nationalist hegemony in Ireland (Mac Laughlin, 1985, p. 30). Like their peers in England and

Scotland, they too took great care to ensure that Poor Relief in Ireland would only be distributed to those who had abandoned all claims to land and property (Driver, 1993, pp. 19–26). In Ireland this had the effect of creating a glut of small holdings on the property market, many of which were rented, or bought up, by 'improving' tenants and landlords, and by independent Catholic farmers. Thus the 'emptying' of the countryside through poverty and emigration greatly extended the geographical range of commercial farming in Ireland and allowed those who stayed behind on the land to add field to field. Similarly, export-led agricultural development later in the century enabled those with viable tenancies to specialise for the market in order to increase production, which in turn edged the 'surplus offspring' on family farms on to the emigrant trails out of Ireland.

From as early as mid-century the indigenous bourgeoisie had been proclaiming Ireland's right to self-determination. They were among the chief benefactors from the Famine-induced restructuring of Irish property relations and post-Famine-induced emigration. Yet so great was the volume of emigration from this nation-building Ireland in the latter half of the nineteenth century that people, not produce, constituted the major export of many rural communities here. Emigration further shattered the community life of rural society in whole tracts of the country. In so doing it paved the way for a far more fragmented, far more individualistic society, one that was more likely to be informed by the class interests of men of property than the shared community interests of the rural poor. Lyons has interpreted the 'headlong exodus' of one million people from Ireland between 1845 and 1851 as 'the instinctive reaction of a panic-stricken people to the spectacle of their traditional way of life breaking into pieces before their very eyes' (Lyons, 1985, p. 44). It was also a continuation of pre-Famine trends, particularly in the midlands and south-east of Ireland, in that emigration was the rational response of the labouring poor to the modernisation of Irish agriculture on the one hand, and the emergence of an international labour market which presented opportunities for working and living abroad on the other. In Ireland, therefore, emigration helped reduce the possibilities of class conflict in the countryside by transferring the discontent in rural, and indeed in urban, Ireland to mainland Britain and North America. It was here that the ethnic, nationalist and social class identities of many of the Irish poor were formed, often for the first time. This was especially the case for those who moved to the industrial towns of lowland Scotland and northern England, as well as those who shifted to the outer limits of the English-speaking labour market in Canada and the United States. Here the Irish swelled the ranks of urban proletariat both as workers in their own right, and as Irishmen and Irishwomen. Not surprisingly they joined the ranks of nationalist organisations as readily as they joined the trade union movement wherever they settled.

An estimated four million people left Ireland between 1855 and 1914. As the century progressed, this outward movement of Ireland's sons and daughters became an irrevocable, permanent move towards countries from which they had little prospect of return (Lyons, 1985, p. 45). The American recession of the 1870s, like the First World War, showed that when the safety valve of emigration from Ireland was temporarily stopped, then the resultant buildup of dissatisfied young adults in the country could often fuel urban and rural unrest by adding manpower, and womenpower, to grassroots movements for social and economic reform in nation-building Ireland (Fitzpatrick, 1984). Generally speaking, however, emigration after the Famine helped to ease class conflict in Ireland. Thus it eased pressure on the land and reduced tensions within families by forcing those without a stake in the land to emigrate overseas, to Britain, North America, Australia and Latin America. Between one-third and one-half of those who left between 1855 and 1914 were between 20 and 24 years old and a significant number of the remainder were teenagers. In one sense these became the new Irish diaspora. However, they could more accurately be labelled a mutant people in the sense that they had one foot still in Ireland and another in their host societies. These emigrants were an estimated 25–30 per cent of the population of the south-west of Ireland between 1881 and 1891. In many western counties they were between 15 and 20 per cent of the population (Cousens, 1965).

Young Irish adults in post-Famine Ireland were not only raised alongside established emigrants' trails to Britain and America. They also forged new trails to the expanding frontiers of the world economy. Their going drained youth from rural communities and contributed to political stability by channelling young adults abroad just when they came of political age. By 1926 most of rural Ireland had literally moved to mainland Britain, the USA, Canada and Australia where they were proletarianised into the core areas of the world economy (Mac Laughlin, 1994a, pp. 23–46). In emigrating, they facilitated the modernisation of Irish agriculture, preserved the territorial integrity of family farms and contributed to a radical re-mapping of the Irish population.

In rural Catholic Ireland outside the north-east all this also allowed strong farmers, especially the middling tenants and 'improving' landlords, to literally 'come to grips' with more and more of the land of Ireland. These groups now began extending their hegemonic grip on the country, at least on that part outside of the north-east where Ulster Unionists were consolidating into a regionally powerful hegemonic group. Elsewhere the rural bourgeoisie of the midlands and south of Ireland allied themselves with an emergent, and far less wealthy petty bourgeoisie of the peripheries prior to becoming a national force in the land. Certainly the number of family farms increased dramatically in the second half of the nineteenth century. By 1901 the socially strategic 'thirty-acre men' who were the backbone of the Home Rule movement constituted one-third of all Irish farmers. Throughout the latter half of the century the focus of their agitation had switched from demands for the economic right of Irish tenant farmers to own and cultivate land in Ireland to the civil and political rights of bourgeois and petty bourgeois nationalist Ireland to self-determination. This sector did not lament the passing of traditional Ireland as a result of emigration but tolerated it because it eased pressure on family farms, halted the drift towards farm fragmentation, and made room for 'graziers and their bullocks' throughout the length and breadth of Catholic Ireland. Emigration on this scale certainly placed Ireland among the leading European exporters of labour between the mid-nineteenth and the early twentieth century. Given the size of the country, and the intensity of the exodus, Irish emigration was at least on a par with some of the greatest migratory movements in modern history, including the shipment of approximately 9.5 million live African slaves to the Americas between 1450 and 1871 (Davidson, 1980, p. 68). Given the fact that the Irish not only gravitated to the urban centres of the east coast of North America but also played a significant role in clearing native Americans from the interior, they were among the chief benefactors of White colonial and capitalist expansion in North America. Irish involvement in bitter 'race wars' against Native and Black Americans is a forgotten chapter in current debates on Ireland's internationalist and anti-colonial legacy.

Malthusian Defences of 'Vanishing' Ireland

Given its scale and social composition, Irish emigration clearly fulfilled a number of important functions, both within nation-building Catholic Ireland and in the world economy. First, it contributed to the Anglicisation of Ireland by transforming the geolinguistic map of Ireland and greatly reducing the number of Irish speakers in the country. Second, it facilitated the commercialisation of Irish agriculture and made Ireland a major emigrant nursery in the world economy. Third, it intensified the eastward drift of political power in Ireland and exacerbated its socio-spatial concentration in the rich agricultural heartlands and in the east of the country. Fourth, emigration, particularly after the Famine, revealed the extent to which socio-economic life in Ireland was determined by globalising forces operating at the level of the international, not just the national, economy. Fifth, together with the Great Famine – and other famines that preceded the 'Hungry Forties' – emigration fundamentally altered power relations in Ireland by removing large numbers of young adults from the land just when they came of political age. Finally, emigration contributed to the abatement of social tensions on family farms in the rich agricultural heartlands and in peripheral areas in the west and north-west of the country as the century progressed. Indeed in rural Ireland as in other rural societies in eastern and central Europe, families were frequently expected to raise young adults for little else than the emigrant trail. The large-scale removal of Mother Ireland's 'surplus' sons and daughters abroad for a long time barred any possibility of a fundamentally social and political revolution in nineteenth-century Ireland.

Several other factors contributed to the transformation of Ireland into a major emigrant nursery in the latter half of the nineteenth century. First, Ireland's entry into a free trade capitalist system dominated by England and the United States hastened the de-industrialisation of the south of the country through the emigration of large numbers of agricultural labourers, artisans and craftworkers. Second, international competition also dictated the further modernisation of agriculture in the south of Ireland and the concentration of industry in and around Belfast city and its environs. However, the progressive diversification of the north-east's industrial base through the addition of shipbuilding, engineering and related industries did not mean that all of those formerly employed in the countryside were now absorbed into Belfast's expanding but deeply sectarian labour market. It was soon apparent that the city was never meant to act as a haven for poor Catholics fleeing poverty and landlessness in the south of Ireland. In 1851 Belfast's population of 87,000 inhabitants was a mere third of Dublin's population. By 1911 the population of the city exceeded that of Dublin by more than 64,000 inhabitants. More significant than this absolute growth were the marked differentials in the growth rates of the Catholic and Protestant population in the city. Between 1861 and 1911 the Protestant population of Belfast quadrupled to 293,704 while the Catholic population increased by 125 per cent to 93,243 inhabitants (Mac Laughlin, 1980).

Finally, the heightened commercialisation and specialisation of Irish agriculture also exposed the cottier class, the middling tenantry and large farmers to the perils of redundancy and international competition throughout the second half of the nineteenth and the opening decades of the twentieth century (Miller, 1985). It exposed the former in particular to the dangers of crop failures and declining prices, and caused the surplus sons, and particularly the surplus daughters, of poor families to be jettisoned on to the emigrant trail at an early age. The commercialisation of farming formalised and revolutionised social relations within the family and gradually paved the way for the destruction of the extended family. This obliged large and small farmers alike to adopt marriage and inheritance patterns which in turn caused their sons, and particularly their daughters, to be 'banished' from nation-building Ireland. As the century progressed, many of those who would formerly have been supported within the family unit, or within the extended family, were forced into seasonal or permanent emigration at a comparatively early age. Many more, particularly young children from poorer families, were literally sold at 'hiring fairs' in order that poor rural and working-class families might supplement meagre cash incomes in areas where opportunities for adults to do this were few and far between (Beattie, 1980, pp. 41–4; 1997, pp. 77–85). A final factor which contributed to the transformation of Ireland into an emigrant nursery in the late nineteenth and early twentieth centuries was the fact that changing market conditions in the world economy caused pronounced shifts from tillage to cattle production and forced more and more young adults on to emigrant trails that literally led to the outer limits of the expanding capitalist system. Thus, just as in the 1980s, the Irish were responsible for 'filling gaps' in the international labour market, and they often literally 'peopled' the frontiers of the world economy. This was particularly the case with Irish emigration to North America, Australia and South Africa.

Marx was among the first to emphasise the links between emigration, capital accumulation and the construction of bourgeois hegemony in the core areas of the peripheries of the British nation in the late nineteenth century (Marx and Engels, 1976, 1950). He argued that the global division of labour which emerged in the latter half of the century favoured the core areas to the detriment of peripheral areas of the world economy. Thus, he added, emigration and core formation, including in Ireland, converted 'one part of the globe into a chiefly agricultural field of production for supplying the other part which remains a chiefly industrial field'. He also stressed the importance of surplus pools of labour in rural Ireland and the Scottish Highlands to the development of the industrial and indeed agricultural cores in Britain and North America. Thus he argued that the Highland clearances and the rural exodus from Ireland served identical ends – the creation of viable fields of agricultural production in Scotland and Ireland and the simultaneous transformation of Scotland and Ireland into 'emigrant nurseries' (Mac Laughlin, 1994a). Certainly by the late nineteenth century Marx's fatalistic prediction that it was Ireland's national destiny to become 'an English sheepwalk and cattle pasture, her people banished by sheep and ox', had largely come true (Marx and Engels, 1976, p. 288). It was against this background that Ireland's middling tenantry and the Catholic middle class gradually acquired hegemonic status in the latter half of the nineteenth century.

This meant that migrants from Ireland not only resolved regional deficits in the supply of labour in Britain, North America and Australia at crucial periods in the development of the world economy in the late nineteenth and early twentieth centuries. The permanent and seasonal proletarianisation of the sons and daughters of the rural poor also provided families back home in 'congested districts' throughout Ireland with cash which contributed to the survival of small farming and working-class communities well into this century. Thus Handley estimated that between 1880 and 1900 almost 38,000 seasonal migrants were still annually leaving Ireland for Britain (Handley, 1947, p. 213). It has been estimated that 18,000 seasonal migrants from the west and north-west of the country were still moving between Ireland, Scotland and the north of England on the eve of the First World War. Many of those from the north-west of the country were engaged in 'tattie hoking' on the 'pratie fields' of lowland Scotland. Their destinations reflected the need to locate in accessible locations with a high seasonal demand for agricultural labour. They may have regarded emigration as a geographical extension of 'hiring out' practices which poor families adopted in order to supplement family incomes and ease pressure on the meagre resources. 'Scottish money', the remittances which young emigrants sent home from Scotland, often accounted for one-quarter of the cash income of poor families in the west and north-west of Ireland up to the First World War (Mac Laughlin, 1987; O'Grada, 1973). It formed the basis of a proto-welfare system which prolonged the life of impoverished rural and working-class communities by literally keeping them alive through the support of young and old alike.

This also meant that emigration was a structural feature of Irish nation-building society which literally contributed to nation-building abroad and fulfilled a wide range of social, political and economic functions. It particularly helped to fill gaps in the labour markets of other expansionist nations in a new international world order. Emigration from underdeveloped rural areas along the Atlantic fringe also contributed to the social disintegration of a pre-modern Ireland and linked the peripheralisation of peasant Ireland to core formation and industrialisation abroad. Far from being peripheral to processes of industrialisation and capitalist produc-tion in the nineteenth century, Irish workers occupied a central position in the international circuits of the global economy. Revolutions in transportation, especially when they affected the costs of travel and broke down the isolation of rural backwaters, facilitated, but by no means caused, the growing internationalisa-tion of the Irish in the late nineteenth and early twentieth centuries. They forced isolated pockets of rural Ireland into the world economy and transformed the core areas of peasant subsis-tence in Ireland into 'emigrants' nurseries' with well-developed links to the international labour market. The annihilation of spatial barriers to the circulation of Irish labour at this time thus forced Ireland deeper into the international labour market (Marx, 1956). Henceforth the solution to unemployment and lack of opportunities within nation-building Ireland would be sought abroad, a trend which still continues to the present day. All this contributed to a commodification and internationalisation of Irish labour and caused new values to be placed on Irish rural and working-class communities as major suppliers of unskilled and highly adaptable workers. Certainly by the close of the century, Marx's fatalistic prediction that Ireland's destiny was to become 'an English sheepwalk and cattle pasture', and that her people would be 'banished by sheep and ox', had largely come true (Marx, 1962, p. 288).

A number of commentators have pointed to the fact that the transition from theories of emigration to theories of nation-building in Ireland in the 1870s was also a very important turning point in Irish and British attitudes towards emigration. In Ireland's case this coincided with the emergence of nation-building classes and increasingly well-organised and disciplined nationalist movements. In Britain it occurred alongside a revival of interest in that country's imperial role. In nation-building Ireland as in expansionist Britain this encouraged a sanitised view of the New World as a land of opportunity, a place eminently suited to meet the socio-economic needs of the Celtic race, especially those who could never hope to secure a living within Ireland. This showed how political attitudes to Irish emigration were refracted through social class and ethnic lenses. As such they shaped, and were shaped by, prevailing political orthodoxies, particularly by nationalist attitudes to Ireland's place in the international community (Black, 1960; Boylan and Foley, 1992). Malthusianists on both sides of the Irish Sea regarded Ireland's rural exodus as a precondition for capitalist modernisation here. By the 1880s Irish emigration was widely perceived as a mathematical demonstration which showed that the best which could be done for the rural poor was to emigrate them altogether. From as early as the mid-nineteenth century Malthusianists were also advocating state support for Irish emigration and suggesting that those leaving Ireland were faring well outside it. They also countered radical interpretations of emigration as a cruel response to 'rancherism' by arguing that emigration was caused by Ireland's proximity to Britain and by revolutions in transportation which drew Ireland closer to Britain and the United States, where, political conservatives argued, the 'troublesome Irish' belonged (Dangerfield, 1979, p. 17).

Malthusian defences of Irish emigration also saw it as a solution to the problems of rural underdevelopment. Moreover, it is important to note that Malthusian justifications for emigration transcended ethnic divisions in nineteenth-century Ireland. Thus the middling tenantry and Catholic priests in impoverished regions throughout Ireland often looked on emigration as an acceptable solution to the poverty of landless families and the cottier classes. Although they could not couch their support for emigration quite so radically or paternalistically as their colonial overlords, they nevertheless realised that the scattering of Mother Ireland's poorest sons and daughters was in everyone's interests. This was particularly true of Catholic priests in the 'congested' west coast where emigration was often perceived as the only solution to rural destitution. Irish social and political leaders here frequently hinted that any long-term curtailment of emigration was impossible because it ran counter to the 'natural' forces of the market and the natural principles of political economy (Tukes, 1889).

Nationalist Reactions to Irish Emigration

However, in order to make political capital from the fact that entire tracts of Ireland were being cleared in order to make room for 'English graziers and their bullocks', nationalists were compelled to ignore the structuring role of emigration in making room for the family farms of the indigenous tenantry (Keep, 1954, p. 417). Instead they Anglicised the causes of Irish emigration and nationalised its solutions. They also systematically refuted each assimilationist premise underlying the progressive Anglicisation of post-Famine Ireland and attributed emigration solely to 'landlordism', 'rancherism' and 'English misrule' in Ireland. Rudimentary though it was, this historicist reaction to colonial rule in Ireland revolutionised social attitudes towards Irish emigration. It also problematised a wide range of other social and economic issues that were supposed to have been resolved through the operation of the laissez faire principles of English political economy in colonial Ireland (Boylan and Foley, 1992). Irish nationalists subverted this discourse by arguing that Anglo-Irish rancherism was the major cause of Irish emigration and that English political economy provided ideological justification for the modernisation of agriculture which caused such widespread emigration. They also attacked as erroneous the assumption that rancherism was necessarily more productive than petit culture (Dewey, 1974, pp. 32–5). They insisted that large-scale agriculture based on the great estates should give way to petit culture centred initially on the tenant holding and subsequently on the family-owned farm. They also suggested that Britain was engaged in a subtle exercise in social engineering in Ireland and that the British government sought to remove the Irish abroad when they were most needed to construct an Irish nation at home (Keep, 1954, p. 419).

According to this 'narrow nationalist' viewpoint, landlordism alone was responsible for emigration and emigrants were victims of alien oppression by 'tyrants' who drove the Irish from their 'happy home'. Indeed in nation-building circles the whole question of Ireland's declining population and involuntary emigration was charged with emotion and linked to the controversy of the 'vanishing Irish' and 'Irish extermination'. However, the view taken of emigration from the pulpit often differed from that taken from the farm gate. While church leaders worried that emigration was becoming a 'kind of self-defacement' and stressed the destructive effects of emigration on local business and community life, small tenant farmers and improving landlords regarded it as a safety valve which eased pressure on the land and on the country's unevenly distributed resources. At best they hoped that emigration would place Irish young adults on a better footing outside than they could ever hope to attain inside the country. As we have already seen, some priests, particularly in 'congested districts', took the view that some level of emigration was unavoidable in the case of young adults from impoverished large families and argued that it was an acceptable solution to the certainty of misery and poverty experienced by such families within Ireland. This meant that many priests viewed emigration through the prism of social class which tempered their nationalism and suggested that the 'new Ireland' was to be built by the 'hale and hearty sons' of the rural bourgeoisie, not by the sons and daughters of the rural and urban poor. In so doing they suggested that the latter should accept emigration as a natural alternative to lack of work at home. Miller has well described the contradictory attitudes to emigration in nation-building Ireland as follows:

> [Blame] for emigration reflected nationalists' and clerics' tortuous efforts *to reconcile traditional social ideals and their own hegemonic imperatives with a social reality which violated those ideals and yet paradoxically both sustained and threatened that hegemony.* On the one hand, many Catholic spokesmen realised that only massive lower class emigration had created the relatively commercialised, urbanised, and bourgeois-dominated 'New Ireland', which had been the precondition for the success of disciplined nationalist movements and the church's devotional revolution ... In addition, Catholic spokesmen also understood that emigration brought specific material benefits to some key elements in Irish society as well as, they hoped, to the emigrants themselves. (Miller, 1985, p. 458; emphasis added)

Church leaders and nationalists also stressed the destructive effects of emigration on the cultural fabric of rural Ireland. In particular they contrasted the pre-Famine emigration of 'pale and panic-stricken people' with the exodus of 'stalwart, muscular, dauntless young braves' leaving Ireland in the late nineteenth and early twentieth centuries. These, they asserted, were 'royally endowed with every attitude that goes to make up a peerless and magnificent manhood' and their going was depriving nation-building Ireland of its very 'bone and sinew' (Kerr, 1943, p. 372). They argued that emigration in the late nineteenth century did not simply involve farm labourers or artisans. It also took away farmers' sons 'who preferred the bustle of life in America to the monotony of country life at home' (Keep, 1954, p. 445). Unlike the 'sad, weeping and melancholy emigrants' of the Hungry Forties, these new emigrants 'did not carry with them one single reminder of their nationality'. Instead they were 'casting off all allegiance to the land' and when they left 'one heard no longer the shout of an everlasting farewell but a ringing cheer'. It was feared that these emigrants were becoming a source of envy to those left behind on the land, many of whom looked at their 'fortunate friends escaping' and hoped that 'when the letter and passage money arrive, they too will be able to leave this land of bondage and follow their friends to the promised land in the wake of the setting sun' (Keep, 1954, p. 457).

Nationalists were also alarmed by the fact that emigration had become so far advanced now that it was becoming a voluntary activity which attracted 'the athletic male population'. Like critics of middle-class emigration today, they were equally concerned about the quality and the volume of Irish emigration, with some leaders even arguing that the genetic pool of the Irish race would literally run through emigration. Church leaders also suggested that emigration was depriving Catholic Ireland of its 'breeding stock' because it was attracting 'country girls' who 'sacrificed their dowries and a certain prospect of marriage for the pleasure of serving in a business house in New York or even going into a situation as housemaids in American families' (Keep, 1954, p. 418). Not surprisingly a whole genre of literature emerged in late nineteenth- and early twentieth-century Ireland which portrayed emigration as the product of 'alien' rule and suggested that some form of self-government would solve Ireland's social and economic problems.

7 Pressing Home the Nation: Print Capitalism and 'Imagined Communities' in the Nineteenth Century

This chapter suggests that the provincial press was one of the most important, and until recently the most neglected, agent of nation-building in nineteenth-century Ireland, as in other European countries. As such it not only reflected nationalist and Unionist thought but directly contributed to two different concepts of the nation, and two different scales of nation-building, at crucial stages in the evolution of Irish and Unionist modernities. Like those that follow it, this chapter adopts a constructionist approach to nation-building. It treats nationalism less as a primordial social force than as a political programme for building the imagined community of the nation in Ireland. Thus it devotes less attention to nationalist and Unionist leaders than to the social modes of incorporation that enabled the latter to literally build the imagined community of the nation from the ground up. Thus it asks, and seeks to answer, such questions as:

- What were the principal means by which nationalism and Unionism were articulated and disseminated in nineteenth-century Ireland?
- What was the role of the print capitalism in this process?
- How did infrastructural change foster two different senses of 'people-hood' in Catholic nationalist Ireland and Unionist Ulster?
- What were the roles of churches and educational establishments in the 'nationalisation' and 'Unionisation' of people at this time?
- How exactly did these institutions 'imagine' the nation, and how did they consolidate nationalist and Unionist support in the contested terrains of Irish nation-building Ireland?

These questions suggest that the proper starting points for a study of nationalism and Unionism in Ireland are not so much the 'great men' who articulated nationalist ideology, but the lesser 'unsung heroes' of nation-building, including rural and small-town nationalists, priests, nuns, clergymen, bishops, Gaelic language activists, authors of political pamphlets, schoolteachers, local historians, antiquarians and especially all those responsible for the success of the Irish provincial press. In examining the roles of these agencies and agents of nation-building this chapter suggests that the nations to which Irish nationalists and Ulster Protestants aspired were not 'fixed historical givens'. They were what E.P. Thompson called 'historical happenings'. Print capitalism and the provincial press were central pillars of nation-building for Unionist nationalists and Irish national separatists alike. This was because the press allowed the new hegemonic sectors in Irish society to imagine themselves either as an Irish nation, or as part of the much larger imagined community that was Great Britain. Before discussing the specificities of nation-building the section that follows examines the role of print capitalism in fostering different imagined communities of the nation in nineteenth-century Ireland.

Print Capitalism, Social Communication and Nation-building

One way of looking at the history of printed language in Ireland is to fuse its development as a language power and administration with the rise of the nation-building bourgeoisie in the nineteenth century. The new self-consciousness of those comprising this sector of Irish society, coupled with the growth of ethnic solidarities, was fostered by great reading coalitions of newspaper readers chiefly in the course of the latter half of the nineteenth century. Their views on nation-building were often fundamentally different from earlier expressions of nationhood. For a start nationalism now probably penetrated further out into the Irish countryside and deeper down the ranks of Irish society than at any previous time in the country's history. As such a sense of 'nationhood' – what we have termed 'peoplehood' – was not just limited to a disinherited Gaelic aristocracy or to the upper echelons of Anglo-Irish society. It was found within all ranks of Catholic and Protestant society. Before this, hegemonic sectors in Irish society, like the ruling classes in pre-bourgeois Europe, generally generated social cohesion within local as well as trans-national worlds. They generally, but not always, also did so outside the realms of the printed word and print languages. In seventeenth-century Ireland for example, as in pre-modern aristocratic societies in central Europe, these groups tended to construct social solidarities around ties of kinship, personal loyalty and clientship. All this was to change quite dramatically with the hegemonic rise of the national bourgeoisie in the nineteenth century. As Anderson has emphasised, here was a class which was capable of replicating and reproducing itself over time and across space (Anderson, 1983, pp. 68–73). This more than anything else was what made the bourgeoisie, including the petty bourgeoisie, such a unique and revolutionary social class in nation-building Ireland and nation-building Europe. The bourgeoisie in general – Ireland included – was a social class that was fragmented along ethnic and national lines. In nineteenth-century Ireland the Catholic bourgeoisie was more and more distinguishable from the British bourgeoisie in the latter half of the century. By the middle of the century clear lines of demarcation were also emerging between the Protestant bourgeoisie of the north-east and their Catholic counterparts elsewhere in the country. What made these sectors such a revolutionary social force at this stage was the fact that they were the first social class to construct sure-footed social solidarities on an essentially imagined basis. Developments in print capitalism and mass education allowed them to do this. According to Anderson the bourgeoisie invited the masses into history chiefly after the French Revolution. They generally did so with invitation cards written either in the vernacular language or couched, as in Ireland's case, in religious terms. Their revolutions were significant because they were not 'made', or even led, by political parties and leaders in any formal sense. Indeed, until the emergence of the post-revolutionary figure of Napoleon, such movements hardly even threw up revolutionary 'leaders' of the kind with which we in the twentieth century are familiar. However, once the national revolution 'happened' in France it entered 'the accumulating memory of print' elsewhere in western Europe, including Ireland. In the course of time it also got to be transferred, via the printed word, first of all into a concept, and later on into a model of revolution. This meant that other peoples, including small nations like the Irish, the Czechs and the Norwegians, could seek to imitate the nation-building programmes of more powerful societies (Hobsbawm, 1962, p. 164). Thus did new models of revolution emerge all across western Europe. To some extent at least these 'pirated' the programme of nation-building inherent in the more conservative doctrines of the French Revolution. They were increasingly also led by identifiable national leaders or modern national 'patriots'.

In Ireland of course, as in central Europe, it is clearly possible to trace the origins of a national – and sometimes even nationalist – consciousness as far back as the sixteenth and seventeenth

centuries (Leerssen, 1996, pp. 8–32; Poliakov, 1974, pp. 34–62;
Warner, 1983, pp. 65–92). However, central to the Gramscian
approach to nation-building adopted in this study, this chapter
suggests that the rise of nationalism as a popular hegemonising
ideology, an ideology of modernity, meant that it affected not just
upper echelons of Irish and Anglo-Irish society. As the next chapter
will stress, it saturated all aspects of social life in Ireland, particularly in the latter half of the nineteenth century. As such also it was
intimately bound up with the coming of age of the nation-building
bourgeoisie and petty bourgeoisie. In Ireland as elsewhere also the
hegemony of these groups was predicated upon the growth of the
popular press. However, it was also linked to the expansion of
Catholic power in the south and Protestant power in the north-
east of the country. Thus it rested upon the ideological impacts of
print capitalism and the churches on the one hand, and the expansion of denominational mass education on the other.

Newspaper publishing in Ireland as elsewhere in Europe,
however, was first and foremost an industry. National and provincial newspapers were not simply the ideological weapons of the
powerful. They had to be profit-making concerns in their own
right. Yet, because they evolved in close dialectical relationships
with the built environments which spawned them, they helped
shape the regional and ethnic milieus within which they operated.
They also, of course, were shaped by their environments. This was
nowhere more evident than in nation-building Ireland, including
Ulster. Here improvements in reporting and newspaper production
meant that only fairly modest amounts of capital were still
required to set up provincial papers in the immediate aftermath of
the Great Famine. Newspapers then often literally were 'family
affairs'. Significantly, after Catholic Emancipation, a new Irish
press emerged which was ready to develop around nationalist and
religious interests. Thus *The Nation* was founded by Thomas Davis,
Charles Gavan Duffy and John Blake Dillon to explain 'how Irish
nationhood was relevant to contemporary events rather than
simply to the country's vast and romantic history' (Smith, 1979, p.
130). At least 30 new papers were founded before 1850, including
historically important journals like the *Catholic Penny Magazine*
(1834), the *Catholic Guardian* (1851) and Frederick Lucas's influential *Tablet* (1840). In *The Nation* Davis defined the modern nation
in terms of its culture, by which he meant its literature, history
and, above all, its language. He claimed that the modern nation
should 'guard its language more than its territory', claiming that a
people without a language of its own was 'only half a nation'. As

he saw it language served a twofold purpose. On the one hand it could act as a barrier against Anglicisation. Indeed he regarded the language as 'a surer barrier, and more important frontier, than fortress or river'. On the other hand language gave a nation its 'vigour, health and great achievements'. As such it was a way of 'unsaxonising' the mind of the Irish people (Boyce, 1991, p. 156). For Davis insisted that:

> The language which grows up with a people is conformed to their origins, descriptive of their climate, constitution and manners, mingled inseparably with their history and their soul, fitted beyond any other language to express their prevalent thoughts in the most national-efficient way. (Griffith, 1918, pp. 54–5)

To lose one's language and to learn that of another nation was, Davis asserted, 'tantamount to losing one's soul'. The 'alien language', therefore, was nothing short of a 'badge of conquest'. He always insisted on the need for a nation to remember its past, to preserve it and keep it 'holy'. Aware of the fact that too close a remembering of the Irish past could be a divisive force in modern Irish society, he was forced to reconcile his ideals of racial purity with the pluralist origins of modern Irish society. Although he could juxtapose the 'Saxon boor' alongside 'the gallant Irish peasant' when it suited his intentions, he was equally cautious of the need not to 'purify' historical records in Ireland too much. 'AE', as George Russell was known, went further than Davis in insisting that the modern nation transcended such mundane national attributes as language, geographical boundaries, religious outlook and even blood ties. Anticipating Benedict Anderson's conception of the nation as an 'imagined community' by almost a century he stated:

> *A nation exists primarily because of its own imagination of itself.* It is a spirit created by the poets, historians, musicians, by the utterances of great men, the artists in life. The mysterious element of beauty, of a peculiar beauty, exists in every nation and is the root cause of the love felt for it by the citizens, just as the existence of spirit, the most mysterious and impalpable thing, is the fountain of the manifold activities of the body. (Russell, quoted in Boyce, 1991, p. 403; emphasis added)

Quite clearly papers like *The Nation* were ideologically proactive and deeply idealistic – in the modern sense of the term. They were also closely associated with cultural nationalists and nationalist intellectuals. Other papers, not least provincial newspapers, were far more banal affairs which mixed cultural nationalism literally with 'the news'. They were also less likely to be identified with any one, or with a coterie, of nationalist ideologues. They were far more likely to be closely identified with prominent nationalist, or Unionist, business families. They also circulated within highly localised worlds and, because they were owned by prominent members of local communities, they were often the chief channels through which the grassroots bourgeoisie – and petty bourgeoisie – expressed their views on a whole range of issues. They not only discussed philosophies of nation-building and the physiology of national differences, but also covered the full gamut of 'the news', especially socio-economic issues of interest to the modernising sectors of a nation-building society. Not only that, in the north as well as the south of Ireland, they quite literally facilitated the elevation of their opinions to the status of hegemonic and quasi-religious, state-centred ideologies. These in turn were disseminated, through the medium of 'their' newspapers, but also of course from the pulpit, to the literate and semi-literate sectors of Irish Catholic and Ulster Protestant society.

By the close of the nineteenth century, newspaper publishing in Ireland had become a relatively expensive affair. If we leave aside the evanescent radical or 'mosquito' press, newspaper publishing was affordable only to those with substantial amounts of capital. The latter now had to have sufficient funds to pay for their expanding staffs and to invest in new and more expensive capital equipment. In late nineteenth-century England, for example, national dailies often operated with a printing staff of 60 employees or more. They also required up to a dozen parliamentary reporters, half a dozen court reporters, and a small band of expensive foreign correspondents scattered throughout the capitals of Europe. In addition to this they had to have a whole crew of provincial reporters and local correspondents. The situation in Ireland, however, was somewhat different in that newspapers here were truly provincial. As recently as the mid-nineteenth century even national papers could be considered 'local' in that they circulated chiefly in and around the 'Pale' of Dublin. They never had near so many foreign correspondents, or such extensive retinues of well-paid reporters, as did their English counterparts. Nevertheless Irish newspapers were by no means simply appendages of a printing industry operating in strict accordance with the principles of laissez faire capitalism. From the start they were, as we have already suggested, pillars of nation-building and important organs of nationalist and Unionist opinion. Given the regionalised social environments within which they operated, it seemed inevitable that they would function as organs of nation-building. In so doing they also performed important integrative functions in Irish society.

They provided the communicative cement which linked together the dispersed bourgeoisie while simultaneously binding them to 'their' communities in great 'reading coalitions'. Given the social contexts within which they evolved it seemed inevitable also that they would adopt either a nationalist or Unionist 'mission civilatrice' by knitting together Protestant Ulster on the one hand, and Catholic nationalist Ireland on the other. This is another way of saying that newspapers were means of social communication and social modes of incorporation. They quite literally shaped the ideological environments of the communities they served. In nation-building Ireland they effectively made it possible for new forms of socio-economic and political activity to come to the fore. Perhaps even more so than in provincial England, newspapers in post-Famine Ireland 'planted in the mind of the individual literate citizen the picture of a world of public events which he could never see or experience for himself' (Smith, 1979, p. 13). In so doing the provincial press helped scatter the seeds of a new form of community, an imagined community, in nation-building Ireland. They literally relocated Catholic Ireland in the modern world of nation-building, while, in the north-east, Protestant newspapers sought to keep Unionist Ulster within the 'historic nation' of the United Kingdom.

'Respectable' and petty bourgeois newspapers in Ireland as elsewhere in western Europe were also engaged in a common defence of the rights of 'propertied' men. They vindicated the rights of Irishmen to own property while simultaneously defending landed property against real or potential attacks from 'unpropertied classes' supported by the radical or 'mosquito' press. This caused a break in the radical tradition of newspaper publishing in Ireland which hastened the demise of the 'unstamped' press and contributed to the marginalisation of the 'mosquito' press. As revolutionary organs which sought to create political frenzy among plebeian sectors of Irish society, radical newspapers often found themselves cut off from the parliamentary tradition in Irish nation-building that was supported by the provincial press in late nineteenth-century Ireland. Here, however, perfectly 'respectable' Catholic newspapers, not least in Protestant Unionist Ulster, were considered constitutionally radical. This was because they challenged ascendancy rule in Ireland and openly advocated the 'breakup' of Britain at a time when it was widely considered

unthinkable that small nationalities should have a separate existence outside a powerful nation like the United Kingdom. They
were deemed all the more radical because they advocated tenant
rights in a country where the landed ascendancy still monopolised
the right to own, and dispose of, property on their own terms.
Here, therefore, the popular press championed the political and
economic rights of Irish tenant farmers, not those of the political
establishment, and certainly not those of the landed aristocracy.
They defended fixity of tenure and pressed for the rights of tenant
farmers to own property, to rent land at fair prices, and to pass it
on to their offspring without undue interference from landlords or
middlemen. Indeed, by the late nineteenth century, provincial
newspapers throughout the south and west of the country were
strongly defending the right of the rural middle classes to run
Ireland. Thus they were the medium through which substantial
farmers defended their right to control the economy and manage
the country's affairs in their interest, not those of the landed elite.

As profit-making concerns in their own right, provincial newspapers, like other publishing concerns, were also catering to the
cultural and ideological demands of an increasingly literate population in nation-building Ireland. Here as elsewhere in Europe the
new papers that emerged in the course of the latter half of the
nineteenth century did not simply come into existence champi-
oning nationalist causes. They catered to a whole variety of other
social needs and opinions. In particular they articulated the worldviews, the cultural and economic interests, of new men of wealth
in Irish society. Because print capitalism in Ireland evolved within
the womb of a class-structured and ethnically divided society, it
fulfilled a range of functions which contributed to the development of national consciousness by articulating and supporting
Unionist and nationalist agendas. These newspapers, whether
nationalist or Unionist, literally nationalised the means of communication. They allowed peoples to imagine themselves as part of a
nation, or more accurately as part of two opposing versions of the
nation as an 'imagined community' in Ireland. They did this in the
dual sense of making English the language of these new imagined
communities, while simultaneously fostering the development of
more unified fields of communication in the north and south of
Ireland. Hence provincial newspapers 'equipped' communities
with the means to 'frame' themselves, to tell their own stories and
to write their own histories. Here as elsewhere in western Europe
they allowed them to store, recall, transmit and replicate a whole
range of information that went into the making of the successful

'imagined community' of the nation in Ireland (Anderson, 1983, pp. 44–5).

In so doing newspapers facilitated the development of new and much wider forms of community here by putting ordinary people 'in touch' with each other, and by permitting them to have a common sense of history and a complimentary image of themselves either as 'Irish people' or as 'successful' Ulster Unionists. In the end, indeed, they helped transform community life into national life by locating local communities in national, even multi-national, communities. As a revolutionary new means of social communication, the Irish provincial newspapers, whether in the north or in the south of Ireland, gave people the memories, the symbols and the habits that constituted the essence of nationalist and Unionist communities. As a means of social communication that was also under the influence of the churches, newspapers foisted a new mission civilatrice on nation-building Ireland. They did this, not least, by inviting readers to take part in the historic act of nation-building. They gave subordinate sectors in Irish society a sense of 'peoplehood', a sense of belonging to large groups that were linked together – within Ireland or to the United Kingdom – by shared political outlooks and common cultural habits. It was not just a question of members of the nation being united by common ties of religion, language and historical experience. Newspapers made people feel that they were also united in the present in great religious and ethnic collectivities. They tied people together in reading coalitions that were quasi-secular counterparts of the great praying coalitions that priests and church ministers helped to construct in 'their' parishes.

Hegel has argued that newspapers served modern man 'as a substitute for morning prayers'. This was not the case in Catholic nationalist Ireland or Unionist Ulster. Here the mass ceremony of attending church and reading the newspaper 'in the lair of the skull', as it were, helped foster two competing and diametrically opposed versions of the imagined community that were deeply rooted in the religious and social life of two quite different parts of the country. Far from acting as substitutes for religion, newspapers often were extensions of highly politicised faiths and dogmas. Observing exact replicas of his own paper being read by his neighbours down the street or across the field, the newspaper reader in Catholic Ireland and Unionist Ulster was continually reassured that his imagined world 'was visibly rooted in everyday life' (Anderson, 1983, pp. 35–6). The high levels of religious influence over reading material, as over education and popular culture, transformed many here into defenders of 'the faith' as well as defenders of 'the nation'. Thus in Ireland as in a number of other European countries – e.g. Spain, Portugal, Poland, Hungary and Tsarist Russia – nationalism was a state-centred ideology which fused with, but most certainly did not replace, religion in the lives of ordinary people.

To explain nations in terms of shared experiences and shared history, however, is to explain them away. People in nineteenth-century Ireland as elsewhere in Europe were never automatically united by 'shared experiences' unless they were in some sense already united through a variety of means of social communication (Deutsch, 1966, p. 19). This is what the provincial and national press and the churches helped the bourgeoisie – and petty bourgeoisie – to achieve. When Ernest Renan (1882, p. 12) referred to the 'possession in common of a rich heritage of memories' and 'a heritage of glory and grief' he captured the two essential elements that also went into the making of the 'soul' of the nation in Catholic Ireland and Unionist Ulster. Newspapers quite literally equipped people in the north and south of post-Famine Ireland with the means to share experiences, to interpret as well as claim the past, and to look to the future with optimism and pride. They simultaneously urged ordinary people to make history in national form rather than simply remaining subjects of other people's histories. In fostering national consciousness newspapermen, like the clergy, also assigned new values to people in nation-building Ireland and Ulster. Catholic newspapers in particular opposed the offensive simianisation of the Irish in English periodicals. This does not mean, however, that they took Irish people for what they were. They reinvented them by continuously exhorting them to become more than what they were. They also stressed their 'worth' as a people by defending the 'worthiness' of national self-determination within Ireland or, as in the case of Ulster Unionists, within the United Kingdom.

Fundamental changes brought about by industrial, commercial and agricultural revolutions in the north and south of Ireland helped people to realise their own immense learning capacities at this time. Their national leaders taught them to appreciate their vast abilities for adaptation to physical as well as social change, and to re-evaluate their powers of discovery, creation and initiative (Deutsch, 1966, p. 179). Thus did Irish nationalism and Ulster Unionism help transform social lethargy into political action in nation-building Ireland. Provincial newspapers in particular transmuted the meaningless fatalities of daily life in local areas into the meaningful continuities of Irish nationalist and British Unionist histories. Even where they were 'new', the nations to which these expressions of nationalism gave voice always appeared to rise Phoenix-like out of an immemorial nationalist or Unionist past. The sense of nationhood which they sought to defend offered hope, and promised security, to the inhabitants of this new Ireland and new Ulster. The nation here, as Anderson noted, always seemed to glide off into 'a blissful and limitless future'. This too helped shatter the narrow parochialisms that characterised Irish, including Ulster, life in earlier centuries. In their place were created two readily identifiable and reasonably well-unified fields of social communication and social exchange. One of these was centred in the Unionist north-east. By the second half of the nineteenth century the expansion of industry here rendered it a place apart from rural Catholic nation-building Ireland. From then on this region identified more and more closely with the 'imagined community' of the British nation and the empire. The rest of Ireland constituted another, albeit 'looser', field of social communication. Here, as in the north-east, print capitalism and the Catholic church also helped foster the development of new regional and national solidarities. These were by no means socially homogenous but drew their members from a whole variety of social class and regional backgrounds.

Hroch has argued that the classic national movement catered to three main demands corresponding to perceived deficits of national existence. These included the development of a national culture; the achievement of civil rights and political self-administration; and, most important of all, the creation of a complete social structure from out of the ethnic group. The latter included, among others, educated elites, a professional intelligentsia, a national bureaucracy, an entrepreneurial class, independent farmers, organised workers and a range of other, more subordinate, social groups (Hroch, 1985, pp. 23–31). By the late nineteenth century the ethnic collectivities of the north and south of Ireland had certainly matured into these complete social structures and social formations. Nationalism and Unionism here were state-centred in the sense that they sought to create or maintain relatively new imagined communities as nations in Ireland. They also nurtured intra-class or 'vertical' relationships within each of these ethnic collectivities, while simultaneously fostering a 'horizontal' or inter-regional sense of comradeship and citizenship in the nation. They gave their adherents a new sense of purpose, a sense of identity, and a new national sense of place.

In selecting English as the commercially viable 'hegemonising' language of Catholic nationalist Ireland and Unionist Ulster, nation-builders rendered this the language of the nation. In so doing they also sought to make it comprehensible to whole new sections of the reading public, not least in the Atlantic fringe of Ireland, and Ulster, where many still spoke Irish down into the closing decades of the nineteenth century. Even then, however, newspapers were a medium of communication which allowed the more prosperous in these communities to 'imagine' themselves as a progressive community. It was not so much the language, or the nationalist message, that mattered most here, but the medium itself. English language newspapers, like popular nationalist histories, political pamphlets and even romantic novels, permitted newly emerging hegemonic groups to communicate both with each other and, more importantly, with those 'below them', often for the first time. That is what we mean when we say that they created 'reading republics' in the ethnicised landscapes of nationalist Ireland and Unionist Ulster. As we have already seen they provided the social cement which held together the country's integrated fields of social communication.

Seeing themselves as gods in the lands over which they presided, newspapermen, priests, ministers and other members of the petty bourgeoisie, strenuously devoted themselves to bringing national civic order out of the social and natural chaos that they encountered in post-Famine Ireland. They insisted that they should lead 'their' people because they could not lead themselves. These groups did not allow themselves to be ground down or tainted by the 'savagery' and 'uncouthness' which they considered were the hallmarks of the rural backwaters and inner-city slums of nation-building Ireland and Ulster. Discussing the 'civilising' role of literacy and the spread of popular culture through newspapers in the nineteenth century, Raymond Williams has suggested that the general extension of printed matter through the press at this time can in one way be regarded as an 'extension'. However, it also had qualitative aspects to it. This was because the true potential of the newspaper industry, and the printing technology which supported it, also led to significant 'internal hierarchies' in the edifices of popular culture. Thus, he added:

> The most serious cultural creation and the most authoritative social knowledge were 'in print'. Access to literacy was determined and directed by institutions formed on these assumptions. 'Correctness', even in the matter of speaking a native language, was similarly deter-

mined. Relative social position and relative command of this skill became regularly associated. Thus the qualitative nature of the expansion (of printed matter) was to an important extent controlled and was never a merely neutral extension. (Williams, 1981, p. 109)

In Ireland the mission civilatrice of the national bourgeoisie appeared to depend on their access to printed matter, especially to the means for distributing and reproducing it on a grand and national scale through the medium of newspapers, and through the churches. It was as if the struggle to master the frontiers of nation-building here was intimately associated on the one hand with ownership of the means of cultural reproduction, and on the other with a quest to escape perdition and to save souls from the fires of an anti-nationalist hell, and from the evils of a banal modernity (Pike, 1997, p. 2). Whether they were farming the land or taming the passions of peasants or inner-city slum dwellers, nationalist and Unionist leaders alike used newspapers, and the pulpit, to 'do God's work'. To these men virtue, including such fruits of virtue as ownership of property, national advancement and economic aggrandisement, depended upon 'good husbandry', hard work, attention to industry, and the systematic and concentrated exploitation of land and labour in a modern nation-state. That was why the language that evolved from print capitalism in Ireland at this time also expressed the social and political interests of the dominant sectors of Irish society. By the close of the century the ideological outlook of these hegemonic groups became the characteristic thinking of society in general in both parts of the country. This was because newspapers allowed for the dissemination of Unionist and nationalist ideology at the local as well as the national market. They provided the means whereby the ideas of ethnically distinct and challenging collectivities got to be fixed and passed on from one generation to the other. This, as much as anything else, gave these ideologies a solidity, and in Ulster a staunchness, which the worldviews of working-class people and the rural poor often seemed to lack.

Press and Nation in Catholic Ireland

There is little doubt that the arrival of the popular press in Ireland as elsewhere in western Europe was widely regarded as a disturbing development. The dissemination of new expressions of popular culture through the medium of newspapers here posed a threat to the high Victorianism of the Anglo-Irish ascendancy. These new cultural expressions, whether in the press or in the church, lacked the authenticity that came with age and time-honoured tradition. Nevertheless, they succeeded in literally 'up-staging' aristocratic values and marginalising the views of the landed ascendancy. Thus the rise of the popular press in Ireland was a cause of alarm to traditional political elites, especially to the relics of the landed ascendancy. In Britain the popular press was the medium through which the nouveau riche thrown up by the industrial revolution battered at the door of aristocratic privilege. Stressing the centrality of newspapers to the rise of the English bourgeoisie, Disraeli once remarked that 'God made man in his own image, but the public is made by newspapers, excise officers and Poor Law Guardians'. A character in one of his novels insisted that 'opinion is now supreme, and opinion speaks in print'. Lord Lyton believed that newspapers embodied 'the prejudice, the passion and the sectarian bigotry that belong to one body of men engaged in active opposition to another'. As such, he added, they expressed 'the truth, the errors and the good and the bad opinion' which they represented (quoted in Lee, 1980, p. 22). In the modernising environment of post-Famine Ireland newspapers, as we have already seen, were at once a democratising and a nation-building force. They were vehicles of national and nationalist communication.

Williams has argued that the point at which ownership of the means of reproduction of popular culture, including newspapers, becomes lodged in the hands of a powerful minority is an important watershed in the political progress of any society. In nineteenth-century Ireland the social and political effects of ownership of the means of propagating, reproducing and distributing nationalist culture through the medium of newspapers, and from the pulpit, were tremendous indeed. In rural Catholic Ireland, as in Unionist Ulster, provincial papers were used to foster 'politically correct' as well as morally uplifting ideological outlooks. They censured some worldviews and privileged others; they helped to control, channel and direct nationalist and Unionist culture. As Williams has argued, the history of newspapers, in the nineteenth century in particular, reveals very high levels of pre-selection of material for massive reproduction (Williams, 1981, p. 106). This helped reduce costs of newspaper production, just as it helped to form a market within which individual choice was displaced by ruling class ideology disguised as majority decision. This enabled those who controlled newspapers, and their markets, to literally bring others in behind them. Marx recognised as much when he wrote:

> The ideas of the ruling class are in every epoch the ruling ideas: i.e., the class which is the ruling material force of society, is at the same time its ruling intellectual force. The class which has the means of material production at its disposal, has control at the same time over the means of mental production, so that thereby, generally speaking, the ideas of those who lack the means of mental production are subject to it. The ruling ideas are nothing more than the ideal expression of the dominant material relationships, grasped as ideas; hence of relationships which make the one class the ruling one, therefore the ideas of its dominance. (Marx, 1974, p. 142)

As it stands this statement suggests that it was the personal power of the ruling class rather than the market forces and structural determinants that rendered theirs the hegemonic ideas of society in general. That is why it is important to stress the all-important structural conditions which favoured the dominance of the ruling class, particularly in the nineteenth century. A whole range of factors facilitated this process, including capital requirements for entry into the publishing industry; size and profitability of newspaper catchment areas; structural links between the publishing industry and other sectors of economy; and institutional relationships of the printing industry with major political parties and powerful social groups.

In whole areas of nation-building Ireland, particularly in disadvantaged rural communities, that ideological dominance was also ensured by the fact that priests, clergymen and schoolteachers derived from the rural bourgeoisie and were often the only mediators between the poor and the ruling class. Print capitalism scarcely made any direct impact upon these subordinate sectors of Irish society. Here it was the clergy and national schoolteachers who constructed the imagined community of the nation. Here also they performed the integrative nation-building roles that newspapers accomplished elsewhere in the country. Priests and church ministers in particular not only policed the morals and the politics of their communities. They so mixed political proselytising with religious and moral instruction that their captive congregations must have found it difficult to know where religious instruction left off and political proselytising began. In so doing these professions greatly extended the appeal of nation-building by bringing isolated rural communities within new national fields of social communication. They literally bound 'their' congregations together, and to each other, while simultaneously linking them with the larger regional and national political and moral systems over which the nation-building bourgeoisie presided. As the chapter that follows shows, the clergy, and the clergy alone, very often were the only arbiters of 'good' political behaviour and 'correct' moral practice in isolated parishes along the Atlantic fringe of Ireland. Their word quite literally was 'gospel', both in a political and spiritual sense. Other ideals, including those who promulgated them, were banished to the outer margins of public opinion. Those who expressed them were often roundly condemned as traitors to the causes of nationalism in the contested terrains of nation-building Ireland.

In Ireland, as in England, Scotland and Wales, the great age of the popular press, for dailies as well as weeklies and national as well as provincial papers, was the period between 1830 and 1890. The most striking feature of Irish newspapers before then was that they circulated in extremely limited numbers and in geographically restricted areas. Judged by modern standards, the individual and the combined output of the press in Ireland before this was extremely small (Munter, 1967, p. 87). There were certainly qualitative and quantitative differences between newspapers published in Ireland in the late eighteenth century compared to those published in the nineteenth century. Unlike in England where newspapers expanded rapidly in the late eighteenth century, prospering both in London and in the provinces, in Ireland only the Dublin journals flourished at this time. The provincial newspapers appeared chiefly at the end of that century and they did not cover the entire country until well into the nineteenth century. As Munter suggests, the explanation is simple enough – Ireland was an impoverished country with a mixed Gaelic and English-speaking society. As such it had a comparatively small reading public. All this was to change around the middle of the nineteenth century when provincial papers flourished all across Ulster and cropped up also in the county towns and agricultural heartlands of southern Ireland. Related to this – and equally important for their success – was the fact that the means for distributing local newspapers greatly improved throughout the latter half of the nineteenth century. Roads were better, railways had developed, newsagents flourished and there were more shops for distributing national and local papers.

As early as the 1760s newspapers in Ireland, especially in the south but also the north-east, were already revealing an increasing concern with Anglo-Irish affairs. This gained impetus alongside a

more general anxiety about freedom of the press and the development of a 'journalistic remonstrance' against English policy in
Ireland. It was not until the mid-nineteenth century, however, that
Irish newspapers began to 'grow up' in the sense of having a
nation-wide distribution and taking an interest in national, and
nationalist, affairs. By that time they were certainly playing an
integral role in the lives of a large body of readers, including town
dwellers, the substantial tenantry and the emergent working class.
In the countryside at large, as we have already seen, they provided
the social cement which knit local communities together. More
significantly still, and despite the earlier ban on printing parliamentary proceedings for much of the eighteenth century,
newspapers were also becoming important agents in the political
education of the reading publics of Ireland and Ulster. By the close
of the eighteenth and the first few decades of the nineteenth
century the cry 'freedom of the press' was added to Irish journalistic vocabulary. By then it was the subject of numerous essays and
political publications. By then also it was clear that Irish newspapers had moved from their first tentative utterances about 'English
misrule' in Ireland to becoming forces for national social and political change. By then also newspaper editors believed it was their
duty to subject the Irish parliament, indeed all politics, to journalistic investigation and to influence decisions by arousing public
interest. Munter suggests that the whole issue of press freedom in
Ireland at this time symbolised:

> a development of great significance, for the newspapers themselves were
> becoming active forces in promoting the political education of the
> public. It was by the medium of the newspaper that ... political news
> travelled quickly, rapidly communicating Dublin events and sentiments
> to provincial areas; for the first time in Ireland something like a modern
> organ of public opinion existed, and for the first time agitation on a
> national scale was feasible. (Munter, 1967, p. 188)

Almost one hundred new papers were issued here between 1830
and 1890. This works out at an average of almost two new titles per
annum. The number of dailies rose from three in 1831 to 19 in
1887. Indeed by the latter decade of the century Ireland was saturated with newspapers. Just as the national population was
declining rapidly through migration and emigration, the number
of newspapers being published here began to increase in leaps and
bounds. In the 1830s there was around one paper per 100,000
inhabitants. By 1890 the equivalent was one per 30,000. These are

very crude estimates indeed but they do point to the fact that Ireland by then had developed into two well-defined and well-integrated fields of social communication, one in the north-east dominated by the Unionist press, the other extending throughout the rest of the country which was more and more under the influence of the Irish nationalist press.

The greatest period of growth in the Irish provincial press occurred in the 1860s. This was when punitive duties were removed from newspapers and taxes were removed from advertising. This in turn meant that newspapers now entered a new phase of mass circulation, particularly in the north-east and in agricultural heartlands and market towns of the south and west of Ireland. They advertised prices of farm produce, set new national social as well as economic standards, expressed the grievances of their readerships, and, outside the north-east at least, gradually articulated an achievable rural capitalist alternative to landed ascendancy rule in post-Famine Ireland. Equally important, the press at this time challenged the highly racist and simianised image of the Irish people in English newspapers and periodicals. Practically for the first time in modern history they proclaimed the Irish a 'civil' people, a people fit for self-government, a people who belonged within the nation-building world on their own terms, not on those of the United Kingdom.

For much of the pre-Famine period print capitalism was very much an urban-based affair requiring relatively little capital. By the last quarter of the century a number of influential provincial papers were already well established. In the west and south of Ireland these included the *Sligo Champion*, the *Connaught Telegraph*, the *Roscommon Herald*, the *Anglo-Celt*, the *Munster Express* and the *Cork Examiner*. These papers linked the petty bourgeoisie of the west with those of the midlands and the east coast. Then between 1880 and 1900 a whole group of new provincial papers were established in the midlands, including the *Leinster Leader*, the *Midlands Tribune*, the *Westmeath Examiner*, the *Kilkenny People* and the *Drogheda Independent*. Even before the Home Rule crisis of the 1880s the north-east already had a whole network of local newspapers. These included the *Londonderry Sentinel*, the *Ballymena Observer*, the *Tyrone Constitution*, the *Ulster Gazette* and the *Impartial Reporter*. Between 1880 and 1900 the *Irish News*, the *Mid-Ulster Mail* and the *Tyrone Courier* were added to this list. Taken as a whole these papers carved out the north-east as a regionally distinctive field of social communication presided over by Protestant landlords, strong farmers, merchants, industrialists and businessmen.

Unlike most pre-Famine newspapers, many of these papers had high levels of circulation and relatively low closure rates. One study of the survival rate of 74 newspaper companies in Ireland between 1856 and 1865 found that 29 aborted after less than one year, 21 lasted between one and four years, and only 7 lasted over 20 years. The nominal capitals of newspaper companies in England at this time were probably not that different to Irish newspapers. In the 1850s 85 per cent of such companies were operating with capital sums of less than £10,000, including 5 per cent operating with sums ranging from a couple of hundred to just over 500 pounds. By the mid-1880s, however, most newspaper companies were operating with much higher levels of nominal capital. The nominal capital of a third of all companies then was over £10,000, including just under 4 per cent with nominal capitals in excess of £100,000 (Lee, 1980, pp. 54–9). Given the fairly small amounts of nominal capital required, it seems safe to suggest that newspaper publishing in Ireland also was by no means beyond the reach of men of modest means, in other words to those who identified with, and often derived from, the substantial tenantry and the urban middle classes.

The largely Tory press which linked Ireland to the wider world of Britain and the empire still circulated in the narrow markets of English-speaking Ireland right down to the beginning of the nineteenth century. These papers were distributed by 'runners', by post and by carriages, usually of the horse-drawn variety. All this was to change dramatically in the post-Famine period. It was then that new more efficient transportation networks emerged and new social classes emerged both in the north-east and in the rest of the country. Henceforth the spread of newspapers was intimately tied up with the hegemonic rise of the bourgeoisie and petty bourgeois ideology and the spread of roads, railways and country shops. Capital, including Irish capital, was now also available in larger quantities for establishing English-speaking Irish newspapers in Ireland. Increases in the numbers attending school and able to read and write in the English language gave these newspapers a wider and deeper circulation than those published in pre-Famine Ireland. Visitors to Ireland at this time repeatedly remarked upon these 'improvements' taking place in education. What they failed to see was that these same improvements were preparing the way for new forms, and new scales, of the 'imagined community' in the north and south of Ireland. By the 1840s and 1850s *The Nation*, operating with a staff of 28 employees, was selling between 4,000 and 7,000 issues. Meanwhile the *Freeman's Journal* was selling approximately

8,500 copies. By the early 1880s Parnell's *United Ireland* was selling as many as 44,000 copies (Hoppen, 1984, p. 458). Not only that, the numbers reading cheap editions of nationalist books, street ballads and pamphlets was also on the increase. By the 1880s many observers in rural Ireland were also struck by the ubiquity of cheap editions of the writings of Charles Kickham, Thomas Davis and T.D. Sullivan, the literary champions of popular nationalism and nationalist culture. By then nationalist reading rooms were spreading out all over the country. These were attracting audiences which were more literate and literally more 'sophisticated' than ever before. All this meant that the strong localisms of the pre-Famine period were now progressively eroded or gradually incorporated into a much wider, more coherent world of nation-building, both in the Unionist north-east and in the Catholic nationalist south and west of the country. Thus increases in news-paper circulation kept pace with the development of new forms of the imagined community in both parts of nation-building Ireland.

By the closing decade of the century proprietors of Irish news-papers were also prominent political leaders and constituted a significant proportion of Nationalist members in the English House of Commons. In 1895 no less than eleven members of the Irish Nationalist Party in the English House of Commons were proprietors of newspapers in Ireland. For these men newspapers were a way into politics, a way of ensuring their election, and a medium for extending the causes of nationalism by bringing as many sectors of the local community behind nation-building proj-ects as possible. Newspapers like *The Nation* and the *Galway Vindicator* were now being read, and run, by people from pros-perous farming backgrounds and the local shopocracy. This meant that Irish rural society was far more open than ever before to the influence of the printed word, especially the press. By the last quarter of the century most towns of any size were capable of supporting two or three newspapers catering to the needs of those living in their hinterlands. These included, for example, Enniskillen, Tralee, Cavan and Monaghan. Indeed places often became towns through their possession of a local newspaper. Thus, writing about Mohill in county Leitrim in 1847, Anthony Trollope stated:

> The idea that would strike one on entering it was chiefly this: why was it a town at all? Why were there, on that spot, so many houses congre-gated called Mohill? What was the inducement to people to come and live there? Mohill is by no means the only town in the west of Ireland

that strikes one as being without a cause. (*Macdermotts of Ballycloran*, 1847, Oxford, 1989, quoted in Legg, 1999)

A decade later Mohill had its own paper, the *Leitrim Gazette* which advertised 'General news of markets, proceedings of local institutions, railway and other public boards [and] reviews of books'.

In the country as a whole the numbers of people able to read papers increased alongside increases in the percentage of children attending school. The latter went from just under 25 per cent in 1841 to almost 60 per cent 40 years later. It was this increasingly Anglicised and literate society which provided the growing audience for newspapers of all kinds. It would be wrong, however, to suggest that the press then was simply a vehicle for nationalist opinion. It has been estimated that half the 'political' papers in Ireland in 1834 were vehicles for Tory opinion. Even as late as 1870 just under half were Tory papers. By then, however, the nationalist press had become highly influential, even if it was not always nationalistic in the sense of disseminating nationalist opinion. As Hoppen remarks, the press at this time:

> must be seen not simply as the engine of nationalist opinion, but as the reinforcer as much as the creator of the tribal political loyalties of Irish society in general. Indeed, what it was most successful in disseminating was not so much nationalism as the metropolitan culture of Dublin and indirectly that of London too. (Hoppen, 1984, p. 458)

In her nation-centred study of the Irish provincial press Legg divides the post-Famine period into three distinct periods (Legg, 1999). Each of these, she suggests, marked the maturation of nationalist and national consciousness in Ireland. Although this periodisation is of doubtful relevance to the quite different social history of the north-east of Ireland, it nevertheless maps out the role of the press in informing national consciousness in rural Catholic Ireland at least. To select the Famine as a watershed in the evolution of the popular press is to immediately indicate that it is national separatism that is being discussed here. Without denying the undoubted effects of the Famine in Ulster, it could be argued that it is a far less useful watershed in studying the politics and social history of the provincial press in the more industrialised and far more urbanised north-east of the country. In dividing the post-Famine half of the nineteenth century into three discrete periods, Legg maps out three stages in the evolution of nationalism-as-national-separatism in Catholic nation-building Ireland. However, she does this in such a way as to suggest the inevitable triumph of small-nation nationalism under the sponsorship of a Catholic provincial press. She completely ignores the anti-separatism of the very important provincial press of Ulster.

The first period in Legg's classification extends from 1850 to 1865. This, she argues, was dominated by 'a desire for atonement in the wake of the Famine and the need to remodel Ireland in a new image'. The second extends from 1865 to 1879 and was said to be remarkable for the birth of 'the emergent nation and the rise of Fenianism and the Home Rule movement'. The third period begins in 1879 and ends in 1890. It witnessed the Land War, the emergence of a radical press, the birth of the 'militant nation' and more and more coercion against the provincial press in Catholic nationalist Ireland. Unionist papers in the Protestant north-east were never considered politically subversive in the way that the Catholic nationalist press was. They were of course equally nation-alistic as the latter. That Catholic papers operated with state-centred and nationalist agendas is clear from their 'mission statements'. In 1850 the *Waterford Chronicle* outlined its political mission as follows:

> To re-model the young mind of Ireland ... to elevate the social and moral condition of this island – to aid her in redeeming her lost char-acter, and to restore both her and her natives to some noble position in the scale of nations and of society. (Quoted in Legg, 1999, p. 21)

In May 1844 the *Belfast Vindicator* argued:

> The newspaper is nowadays what the preacher was some 200–300 years ago. It is the guide, counsellor and friend. It is our best moral police. It exposes abuses, unmasks jobs, censures vice, lashes tyranny ... in all free countries it is the great agent of political education, the chief bulwark of liberty and the most active pioneer of public intelligence. (Quoted in Legg, 1999, p. 51)

Provincial papers like these were not considered as subsidiary or even inferior to the national press. They not only performed essen-tial roles in the development of national consciousness. They also pointed to the different varieties of nationalist thought and the different concerns of nationalist and Unionist nation-builders. Gladstone argued that the local press was a 'great instrument of power ... which forcibly altered the vision of Ireland and ... helped create a new self-image of Ireland in the next century' (Legg, 1999, p. 175). Archbishop Croke constantly referred to the role of the press in the 'improvement of our national character'. As he saw it the provincial press was 'an auxiliary to a national movement'. These ideals also underlay the philosophy of those who ran the press from the late 1860s up to the eve of the Land War. Moriarty, Bishop of Kerry, writing to William Monsell MP in March 1868 stated:

> The minds of the Irish people are in the hands of the Irish priests. They have a platform where no other voice is heard. They have a press which supports their views. Their newspapers are extensively read, and the people read no other ... the clergy are the intermediate class between the gentry and the people. (Quoted in Legg, 1999, p. 72)

As Legg rightly points out, the new men who entered provincial journalism after 1860 came with the fixed purpose of having a voice in politics. Growing numbers of nationalists saw journalism as a respectable way to live because, unlike landowning and shop-keeping, it did not depend on exploiting others (note altruism) and unlike the law it could not be seen as supporting the government. Newspapers, Legg suggests, were 'part of the theatre of the nation' in Ireland. They were 'the signal to the local residents, to tradesmen, to visitors that their town, their county is of distinct importance' (Legg, 1999, p. 172). She fails to emphasise that, in the north-east of Ireland, local papers were theatres where Irish national separatism was vehemently rejected, where the Union was defended, and where a quite different and less anomalous conception of the nineteenth-century nation was articulated.

8 Pamphlet Wars and Provincial Newspapers in Protestant Ulster

A Protestant Press for a Protestant People

As we have already seen, Legg's account of the provincial newspapers in post-Famine Ireland emphasises the centrality of the press to the nation-building process – but only in Catholic nationalist Ireland. In adopting an Irish nation-centred approach to the history of the provincial press in Ireland she completely ignores the role of the provincial press in promoting Unionist nationalism in Protestant Ulster. Yet, even before the Famine, this part of the country arguably had the most well-developed provincial press in the country. As we have already seen, it certainly constituted a quite distinctive field of social communication. It had its own network of provincial papers, its own style of political reportage, its own 'reading publics', and its own provincial catchment area broken down into smaller areas within which provincial newspapers flourished. In focusing exclusively upon Catholic Ireland, Legg's study treats Unionist Ulster as if it did not exist or did not possess a provincial press that strongly opposed Irish nationalism but staunchly supported its own brand of Unionist nationalism. Given the vibrancy of the provincial press in late nineteenth-century Ulster this is a strange omission indeed.

Taken together, mid-Ulster and east Ulster in particular possessed some of the leading provincial newspapers in the country. It has often been remarked that this region was ethnically and economically distinct from the rest of Catholic nationalist Ireland, including the Catholic west of Ulster. For that reason it also constituted a different and well-integrated field of social communication in an otherwise Catholic nation-building Ireland. Conservative papers like the *Belfast Newsletter*, the *Ballymena Observer*, the *Coleraine Constitution*, the *Londonderry Standard*, the *Sentinel*, the *Fermanagh Times*, the *Mid-Ulster Mail* and the *Ulster Gazette* effectively forged Ulster Protestants into separate reading publics that were strongly supportive of the Union and passionately opposed to Irish Home Rule. The Press Directory or official monitor of newspaper opinion and influence in Ireland in the 1850s through to the 1880s constantly referred to the fact that many local papers here were leading advocates of 'loyalty to the Throne and maintenance of the Union'. The *Banner of Ulster*, the organ of the General Assembly of the Presbyterian Church, upheld 'the opinions of all the Evangelical Protestant Dissenters in Ireland'. Throughout the 1870s the conservative Belfast *Evening Telegraph* devoted itself to 'questions affecting the moral and social conditions of the working classes'. The *Belfast News-Letter*, another leading conservative journal which circulated throughout the province, was an advocate of the industrial, agricultural and commercial interests of Ulster. The *Belfast Weekly Telegraph*, which also circulated throughout Ulster, devoted itself to 'the development of sound Protestant and Constitutional opinions, the advancement of religion among the masses, and the cultivation of freedom and independence among its readers'. By the mid-nineteenth century the *Fermanagh Mail* had already adopted as its motto 'The Crown and the people not a class'. The *Fermanagh Reporter*, which also circulated in Tyrone, Cavan, Monaghan and Leitrim, defended the 'common Protestantism of the Reformation'.

These and other Protestant papers mapped out the ideological contours of Protestant Ulster in Catholic nation-building Ireland. There was a remarkable congruence between their catchment areas and the political boundaries of loyalist Ulster. Unlike in Unionist enclaves in the south of Ireland, the Unionist press here – whether Liberal Unionist or Conservative Unionist – was read by a whole cross-section of Protestant society, not just by the landed ascendancy. Thus these newspapers were not just organs of ascendancy rule that operated in the interests of landed elites. Because they were read in Unionist reading rooms and distributed by Protestant newsagents throughout the north-east they percolated into the plebeian worlds of Protestant small farmers and the urban working class. They were widely read by the petty bourgeoisie and also reflected the interests of the respectable Presbyterian middle classes. They particularly helped create the inter-class and inter-regional reading republics. The latter not only set Ulster Unionists apart from Irish nationalists – they equipped them with ideological tools with which to establish Unionist hegemony and defend the territorial integrity of the United Kingdom in Protestant Ulster. The provincial press here gave northern Protestants an Ulster identity and allowed them to construct images of themselves as defenders of civilisation against the Balkanising evils of Irish nationalism. This meant that hegemonic sectors both within Ulster and in

Britain had a very effective machine for channelling anti-Home Rule agitation in northern Ireland. From the 1880s Protestant papers constructed Irish nationalists as 'political wreckers' hell bent on the destruction of civil liberties and social progress in Unionist Ulster. They equated rural radicalism in the west of Ireland with continental agrarian socialism. They condemned physical attacks on landlordism in the south of Ireland as 'agrarian outrages'. They argued that rural unrest and civil disobedience were simply 'foretastes' of the kind of government that Home Rulers would impose on the industrious north-east of Ireland if Unionists here were not everywhere on their guard.

Just because Protestant Ulster had a provincial press which was vehemently opposed to Home Rule that did not mean that Unionism here was a form of narrow nationalism. To argue that is to miss one of the central tenets of Ulster Unionism. As this chapter and other chapters have consistently argued, Ulster was not a separate terrain of national separatism. It was the arena when Unionism was most successfully defended, the place where 'big-nation' nationalism had greatest appeal, across a whole spectrum of social groupings. Thus Unionism here was not simply a sectarian ideology with negative 'Catholic bashing' associations. It stressed the economic superiority of Protestant Ulster over the rest of the country, including Catholic Ulster. It emphasised Protestant Ulster's connections with Britain and the British Empire. It high-lighted the long-standing historical relationships between Protestantism and Ulster from well before the plantation of the province in the early seventeenth century. It emphasised the organic links between 'Honest Ulstermen' and Protestant Ulster. It stressed the 'civil liberties' and traditional Protestant values of this part of the province. It used these to explain Ulster's modernity and its industrial and commercial virtues. Thus, to suggest that this part of the country had a 'Protestant identity' is not to suggest that this was a terrain of 'narrow nationalism'.

This was not the case at the height of the Home Rule crisis in the 1880s or on the eve of Irish partition in the early 1920s. Protestant 'identity' was not singular and could more accurately be discussed in the plural. It was multifaceted rather than monolithic. It included the sectarian tradition of sections of the Protestant working class; the conservative fundamentalism of Protestant farmers; the elitism of the Province's large farmers and great estate owners; the liberalism of the Protestant merchant class; and the radicalism of Ulster's Presbyterian communities. Moreover, and contrary to Gibbon, the modernity of Unionism here was not confined to Belfast and its environs. As Anderson has convincingly shown, from the 1880s onwards it was extended to the rest of Protestant Ulster through the medium of Protestantism which was then considered the religion of a superior or 'chosen' people. Provincial newspapers played a crucial role in this process. They transmitted material from national newspapers, they provided detailed reports of parliamentary proceedings, they allowed political speeches to be reported verbatim, and they gave coverage of meetings and other activities both in Britain and in other parts of Ireland. As a result local newspapers here as elsewhere in nation-building Ireland were politically close to their readers. They accurately reflected a diversity of Protestant Unionist opinion which they both 'led' and 'followed'.

The Pamphlet War

During the height of Home Rule agitation provincial papers all across Protestant Ulster called on prominent Unionists to look to the interests of their less well-off brethren in order to defend themselves against the forces of Irish nationalist disorder. In appealing to Protestant employers to employ only Orangemen and not allow them to emigrate, the *Ulster Gazette* described Ulster as a loyal province under siege from evil forces of Irish nationalism. The north-east, it was argued, could not 'spare one loyal man, threatened as it is on all sides with Home Rule and civil war' (Anderson, 1989). In June 1886 the Conservative Unionist *Fermanagh Times* praised the 'industrious Protestants' of 'loyal and enterprising Ulster' and contrasted them with the 'thriftless and labouring classes' who supported the Irish Nationalist Party in Ulster. In a widely circulated Unionist pamphlet published in 1888, one writer put the case for resisting the 'breakup' of Britain so well that it deserves to be quoted at length.

> When the whole current of a nation's history has for centuries been set in one direction, I think there is at least a prima facie case against an attempt to turn the current in the opposite direction. Now, the history of these islands since the English Conquest of Britain has been one steady movement towards consolidation and Unity. First of all, the various English kingdoms were gradually united into one, and consolidated under the rule of one King and one Parliament. Next the Welsh Principalities, which had maintained their independence and their separate government, and which were alien in race and language to their English neighbours, were incorporated with England, and brought

under the rule of the English kings and English law. Next came the union of the kingdoms of England and Scotland under one crown; and in due time came their union under one parliament. The unity of great Britain was not accomplished as a matter of sentiment or affection ... . As an Irishman, I can understand and sympathise with independence; but I protest that, as an Irishman I cannot conceive how Irishmen could contentedly sit down, as tributaries of an Empire in whose glories they had no share, to administer for a foreign power the affairs of a conquered province. That would be, to my mind, a disastrous surrender of the political future of our country; and it could not be carried out without degrading to the parochial level the political instincts and political capabilities of Irishmen. ('Home Rule Nutshell', 1912, p. 87)

Unionist pamphlets and provincial newspapers in Ulster frequently fused racism with Unionism in such a way as to depict those who sought the breakup of Britain as 'irrational nationalists', as a people who were considered genetically unfit to rule themselves because they belonged with the 'lesser breeds', and not with the 'Lords of Humankind'. The bulk of nationalist support in Ulster was said to derive from 'illiterates [who] voted to a man, or rather to a being in the shape of a man ... of a class absolutely degraded from an educational point of view, and consequently the natural dupes of adventurers'. The *Fermanagh Times* found it 'impossible to imagine Ulstermen receiving their laws from ... penniless adventurers who would be scouted from the public life of even a South American Republic'. The revolutionary slogan of eighteenth-century American nationalists which insisted on 'no taxation without representation' was also adopted by 'Honest Ulstermen' to suit their needs. Thus the pro-Unionist *Londonderry Sentinel* claimed that Gladstone's support for Irish Home Rule favoured the 'five-sixths of disloyal, bigoted ... and largely incapable inhabitants' against the 'numerical minority who contribute five-sixths of the entire taxation of the country'. Thirty years later this paper was making similar arguments in order to defend a threatened disenfranchisement of Catholics in the 'Maiden City' of Londonderry. In its issue of 25 January 1913 it stated:

In Derry more than two thirds of the nationalists are paid by Protestants, and on the liberal principle of no taxation with representation that is exactly what we have got. Why should we trust the Catholics to run the town on our money? Compare the nationalists of Derry and the municipal services rendered with any city or town in Ireland managed by a Catholic Corporation and you will see that they [i.e. Derry Catholics] substantially benefit by the Protestant Board in office. (*Londonderry Sentinel*, 25 January 1913)

Newspapers like this conferred a sense of quasi-racial superiority on Ulster Protestants and caricatured Catholics in the north as 'dupes' of southern 'nationalist fanatics'. One such pamphlet claimed that those in favour of Home rule included:

> The dynamiters of America.
> The Fenians and Invincibles of Ireland.
> The illiterate voters of Ireland.
> The idlers, the grumblers, and the disaffected.
> The mutilators of cattle.
> The boycotters, and other systematic law-breakers.
> The moonlighters and other perpetrators of outrage.
> The placehunters who see no other prospect of earning money.
> ('Dishonesty and the Home Rule Bill', n.d., p. 1)

On the other hand the history of Ulster Protestants, particularly the Scots Presbyterians, was depicted as a 'success story of which any Scotsman at home or abroad may be proud'. Defending the racial superiority of 'Scottish Ulster' over Catholic Ulster and Catholic nation-building Ireland, one Unionist historian argued that the 'men of Ulster' had:

> an inalienable right to protest, as far as they are concerned against the policy of separation from Great Britain, to which the Irish – with the genius for nicknames which they possess – at present give the name Home Rule. (Women of the North West, n.d., p. 13)

In one of the earliest expressions of blood and soil 'big-nation' nationalism in Ireland this same author went on to claim that because they were upholders of 'the old ideals' Scots Ulster Presbyterians should: 'multiply and replenish the earth ... until the globe is circled round with colonies which are of our blood, and which love and cherish the "old lands of the mountain and the flood"' (Harrison, 1923, p. 97).

What made 'Ulster Scotsmen' worthy of respect from 'the parent stock' in the eyes of the author of these sentiments was their contributions to the progress of civilisation in general, but particularly in Ulster. Omitting the impoverishment of entire tracts of Catholic Ulster, and glossing over the social disparities within the world of Ulster Protestants, Harrison contended that 'the portion of Ireland which these Scotsmen hold is so prosperous and contented that it permits our statesmen to forget that it is a part of that most "distressful country"'. Focusing on the divergent status of Protestants and Catholics within Ulster he stated:

> There is a deep, strongly marked difference between the Ulster men, and
> the Irish, and that difference is not accidental, not the divergence
> arising out of different surroundings, not even springing from antago-
> nistic religious training, but is the deeper, stronger-marked cleavage of
> differing race. (Harrison, 1923, p. 99)

He then went on to elaborate a racial theory of origins and an evolutionary theory of social progress which attributed the economic
development of the north-east of Ireland to racial superiority of its
Protestant inhabitants. In tones reminiscent of racist defences of
English civilisation in seventeenth-century Ireland, Harrison, like
many others who wrote for the provincial press in Ulster, warned
against the dangers of mixed marriages and cultural miscegenation.
A loyal province in a 'disloyal land', nineteenth-century Ulster
society also was depicted as 'cleft society' which contained many
pockets of anti-Unionist resistance. Thus Harrison argued:

> The distinction between the native Irish and Scottish descendants in
> Ulster was a cleavage that was as distinct as that between the two vari-
> eties of any other animal and, say, between the mastiff and the
> stag-hound. Of course intermarriage gradually shades off the difference
> of type, but take the Scots of Ards of Down, who have probably scarcely
> intermarried with the Irish in the 300 years they have been in the
> island, and contrast them with the inhabitants of west Donegal, who
> have probably mixed their blood with the English, and you see the
> difference. (Harrison, 1923, p. 112)

As such, Honest Ulstermen could ill-afford to lose the blood of
Protestant Ulster through intermarriage with Roman Catholics.
Neither, it was argued, could they risk ethnocide through cultural
dilution or cultural mixing.

Warning Protestants to 'be on their guard' some four years after
the Northern Ireland state was established, the Unionist leader Sir
James Craig referred to Northern Catholics as 'past masters at
getting their foot in the door'. Addressing a crowd in Derry, the
'Maiden City' of Unionist history, he went on to state:

> I have watched for twenty four years the skilful manner in which that
> party conducted all their operations, and I know that they are no less
> dangerous when all looks quiet and peaceful. I know very often what is
> going on behind backs. (*Northern Whig*, 31 March 1925)

In terms reminiscent of Unionist suspicions about direct rule from
Westminster today, he followed up this statement of political

paranoia with an assurance that Unionist leaders in Northern Ireland were:

> trying to arrange everything so that, whatever Government may be in power in Great Britain, whether it be antagonistic to us in Ulster or not, the machinery will be so sound that all of us may rest safely in our beds knowing that no further attacks can be made upon our liberties. (*Londonderry Standard*, 4 April 1925)

Unionisation of Ulster

Statements like these, issued at sites sacred to the cause of Unionism throughout Ulster, were widely disseminated in the provincial press and for that reason constituted an integral element in the 'common sense' of Unionist Ulster. They were especially remarkable for the way in which they equated political power with geo-power. They were not only loaded with local, national, imperial and even global significance for Ulster Protestants – they helped to elaborate a geopolitics of Unionism which reminded Protestants, especially those at the outer limits of Unionist Britain, that they had duties and responsibilities, and an obligation to be alert to 'incursions' of Catholic nationalism from inside as well as outside Ulster. Like modern Unionists who have constantly stressed the need for vigilance and more security in border areas around Fermanagh, Tyrone and Derry, they cast Unionists in such places as political gatekeepers, as key figures in the maintenance of the territorial integrity of the United Kingdom. With Union safely maintained by its supporters in these symbolic sites of Ulster Unionism, the integrity of the nation-state itself was ensured.

Others maintained that preservation of the Union in Ulster would lead to the downfall of the Irish nation. This was the view of the conservative *Ballymena Observer* which in April 1886, stated that 'Ulster – Protestant Ulster – is the milch cow of the whole country. Should Ulster be dissevered ... the Dublin Parliament would not have revenue enough to pay its way'.

Years later while addressing a pro-Union rally in Londonderry, the Church of Ireland bishop of the city declared:

> We, Unionists of Londonderry, hereby record our solemn protest against the establishment of a Parliament in Dublin ... as we believe that the granting of any measure which would deprive the loyalist minority in Ireland of the protection of the Imperial Parliament would be disastrous

to the welfare of our country, and ultimately lead to the destruction of our great empire. (Speech of Bishop of Derry, n.d., p. 1)

Around the same time a Unionist handbook which was widely quoted in the provincial press in Ulster asserted that:

The opposition to Home Rule is the revolt of a business and industrial community against the domination of men who have no aptitude for either. The United league is remarkably lacking in the support of businessmen, merchants, and manufacturers, leaders of industry, bankers and men who compose a successful and prosperous community. (Unionist Party Handbook, 1912, p. 36)

When referring to 'prosperous Ulster' the Unionist press here in the 1880s made it clear that it was referring to Protestant Ulster alone. They considered the rest of the province backward both because it had less good land and far less industry than eastern counties like Antrim and Down, and because it was predominantly Roman Catholic. Thus when the Monaghan *People's Advocate* produced statistical data refuting assertions that this was the wealthiest province in the country the Conservative *Weekly News* in Cavan replied that: '[the] Nationalists know that when people speak of Prosperous and intelligent Ulster, it is to the Protestant divisions of the province that they more particularly refer' (quoted in Anderson, 1989, p. 26). On 15 July 1886, the Liberal Unionist paper *The Northern Whig* insisted that 'Our commercial and manufacturing classes are devoted to the Union because they know that trade and commerce would not flourish without the Union'.

Liberal and Conservative Unionists alike then insisted that Home Rule would result in 'a flight of capital, the ruins of thousands of industrious families, large destruction of banking, commercial and industrial enterprises, and a prohibitive interest for loans for public works of any kind'. Statements like these not only fostered political paranoia in Unionist Ulster. They encouraged northern Protestants to be self-reliant in their defence of the Union in Ulster. One speaker at a widely publicised Unionist rally in Derry in 1893, addressing his remarks to English political leaders as much as to those listening to him, suggested that Home Rule for Ireland would affect the English as well as 'Honest Ulstermen' in Ulster. The English, he predicted, would find:

that peace will be neither with Ireland or England. They [i.e. the English] will have propitiated the Nationalists, who will soon discover that a country without capital or credit is not a good milk cow. They

will have alienated the Protestants throughout Ireland, and we in
Ulster, the descendants of these sent here originally to plant religious
loyalty and civilisation, because we have fulfilled our missions, because
as hard-working, God-fearing men and women, we who have brought
order out of disorder, are to be handed over to the tender mercies of the
merciless with cynical indifference. ('Women of the North West', n.d.,
p. 2)

There clearly was a strong territorial imperative in the propaganda
war that was waged in these Unionist pamphlets. Political
pamphlets, posters and postcards, perhaps more so than Unionist
history books, fostered a sense of Unionist identity that rendered
the north-east of Ireland a Protestant homeland, one that had its
own Protestant capital in Belfast city. Belfast was regularly characterised as a 'fighting city', a city that thrived on the Union with
Britain. One pamphlet claimed that Belfast's progress in the nineteenth century was a 'standing contradiction to Irish nationalist
claims that the Act of Union had been the cause of all Ireland's
problems'. It went on to argue:

That a provincial town, remote from the great centres of coal and iron,
should thrive and prosper during the very period when we are assured
that, for political causes, Ireland was bound to decay, would in any case
be provoking. But Belfast has not merely held its own as an Irish town;
it has taken its place as one of the great world centres of industry and
commerce, challenging the supremacy of the Clyde in ship-building,
and of Belgium and France in linen-weaving, holding its own with all
comers in a score of smaller industries, and attaining the position of
third Customs port in the United Kingdom. ('The Capital of Ulster',
n.d., p. 2)

Addressing a widely publicised Unionist rally in 1912 the Marquis
of Londonderry contended that Irish nationalists had made Home
Rule their 'idol'. He proceeded to denounce everyone who
'worshipped at its shrine', including those who attributed 'all Irish
shortcomings' to the Act of Union. He added:

Ulstermen, bearing in mind their progress since the Union, not unnat-
urally decline to accept so absurd an argument. The Union has been no
obstacle to their development; why should it be a barrier to the rest of
Ireland? Ulstermen believe that the Union with Great Britain has
assisted the development of their commerce and industry. They are
proud of the progress of Belfast, and of her position in the industrial and
shipping world. ('Home Rule Nutshell', 1912, p. 96)

Another Belfast working-class Unionist put this argument in simpler terms when he flatly stated that: 'the commercial and social status of the Protestants is due solely to the merits of Protestantism' (quoted in Bell, 1978, p. 97). Casting serious doubt on the ability of 'Catholic Ireland' to go it alone without 'prosperous Ulster' the Duke of Abercorn in September 1911 stated that:

> Without Ulster Ireland would be poor indeed – a country without a great port, without a commanding manufacturing industry, without the social stability that comes from diversification of occupation. To hand over this large and virile population of Protestants to the Irish nationalists, mitigated by a caucus of subsided politicians, will be the first and obvious result of a ... Home Rule Bill – a Bill which will be drafted by an orator who stands where Parnell stood, who talked about the 'union of hearts' as cant and who ... regarded all concessions to Ulster Unionists as valueless except in so far as they 'pushed on the great goal of National Independence'. ('Home Rule Nutshell', 1912, p. 87)

The claim that Protestantism was at the root of Ulster prosperity was taken seriously by the many Unionists who read such pamphlets. One of these, entitled 'Political Ulster', stated that:

> Ulster had no wish to boast of her industrial superiority to the other provinces of Ireland, but it is an indisputable fact. Wherever similar industry and wealth are to be found in the rest of Ireland they are similarly arrayed on the Unionist side.

It was then asserted that 'Political' or 'Unionist Ulster' was 'justified in her claim to be the most prosperous, the best educated, and the most orderly and enlightened province in Ireland' ('Political Ulster', n.d., p. 1). In September 1911 the Right Honourable Thomas Andrews, reflecting on Gladstone's Home Rule Bill, asked a mass rally of 'Honest Ulstermen' at Craigavon, near Belfast:

> Where in the British Empire would they find prosperity such as existed in the great City beside them and in its neighbouring counties? Where outside the North East of Ulster would they find an industry worth the name in Ireland?

He went on to state that they as 'law-abiding loyal citizens' who could 'claim every prosperity' were:

> asked to trust their lives and fortunes in the hands of men who never succeeded in anything save agitation. They, the loyal men of Ireland ... would never be enslaved by the enemies of the Empire – which they had

done their share in building up ... They claimed their birthright as citizens of the greatest Empire the world had yet seen ... They would remain as they were today – an integral part of the United kingdom, with which they have prospered and lived happily as loyal subjects of their King. ('Home Rule Nutshell', 1912, p. 79)

These Unionists were prepared to accept that Ulster was neither uniformly prosperous nor even predominantly Unionist. They simply asserted that 'Political Ulster' was superior to Catholic Ireland. When Irish nationalists pointed out that parts of Ulster were Catholic and underdeveloped these same Unionists replied that:

> these statements are literally true of the entire province, burdened as it is with Donegal, where thirty one per cent of the population over five years old are illiterate. But they do not affect the Protestant and Unionist population, for more than seventy two per cent of the illiterates belong to the Roman Catholic minority.

From this they advanced to the argument that:

> There are two Ulsters. The geographical province of Ulster contains nine counties; but of these three – Cavan, Donegal and Monaghan – are Ulster counties only in name. Like Leinster, Munster and Connaught, they are occupied mainly by a Celtic and Catholic population. Indeed Donegal contains a larger proportion of Irish-speaking inhabitants than any county in Leinster, and strictly belongs to the same natural region as Connemara. The remaining six counties – Antrim, Down, Armagh, Londonderry, Tyrone and Fermanagh – may be called 'Political Ulster'. When Unionists speak of 'Ulster' it is political Ulster they mean. Political Ulster contains 76.3 per cent of the population of the whole province. ('About Ulster', n.d., pp. 1–2)

The political pamphlet war that erupted on the Ulster scene at regular intervals when Home Rule was being debated made three basic arguments that are worth noting here. First, it was argued that, regardless of religion or politics, Belfast was the natural and true capital of the province of Ulster and the primate city of 'Political Ulster'. If anything indeed, Ulster Unionists valued Belfast more than Irish nationalists did Dublin. This was because Unionism was far more urban in ethos than Irish nationalism – with all its associations with the rural and with rural fundamentalism – ever was. Irish nationalists tended to treat city life as a source of contagion and moral debasement. Ulster Unionists were proud of 'their' towns and cities, including 'outlying' towns and cities like Londonderry, Lisburn, Enniskillen, Omagh, Portadown, Carrickfergus and Bangor. These towns and cities, as we have seen, were considered to be 'Unionist in their bricks and mortar'. Belfast in particular was lauded as a great urban Protestant achievement in an otherwise 'backward' rural Ireland. It quite 'naturally' belonged within urban Britain. It literally was considered, at least by Unionists, as an 'imperial city'. It had powerful trading links with Great Britain and the British Empire, and it contributed to the construction of an imperial world. Thus it was claimed that Belfast built the ships that gave the British their naval – and trading – supremacy on the world oceans, and helped to conquer an imperial world for Great Britain.

Second, it was sometimes admitted that while Belfast's political influence might not encompass the entire province, it at least spoke for 'Political Ulster', especially for the Unionist heartlands of east and mid-Ulster. It reigned supreme over a Unionist landscape wherein Gaelic-speaking areas, as for example in counties Derry, Tyrone and Antrim, were deemed not to exist. Instead this was a landscape where 'Protestant towns' and neat farmsteads were considered 'proofs' of Protestant achievement and symbols of Unionist power. The former were also, of course, urban constellations of Unionist power. They rarely if ever were modern urban meeting places, locations where people from different religious or ethnic backgrounds met to share each others' social or religious outlooks. Even more rarely were they places where Catholic nationalists met with Ulster Unionists on equal terms. Indeed, in living memory the streets of not a few 'Ulster towns' were not common but were narrow grounds, places where 'Ulster Protestants' walked on one side, while 'Roman Catholics' walked on the other.

Finally, towards the end of this 'pamphlet war' which politicised and Unionised Ulster, it was claimed that there was not one but two Ulsters. One was developed, Unionist and Protestant and comprised the six counties of 'Political Ulster'. The other was Ulster only in name and also contained rural underdeveloped counties like Donegal, Cavan and Monaghan. Thus there was a powerful nation-building, territorial imperative behind Ulster's pamphlet war at the turn of the century. Pamphlets, perhaps more so than 'Unionist' histories, claimed 'Political Ulster' for Britain and made Belfast its natural capital. Belfast it was argued always was a 'fighting city' which thrived on the Union with Britain and the Empire. James Wender Good, one of the few liberal Unionist historians of his day, referred to it as such. He wrote:

the cocksure perkiness of its red-brick houses and its monstrous array of factory chimneys, flaming plumes of smoke above the diminished spires of churches, symbolises commercialism exulting in the overthrow of all that is simple and comely in life. (Good, 1919, p. 79)

His characterisations of the city and the 'Belfastman' are so richly symbolic that they deserve to be quoted at some length. In his appropriately titled book *Ulster and Ireland*, Good indeed claimed that:

> The combativeness of Belfast is equalled only by its self-assertiveness ... The Belfastman makes his very faults a panache, and he does not defend them like the Gasson with a sword, he shoots off facts and figures at his opponents for all the world as if he were an animated Lewis gun. Nor is the Belfastman's 'guid conceit' of himself a piece of arrogance. He is conscious of having created something unique of its kind in Ireland, and any attempt to belittle that achievement brings him into the field, horse, foot and artillery, ready and panting for battle. Strange as it may seem to outsiders, the Ulsterman is firmly convinced that to have woven better linen and built bigger liners than his rivals is proof of the soundness of his politics and the truth of his religion. And when the manner in which he weaves his linen or builds his ships is questioned, he feels his politics and religion are being questioned. Protestantism, he contends, is the only key to the riddle why Belfast advances as Galway recedes and all those who reject this solution do so because they are unwilling to face unpalatable facts. (Good, 1919, p. 83)

In terms reminiscent of present-day pleas for power-sharing, he called on Protestants to sink their differences with Catholics and to bring an end to religious hatred and ethnic supremacy. He insisted that both the latter were more characteristic of life in the inner city than 'the simple and comely life' which he found in the Ulster countryside, and in its towns and villages. Referring to Edward Carson's anti-Home Rule movement, Good insisted that:

> The towns provided the driving force for the Carson crusade, and prejudices flourish more rankly in the back streets of Belfast and Portadown than in the fields of Tyrone and Antrim. In the country Orange and Green generally live and work apart, and come into collision only on the high days of their respective creeds, when bad whiskey has perhaps more to do with their broils and battles than either King William or the Pope. In the towns, though factions reside for the most part in separate quarters – the Ghetto principle still survives in Ulster – the chances of friction are naturally greater, and a tiny spark can provoke a shattering explosion. The real reasons why hostility should have developed so strongly lies deeper down; and its roots are to be found, I believe, in

economic rather than political causes. On the land ... the Catholic inside the last generation has attained a status equal to that of the Protestant, and in attaining it, has established an identity of interests which, though it may be obscured by party or religious differences, exercises a potent influence. In industry, on the contrary, the Catholic still is regarded as a 'have not' whose efforts to better his position are denounced as inspired by a desire to dispossess 'haves'. In a word, capitalism to-day has stepped into the position vacated by aristocratic landlordism; and by playing the racial and religious prejudices of the workers uses one section to depress the other, while it profits by exploiting both. Just as the Protestant tenant in other generations was protected by the Ulster custom, so the Protestant workers in Ulster have gradually established for their members a definite status in the industrial world. Nationalists are strongest in the ranks of unskilled labour; and, until the war transformed the existing system, it was precisely amongst unskilled workers that the leaven of a new gospel was fermenting most vehemently. They were demanding their 'place in the sun', in the shape of a living wage and the safeguards which the members of skilled traders had through their organisations managed to secure by dint of persistent agitation. (Good, 1919, pp. 83–4)

Good and his Liberal Unionist contemporaries failed to appreciate that, once adopted, Protestantism could not readily be discarded as a symbol of Unionism, or as a cultural marker which set 'prosperous' and 'Political Ulster' apart from 'illiterate Catholic Ireland'. Falling back on social Darwinism, environmental determinism and race-thinking to explain away lack of 'development' in Catholic areas, one pamphleteer insisted that:

Roman Catholicism strikes an outsider as being in some of its tendencies non-economic if not actually anti-economic. These tendencies have, of course, fuller play when they act on a people whose education has been stunted. The reliance of that religion on authority, its repression of individuality, and the complete shifting in what I call the human centre of gravity to some future existence ... appear to me calculated ... to check the growth of qualities of initiative and self-reliance, especially among a people whose lack of education unfits them for resisting the influence of what may represent itself to such minds as a kind of fatalism with fatalism as its paramount virtue. ('Home Rule Nutshell', 1912, p. 57)

Unionists like these claimed that 'Gaels have not the business turn of mind and do not build factories' ('Prosperous Ulster', n.d., p. 2). Referring to the United Irish League, a prominent Irish nationalist organisation with branches in the province, one Unionist writer stated:

On its roll of membership there are no landlords or ex-landlords, few merchants, fewer manufacturers. There are few of the men who are managing the business of Ireland in city or town connected with the League. The bankers who regulate our finances, the railway or transit men who control our trade, internal and external, even the leading cattlemen who handle most of our animal produce, are not to be found in its ranks. ('Case Against Home Rule', 1912, p. 165)

Such statements showed that Protestant support for the Union was firmly planted in anti-Catholic race-thinking and in highly congratulatory self-images of themselves as a 'superior' – even 'chosen' – people. It was not simply a mechanistic or irrational response of a bigoted minority to the rise of Irish nationalism. More importantly still, Unionist political pamphlets showed Irish nationalists that theirs was not the only programme of nation-building that had a right to exist in nineteenth-century Ireland. Ulster Unionists regularly couched their opposition to Irish nation-alism in terms that were supportive of 'big-nation' Unionist nationalism. Contrary to Irish nationalists, opposition to nation-alism-as-national-separatism here was not a British conspiracy to kill Irish Home Rule by dividing the country along religious lines. It was less the product of the uneven development of capitalism than a product of the uneven development of 'big-nation' nation-alism in Ireland. That is why the geopolitical statements which we have been discussing were also statements of 'geo-power'. This term is generally used to describe the functioning of geography as a body of knowledge used in the service of the state. However, it also refers to an ensemble of technologies of power concerned with the management and political cohesion of territorial space. That is precisely how Unionists viewed the governability of the north of Ireland after the rise of Irish Home Rule. They not only fought Irish nationalism in order to resist the Balkanisation of Britain and the Empire. Like their seventeenth-century counterparts in the south of Ireland they perceived themselves as the defenders of civilisa-tion itself. For these Unionists the art of good government raised not just Machiavelli's concerns about the moral conduct of the prince as governor of society. It moved well beyond this, and beyond an interest in the rationality of rulers, to much more gener-alised concerns about management of the local economy by keeping 'Political Ulster' as part of the United Kingdom. It was about monitoring the personal conduct of all citizens of the state, not least the conduct of Roman Catholics and all those considered disloyal to the state. In the end this monitoring and government of personal conduct was literally reduced to an all-encompassing, panoptical government of the lives and souls of ordinary people, not least those in Catholic nationalist areas located inside 'Political Ulster'. Unionists were also concerned with the governability of Unionist Ulster because they believed that, having 'brought' prosperity to the north-east of Ireland, having carved this region out as a place apart from rural underdeveloped Ireland, they, and they alone, were responsible for the maintenance, reproduction and management of that regional enclave as part of the United Kingdom. That is why issues like security, defence of territory, the proper management of the economy, 'good' government, and the containment of anti-Unionist 'disorder' have always been of such concern to 'Political Ulster'.

9 The Surveillance State and the Imagined Community

Mapping the Imagined Community of the Nation

Although Anderson points to peculiarities of nation-building in late colonial societies, the examples he chooses are largely drawn from new nations that made the transition from colonialism to nationhood since the 1950s. His insights, however, may also be applicable to Ireland in the latter half of the nineteenth century and the opening decades of the twentieth century. Thus, as he sees it, the state in this century has been directly, and indirectly, responsible for fostering whole new styles of 'imagining' which in turn have helped construct 'imagined communities' of nations all across Asia and Africa. This is because the modern state has not merely aspired 'to create, under its control, a human landscape of perfect visibility' (Anderson, 1983, p. 187). It also forged a whole range of other forms of communication and surveillance – apart from the newspapers and periodicals so much discussed in Anderson's work – that allowed the state to literally monitor modernity (Giddens, 1985; Giddens et al., 1994). All this has involved radically new ways of organising time and space in the modern world system. In particular it fostered new ways of becoming 'visible'; it gave everyone, and everything, within the state's domain a label, a serial number, a place or a name; and it thereby made everyone, and everything, highly visible on the procedural landscape of the modern nation-state.

These styles of 'imagining', together with the new socio-spatial configurations which they helped to nurture, did not materialise out of thin air. They were products of the new systems for monitoring and literally itemising people on the procedural or 'programmed' landscapes of the modern nation-state and its territorial possessions. They clearly also proceeded from new ways of arranging, mapping or 'imagining' countries. Thus they equally resulted from new methods for categorising land, depicting places, classifying resources and monitoring people in nation-building, and in colonial societies. Viewed thus the modern 'imagined community' of the nation was not just a cultural construct, which is what cultural nationalists insist. It was a scientific construct in that it was equally the product of census collection, cartography, land surveying, and the relentless driving force of modern – and increasingly national – capitalism. All this partially facilitated a transition from 'colony' to 'nation' in many Third World countries from the 1950s onwards.

In nineteenth-century Ireland also, however, as in twentieth-century Burma and Indonesia, mapping the nation and collecting data on its population size and distribution were not just exercises in cartography and demography. They made visible, often for the first time to many people, the crude outlines of the nation as a territory and as a social formation with sufficient political and economic potential to suggest that the Irish could stand alongside other nations. Cultural geographers in particular have pointed to the role of maps and map-making in the construction of this imagined community of the nation. In a recent study of the role of cartography in mapping national identities in England, Daniels has stated: 'to imagine a nation is to envision its geography'. As he sees it there is 'seldom a secure or enduring consensus about a nation's geography, about which places are representative, which central, which peripheral, about how they are co-ordinated both within the nation and in relation to the world at large' (Daniels, 1998, p. 112).

Certainly in nineteenth-century Ireland cartography and the collection of statistics on a whole range of natural, social and physical phenomena equipped nation-builders with the means whereby they could 'imagine' and literally 'visualise' the modern Irish nation for the first time. The maps and statistical charts drawn up at this time allowed hegemonic sectors in Irish society, including Ulster, to visualise the nation as an expression of modernity, to see it as a forward-looking political community, not just a backward-looking historical and cultural community. These cartographic exercises, I would argue, gave rise to a scientific literature which was every bit as important a nation-building force as 'nationalist literature', in the narrow and commonly understood meaning of that category, ever was. Both genres of literature, one scientific, the other cultural and 'literary', helped shape the very contours and grammar of nation-building. As such they made possible the concrete expressions of 'Irishness', and 'Ulsterness', in the contested terrains of nation-building Ireland. The concretisations of the nation in Ireland, as in Ulster, owed much to the British state's peculiar way of viewing Irish geography, interpreting Irish history, and exercising political power over Ireland and its 'natural' resources.

Maps as Images of the 'Imagined Community' in Ireland

Because they were concerned with the recording and transliteration of Gaelic placenames, and with their replacement with English ones, Irish cartography, ethnography, archaeology and other 'scientific' literature dealing with the social and physical geography of the country were especially crucial to the modernisation and 're-nationalisation' of Ireland in the nineteenth century. Indeed, as practised here, these disciplines revealed that the struggle to become a people and a country was enacted as much in geography and nationalist history as in the political arenas of either Ireland or mainland Britain. Maps, whether of 'Ireland' or of 'Ulster', literally were the locus of competing and conflicting images of Ireland and 'Irishness'. Much of the work of the Ordnance Survey simply resulted in Gaelic placenames being transliterated or replaced with English ones. Thus for example it has been likened to an 'eviction of sorts' (Kiberd, 1995, p. 614). Thus map-making as much as any nationalist literature was also a Foucauldian discourse in power. It enabled the Irish to literally name Ireland and Irish places. As such it was inextricably intertwined in a wider project of 'claiming' Irish history and naming Ireland for the Irish people. Viewed thus the six-inch map in Ireland was every bit as important to nineteenth-century Irish nation-builders as the literary gleanings of cultural nationalists ever were. Both substituted for the poverty and foulness which heretofore ranked highly in English depictions of the Irish countryside and Irish people. They allowed the country to become a Motherland, or at least a home fit for 'successful' Irish people. Just as nationalist history allowed the Irish to 'seize hold' of memories of themselves at crucial junctures in the construction of an Irish modernity, Irish map-making allowed them to seize hold of the country in the face of an Anglo-centric modernity (Benjamin, 1990, p. 257). As nation-centred projects they literally allowed the Irish to 'strike back' against the forces of Anglicisation in a nation-building Ireland. Friel's play *Translations* captures the complexities of this struggle very well indeed when it suggests that the entrepreneurial sectors of Irish society may not have lamented the passing of Gaelic Ireland through the loss, or transliteration, of Irish placenames through a process of Anglicisation (Friel, 1981).

For these sectors of Irish society the English language may indeed have been 'a necessary sin, but a convenient language to sell pigs in'. The play also implies that the Irish middling classes willingly collaborated in the 'eviction' of Gaelic placenames from modernising Ireland. Far from bemoaning the passage of the Gaelic geography of the country, the more pragmatic among them welcomed the act of transliteration precisely because they saw this as part of a wider process of modernisation from which they themselves could benefit. They may also have looked on Gaelic names as the more parochial remnants of a society that had to be forgotten if Ireland was ever to be transformed into a cohesive, modern nation-state. It was as if they considered the modernisation of Ireland as adequate compensation for the cultural loss and 'disinheritance' which ensued from this process of transliteration. They were willing to literally let Gaelic placenames go because they saw in English a language filled with opportunities, and because they perceived Gaelic as the language associated with poverty, backwardness and defeat.

By engaging in a cartographic rebellion against Britain's constructs of 'Ireland' and all things 'Irish', map-makers here were tentatively also claiming Ireland for the Irish. Thus for example in outlining the topography and geological structure of the country they were inadvertently also laying the scientific basis for the imagined community of the nation in Ireland. Thus the 'nation' here was not simply a cultural construct or the product of a cultural renaissance. It was equally a cartographic and scientific construct, the product of scientific revolutions that had been germinating since the mid-eighteenth century. Yet, however banal the maps, the 'memoirs' – i.e. field reports drawn up by OS officials working throughout the country – and other 'scientific' accounts of local places here appeared, they contributed as much to the 'awakening' of a sense of place and a sense of nationhood as the 'cultural renaissance' and the 'Celtic revival' ever did.

Modern Irish cartography commenced in the mid-1820s when the Ordnance Survey set out to fix the boundaries and spell out the names of some 69,000 townlands. These of course also formed the basis of land valuation and provided the early basis for a modern taxation system in Ireland. In 1825 the Ordnance Survey, under the directorship of Richard Griffith, set out to produce a major new national map of Ireland. Moreover, the country was to be mapped not on the traditional scale of one inch to the mile that had been used in England and Wales, but on the far more generous six-inch scale. One writer has suggested that the choice of a six inch to one mile scale for these maps was not dictated by any detailed knowledge of the peculiarity of Irish circumstances but was instead a 'cartographical expression of the union of the two kingdoms' (Andrews, 1975, p. 24) As such, it could be argued, it was as much a cartographic expression of 'big-nation' British nationalism in Ireland as an expression of cartographic imperialism. It was intended that the new maps would provide a data bank that would allow the state to get to the heart of social unrest in 'unruly' Ireland. Thus maps were to act as a basis for social planning in Ireland. They were to provide an understanding of the rapid pace of socio-economic and demographic change in a country on the brink of modernity. Map-making here therefore was not undertaken simply for the sake of it. It was part of a much wider utilitarian, state-centred project aimed at bringing Ireland closer to Britain by equipping the state with the cartographic means to monitor and project social and environmental change in Ireland. Another leading cartographer here felt 'the general Disposition of the Minerals of a Country' to be 'so important in every Branch of Domestic and Political Economy connected with its improvement' that 'very particular attention' should be directed towards this subject (Lt Colonel Thomas Colby, quoted in Davies, 1983, p. 87).

Certainly Ireland was one of the earliest European nations to use maps in order to assess the country's development potential. Irish nation-builders, including some of the country's leading academics, used these maps to project a favourable image of the country in the international arena. As far back as the eighteenth century there had already existed a map-making tradition in Ireland which rebelled against earlier British caricaturisations of the country as a place lacking in developmental potential. Many of these Irish cartographers were part of a European-wide utilitarian intellectual revolution which saw natural scientists taking a far more perceptive interest in the flora and fauna, and especially in the mineral wealth and the geological structure, of 'their' own countries. This occurred alongside two other developments, one scientific, the other social, which further contributed to growing interest in natural history as a basis for nation-building. This was particularly evident in the high levels of interest shown in the physical and geological structure of national space from the late eighteenth century onwards. On the one hand there was a rapidly developing and purely scientific interest in rocks as keys to understanding the complex history of the earth's surface. This, however, was accompanied by social and economic developments, such as population growth, increasing industrialisation and commercialisation, which caused the work of scientists to be of general interest to nation-builders.

As a result, new men of science, especially geologists and physical geographers, focused more pragmatically on rocks not just as

keys to understanding the geological structure of the earth's
surface, but as natural resources and natural attributes of national
space. Thus coalfields were mapped with a view to enhancing
industrial production, including the production of steam-engines.
The distribution of brick-clays was mapped partly to cater to the
building needs of expanding cities, including those of a highly
lucrative and labour-intensive construction industry. The distribution of water supplies (especially clean water) was meticulously
mapped so that those concerned with the health and sanitary
conditions of burgeoning population centres would be in a better
position to enhance the social fabric of the nation. At another level
the 'natural' resources of national spaces – what Adam Smith
referred to as the 'wealth of nations' – were mapped with a view to
arranging nations in a hierarchical international ordering of
nation-states. Indeed, aside from England, France and the Dutch
Republic, Ireland was one of the earliest nations in the European
world to display a concern for its international image by fostering
a scientific interest in its physical resources and geological structure. From as early as the 1740s onwards, Davies suggests:

> a group of Irish gentlemen began to feel disquiet at the regular presen-
> tation of their land as one populated by people who were primitive,
> barbarous, superstitious and unruly. In short they saw the image of
> Ireland being offered to the world through foreign publications as a
> grotesque caricature of reality. Looking across the water they saw that
> the English natural historians ... had offered accurate accounts of their
> chosen territories; why, the Irishmen reasoned, should the same not be
> done for Ireland? (Davies, 1983, p. 1)

Quite clearly we cannot 'claim' that these 'gentlemen' were Irish
nationalists, although we may be on firmer ground in claiming
them for the cause of nation-building in Ireland. They probably
bridged the gap separating the 'big-nation' English nationalism of
the Anglo-Irish aristocracy on the one hand, and the national separatism of nineteenth-century Irish nationalists on the other. What
we do know is that throughout the closing decades of the eighteenth century and on into the opening decades of the century
that followed, geologists, cartographers, demographers, physical
geographers and ethnographers all collected statistical material
which helped nationalists and natural scientists alike to literally
put Ireland on the map of western Europe.

   As early as the mid-eighteenth century the group of geologists
and cartographers already referred to even set themselves the task
of amassing sufficient material for the compilation of a national

geography of Ireland that would be comparable to William Camden's late sixteenth-century publication *Britannia*. They intended to have their endeavours published as *Hibernia*, or *Ireland Ancient and Modern* (Davies, 1983, p. 2; Cormack, 1997, p. 41). Although this particular project met with disappointment in that the Irish atlas was not actually published, this did not stop them preparing for circulation a list of questions to be sent to 'learned gentlemen' in 'several counties' of Ireland seeking information about a whole range of natural and social phenomena. This list solicited information about 'epidemical diseases, meteors, holy wells and petrifying springs, tides and currents, tempests and hurricanes, thunder and lightning, echoes, rivers (whether stony, gravelly, sandy, muddy), waterfalls, the character of the lakes, the height and trend of mountains, whether they be any volcanoes, promontories (whether hawks, eagles, &c. breed in them), soils, mines, woods, insects, birds, archaeology and manufactures' (Davies, 1983, p. 2). Had they received the co-operation they hoped for in this project they would have gone a long way towards 'charting' the Irish nation, even at this early stage in the evolution of Irish modernity.

Map-making as Cartographic Rebellion

Certainly the material which these 'gentlemen', and others, collected subsequently facilitated a mapping of the national territory in great detail. This not only resulted in the emergence of new geographical and scientific images of Ireland and the Irish, and indeed of Irish geography and Irish cartography. It also enabled a nation-centred and increasingly Irish intelligentsia to react against the essentialising or 'fixed' visions of 'their country' as a barbarous and underdeveloped appendage of the English nation-state. Now Irish 'gentlemen' set about literally 're-mapping' Ireland and rewriting the geography and ethnography of Ireland. In the process they acquired a corporate identity and a professional status for themselves as national 'figures of learning' in nation-building Ireland. Later on the institutionalisation of map-making and physical geography in the Department of the Ordnance in the 1820s and 1830s augmented the number of Irish-speaking civilian scholars employed in consulting Irish documents. The latter also set about interviewing Irish people about a whole range of phenomena, including local history, placenames, social ecology and human geography (Daniels, 1998, p. 121).

One result of all this was that the geographies which these men compiled were the radical opposites of the 'fabulous' geographies of Ireland compiled during the seventeenth century. This latter tradition, as we have seen, provided the cartographical underpinnings for a whole system of English rule, and English nation-building, in seventeenth- and eighteenth-century Ireland. They implied that all the latent characteristics of the Irish people were unchanging because they were rooted in the geography of the country as a 'barbarous place'. They also suggested that Ireland was a country which literally undernourished its inhabitants while simultaneously defining their specificity by branding them with all the essential characteristics of an 'inferior' and 'lawless' people. English statesmen, including many among the landed aristocracy in Ireland, had always fostered this elitist and extremely covetous tradition in geographical thinking here which rendered Ireland either into a 'home country' of England or transformed it into a meagre 'possession' of a wider imperial Britain. This was the tradition which was reversed in the course of the nineteenth century by a native Irish intelligentsia seeking to describe Ireland as a country in its own right, a country capable of imagining itself as a self-governing nation managed by an Irish bourgeoisie.

The great age in this latter tradition of Irish map-making extends roughly from the mid-1850s to the late 1880s – a period when more geological maps were produced than in any other in the country's history. Moreover, the number of geological papers published in scientific journals then reached a level that was not exceeded until the 1960s (Davies, 1983, p. 159). Nationalist historians and cultural nationalists have all too frequently portrayed post-Famine Ireland as a 'damnable place', a country in the throes of an identity crisis brought on by economic stagnation and political repression, a land, in nationalist eyes at least, of rack-renting landlords and wholesale emigration. Yet this was a period of great intellectual and scientific advance. The 1850s through to the 1890s in particular saw huge advances in academic disciplines here, especially in the fields of geology, political economy, geography, anthropology, ethnography and history. Aside from the many 'mental maps' of Ireland which this produced, the Geological Survey in the 1860s alone mapped an average of over 2,000 square kilometres of new territory each year. By July 1869 the Survey had published 117 of the 205 one-inch sheets needed to cover the whole of Ireland. Moreover, interest in matters scientific and geological at this time was not confined to those with a narrow 'nationalistic bent'. As Davies suggests:

from 1854 onwards geology was one of the subjects covered by courses of public lectures given throughout Ireland under the auspices of the Department of Science and Art. Attendance at many of these courses was free of charge and attendance was often large ... . At the centre of all this Irish interest in geology there stood the Geological Survey of Ireland, then, as now, by far the largest Irish institution devoted to the earth sciences. Its officers dominated the Irish geological scene [and] between 1850 and 1869 mapped in detail the geology of more than half of Ireland. (Davies, 1983, p. 160)

The new maps and geographies – mental or otherwise – which these men constructed therefore allowed whole new sections of Irish society – not just the substantial middle classes – to reject negative portrayals of the Irish as a lawless and childlike people inhabiting an underdeveloped country on the edge of western Europe. Instead they portrayed Ireland as a fair and pleasant land, a country deserving of scientific interest in its own right, a country which Irish nation-builders, including Irish scientists, insisted should – and could – be ranked among the civilised nations of nation-building Europe. In so doing amateur and professional geographers, geologists, natural historians and nationalist historians painted Ireland in entirely new and far more optimistic colours, even if many among them did not paint it in the nationalist colours of Orange and Green used by nationalist and Unionist historians later in the nineteenth century. In challenging the prerogative of the aristocracy to represent, and therefore to own and control Ireland, they were inadvertently laying the basis for a scientific tradition which insisted that the Irish were a people as human and worthy of respect as any other nationality in western Europe. Far from being mere 'serial numbers' in a wider 'colonial' scheme of political control, the Irish now viewed themselves as a people deserving of social and political rights, just like other nationalities in nation-building Europe.

All this involved a reaction against what Abdel-Malek has termed 'the hegemonism of possessing' that was such a distinctive feature of colonial thought elsewhere in nineteenth-century Europe. This was also to result in a radical disavowal of an Anglo-Irish elitist hegemonism which had defended Britain's right to 'own' Ireland and 'manage' its people. While Davis and the Young Irelanders were not the first to react against this hegemonism, they were among the most popular political defenders of cultural nationalism in their day. However, Davis returned again and again to the problematic of mapping the country's Irishness by mapping only its Gaelic landscapes and Gaelic placenames. He was convinced that any racial purity that might have existed in Ireland in the mid-nineteenth century had long ago been melted down by racial and ethnic intermingling. Yet, as Boyce points out, there was 'an air of self-defensiveness' in his pleas for the 'Milesian, the Dane, the Norman, the Welshman, the Scotchman, and the Saxon', to 'combine, regardless of their blood'. Thus, despite his love of things Gaelic, he could never bring himself to admire the complete Gaelicisation of the Irish landscape that could sometimes underlie the cartographic ambitions of cultural nationalists. Thus Boyce suggests:

> Davis wished to apply racial concepts to Anglo-Irish relations, but not to relationships within Ireland itself; he wanted to erect linguistic and cultural barriers between Ireland and England, and at the same time use those same weapons to break down barriers between the descendants of Englishmen and Irishmen living in Ireland. What was an obstacle in one context, must become an open door in another. From his starting point of cultural distinctiveness, therefore, Davis arrived at the conclusion that Irishness was the product, not of race, but of environment; and only by accepting that the uniqueness of the Irishman was the product of the uniqueness of Ireland (more particularly of Celtic but not Catholic, Ireland) could a truly united nation be achieved. (Boyce, 1991, pp. 157–8)

Mapping the Subject

Nevertheless, by the close of the century many others, apart from Davis and the Young Irelanders, were engaged in a much more pragmatic 'mapping' of Ireland and the Irish environment with a view to emphasising the Irishness of the Irish nation. By then the new detailed maps and memoirs of Irish counties, including Irish placename surveys, produced by the Ordnance Survey gave the Irish a deeper sense of local and national identity. Even Connolly argued that, despite the common interests of workers as workers the world over, each country, and especially the Irish, had a right to work out 'its own salvation on the lines most congenial to its own people'. He went on to suggest that 'the racial characteristics of the English and Irish people are different'. He even added that:

> Their political history and traditions are antagonistic, the economic development of the one is not on a par with the other, and, finally, although they have been in the closest contact for seven hundred years, yet the Celtic Irishman is today as much of an insolute problem to even

the most friendly English as on the day when the two countries were first joined together in unholy wedlock. (Connolly, quoted in Edwards, 1981)

In this statement Connolly was drawing on over half a century of 'mental mapping' and indigenous scientific thought which also insisted on the distinctiveness of the Irish people and heightened Ireland's sense of national identity. Indeed, writing around the same time as Connolly, Alice Stopford Green suggested that the 'memoir survey' was the first 'peripatetic university' that Ireland had seen since the wanderings of her ancient scholars in the sixteenth and seventeenth centuries. She went on to argue that:

Passionate interest was [now] shown by the people in the memorials of their ancient life – giant rings, cairns, and mighty graves, the twenty nine thousand mounds or moats that have been counted, the raths of their saints and scholars – each with a story on the lips of the people. (Green, 1911, p. 45)

It is not too much to conjecture that the new maps and map-making traditions sponsored by the Ordnance Survey were at least in part influential in this area. Certainly Ordnance Survey 'memoirs' gave the Irish the power 'to transform discourses of national identity, to chart history as a sequence of settlement patterns or distribution of antiquities, economy as a topography of peaks and depressions, citizenship as a pattern of property owner-ship or rights of way'. As such they possessed the potential to realise their political claims and to act as 'powerful instruments of statecraft' (Daniels, 1998, p. 129).

Although he recognises the role of cartography, statistical surveys and ethnography in laying the intellectual foundations of the imagined community of the modern nation, Anderson attaches most importance to mass education and print capitalism in cultivating the new imagined community of the nation. He suggests that the unified fields of communication created by the popular press and the national educational system then provided the basic morphology out of which emerged the modern nation-state. In arguing that nationalism sounded the death knell of tradition and the birth of modernity, he gets the story of nation-building in nineteenth-century Ireland seriously wrong. The clergy here gravitated towards nation-building as a strategy for ensuring their own survival by ensuring the survival of the belief systems and social systems that spawned them. A central weakness of

Anderson's thesis as applied to Ireland is his contention that the imagined community grew out of, and in opposition to, larger cultural systems. He neglects the role of state-centred cartography, including 'mental map-making', in the construction of unified fields of communication in many nineteenth-century nations, including Ireland. He also fails to see how nation-building and nationalism in a small nation like Ireland were at once reactions against cartographic expressions of 'big-nation' British nationalism on the one hand, and Unionist defences of this same genre of nationalism on the other.

The imagined community of the nation here was never simply a product of 'print capitalism' as Anderson implies. It was a territorially based economic and political discourse mapped out and articulated by, and indeed for, a national and provincial bourgeoisie, including the petty bourgeoisie in the countryside. Here nationalism was an Angel of History which crept at a much slower pace, and often marched to a quite different tune, than it did in Europe's larger nations, especially Britain and Germany. Anderson's work clearly points to the significance of print capitalism in fostering the unified fields of communication which underpinned the imagined community in the nineteenth century. Together with Hobsbawm he suggests that the progress of schools, and universities, measured that of nationalism then. Certainly the national press and universities, were, as we have already seen, among the most conspicuous champions of nationalism and nation-building in nineteenth-century Europe. In Ireland, however, these important integrative roles were performed by individuals from a whole range of institutions, including map-makers working with the Ordnance Survey, priests and clergymen living in close proximity to 'their people', reporters and newspapermen writing in the provincial and national press, and schoolteachers teaching in national and secondary schools throughout the country. In the Unionist north-east, as in the rest of Catholic Ireland, all of these were under the tight tutelage of Catholic and Protestant religious leaders on the one hand, and Unionist or Catholic cultural nationalists on the other. Using visual as well as aural techniques, the churches also mediated the central conceptions of European Catholicism, and Protestantism, to the masses, to 'their people'. In so doing they performed very personal and very particular roles in the communities that they served. Now members of the imagined communities of Christians were also members of the imagined community of the nation in the north as well as the south of Ireland.

Thus, contrary to Anderson, nationalism in Ireland did not grow out of the dusk of religious modes of thought. If anything it contributed to the growing power of the churches and boosted their political power while heightening the appeal of simple religious beliefs among ordinary people. As a result Ireland was shared out among two different mappings of modern Christianity. In the Protestant north-east, as in rural Catholic Ireland, traditional conceptions of spirituality and temporality did not break down under the spreading influences of a sceptical modernity. If anything they were hardened by it. Old everyday certainties of pre-modern life – belief in an afterlife, respect for authority, particularly that of the church, and belief in the sacredness of life – all acquired new meaning in nation-building Catholic Ireland as well as in Unionist Ulster. Hence nationalism acquired the status of a state-centred religion. In the eyes of many, nationalism was practically indistinguishable from religion. Like Puritans in early colonial America, priests and other religious leaders here often marvelled at their own ability to overcome Nature as a miracle of grace. They looked upon the survival of religious beliefs in these outer fringes of 'pagan' Europe almost as a miracle, one to be defended through a defence of the Christian nation-building projects of Catholic nationalists and Protestant Unionists (Pike, 1997, p. 23).

Ireland was not only depicted as a country divided by religion. It was torn between two different maps of religious modernity. One was centred on Rome and the 'foreign mission' fields. The other was centred on Britain and the Empire. Not surprisingly the identities of the men who defended this fragmented mapping of a 'divided Ireland' were intimately wound into the very landscapes which they mapped out in their minds, and upon which they toiled to bring 'their people' closer to 'their' God and 'their nation'. Thus nationalism and Unionism in Ireland were part of, and never apart from, the landscapes on which religious faith collaborated with men of intellect to achieve their nation-centred ends. By the end of the century the minutely mapped landscapes of rural and urban Ireland were perceived not as wildernesses, or even as natural places, but as organic parts of two different versions of the nation-state in Ireland, one of which was an integral part of the United Kingdom. These were at once political and sacred places, sacred to God and Ulster, sacred to Catholicism and to the Irish nation. Church leaders on all sides openly discouraged expressions of radical nationalism as fascism. In so doing they acted as a counterweight against tendencies of over-centralisation of the state that marked many European nations in the late nineteenth and early twentieth centuries (Kenny, 1997, p. 185). Irish citizens were clearly commended for giving unto the nation that which rightly belonged to the nation – love of country and love of its Catholic patriots – but they were also commanded to put respect for the teachings of the church over and above the teachings of the state whenever, and wherever, there was a divergence between the two. In other words they were expected to keep their love of the nation-state in check. As Kenny has argued:

> Catholicism was seen as the moral teacher in forging the new national identity of Eire, since Catholicism was the crucible of the historic Irish identity ... As the French State taught Frenchness through a careful and deliberate system of inculcating French Republican ideals through schools, the army, the civil service and other national institutions, so in Ireland Catholicism now taught Irishness through a less explicit but emphatically meaningful set of uplifting parables of what a patriotic Irishman should be. (Kenny, 1997, p. 168)

Periodicals like the aptly-named *Ireland's Own* and *The Irish Sacred Heart Messenger*, and especially the pamphlets of the Catholic Truth Society, played a crucial role in mapping out this simple Catholic Ireland. They defined patriotism as love of country and as a social obligation which required citizens to improve the nation by improving themselves and by striving to live up to the ideals of Catholic nationalists in particular. This view of patriotism was not unlike Greek and Roman conceptions of patriotism in that it evoked 'a sense of commitment to, and affection for, the political institutions and way of life that sustain the common liberty of a people' (Viroli, 1997, p. 185). Mobilised alongside nationalism, patriotism reinforced the cultural, linguistic and ethnic homo-geneity of the Irish nation. Map-making contributed to this process by cultivating a proprietorial sense of place, by fostering a sense of identity, and by nurturing a geography of exclusion which insisted that Ireland belonged only to the Catholic Irish. At their most extreme these cartographic expressions of national patriotism unified and even 'purified' the nation and depicted the territory of the other as 'enemy territory'.

In Ireland also, however, this view of patriotism was frequently softened by nationalists, not least by priests, nuns, local doctors and schoolteachers who extolled the not yet common virtues of cleanliness, hard work and good husbandry. They inculcated respect for all that was good in English 'high culture', especially in English literature and suggested that a good Irishman should have a sense of honour and a strict sense of honesty. Women were exhorted not to spend their time in 'idle gossip', and to put their energies instead into the family and into constructive community activities. Thus cultural associations were fostered, musical, dramatic and debating societies were encouraged, all of them under the strict control of the Catholic church. As Kenny points out, the real passion of the Irish countryside in the first half of the twentieth century was debating societies. These more than anything else provided a refined form of entertainment and pleasure that was otherwise often absent from rural areas and small towns. The chapter that follows shows how local nationalists acquired west Ulster for the Irish nation by nationalising people and places here, and by edging themselves into hegemonic positions in this rural underdeveloped corner of Catholic nation-building Ireland.

10   Local Politics and Nation-building: The Grassroots of Nationalist Hegemony

This chapter offers a critical account of nation-building and nationalism in one Irish county. It literally illustrates, in a specific socio-historical epoch and in a concrete geographical milieu, the theories of nation-building discussed so far in this work. It differs from more conventional local histories of nationalism to the extent that it does not take for granted the nationalist 'credentials' of the communities it seeks to study. Without devaluing the local or prioritising the national, it fuses local detail with broader theoretical perspectives in order to understand how nations have literally been constructed from the ground up. It particularly applies the theoretical logic of Gramsci's cultural Marxism to an analysis of the nation-building roles of the Catholic intelligentsia in the nationalisation of local communities and regional landscapes in the north-west of Ireland in the post-Famine period.

Towards a Gramscian Geography of Nationalist Hegemony

Gramsci was among the first to outline a historical and geographical approach to state-formation and nation-building within a materialist framework (Gramsci, 1977, pp. 34–45; Mac Laughlin and Agnew, 1986, pp. 248–51). The category of hegemony occupied a central position in his analysis of capitalist and pre-capitalist societies. It referred to the cultural as well as the economic modes of incorporation adopted by dominant sectors of class-structured, including nation-building, societies. The latter used this dominance to establish control over their social subordinates and to legitimise their monopoly of state apparatuses of local government and education (Gramsci, 1977, pp. 56–9). As used by Gramsci the concept 'hegemony' is not simply synonymous with ideological domination or manipulation. It constitutes instead the very substance and outer limits of 'common sense' for most people. As such it corresponds to the reality of social experience very much more clearly than any notion derived from simplistic Marxist formulae about the role of the 'base' and the 'superstructure' in 'determining' social behaviour (Williams, 1980, p. 80). Gramsci's mode of theorising clearly recognised the centrality of human agency in nation-building and historical social change. As we have seen, he particularly insisted that the dialectic was much more than the blind clash of 'physical forces' that it was in orthodox Marxist-Leninist accounts of nation-building and state-formation (Mac Laughlin, 1986a, p. 269). He viewed it instead as an historical movement to which real people contributed by claiming territory as their own, constructing their own 'homelands' and literally making their own history and nationalist mythologies. This allowed Gramsci to evade the voluntarism of idealist accounts of social and historical change, and the determinism of structuralist explanations of social change by building a model of social behaviour which recognised the powerful and powerless in nation-building societies as both 'determined' and 'determining' agents of regional and historical development. Thus to Gramsci, writing in an Italian context, a hegemony had distinctive geographical correlates. It was rooted to places and was never just a question of how a state related to society in any abstract terms. Thus the manner in which the largely peasant Mezzogiorno had been integrated into the Italian nation-state in the late nineteenth century particularly attracted Gramsci's attention. Northern industrialists, he argued, in alliance with southern landowners established hegemonic control over all of Italy by using the southern intelligentsia as local intermediaries between peasants and landowners (Gramsci, 1957, pp. 25–96).

As we have also seen, Gramsci's approach is suited to an analysis of nation-building in a region like post-Famine Donegal for a number of reasons. First, unlike Marx, he cast a sympathetic focus on rural societies and recognised the rural poor as important actors in the political arena. He showed for example that, through their associations with the clergy and the petty bourgeoisie in general, better-off peasants and small farmers often had a crippling effect on working-class movements for revolutionary change in a nation-building society like late nineteenth-century Italy (Gramsci, 1957, p. 58). Second, he explained the anomaly of subordinate social classes being led by a conservative clergy and a petty middle-class intelligentsia in terms of the social class origins of both these groups, especially the close links between the rural poor and their 'betters' among the clergy and the intelligentsia. Thus he argued that the nationalist intelligentsia, especially the clergy, often acted as social mediators between dominant and subordinate social classes in class-structured and nation-building societies. The landless poor and small farmers in turn, he argued, often regarded priests, teachers and others set above them in a deeply ambivalent manner. On the one hand they looked up to them as their political 'betters' and 'natural' leaders, not least because so many of them were their own 'flesh and blood' (Gramsci, 1977, pp. 2–23, 44–51). This was the case not only in the impoverished south of Italy in the late nineteenth century but also in Catholic areas of Ulster, including Donegal, where priests, teachers, doctors and local newspapermen carried huge amounts of 'cultural baggage'. They also wielded enormous social and political influence and acted as social intermediaries between the rural poor on the one hand and the local petty bourgeoisie and other nation-building social groups on the other. Having a son, or daughter, in the clergy or religious orders, in the teaching profession or indeed in any other white-collar profession in the county gave families here, as in rural Italy, a great deal of status and influence in the local community.

However, Gramsci also recognised that the rural and working-class poor could also envy – even despise – 'their' clergy and their political 'betters'. They envied them especially for their 'easy' way of life, and for the fact that these groups often identified with dominant social classes rather than siding with 'their own kind', namely those from whom they had literally sprung. As the case of late nineteenth-century Donegal clearly shows, it was more commonly the case that the local intelligentsia, including the clergy, were central to the consolidation of petty bourgeois nationalist hegemony at local level. In so doing they cultivated highly deferential attitudes among the poor, fostered a sense of national identity and national patriotism, and helped prevent outbreaks of class conflict by quelling social unrest and literally managing 'their people'.

Finally, Gramsci insisted that the rural poor were often as much subjects as objects of their political history, and their own historical geography. He showed that nation-building was never simply the prerogative of 'Great Men' or intellectual elites operating outside of time and space. It was instead something towards which the lesser intelligentsia, the rural poor and the working class could contribute by forging strong organic links with national-popular masses (Joll, 1977, p. 124).

The remainder of this chapter suggests that nationalist hegemony in post-Famine Donegal was not simply the product of

ethnic geography or ideological manipulation. It was instead literally rooted in the political and symbolic landscapes and economic
structures of Donegal. Thus nationalist hegemony here described a
process of structural and cultural negotiation which allowed
certain social groups, notably well-off farmers, the 'shopocracy',
petty industrialists and a small professional class, to exert moral
leadership, through the clergy and schoolteachers, over the rest of
Donegal society in such a way that their ideological outlook came
to be regarded as 'common sense' by society in general. Nationalist
hegemony here also rested on a set of cultural, economic and political strategies whereby these small-time nation-building power
elites claimed to represent 'their kind'. From their socially strategic
positions within local communities they set about imposing their
norms of political and cultural behaviour on the rest of Donegal
society. Indeed, as I have argued elsewhere, they made these the
ideals to which their social subordinates in particular should and
could aspire (Mac Laughlin, 1993b, pp. 97–112).

Thus nationalism in Donegal was not so much an autonomous
social force imposed from above by an altruistic nationalist intelligentsia. It was a political mass movement that developed out of the
county's socio-economic and political geography and intersected
with nation-building forces operating at national – and sometimes
even international – levels. As such it released Donegal's rural poor
from the 'idiocy of rural life' and gave many of those at the bottom
of rural society here a new national sense of place, and a sense of
worth, in nation-building Ireland (Marx, 1950, pp. 231–5). In
keeping with the logic of previous chapters, the sections that
follow examine the role of nationalist history in the nationalisation of people and places in the latter half of the nineteenth
century and the opening decades of the twentieth century.

The Nationalisation of Local Places

Gellner has suggested that nationalism is an attribute of people
rather than places (Gellner, 1972, 1983). This was only partially the
case in late nineteenth-century Donegal where, largely as a result
of local nationalists among the clergy and other sectors of the
intelligentsia, nationalism was also transformed into a sensitive
attribute of places and reflected the socio-regional contexts within
which it evolved. As such it constituted what we have described as
a Balkanising force and set the county apart from Unionist Ulster
while simultaneously uniting it with the rest of nation-building

Ireland. However, contrary to Irish nationalists and Ulster Unionists, places here were neither 'primordially' and 'naturally' Unionist nor nationalist. This is what most local and nationalist historians have insisted, at least until recently. It was precisely also what one Unionist politician suggested when, claiming Derry city (much of which was then actually located on Donegal soil) for Unionist Ulster, he insisted that:

> No candidate or truthful person can deny that the city of Derry is Unionist. It is Unionist in its representative citizens, in its industry and in its social life, aye, its very bricks and mortar are Unionist. (*Londonderry Standard*, 25 March 1912)

However, it is possible to propose an alternative perspective on nationalism and Unionism to that held by Irish nationalists and Unionists, and to treat state-centred farmers in late nineteenth-century Ireland as propagators and enforcers of regionally based hegemonies (Mac Laughlin, 1993b, pp. 392–5). This perspective at least allows for a critical geography of nationalism and Unionism in Ireland and Ulster and does not take national or Unionist geographies as socio-spatial, historical 'givens'. Irish nationalism and Unionism certainly had clearly identifiable heartlands and 'shatter-belts' in late nineteenth- and early twentieth-century Ulster. Just as there were areas over which nationalists and Unionists fought for hegemonic control, there were others where Irish nationalism and Ulster Unionism literally had to be constructed from the ground up. Indeed within Ulster it is possible to identify three distinct zones where nationalism and Unionism evolved and were either hegemonically successful, or failed to develop. First, there was the predominantly Presbyterian and prosperous heartland of eastern Ulster, the heartland of Unionist Ulster where Unionist hegemony was practically unchallenged. Second, there was the mixed Catholic and Protestant 'shatter-belt' of mid-Ulster. This was a 'contested terrain' over which Irish nationalists and Ulster Unionists struggled to assert political and cultural hegemony. Finally, there was the 'other Ulster', the overwhelmingly Catholic and underdeveloped west of the province, a region that was of peripheral interest to Ulster Unionists but of considerable strategic and symbolic significance to Irish nationalists ever anxious to acquire '*lebensraum*', or 'living space', for an Irish Catholic nation.

In Ireland as elsewhere in Europe there was a fundamental difference between the movement to found the nation-state and 'nationalism', in the sense that one was an ideological programme for constructing a political artefact claiming to be based on the other. In ethnically divided Ulster as elsewhere nationalists, including historians and antiquarians, played a crucial role in the nationalisation of people and places, not least in Donegal and the 'Other Ulster'. Thus Catholic priests and cultural nationalists here sought to contain Unionist influence and to resist the encroachment of Unionist power beyond the heartlands of east and mid-Ulster into the county's rich agricultural heartlands. Protestant influence was especially strong in the latter, especially in the Laggan Valley stretching out from Letterkenny, where Catholics were between 50 and 65 per cent of the population on the eve of the Great War (Census of Population, 1911). This part of the county was considered a contested terrain of nation-building and was caught between rural underdeveloped west Donegal on the one hand, and Unionist east Ulster on the other. In his *In the Days of the Laggan Presbytery* the Reverend G.A. Lecky suggested:

> It should be remembered that there are two Donegals – an outer and an inner. The former, which is almost wholly Roman Catholic, and from which the county to a large extent takes its character and complexion in the eye of the public, consists of extensive mountainous districts that lie along the western seaboard, and at some points run far inland. The latter consists of the more flat and fertile country that lies between the mountains and the river Foyle – the eastern boundary of the county. It is largely Protestant and from a very early period in history has been known as the Laggan, i.e. the low and level country. (Lecky, 1908, p. 8)

Local historians and antiquarians like Lecky mobilised history behind their constructions of a national identity. In so doing they helped create national styles, just as they established the ethnic lineage and political legitimacy of nation-building in the county. In underpinning the political legitimacy of nation-building here, they also 'nationalised' folk culture and insisted that the growth of strong nations was a moral evolution as spontaneous and uncontrollable as the evolution of the human organism.

Myth and myth-making were mixed in equal proportions both in regional and nationalist history, and in the state-centred ideology which this spawned. Thus, far from disproving myths and dispensing with tradition, local nationalist historians and the intelligentsia nourished the political imagination of their communities with myths and folk history and introduced a strong element of tradition into the political consciousness of nineteenth-century Donegal society (Anderson, 1983, pp. 34–9). In post-Famine Donegal nationalist myths and folk beliefs often supplemented, but less frequently substituted for, religious modes of explanation for social change and historical development. Here also they gave the rural poor a new national sense of place by elevating the 'native', including the native landscape and native iconography, to a new position in modern nation-building Irish society. The writings of Daniel Corkery best exemplify this genre of nationalist literature. Corkery described the symbolic and cultural significance of 'the sterile tracts' and 'back places' of counties along the Atlantic fringe of Ireland to the whole process of nation-building as follows:

> The hard mountain lands of West Cork and Kerry, the wild seaboard of the West, the back places of Connemara and Donegal – in such places only was the Gael at liberty to live his own way. In them he was not put upon. Big houses were few or none. Travellers were rare; officials short at the very aspect of the landscape; coaches found no fare. To reach them one must, leaving the cities and town behind, venture among the bogs and hills, far into the mountains even, where the native Irish, as the pamphleteers and politicians loved to call them, still lurked. (Corkery, 1924, pp. 19–24)

In Donegal cultural nationalists and local historians also regarded the west of the county in particular as the very 'core of Gaeldom'. Here, they argued, were the perfect specimens of an Irish race, the remnants of a folk society and 'the mental heirs of the historic past'. In quasi-racial accounts of the history of Celtic civilisation 'back places' like Donegal, Galway and Mayo were valued because they were a world apart from urban Ireland, and urban Britain. They were inhabited instead by a people set apart from Ireland's 'West Britons' by their linguistic heritage and social psychological characteristics. Thus, in *Education and the Nation*, a Catholic Truth Society pamphlet published in 1901 and which circulated widely among Donegal priests right up to the time of Irish partition, the Reverend J. Fahy argued that, 'in spite of severe privations', the inhabitants of 'core areas of Gaeldom' like west Donegal were:

> among the finest specimens of the race; mentally, in spite of want of education – perhaps because of that want – they are the equals or the superiors of their English-speaking neighbours. Classed as 'illiterates', because unable to speak or write English, they are equipped with a store of folk-lore, proverbs, and legends, and endowed with an acuteness whose neighbours entirely lack. Masters of vocabulary ten times greater than that of the English peasant, they speak their language with a fluency and accuracy he knows nothing of and many of the best English speakers never attain. In respect of courtesy, reverence, or morality, there is no comparison between them. (Fahy, 1901, p. 7)

In stressing the centrality of the Irish language both as a basis of national identity and as a defence against cultural imperialism, the Bishop of Raphoe in the east of the county urged his flock to take their example from the Gaelic-speaking 'people of the mountain', where, he stated, 'The language is still in the air there. It is in the blast that blows from the mountains, and it is our duty to see that it is the breeze that fans the plains' (*Irish Catholic Directory*, 1915, p. 519).

Another local nationalist referred to the inhabitants of north and west Donegal as 'the people of the rock' (O'Gallchobair, 1975, p. 45). They possessed all the characteristics of the peasants in Carlo Levi's *Christ Stopped at Eboli*, a classic account of peasant life in southern Italy in the 1930s (Levi, 1982, pp. 35–7). Indeed Levi's portrayal of relations between the rural poor and the state in this part of Italy could equally be applied to the rural poor of Donegal in the late nineteenth century. In Levi's classic the rural poor 'existed outside the framework of time' and were 'confined to that which is changeless and timeless'. Thus, he argued:

> Governments, Theocracies and Armies are stronger than peasants. So the peasants have to resign themselves to being dominated, but they cannot feel as their own the glories and undertakings of a civilisation that is radically their enemy. The only wars that touch their hearts are those in which they have fought to defend themselves against that civilisation, against history and government. These wars they fought under their own pennants, without military leadership or training. The peasant world has neither government or training; its wars are only sporadic outbursts of revolt, doomed to repression. Still it survives, yielding up the fruits of the earth to the conquerors, but imposing upon them its measurement, its earthly divinities and its language. (Levi, 1982, p. 35)

Myths, mythical history and folklore allowed local people here to write their own histories and appropriate the past. Thus for example in nineteenth-century Russia 'Saintly Princes' and 'Princely Saints' featured prominently in the political landscape, and were also 'beatified' in the history books (Cherniavsky, 1961, pp. 91–4). This was also the case with the Reverend William James Doherty's Catholic nationalist study, *Inis-Owen and Tirconnell: An Account of Antiquities and Writers* which was published in 1895 (Doherty, 1895). Born in Buncrana in the north-east of the county in 1864, his account of the local history of Donegal is a roll call of Catholic patriots and a celebration of its prehistoric Gaelic past. Doherty argued that, prior to the Young Irelanders in the mid-nineteenth century:

The History of Ireland had to be written to satisfy the English conscience, generally by showing that everything noble and exalted had been done by English statesmen, and their army of heroes and divines sent for the reclaiming, extirpation, extinction, and good example to the Irish savage. (Doherty, 1895, p. 488)

Eulogising the Donegal-born Franciscan John Colgan for his patriotism in recording so much Irish ecclesiastical history, he stated that:

Ireland, though the possessor of ancient historical manuscripts, unsurpassed by those of any other nation in their present spoken language, had been unable from the vicissitudes of ever recurring conquests, to do much more than preserve her historic treasures from extinction. Her ancient manuscripts like her people, breathed an heroic and lively imagination. Full of sentiment, with Christian feeling even to exultation. This tended to impress on the Irish mind that strong veneration which at all times has ever been rendered to the patron saints of Ireland. These manuscripts were interwoven with a crowd of traditions, the very framework of the history of every ancient nation, so difficult of comprehension to the uninitiated critic, and which has found a place in the lives of several of her saints. (Doherty, 1895, p. 85)

Doherty also stated that his original objective in writing this type of history was to provide 'a popular and homely rendering of John Colgan's place as a writer of the seventeenth century'. In *Inis-Owen and Tirconnell* this was extended to include 'other prominent writers of Donegal, who, in ancient and modern times, by their genius and learning, at home and abroad, have upheld the name, and extended the fame of the Irish race' (Doherty, 1895, p. 10). This in turn brought the author on a literary tour de force through the county which included not only Donegal's most famous saints and scholars, but also those who were only remotely connected with the county by accident of birth. Here also the recording of history was the work of amateurs, not least Catholic priests and self-taught antiquarians who literally 'Christened' places in Donegal and claimed them for nationalist rule. Thus, writing on 'the place occupied by Donegal in early Christian civilisation', Father Doherty stated:

we find her present from the first, sending forth apostles of religion, recording in the pages of history its progress, successes and vicissitudes, founding schools and universities abroad to impart knowledge, and extending literature. The children of Donegal rescued many treasured relics of antiquity, thereby contributing towards the distinction we claim as a nation, as pioneers in the cause of progress, Christianity, and civilisation throughout Western Europe. (Doherty, 1895, p. 7)

That this type of cultural nationalism still informed local history in Donegal until recently is evident in the following statement from Brian Bonner's *Our Inis Eoghain Heritage* published in 1972 (Bonner, 1972). The author's stated aim in this historical account of this Donegal peninsula was 'to make the people ... aware of the achievements, the sufferings and the heroism of their ancestors'. He went on to add:

The example of the past generations will, it is hoped, help them to retain their true sense of values and so stimulate a better informed line of action in community life. The earnest hope is that the present inhab- itants of Inis Eoghain will become more fully aware of their rich inheritance and appreciate adequately its great and unique character. They will then, no doubt, take steps to restore what has been lost and retain, from deep conviction, what is best in their traditional mode of life. A renewed and dynamic community will be the result. Inis Eoghain will thus be able to make a major contribution to the whole Irish nation in the coming years, as it did so effectively once before, in the period following the introduction of Christianity. (Bonner, 1972, pp. 1–2)

For Bonner, as for many Catholic nationalist historians in the late nineteenth century, the writing of history clearly was a strategy for dispelling 'a superficial sense of values'. It was a way to protect 'an old and precious order of things' from 'a new and materialistic culture devoid of spiritual values'. Thus Bonner insisted that only a proper recording and reading of history would set Inis Eoghain apart from 'that pagan, de-Christianised society which is such a disturbing feature of the present day' (Bonner, 1972, p. 1).

Like local historians in nineteenth-century Russia, 'priestly' nationalists in Donegal sanctified and nationalised the very land- scapes of Donegal (Cherniavsky, 1961; Doherty, 1895). In so doing they peopled them with nationalist heroes and local saints. Discussing the role of iconography in nation-building, Johnson has argued that public statues function as 'points of physical and ideo- logical orientation' on the landscape. As such they provide insights into 'how the public imagination is aroused and developed in the on-going task of nation-building' (Johnson, 1997, p. 348). Public statuary, in other words, whether in town or in the countryside, act as circuits of collective nationalist memory. As Johnson remarks, they form the material bases which allow for the emergence and structuring of 'nationalist imaginings'. We can see this clearly in late nineteenth-century Donegal. Discussing the rebellion of Cahir O'Doherty against English rule under Sir Arthur Chichester in Donegal in the opening years of the seventeenth century, the author of *Inis-Owen and Tirconnell* claimed that the 'crumbling ruins' of the castle of O'Doherty were more worthy of respect than the 'alabaster monument' erected to the memory of Chichester (Doherty, 1895, p. 7).

Local historians and antiquarians like Doherty not only provided 'points of physical and ideological orientation' on the landscape of nineteenth-century Inis-Owen. They literally made the place ring with the sound of a nationalist history by making it reverberate with calls from a heroic and largely mythical past. They replaced the landscape of the 'big house', and of the settler, with a native landscape rich in Gaelic iconographic detail. In particular they reconstructed the pre-plantation and Gaelic landscapes of Inishowen to make them immediately recognisable, and respected, by the poorest inhabitants of late nineteenth-century Donegal. They pointed to the high densities of Gaelic iconography in the county, and to the historical depth of the Celtic traditions here. In imprinting this nationalist geography on the consciousness of local communities, cultural nationalists like Doherty helped instil a strong sense of place in the inhabitants of rural Donegal and taught them to revere an 'unsaxonised' version of the past.

Thus Michael Harkin, also of Inis-Owen, was equally aware of the role of local history and ethnic geography in the cultivation of a nationalist sense of place among the poor of north Donegal. Writing on the history, traditions and antiquities of Inishowen in 1867, he described his philosophy of history as follows:

I wished to draw the attention of the people of Inishowen to the prominent and proud position which this territory holds in the ancient history of our country; to the illustrious line of princes of the Kinel-Owen, born and reared within the wall of Aileach, who wielded monarchical sceptre, who proved themselves the fathers of their people and the defenders of the rights of their country; to notice the old druidical temples, and other remains of pagan times, as illustrating the colonisation of the district and the form of worship of that remote period; *to show the childlike docility with which its people received the light of the gospel, and to point to the churches and monasteries which they founded*; to call to remembrance the struggles which our fathers sustained with the Dane and Saxon, successfully against the first, and though to the other they were forced to yield, it was not until after a most obstinate defence, when all Ireland besides had been subdued, and more than four centuries after Henry II received the submission of the southern princes. (Harkin, 1867, p. 199; emphasis added)

Meanwhile Stephen Gwynn, whose *Highways and Byways in Donegal and Antrim* appeared in 1899, argued that although the county had long been 'a worthless appendage of the Empire' under English rule, it would one day be of considerable strategic and economic significance to nation-building Ireland. Thus, in a statement which could equally have come from the German geographer Ratzel because of its reference to 'breathing space' or *lebensraum*, Gwynn argued that Donegal could never be:

> a thriving county, but it may cease to be clouded by the shadow of famine. *While human beings in these islands increase and multiply as they are doing, every year will give an added value to these lonely places which become the breathing spaces and playgrounds of our laborious race.* (Gwynn, 1899, p. 4; emphasis added)

Like other Victorian visitors to Donegal, Gwynn was 'enchanted' by its 'remote, lonely, and storm-beaten character', and by the fact that 'many districts here are so wild and barren that no industry of man has yet reclaimed them' (Gwynn, 1899, p. 15).

Nationalist myths, heroic geographies and religious histories like these performed a number of other functions in rural counties like Donegal. First, in recalling the past in heroic terms they mobilised popular support for the nationalist cause and bolstered the political confidence of nationalists throughout the late nineteenth and early twentieth centuries. Second, they gave the struggling nationalist movement in Donegal an ancient and respectable lineage by 'ethnicising' the historical record and reducing all past struggles to clear-cut conflicts between native 'insiders' and foreign 'outsiders'. Finally, they portrayed the local bourgeoisie, especially the Catholic clergy and their secular associates, as 'natural' leaders, as people who knew what was best for all sectors of Donegal society. They praised them for thwarting foreign rule, and for leading 'their people' out of the 'idiocy of rural life' on to national pathways of political righteousness.

It could also be argued that nationalism in late nineteenth-century Donegal was not just a cultural phenomenon. It was a local and regional expression of a European-wide tradition of race-thinking used by nationalists to rank their nations in a hierarchical world order of nation-states. In an ethnically divided nation like nineteenth-century Ireland local nationalists also emphasised the dangers of cultural miscegenation and stressed the centrality of nation-building to the preservation of local customs. This was particularly the case in Ulster where national separatism, as in Irish nationalism, and 'big-nation' nationalism as in Ulster Unionism, also reflected the political and economic concerns of regionally based social blocs and ethnic collectivities. Nationalism in such an area was also inherently geographical. It had clear-cut territorial imperatives, it evolved within geographical domains and, as a nation-building force, it altered the very contours of the built environment. Thus it not only attacked the Unionism at the heart of Anglo-Irish historiography for suggesting that 'the mere Irish' – especially those in a poor county like Donegal – were unfit to govern themselves and should therefore be governed by 'successful Protestants' and their Anglo-Irish 'betters'. It also condemned the 'rancherism' of the latter, believing that laissez faire rural capitalism under the hegemony of this ethnic and religious minority was contrary to the best interests of the Irish people, not least those living in the west and north-west who were forced to leave Catholic nation-building Ireland in search of work in Britain and North America. Thus, whereas English political pamphlets 'simianised' the 'Paddy' and caricatured Irish politics as irrational, local nationalists in Donegal as elsewhere in the country literally characterised 'English rule' as a 'foreign imposition', as a crime against Irish farming and Irish civilisation (Curtis, 1971, pp. 120–8; Mac Laughlin, 1999f, pp. 50–73).

Legitimising Nationalism: Local Custom versus 'Alien' Rule

Describing the poor condition of farming in Donegal in the aftermath of the Great Famine, the Inishowen historian Micheal Harkin argued that:

> The cause of all this misery is palpably plain, though many pretend not to see it. Ireland is an agricultural country. The few who own the soil till it not, and the millions who till the soil own it not; and while tillage and occupation impart increased value to the land, landlord-made law steps in and says to the tenant – I disown your improvements or I leave the landlord to appropriate them to himself, to rent you for them, and tax you for your own industry; you are his serf, his engine, his machine; the trust which the legislature confers on you is partially his; you are wholly and completely in his power, and he may evict and exterminate you without let or hindrance. (Harkin, 1867, p. 46)

Harkin, the son of a local small farmer was ideologically much closer to Donegal's petty bourgeoisie than he was to the landless poor. He suggested solutions to the social and economic problems of post-Famine Donegal which stopped well short of any radical restructuring of social class and property relations in the county. Steering a clear course between the extremes of laissez faire rural capitalism on the one hand, and what he saw as the doctrinaire socialism of continental Europe on the other, he argued that:

> In treating of the relations which should exist between landlord and tenant in Ireland, I wish at the very outset not to be understood as advocating socialism; for God forbid I should be found on the side of socialism, or to advocate the doctrines of Rousseau, nor those of Diderot or D'Alembert, as circulated through the medium of the infidel Encyclopaedia, and which led to the horrors of the revolution. (Harkin, 1867, p. 47)

He also made repeated historicist claims that the rightful rulers of Donegal were not 'alien landlords and their agents' but 'the descendants of its old Celtic tribes'. Like the late nineteenth-century Basque separatist Sabino de Arana, Harkin also made attachment to place and rootedness in rural society here the legitimate basis for nationalist rule in Donegal (Heiberg and Escudero, 1977, pp. 32–47). Central to both of these defences of national separatism was the concept of race as the foundation of the nation. In Donegal, as in the Basque country, nationalism was an historic 'obligation'. Like Sabino de Arana, founder of the Partido Nacionalista Vasco in the mid-1890s, local nationalists in Donegal also transformed elements from folk history and folk memory into symbols of nationalist legitimacy. These symbols in turn were destined for use in a nationalist struggle over ownership of the cultural, economic and political resources of the county.

Thus the local historian Harkin pointed out that 'the title deeds of many of our landed properties do not extend beyond the revolution of 1688' and argued that most large landholders in Donegal 'derived their grants from the confiscation of Ulster' (Harkin, 1867, p. 45). In so doing he exaggerated the historical lineage of nationalism in Donegal by repeatedly suggesting that the 'Irish nation' here had been suspended through Plantation of Ulster in the early seventeenth century. He also claimed that:

> the title deed of occupancy is as good as any title which the Crown can confer, and should shield the inhabitants of the country from the irresponsible exterminator; should warrant the law to secure them the full

value of the improvements which their labour or capital, or both, have
conferred upon the soil. (Harkin, 1867, p. 47)

Ignoring the role of middling tenantry in consolidating rural capitalism in Donegal, local historians and political leaders like Harkin
went on to systematically refute each assimilationist premise
underlying the Anglicisation and modernisation of Donegal
society in the nineteenth century. Inchoate though it was, this
historicist reaction to 'English misrule' in nation-building Ireland
revolutionised the treatment of many questions concerning social
life and work in Donegal, including the political future and future
development of the county. In so doing it constructed a new political landscape here. It also created a new historical agenda and
reopened questions that were supposed to have been settled with
the introduction of 'progressive' farming techniques from the early
nineteenth century onwards (Beattie, 1980).

Discussing the role of historicist claims and Celtic agrarian legislation on nationalist politics in general, Clive Dewey has argued
that such historicists, in late nineteenth-century Ireland as well as
Scotland, shifted the cause of agrarian conflict from population
pressure to a conflict of laws – a conflict between Celtic custom
and English commercialism (Dewey, 1974, pp. 30–71). He also
showed that confident rationalist conclusions were embodied
across the whole spectrum of social issues, and has argued that
nationalist historians attacked as erroneous the assumption that
rancherism was necessarily more productive than 'petit culture' in
rural Ireland and Scotland (Dewey, 1974, p. 32). Thus, after considering the options available for the alleviation of poverty in late
nineteenth-century Donegal, one state official argued:

> What seems to be needed for the relief of these districts is the establish-
> ment on a permanent basis of an emigration department, which, with a
> competent staff, and the co-operation of a voluntary committee,
> combined with systematic and careful oversight at ports of departure
> and arrival, shall from year to year, and not spasmodically, deal with all
> applications for assisted emigration, and advise or make grants in each
> case as may seem for the best. (Tukes, 1889, p. 44)

The wife of one prominent landlord in south Donegal also
suggested that the only remedy for the endemic poverty of
Donegal at this time was for the people:

> to rely on their own industry and efforts, instead of becoming public
> beggars, or beseeching the Government to help them – in other words

requesting the Government to hand over to them the result of other people's labours. If a healthier tone could be infused, and the people roused from their old indolent ways, Donegal's great curses – misrepresentations, beggings, and laziness – would vanish, and we should hear no more pitiable appeals. Doling out meal, abusing landlords, and blaming Government can never be the cure for the evils from which these congested districts suffer. At present there is neither industry nor the desire for improvement. When seasons do not fail the people can exist, and are happy, and do not care for settled work. They have their warm cabins, and all the winter the men lounge about doing nothing. To get the people away from the crowded districts and into more profitable fields of labour, if possible at home, if not, abroad, is the only cure for Donegal. Thousands of girls could find employment in the factories of Belfast and vicinity, but as long as meal can be had for the asking, the people will not exert themselves. (Maurice, 1886, p. 56)

This statement is all the more remarkable because it referred to subjects of the Crown in an Ulster county in terms redolent of the paternalism, racism and ethnocentrism normally reserved for subordinate communities in colonial Africa and India. In the event, many of the poor 'vanished' from Donegal (although not chiefly to Belfast), running off instead to England, Scotland, and North America with hardly enough English to write their names (Mac Laughlin, 1993b, p. 149–70). Thus local nationalists here made political capital out of the fact that from the late nineteenth century onwards Donegal became an 'emigrant nursery' which exported 'surplus' labourers, not just the products of surplus labour, to the core areas of world capitalism in order to make room for 'graziers and their bullocks' in rural Catholic Ireland (Keep, 1954, p. 413).

Forging a National Imagination in Late Nineteenth-century Donegal

Cultural nationalists and the nationalist intelligentsia in late nineteenth-century Donegal also coupled a concern with tenant right and legislative reform with a concern for denominational education. Thus they extolled the virtues of Catholic teaching as the best means for transforming the county's rural poor into citizens of an Irish Catholic nation. As Eugen Weber's study of the transformation of French peasants into French citizens has shown, Irish nationalists in Donegal were in no way exceptional in regarding national schools as social modes for incorporating the rural poor into a bourgeois nationalist world in the late nineteenth century (Weber, 1977). Thus in Donegal, as in rural enclaves elsewhere in Ireland, local historians and the nationalist intelligentsia defended nationalist education because it was their own creation. They defended it also of course because it provided employment for their own kind among the Catholic petty bourgeoisie while simultaneously disciplining the children of the poor and disseminating 'good taste' and the 'Three Rs' to those occupying the lowest ranks of late nineteenth-century Irish society.

Thus, by the opening decades of the twentieth century, a Catholic education was widely regarded as a hedge against Music Hall culture, and socialism and other radical ideas emanating from Scotland and England. They also defended Catholic schools because these imparted a moral code and educational values which eclipsed any training in 'the mechanical arts'. From a cultural nationalist perspective indeed, state education under English rule had been little more than a veiled attempt 'to steal their love of the their faith and the love for their motherland from the young hearts of little ones'. In his book *Catholicity and Progress in Ireland*, a veritable handbook of Irish Catholic nationalism published in 1905 and familiar to priests and nationalists throughout Donegal at the time, the Reverend O'Riordan claimed that:

> Irish Catholic children, while their hearts were plastic, were brought under un-Catholic influences, and were trained to think of Ireland as a western province of England with no more national individuality than an English shire. ... The effect of the thing called National Education on the Irish mind and character has been to lessen or to destroy that genuine idea of patriotism which is a positive principle of thought and action. (O'Riordan, 1905, pp. 446–7)

Donegal nationalists adapted such arguments about national education to local conditions. In so doing they made them the guiding principles of nationalist education in this corner of nation-building Ireland. Thus Michael Harkin was a strong advocate of Catholic education who preferred to have the children of Inishowen steeped in Catholic values, and in Celtic beliefs and mythology, rather than having them 'raised in a knowledge of the mechanical arts'. Thus Harkin argued:

> Education does not consist in reading, writing, music and the like. These are mere mechanical arts. They form part of the grand educational system, but it is only a subordinate one. Religion should be the beginning, the middle and the end of all educational systems. (Harkin, 1867, p. 167)

For laymen like Harkin, as for priests throughout Catholic nation-building Ireland, education was not only about 'book learning'. These men cultivated a whole new conception of education for the Catholic poor, one that emphasised the need to produce good citizens, citizens who would participate in the activities and public life of the new Irish nation. Indeed they reformulated a classical conception of education and adapted it to the needs of Catholic nation-building Ireland. Like Cicero and Aristotle, they insisted that an individual personality only attains intellectual and moral maturity through participation in the life of the polis. In so doing they transformed the humanism of the medieval world into a civic humanism. Where the former preached social aloofness and dedication to the other world, the latter was firmly rooted in this world of nation-building. Thus civic humanism merged with nationalism and insisted that citizens of the nation had a responsibility to live up to the ideals set out by the state.

Later in the century Catholic priests the length and breadth of the west of Ireland echoed Harkin's views, arguing that 'imparting knowledge without religion' meant that schools were 'only making so many clever devils'. They also stressed the role of schools in the formation of national character, insisting that:

> A nation is what its schools have made it. Schoolmasters are the teachers of the race – as they mould the child's mind, so is the nation moulded. The school is the nation's home, where its children are trained; as home-life leaves its impress on the family, so is the imprint of the school left on the civic and national life. The schoolboys of today are the men who will rule our destinies tomorrow. (Christian Brothers Handbook, 1952, p. 11)

In 1905 the Catholic Bishop of Derry, whose diocese extended into north Donegal and supplied the county with many of its priests, exhorted local priests and teachers in the following terms:

> In their anxiety about secular education men appear to forget that there is a knowledge of greater importance than that which facts of history or scientific knowledge can impart. They seem to lose sight of the truth that man is not a mere animal, but he possesses an immortal soul, the salvation of which is the supreme good. (Lenten Pastoral Letter, 1905)

In making statements like these, cultural nationalists and the Catholic clergy were literally making local communities their own, while making them also part of nation-building Ireland. As we have already seen, this gave local people here an elevated status of their own worth in the new Ireland. Henceforth, they were convinced by their priests, the rural poor were a step above the 'accomplished linguist', the 'eloquent orator' and 'successful businessman'. Listening to the oratorical eloquence of their priests, the rural and small town poor in turn learned to respect the authority of their priests just as they were impressed by the breadth of their knowledge of spiritual and worldly matters. Thus the author of 'The Literature Crusade in Ireland', a Catholic Truth Society pamphlet which circulated widely in Donegal, Derry and Tyrone on the eve of partition, stated that:

> Since the barrier of the Irish language was broken down, and since Ireland has become practically an English-speaking country, there is no natural breakwater to prevent the flood of English literature flowing through the land. Day and night it is constantly coming, and in ever-increasing quantities. Some of the new Crusade have been struck by the number of cross-channel publications which find their way to the small towns and villages of Ireland. The larger towns have been almost deluged with them. (Murphy, 1912, p. 21)

This author also warned against the dangers of secularism in Catholic Ireland. He stressed the relationship between 'literature and infidelity' and insisted that the connection between the two was 'only too often lost sight of by the petty philosophers of our own day'. He went on to argue that:

> There is indeed a striking contrast between the profound respect with which the great minds of all time have approached the deep questions of pure existence, and our relations with our Creator, and the flippancy with which many of your modern quill drivers treat of them. Yet the disrespect of up-to-date novelists and review writers will have its effect on the unthinking, and even the best literature crusade imaginable will not save them from moral ruin. If the 'little philosophy' which is only too often apparent in the flippancy and shallowness of current literature does not openly preach atheism, it very often attacks us Catholics, and everything that is dear to us. This is especially the case since so much of the Press has got into Masonic hands. (Murphy, 1912, p. 18)

That it was not so much 'foreign' literature and secular ideology but the 'baser elements' of both that chiefly worried cultural nationalists and priests here is clear from the following statement from the Reverend J. Fahy. Fahy's writings were familiar to priests and other cultural nationalists in Donegal. He stated that:

> We have no quarrel with the best forms of English life, manners and literature. They are no doubt excellent and they suit English people. But

it is exactly the worst forms which Ireland absorbs and assimilates, and which eat into her marrow, transmuting our people beyond the power of pulpit or platform to resist. (Fahy, 1901, p. 7)

In rural Catholic Donegal, as in Catholic enclaves elsewhere in Ulster, Catholic literature, especially Catholic newspapers, were considered a means for protecting 'the unthinking' from 'pernicious influences' of 'foreign literature'. As we have seen, they also created a unified field of communication which linked the isolated Catholic population of Donegal and other parts of Ulster to the rest of Catholic Ireland. Catholic newspapers and political pamphlets here provided cultural nationalists with an alternative to the hegemonic culture of English secularism and Protestant Unionism. They also, of course, provided priests and local nationalists alike with the means to tighten their hegemonic control over 'their own people'. This concern to resist Anglicisation and contain class conflict was especially evident in the county's small towns and villages. This was particularly the case in the vicinity of Derry where shirt factories were spreading industry and labour unrest to the countryside in the opening decades of the twentieth century. Here, it was suggested,

the Gael has been crying for help to beat back the Anglicisation he saw dragging its slimy length along – the immoral literature, the smutty postcards, the lewd plays and suggestive songs were bad, yet they were mere puffs from the foul breath of a paganised society. (Phelan, 1913, p. 773)

Worse than the 'full sewerage' of immoral literature in such areas was 'the black devil of Socialism, hoop and horns', which, priests and cultural nationalists here argued, was 'invading' Donegal and other Ulster counties. Thus the Reverend Phelan, whose speeches regularly appeared in newspapers which circulated throughout east Donegal, argued that:

Our workmen are Catholic, but borrow their thoughts, phrases and standards from the infidel socialism. They denounce the power which denies their country the right to manage their own affairs, and then hitch themselves on to English trade unions and ask foreigner to dictate to Irish trade. (Phelan, 1913, p. 773)

In arguing thus, Catholic employers and the clergy reminded workers of their duty to give employers a 'fair' day's work for what they deemed a 'fair wage', treated trade unionism and labour unrest as a threat to nationalist unity in Donegal, and extended patriotism from the political realm to the workplace.

The 'Natural Leaders' of the Nation

Portraying the rural bourgeoisie as the natural defenders of Donegal's moral economy, writers like Harkin, Doherty and Gwynn also portrayed the Hungry Forties as the final indictment of landlord rule in Ireland. In so doing they completely ignored the parsimonious response of Catholic tenant farmers, and shop-keepers, to rural poverty during and after the Famine. Both these social groups held strategically important positions in mid-nine-teenth-century Donegal society, not least as Poor Law Guardians responsible for indoor and outdoor relief. Like their social class peers in England and Scotland, they took great care to ensure that the local poor would not become a burden on the local rates, and, like their peers across the Irish Sea, often insisted that relief be distributed only on condition that its recipients abandon all claims to land and other property. In mid-nineteenth-century Donegal as elsewhere in underdeveloped Ireland this led to a glut of small holdings on the market and these were frequently bought up, or rented, by 'improving' tenants and independent small farmers. Thus did the disintegration of peasant society augment the socio-economic status, and heighten the political status, of improving tenant farmers and consolidate bourgeois nationalist hegemony in late nineteenth- and early twentieth-century Donegal (Mac Laughlin, 1985, pp. 26–38). The 'emptying' of the county through emigration also extended the range of commercial farming in the county and consolidated the power of the 'thirty-acre men' and the petty bourgeoisie throughout Donegal.

Thus the proletarianisation of Donegal's rural poor into overseas labour markets allowed those who stayed behind to add field to field, and to enter the ranks of the small but substantial propertied classes. As early as the mid-nineteenth century members of this social class in west Donegal were already proclaiming Ireland's right to self-determination. Thus in 1845 the Guardians of Glenties Poor Law Union in the south-west of the county claimed:

> The Irish Nation in extent of territory, in fertility of soil, in the number and industry of its inhabitants furnishes abundant means for the main-tenance of an independent legislature and requires such legislature for the due attention to the local interests and general prosperity of Ireland. (Minutes of Glenties Poor Law Union, 26 September 1846)

By the late nineteenth century this petty bourgeoisie owed its hegemonic status to its economic strength, and to the fact that it had by then practically monopolised political and cultural life in Donegal. Thus it had largely controlled the market for agricultural produce. It practically dominated local government and was on the verge of securing property rights from the beleaguered landed ascendancy. As we have already seen, it had long sought to ensure that Poor Law rates would not pose an obstacle to development in the county, including the development of modern farming practices with their revulsion against farm fragmentation.

By the turn of the century the Catholic petty bourgeoisie in Donegal had clearly come of age, and were dominant in the professions as well as in economic life. This is well borne out by an analysis of the social class structure of Donegal in Table 10.1 which shows that Catholic representation in selected professional and commercial occupations in Donegal increased quite significantly between 1881 and 1911. These figures also show that Donegal had become a more commercialised society at the end of this period, and that the Catholic middle class, although still quite small by 1911, had benefited significantly from the breakdown of peasant society and the emergence of native capitalism. There were a number of occupations where Catholic strength was on the increase, notably civil service officers and clerks, and parish, county and Poor Law Union officials. Catholics were also dominant in the teaching profession, and were increasingly dominant in the merchant class. However, as Table 10.1 shows, Donegal's middle class was still very small in the late nineteenth and early twentieth centuries and Catholic priests constituted a very significant social force in the county. The total number of Catholics in these occupations was only 1,266 in 1881, and Catholic representation in this broad socio-economic grouping increased by 25 per cent in 1911 (Census of Population, 1881, 1911). Priests as a percentage of listed occupations in 1881 and 1911 were 10.6 per cent and 11.2 per cent respectively. However, taken together, priests, schoolmasters and teachers formed a cohesive intelligentsia and accounted for just over 35 per cent of all Catholics in the occupations listed in Table 10.1 in 1881 and 1911. However, they were over 25 per cent of all Catholics in a middle-class socio-economic grouping comprising civil service officers and clerks, county and local officials, parish and Union officials, barristers, physicians, teachers, civil engineers, merchants, brokers, auctioneers and bankers. The fact that they had state-centred interests and were engaged in national and county politics, meant that the rural bourgeoisie were a class apart from their social subordinates in Donegal who struggled against the vicissitudes of rural capitalism.

Table 10.1: Catholic Representation in Selected Occupations, Donegal, 1881–1911

Occupation	1881		1911	
	Total Employed	% RC	Total Employed	% RC
Catholic priest	88	100%	121	100%
Schoolmaster/Assistant	241	73%	301	80%
Teacher/Professor	74	51%	26	66%
Civil Service official	54	39%	101	48%
County and local official	53	23%	73	36%
Parish/Union/district officer	39	33%	53	76%
General shopkeeper	262	77%	336	85%
Merchant	145	61%	160	67%
Broker	15	47%	33	58%
Commercial traveller	12	58%	39	64%
Commercial clerk	69	55%	87	49%
Banker	3	00%	1	00%
Bank service	44	16%	52	25%
Auctioneer	18	72%	20	15%
Barrister/Solicitor	25	20%	42	36%
Law clerk	47	49%	39	49%
Physician	62	29%	64	45%
Civil engineer	14	14%	17	41%
Insurance agent	1	00%	28	75%
Total	1,266	60%	1,593	68%

Source: Census of Population, County of Donegal, 1881, 1911. Her Majesty's Stationery Office, Dublin.

Priestly Politics and Nationalist Hegemony in Donegal

The population of Donegal in 1881 was 206,035, of whom 76 per cent were Roman Catholics. Twelve per cent of the population belonged to the Church of Ireland, and a further 10 per cent were Presbyterians (Census of Population, 1881). By 1911 the population of the county had dropped by almost 20 per cent, but Roman Catholics still constituted 79 per cent of the total population of 168,537. The Church of Ireland congregation had by then dropped to only 10.7 per cent, and Presbyterians were a mere 8.9 per cent of the total population (Census of Population, 1911). This meant that the ratio of clergy to the population here increased significantly for all denominations in this period. However, this was particularly the case for the Catholic population of the county. Thus the number of priests and nuns in the county at this time increased by 38 per cent and 124 per cent respectively. This in turn meant that the overall ratio of priests and nuns to the Catholic population had risen sharply, from a ratio of 1 to 1,260 in 1881 to a ratio of 1 to 652 in 1911. The ratio of priests to people had risen from 1 priest to 1,791 Catholics in 1881 to just under one in 1,000 in 1911. With equally strong ratios of clergymen in the Protestant population of Donegal and Ulster in general it is little wonder that late nineteenth-century Ireland, including Ulster, has been labelled a 'priest-ridden' or clerically-dominated society.

As leaders of 'their people' priests in particular were responsible for instilling a sense of patriotism in the Donegal poor while simultaneously reminding them of their Christian and political duties as Irishmen and Irishwomen to support Catholic nationalists. Far from being mere instruments in the hands of the petty bourgeoisie, Catholic priests occupied socially strategic positions within the petty bourgeois world and were at once structured by, and had a powerful structuring influence within that world. Their social position also meant that they not only informed but frequently formed the political and moral outlook of those under their care, including the petty bourgeoisie. Their numerical strength and political pragmatism cast Donegal priests in the role of 'organisational men' in the late nineteenth century and early twentieth century. One priest-historian described priests in a neighbouring diocese in county Tyrone in the early twentieth century as follows:

> they were men of zeal and activity and solid piety. It is administrative and apostolic activity that they favour rather than literary and intellectual activity. In this they differ from their confreres in mainland Europe. They prefer to build and develop church, school and parochial house, as generally their predecessors did when they restored the faith to Western Europe in the eighth and ninth centuries ... Above all they are people's priests, sprung from the people and though coming back to them after years of higher education in seminary or university in Ireland or abroad, they are at one with the people. ... They were never revolutionaries though sometimes innovators. They adhered to what was tried and found to be good. (Donnelly, 1978, pp. 113–17)

A better description of priests as a Gramscian 'organic intelligentsia' could scarcely be found. However, this depiction of priests as men who were 'at one with their people' requires considerable qualification in the case of rural Donegal. Far from simply being 'sprung from the people', priests in Donegal tended to derive from small farming and middle-class families as these alone could afford the expense of training a son for the priesthood. As the organisers of their communities, Catholic priests were also able to dictate social and political morality in Donegal. Thus they used their considerable social influence to police the political consciousness of their communities and, like their political confrères in the richer heartlands of the south of Ireland, supported the political objectives of the rural middle class against the landed ascendancy during the Land War in the 1880s. They also condemned all expressions of rural radicalism when this threatened the interests of the middling tenantry, and preached the politics of moderation and national consensus. To have acted otherwise would have been to attack the social and political edifice upon which they depended.

Recent studies of the social outlook and political role of priests throughout late nineteenth- and early twentieth-century Ireland have stressed the fact that priests often acted as social and political mediators between dominant and subordinate sectors of rural and urban society. This was particularly the case in Donegal where priests were the chief, and often the only, mediators between the rural poor and the emergent bourgeoisie. In his political portrait of priests in mid-nineteenth-century Tipperary, O'Shea has argued that the priesthood here by the 1860s had:

> largely come to grips with spiritual and ecclesiastical problems. Aided by synodical guidelines these priests imposed a large measure of Catholic discipline on society, as well as making frequent examinations of their consciences. Following the dramatical upheaval of the Famine, ... they found themselves in a society dominated by their own kith and kin, the tenant farmers who were the bastions of this church spiritually and financially. Not only could the clergy identify with this class on a social and spiritual level, but their respective politics were ... comfortably compatible. (O'Shea, 1983, p. 215)

O'Shea has shown that a mixture of Catholic theology, social class influence and public opinion directed the socio-political actions of priests in Tipperary. He also argued that it was precisely through their affinity with the middling tenantry that priests were 'sucked into the vortex of politics'. However, while O'Shea has painted an excellent portrait of 'priestly politics' in one of the richer heartlands of post-Famine Ireland, he fails to allow for regional differences in the social class origins and political functions of priests in the peripheral counties like Donegal, Mayo, Clare and Kerry. His categorisation of Tipperary priests as a 'peasant priest-hood' is particularly inappropriate, given, as he himself has shown, that most priests here derived from the substantial tenantry and from the middle-class shopocracy.

Preliminary analysis of the social origins of priests in late nine-teenth- and early twentieth-century Donegal suggests that here, as in other rural Ulster counties, Catholic priests were of humbler origins than their confrères in the richer heartlands of southern Ireland. They were as likely to derive from medium as from large farms throughout Donegal, Derry and Tyrone, and a significant proportion originated from an emergent middle class comprising shopkeepers, publicans, grocers, hoteliers, butchers and clerical workers (Daly, 1980, pp. 26–34). Their humbler social class origins not only reduced the social distance between priests and poorer parishioners in Donegal. It also made it all the easier for them to act as an organic intelligentsia who not only represented but actively articulated what they considered the best interests of 'their' people. Those Donegal priests raised in the mixed nation-alist and Unionist shatter-belt of mid-Ulster were often brought up with an awareness of the second-class status of Catholic national-ists in Unionist Ulster and brought to their pastoral duties in Donegal a missionary zeal to simultaneously elevate and nation-alise those under their care.

However, in Donegal, as elsewhere in rural Ireland, the Catholic clergy was not a monolithic group, and the politics of its members could range from political indifference, through Romantic nation-alism, to constitutional nationalism. Thus, while the overtly political clergy could present themselves as 'at one with their people', they shared the social class outlook of the substantial tenantry and petty middle class from whom they derived and the politics of both groups were almost completely compatible. Moreover, even the politically indifferent among the clergy could be classified as nationalists in the wider sense of being nation-builders who instilled nationalist sentiments in those under their charge and defended nation-building as a political project that was above party politics.

By the turn of the century Catholic priests in Donegal were not only urging Catholics to vote for Catholic candidates. They made patriotism and loyalty to Catholic Ireland a moral obligation binding on all Catholics in Donegal. As one nationalist priest whose views were widely publicised throughout Catholic Donegal in his day stated:

Patriotism is a Christian virtue, just as really as truthfulness, obedience, gratitude are virtues. It is a virtue that binds us in conscience, in the first place, *to honour and reverence the country of our birth, and in the second place, to make sacrifices proportionate to the need of our country when she requires them.* (Burbage, 1913, pp. 593–4; emphasis added)

In another Lenten pastoral letter read at all masses in one Donegal diocese on the first Sunday of Lent 1901, the local bishop prayed that 'God in his mercy would send a man who will not seek his own exaltation but to raise Ireland and her people to her proper place among the nations of the world'. He also urged his priests to play an active role in nation-building and insisted that:

with us the cause of faith and fatherland have ever been inseparably intertwined; that priests and people have worked together as one body; and we have reason to fear those who would try to separate them now, and to teach the people that politics and religion are no longer one, but two distinct issues. (Lenten Pastoral Letter, 1901)

In March 1913 the Bishop of Raphoe in east Donegal was similarly stressing the links between priests and their people, and prayed that:

under God's grace and mercy, the bonds between priests and people, so indispensable to national concord, would never be broken, while the Irish priest found, as he did, his place by preference among the poor and the toilers, giving them the priceless sympathy of his warm heart. (*Irish Catholic Directory*, 1913)

Bishop O'Doherty of Derry defended political caution, gradualism and a constitutional route to national self-determination as preferable to any radical break with the past, including, not least, any radical break between priests and 'their people'. Thus he argued:

It is with nations as it is with individuals, nature knows no harsh transition. A crushed bone does not recover in a day. We could only abandon ourselves to despair if, without remembering our respective historical conditions, we were to compare our historical conditions with that of any of the European nations whose homes are hives of industry and whose traditions of industry are the growth of centuries. Their government was sunshine and love, when ours was a boulder from an iceberg when it was not a gibbet. (*Irish Catholic Directory*, 1915, p. 519)

From sermons like these a paternalism or hegemony was constructed which was accepted by both the dominated and the dominant, and afforded a fragile bridge across the social contradictions separating priests and the rural poor, and separating also the rural poor and the rural middling classes. For men like O'Doherty, as indeed for the priests and nuns under his charge, Catholic nationalism was not only a strategy for undermining solidarity among the poor by linking them to their social and political 'betters' – it was also, as we have already seen, a cultural defence against 'pernicious' influences from England and Scotland.

Bishops and priests in Donegal frequently defended Catholicism against Unionist charges that Irish Catholics were innately inferior to Ulster Protestants and that 'Catholicity' was an obstacle to social and economic development. The fact that they were responsible for building schools, churches and parochial halls throughout the county made it easier for Donegal's poor to see priests as socially progressive and worthy of respect. To many indeed it appeared that they were literally constructing a Roman Catholic Ireland among the hills and fields of Donegal. Thus the parish priest of Buncrana in north-east Donegal described the relationship between Roman Catholicism and Irish nation-building as follows:

> We are the children of long ages of struggling and servile existence. Throughout a struggle which would have crushed the heart of any other people we clung to the jewel of religion though we lost the casket, nationality; and if our national character has not been preserved so well as our National Faith, we have surely good reason as a people to thank God that so many splendid virtues have survived the wreck. It is from the records of our past enforced degradation that we acquire confidence in our future destiny. The degradation of a country is the work of centuries, and though its freedom can be achieved with the swiftness of a storm, yet the recovery of a nation's liberty is often a gradual, uphill work. (*Derry Journal*, 5 June 1905)

Sermons like these were regularly preached to captive congregations attending Sunday mass throughout Donegal in the late nineteenth and early twentieth centuries. They not only suggested that patriotism was a Christian duty and that nationalism was the epitome of political virtue – they made the poor of Donegal defer to 'their betters' in matters political, and made it difficult for those attending mass on Sunday to know where religion left off and where middle-class social morality and nationalist politics began.

This chapter has focused on nation-building and nationalism in Donegal in order to redress an imbalance in existing literature which has tended to adopt either a national focus, or has concentrated on historic heartlands of Irish nationalism outside Ulster.

Thus it has been a study of failed Unionism and successful nationalism in a forgotten 'other Ulster' beyond the heartlands of
Unionist and Irish nationalist power. This 'other Ulster' was far
less urbanised, and indeed less commercialised, than the industrialised east of the province. It was also far more homogeneous than
the mixed Catholic and Protestant shatter-belt of mid-Ulster, the
great 'contested terrain' over which Unionists and nationalists
struggled to assert hegemonic control. By the late nineteenth
century it was both politically and economically integrated into
nation-building Ireland and was nationalised from within by
Catholic priests and teachers and other 'local heroes' of the
nationalist cause. Winning the plebeian sectors of Donegal society
to an acceptance of the statist goals of the nationalist bourgeoisie
proved a more difficult task than the latter had anticipated.
However, it was made all the easier after the Famine depleted the
ranks of the plebeian poor and hastened the 'kulakisation' of
Donegal society by facilitating the emergence of a petty bourgeois
rural sector.

It was in this way that nation-building forces operating at the
national level intersected with those operating at the local level to
form a social bloc of bourgeois and petty bourgeois interest groups
capable of exerting hegemonic control over the political and
economic life of the county and the country. This was achieved
not so much by the conversion of the rural poor to the political
creed of the petty bourgeoisie as by a 'long revolution' led by
priests, teachers, merchants and substantial farmers. Cultural
nationalists here also forged local links with national identities by
literally highlighting relics on the Celtic landscape and stressing
the authenticity of local over 'foreign' customs. Thus priests and
their lay subordinates used chapel and school to 'nationalise' the
rural poor and to 'Gaelicise' the landscapes wherein they lived and
laboured. Far from being political mediators who carried the
gospel of nationalism from dominant to subordinate sectors in
Donegal society, Catholic priests here were organisational men in
their own right. The cultural and ideological markers which they
used to define Irishmen and Irishwomen accorded well with the
political and economic interests of the petty bourgeoisie from
whom they derived. Moreover, their socially strategic, and
frequently unchallenged, positions in Donegal society meant that
they were able to lay the bare architectural framework of Irish
nationalism in such a way that alternatives to their worldview
were literally unthinkable. Thus they facilitated the ethnicisation

and modernisation of Donegal society and made ethnic identity superior to class identity by treating class conflict as 'foreign' to Catholic nationalist Ireland. In so doing they channelled class identities into ethnic moulds, upheld the subservient sectors of rural society as paragons of nationalist virtue, and 'sanctified' people and places for the cause of nationalism.

Bibliography

Abdel-Malek, A. (1963) 'Orientalism in Crisis', *Diogenes*, vol. 44, pp. 107–8.
Adams, F. (1914) *Conquest of the Tropics: The Story of the Creative Enterprises Conducted by the United Fruit Company* (New York: Doubleday).
Agnew, J. (1982) 'Sociologizing the Geographical Imagination: Spatial Concepts in the World Systems Perspective', *Political Geography Quarterly*, vol. 1.
Agnew, J. (1983) 'An Excess of "National Exceptionalism": Towards a Political Geography of American Foreign Policy', *Political Geography Quarterly*, vol. 2.
Agnew, J. (1987) *Place and Politics* (London: Allen and Unwin).
Agnew, J. and Duncan, J. (1981) 'The Transfer of Ideas into Anglo-American Geography', *Progress in Human Geography*, vol. 5, no. 1.
Akbar, M.J. (1985) *India: The Siege Within* (Harmondsworth: Penguin).
Althusser, L. (1969) *For Marx* (London: New Left Books).
Althusser, L. (1977) *Lenin and Philosophy* (London: New Left Books).
Anderson, B. (1983) *Imagined Communities* (London: Verso).
Anderson, J. (1973) 'Ideology in Geography', *Antipode*, vol. 5, no. 3.
Anderson, J. (1986) 'On Theories of Nationalism and the Size of States', *Antipode*, vol. 18, no. 2.
Anderson, J. (1989) 'Ideological Variations in Ulster during the first Home Rule Crisis', in Williams, C. and Koffman, E. (eds) *Community Conflict, Partition and Nationalism* (London: Routledge).
Andrews, C.S. (1975) *Man of No Property* (Dublin: Wolfhound).
Andrews, J. (1975) *A Paper Landscape* (Oxford: Oxford University Press).
Andrews, J. (1997) *Shapes of Ireland: Maps and Mapmakers* (Dublin: Templeogue).
Andrews, T. (1982) *A Man of No Property* (Dublin: Macmillan).
Ardey, R. (1968) *The Territorial Imperative* (London: Fontana).
Baddeley, O. and Fraser, V. (1992) *Drawing the Line: Art and Cultural Identity in Contemporary Latin America* (London: Verso).
Balibar, E. and Wallerstein, I. (1991) *Race and Nation* (New York: Sage).
Barker, D. (1993) 'Off the Map: Charting Uncertainty in Renaissance Ireland', in Bradshaw, B. et al. (eds) *Representing Ireland* (Cambridge: Cambridge University Press).
Beames, M. (1982) 'The Ribbon Societies: Lower Class Nationalism in Pre-Famine Ireland', *Past and Present*, vol. 97.
Beames, M. (1986) *Peasants and Power* (Brighton: Harvester).
Beattie, S. (1980) 'The Congested Districts Board and Inishowen, 1891–1922', *Derriana*, Journal of the Derry Diocesan Historical Society.

Beattie, S. (1997) 'Laggan Farm Accounts', *Donegal Annual*, no. 49.

Bell, G. (1978) *The Protestants of Ulster* (London: Pluto).

Benjamin, W. (1990) *The Bonds of Love* (London: Virago).

Beresford Ellis, P. (1975) *A History of the Irish Working Class* (London: Pluto).

Bernal, J. (1969) *Science in History* (Harmondsworth: Pelican).

Bhabha, H. (1990) *Nation and Narration* (London: Routledge).

Billig, M. (1995) *Banal Nationalism* (London: Sage).

Bishop of Derry (n.d.) Speech in unpublished manuscript (Derry: St Columb's College).

Black, R. (1960) *Economic Thought and the Irish Question* (Cambridge: Cambridge University Press).

Blaut, J. (1987) *The National Question* (London: Zed Press).

Boate, H. (1652) *Ireland's Naturall History* (Dublin: Ms., National Library).

Bonner, B. (1972) *Our Inis Eoghain Heritage* (Dublin: Foilseachain Naisiunta Teoranta).

Bowler, P. (1989) *The Invention of Progress* (London: Blackwell).

Boyce, D. (1991) *Nationalism in Ireland* (London: Routledge).

Boylan, T. and Foley, T. (1992) *Political Economy and Colonial Ireland* (Oxford: Oxford University Press).

Branch, M. (ed.) (1985) *Kalevala: The Land of Heroes* (London: The Athlone Press).

Breuilly, J. (1982) *Nationalism and the State* (Manchester: Manchester University Press).

Bull, P. (1996) *Land, Politics and Nationalism* (Dublin: Gill and Macmillan).

Burbage, C. (1913) 'The Obligation of Patriotism', *Catholic Bulletin*, vol. 3, no. 11.

Calder, A. (1981) *Revolutionary Empire* (London: Jonathan Cape).

Canny, N. (1991) 'The Marginal Kingdom', in Bailyn, B. and Morgan, P. (eds) *Strangers Within the Realm* (Chapel Hill: University of Carolina Press).

Carr, E. (1945) *Nationalism and After* (London: Macmillan).

Chatterjee, P. (1986) *Nationalist Thought and the Colonial World* (Delhi: Oxford University Press).

Cherniavsky, M. (1961) *Tsar and People: Studies in Russian Myths* (New Haven: Yale University Press).

Clark, C. (1992) *Economic Theory and Natural Philosophy* (New York: Edward Elgar).

Clark, M. (1998) *Modern Italy* (London: Longman).

Clark, S. (1978) 'The Importance of Agrarian Class Structure and Collective Action in Nineteenth Century Ireland', *British Journal of Sociology*, vol. 29.

Clark, S. (1979) *The Social Origins of the Land War* (Princeton: Princeton University Press).

Clark, S. and Donnelly, J. (1983) *Irish Peasants* (Manchester: Manchester University Press).

Clayton, P. (1982) *The Rediscovery of Egypt* (London: Thames and Hudson).

Colletti, L. (1975) *Introduction to Marx's Early Writings* (Harmondsworth: Pelican).

Connell, K. (1968) *Irish Peasant Society* (Oxford: Oxford University Press).

Connolly, J. (1948) *Socialism and Nationalism in Ireland* (Dublin: Three Candles Press).

Connolly, J. (1971) *Labour in Irish History* (Dublin: New Books).

Connolly, S. (1982) *Priests and People in Pre-Famine Ireland 1780–1845* (New York: St. Martin's Press).

Connolly, S. (1995) 'Popular Culture: Patterns of Change and Adaptation', in Connolly, S., Houston, R. and Morris, R. (eds) *Conflict, Identity and Economic Development: Scotland and Ireland 1600–1939* (Preston: Carnegie).

Corbin, A. (1986) *The Foul and the Fragrant* (New York: Berg).

Corkery, D. (1924) *Hidden Ireland* (Dublin: Gill and Macmillan).

Cormack, L. (1997) *Charting an Empire* (Chicago: Chicago University Press).

Cousens, S. (1965) 'Regional Variations in Emigration from Ireland between 1821–1841', Institute of British Geographers, Transactions and Papers, vol. xxxv.

Craske, M. (1997) *Art in Europe, 1700–1830* (Oxford: Oxford University Press).

Crinson, M. (1996) *Empire Building: Orientalism and Victorian Architecture* (London: Routledge).

Cubitt, G. (ed.) (1998) *Imagining Nations* (Manchester: Manchester University Press).

Cullen, F. (1997) *Visual Politics: the Representation of Ireland, 1750–1930* (Cork: Cork University Press).

Curtis, L. (1971) *Apes and Angels* (Newton Abbot: David and Charles).

Daly, E. (1980) 'Priests of Derry, 1820–1905', *Derriana*, Journal of Derry Diocesan Historical Society.

Dangerfield, G. (1979) *The Damnable Question* (London: Quartet).

Daniels, S. (1998) 'Mapping National Identities' in Cubitt, G. (ed.) *Imaging Nations* (Manchester: Manchester University Press).

Davidson, B. (1980) *The African Slave Trade* (New York: Atlantic Little, Brown).

Davies, G. (1983) *Sheets of Many Colours* (Dublin: Royal Dublin Society).

Davis, H.B. (1978) *Nationalism and Socialism: Marxism and Labour Theories of Nationalism to 1917* (New York: Monthly Review Press).

de Cortazar, F. and Espinosa, J. (1994) *Historia del País Vasco* (San Sebastian: Txertoa).

De Paor, M. (1993) 'Irish Antiquarian Artists', in Dalsimer, A. (ed.) *Visualising Ireland* (New York: Faber).

Deutsch, K. (1966) *Nationalism and Social Communication* (New York: MIT Press).

Dewey, C. (1974) 'Celtic Agrarian Legislation and the Celtic Revival', *Past and Present*, vol. 64.

Dijkink, G. (1996) *National Identity and Geopolitical Visions* (London: Routledge).

Doherty, W. (1895) *Inis-Owen and Tirconnell: An Account of Antiquities and Writers* (Dublin: Traynor).

Donnelly, P. (1978) *A History of the Parish of Ardstraw West and Castlederg* (Strabane: Mourne Printers).

Driver, F. (1993) *Power and Pauperism* (Cambridge: Cambridge University Press).

Duden, B. (1992) 'Population', in Sachs, W. (ed.) *Development Dictionary* (London: Zed).

Duffy, C. (1882) *Bird's-Eye View of Irish History* (Dublin: Duffy).

Duffy, P. (1985) 'Carleton, Kavanagh and the South Ulster Landscape', *Irish Geography*, vol. 18.

Duffy, P. (1994) 'The Changing Rural Landscape', in Kearney, B. and Gillespie, R. (eds) *Art Into History* (Dublin: Town House).

Dunne, T. (ed.) (1992) *The Writer as Witness* (Cork: Cork University Press).

Eagleton, T. (1995) *Heathcliff and the Great Hunger* (London: Verso).

Edwards, R.D. (1981) *James Connolly* (Dublin: Gill and Macmillan).

Elias, N. (1978) *The Civilising Process* (London: Blackwell).

Elliot, M. (1982) *Partners in Revolution: The United Irishmen and France* (New Haven: Yale).

Engels, F. (1987) *The Condition of the English Working Class in 1844* (Harmondsworth: Pelican).

Epstein, A.L. (1978) *Ethos and Identity* (London: Tavistock Publications).

Fahy, J. (1901) *Education and the Nation* (Dublin: Catholic Truth Society).

Falkiner, F. (1909) *Literary Miscellanies* (Dublin: Hodges Figgis).

Fitzpatrick, D. (1982) 'Geography of Irish Nationalism', *Past and Present*, no. 78.

Fitzpatrick, D. (1984) *Irish Emigration, 1801–1921* (Dundalgan: Dundalgan Press).

Fitzpatrick, D. (1998) *Politics and Irish Life* (Cork: Cork University Press).

Foster, R. (1988) *Modern Ireland* (London: Penguin).

Fox, E. (1975) *History in Geographic Perspective* (New York: Norton).

Friel, B. (1981) *Translations* (London: Faber).

Fromm, E. (1968) *The Sane Society* (New York: Rheinhart).

Garvin, T. (1981) *Evolution of Irish Nationalist Politics* (Dublin: Gill and Macmillan).

Gellner, E. (1972) *Thought and Change* (New York: World University Press).

Gellner, E. (1983) *Nations and Nationalism* (London: Blackwell).

Genovese, E. (1976) *Roll Jordan, Roll: The World the Slaveholders Made* (New York: Vintage).

Gernon, L. (1620) *A Discourse on Ireland* (Dublin: Ms., National Library).

Geyl, P. (1932) *The Revolt of the Netherlands* (London: William and Norgate).

Gibbon, P. (1979) *The Origins of Ulster Unionism* (Manchester: Manchester University Press).

Giddens, A. (1985) *The Nation State and Violence* (London: Routledge).

Giddens, A., Beck, U. and Lash, S. (1994) *Reflexive Modernisation* (Cambridge: Polity Press).

Gillespie, R. (1986) *Natives and Outsiders* (Dublin: Academic Press).

Gillespie, R. (1993) 'Describing Dublin: Francis Place's Visit, 1698–1699', in Dalsimer, A. (ed.) *Visualising Ireland* (New York: Faber).

Gillespie, R. (1997) *Devoted People: Belief and Religion in Early Modern Ireland* (New York: Manchester University Press).

Good, J. (1919) *Ulster and Ireland* (Dublin: Maunsell).

Gramsci, A. (1957) *The Modern Prince and Other Writings* (New York: International Publications).

Gramsci, A. (1966) *La Questione Meridionale* (Rome: Riuniti).

Gramsci, A. (1971) *Selections from the Prison Notebooks* (London: Lawrence and Wishart).

Gramsci, A. (1977) *Selections from Political Writings* (London: Lawrence and Wishart).

Green, A. (1911) *The Making of Ireland and its Undoing* (Dublin: Duffy).

Griffith, A. (1918) *The Resurrection of Hungary* (Dublin: Duffy).

Gwynn, S. (1899) *Highways and Byways in Donegal and Antrim* (London: Macmillan).

Gwynn, S. (1924) *The History of Ireland* (London: Macmillan).

Hamilton, E. (1917) *The Soul of Ulster* (London: Hurst and Blackett).

Handley, J. (1947) *The Irish in Modern Scotland* (Cork: Cork University Press).

Harkin, M. (1867) *Inishowen: History, Traditions and Antiquities* (Londonderry: Journal Press).

Harrington, J. (1991) *The English Traveller in Ireland* (Dublin: Wolfhound Press).

Harrison, J. (1923) *The Scot in Ulster* (Edinburgh: Blackwood).

Harrison, J. (1977) 'Big Business and The Rise of Basque Nationalism', *European Studies Review*, vol. 7, pp. 371–91.

Harvey, D. (1982) *Limits of Capital* (Oxford: Oxford University Press).

Harvey, D. (1992) *Condition of Postmodernity* (London: Blackwell).

Hayes, C. (1953) *The Historical Evolution of Modern Nationalism* (New York: R.R. Smitty).

Hechter, M. (1975) *Internal Colonialism: The Celtic Fringe in British National Development, 1536–1966* (Berkeley: UCLA Press).

Heiberg, M. (1989) *The Making of the Basque Nation* (Cambridge: Cambridge University Press).

Heiberg, M. and Escudero, M. (1977) 'Sabino de Arana, la logico del nacionalismo', *Materiales*, vol. 5 (Barcelona).

Hill, C. (1967) *Reformation to Industrial Revolution* (Harmondsworth: Pelican).

Hiro, D. (1994) *Between Marx and Mohammed* (London: Harper Collins).

Hobsbawm, E. (1958) *Primitive Rebels* (Manchester: Manchester University Press).

Hobsbawm, E. (1962) *The Age of Revolution, 1789–1848* (New York: Mentor).

Hobsbawm, E. (1969) *Bandits* (Harmondsworth: Pelican).

Hobsbawm, E. (1977) 'Some Reflections on the Break-up of Britain', *New Left Review*, vol. 105.

Hobsbawm, E. (1982) 'Working Classes and Nations', *Saothar*, vol. 7.

Hobsbawm, E. (1988) *The Age of Capital, 1848–1875* (London: Cardinal).

Hobsbawm, E. (1990) *Nations and Nationalism since 1780* (Cambridge: Cambridge University Press).

Hobsbawm, E. (1992) *The Age of Empire* (New Delhi: Rupta Publications).

Hobsbawm, E. and Ranger, T. (1996) *The Invention of Tradition* (Cambridge: Cambridge University Press).

Hofstadter, R. (1955) *Social Darwinism in American Thought* (Boston: Beacon).

Hoppen, K. (1984) *Elections, Politics, and Society in Ireland 1832–1885* (Oxford: Clarendon).

Horne, A. (1984) *The Fall of Paris* (Harmondsworth: Penguin).

Hroch, M. (1985) *Social Conditions of National Revival in Europe* (Cambridge: Cambridge University Press).

Hudson, W. (1979) 'The Historian's Social Function', in Moses, J. (ed.) *Historical Disciplines and Culture in Australia* (Queensland: University of Queensland Press).

Huttenbach, E. (1990) *Society, Nationality, Policies* (London: Mansell).

Ignatieff, M. (1993) *Blood and Belonging: Journeys in the New Nationalism* (London: BBC).

Ignatieff, M. (1998) *The Warrior's Honour* (London: Chatto Windus).

Inglis, T. (1962) *West Briton* (London: Faber).

Isaacs, H. (1975) *The Idols of the Tribe* (New York: Harper and Row).

Johnson, N. (1997) 'Cast in Stone: Monuments, Geography and Nationalism', in Agnew, J. (ed.) *Political Geography* (London: Arnold).

Joll, J. (1977) *Antonio Gramsci* (Harmondsworth: Penguin).

Jordanova, L. (1998) 'Science and Nationhood: Culture of Imagined Communities', in Cubitt, G. (ed.) *Imagining Nations* (Manchester: Manchester University Press).

Kearney, B. and Gillespie, R. (eds) (1994) *Art into History* (London: Town House).

Kedouri, E. (1960) *Nationalism* (London: Hutchinson).

Keep, G. (1954) 'Official Opinion on Irish Emigration in the Later Nineteenth Century', *Irish Ecclesiastical Record*, vol. lxxxi.

Kelly, F. (1993) 'Fancis Wheatley', in Dalsimer, A. (ed.) *Visualising Ireland* (New York: Faber).

Kenny, M. (1997) *Goodbye to Catholic Ireland* (London: Random House).

Kerr, B. (1943) 'Irish Seasonal Migration to Britain, 1800–1830', *Irish Historical Studies*, vol. 3, no. 43.

Kiberd, D. (1995) *Inventing Ireland* (London: Cape).

Kiernan, V. (1972) *The Lords of Humankind* (Harmondsworth: Pelican).

Kohn, H. (1955) *Nationalism: Its Meaning in History* (Princeton: Van Nostrand Press).

Konvitz, J. (1987) *Cartography in France, 1600–1848* (Chicago: Chicago University Press)

Kropotkin, P. (1930) *Memoirs of a Revolutionist* (Boston: Houghton Mifflin).

Kropotkin, P. (1939) *Mutual Aid* (Harmondsworth: Pelican).

Landsberger, H.A. (1974) *Rural Protest: Peasant Movements and Social Change* (London: Kegan Paul).

Larkin, E. (1972) 'The Devotional Revolution in Ireland, 1850–1875', *American Historical Review*, vol. 77, no. 3.

Laski, H. (1944) *Faith, Reason and Civilization* (London: Gollancz).

Lecky, G. (1908) *In the Days of the Laggan Presbytery* (Dublin: Maunsell).

Lee, A. (1980) *The Origins of the Popular Press, 1855–1914* (London: Croom Helm).

Lee, J. (1981) *The Modernisation of Irish Society* (Dublin: Gill and Macmillan).

Lee, J. (1993) *Ireland 1912–1985* (Cambridge: Cambridge University Press).

Leerssen, J. (1996) *Remembrance and Imagination* (Cork: Cork University Press).

Legg, M.L. (1999) *Newspapers and Nationalism* (Dublin: Four Courts Press).

Lenin, V.I. (1966) *Imperialism* (Peking: Foreign Language Press).

Levi, C. (1982) *Christ Stopped at Eboli* (Harmondsworth: Penguin).

Lewis, A. (1958) 'The Closing of the European Frontier', *Speculum*, vol. xxxiii.

Lloyd, D. (1993) *Anomalous States* (Dublin: Lilliput).

Lloyd, D. (1997) 'Outside History: Irish New Histories and the "Subalternity Effect"', in Amin, S. and Chakrabarty, D. (eds) *Subaltern Studies IX: Writings on South Asian History* (New Delhi: Oxford).

Lovell, T. (1980) 'The Social Relations of Cultural Production', in Clarke, S. et al. (eds) *One Dimensional Marxism* (London: Allison and Busby).

Lydon, J. (1984) *The English in Medieval Ireland* (Dublin: Macmillan).

Lyons, F.S.L. (1985) *Ireland Since the Famine* (London: Fontana).

McClintock, A. (1995) *Imperial Leather: Race, Gender and Sexuality in the Colonial Conquest* (New York: Routledge).

Macfarlane, C. (1833) *The Lives and Exploits of Banditi and Robbers in all Parts of the World* (London: Edward Nelson).

Mackenzie, J. (1986) *Imperialism and Popular Culture* (Manchester: Manchester University Press).

Mac Laughlin, J. (1980) 'Industrial Capitalism, Ulster Unionism and Orangeism', *Antipode*, Radical Journal of Geography, vol. 12, no. 1.

Mac Laughlin, J. (1983) 'Ulster Unionist Hegemony and Regional Industrial Policy in Northern Ireland, 1945–1972', Occasional Papers Series, no. 81, Department of Geography, Syracuse University, New York.

Mac Laughlin, J. (1985) 'Regional Social History, the Nationalist and the Famine', *Journal of Northwest Archaeological and Historical Society*, vol. 1, no. 1.

Mac Laughlin, J. (1986a) 'The Political Geography of Nation-Building and Nationalism in Social Sciences: Structural Versus Dialectical Accounts', *Political Geography*, vol. 5, no. 4.

Mac Laughlin, J. (1986b) State-Centred Social Science and the Anarchist Critique: Ideology in Political Geography', *Antipode*, Radical Journal of Geography, vol. 18, no. 1.

Mac Laughlin, J. (1987) 'Nationalism as an Autonomous Social Force: Critique of Recent Scholarship on Ethnonationalism', *Canadian Review of Studies in Nationalism*, vol. xiv, no. 1.

Mac Laughlin, J. (1988) 'Reflections on Nations as Imagined Communities', *Journal of Multicultural and Multilingual Development*, vol. 9.

Mac Laughlin, J. (1990) 'Difficulties in Dating Nations', *Journal of Multilingual and Multicultural Matters*, vol. 11, no. 6.

Mac Laughlin, J. (1993a) 'Towards a Critical Political Geography of Irish Partition', *Espace, Populations, Societies*.

Mac Laughlin, J. (1993b) 'Place, Politics and Culture in Nation-building Ulster: Constructing Nationalist Hegemony in Post-Famine Donegal', *Canadian Review of Studies in Nationalism*, vol. XX, nos. 1–2.

Mac Laughlin, J. (1994a) *Ireland: the Emigrant Nursery and the World Economy* (Cork: Cork University Press).

Mac Laughlin, J. (1994b) 'Emigration and the Peripheralization of Ireland in the Global Economy', *Review Journal of the Fernand Braudel Center*, vol. xvii, no. 2.

Mac Laughlin, J. (1995a) *Travellers and Ireland: Whose History, Whose Country?* (Cork: Cork University Press).

Mac Laughlin, J. (1995b) 'The Politics of Nation-building in Post-Famine Donegal', in Nolan, W. et al. (eds) *Donegal: History and Society* (Dublin: Geography Publications).

Mac Laughlin, J. (1996) 'The Evolution of Anti-Traveller Racism in Ireland' *Race and Class*, vol. 37, no. 3.

Mac Laughlin, J. (1997a) 'The Devaluation of Nation as "Home" and the De-politicisation of Irish Emigration', in Mac Laughlin, J. (ed.) *Location and Dislocation in Contemporary Irish Society: Emigration and Irish Identities* (Cork: Cork University Press).

Mac Laughlin, J. (1997b) 'The Political Geography of Anti-Traveller Racism in Ireland: The Geography of Closure and the Politics of Exclusion', *Political Geography*, vol. 17, no. 4, pp. 417–35.

Mac Laughlin, J. (1997c) 'European Gypsies and the Historical Geography of Loathing', *Review Journal of the Fernand Braudel Center*, vol. xxii, no. 1.

Mac Laughlin, J. (1997d) 'Emigration and the Construction of Nationalist Hegemony in Ireland: The Historical Background to "New Wave" Irish Emigration', in Mac Laughlin, J. (ed.) *Location and Dislocation in Contemporary Irish Society: Emigration and Irish Identities* (Cork: Cork University Press).

Mac Laughlin, J. (1997e) 'The Gypsy as "Other" in European Society: Towards a Political Geography of Hate', *The European Legacy*, vol. 4, no. 3.

Mac Laughlin, J. (1998) 'Racism, Ethnicity and Multiculturalism in Contemporary Europe', *Political Geography*, vol. 17, no. 8.

Mac Laughlin, J. (1999a) Review, *Dublin Slums 1800–1925*, Prunty, J. (Dublin: Irish Academic Press), *Irish Studies Review*, vol. 7, no. 2.

Mac Laughlin, J. (1999b) 'Nation-building, Social Closure and anti-Traveller Racism in Ireland', *Sociology: Journal of British Sociological Association*, vol. 33, no. 1.

Mac Laughlin, J. (1999c) 'Sixteenth Century English Geographers: Earth Scientists as an Organic Intelligentsia', *The European Legacy*, vol. 4, no. 2.

Mac Laughlin, J. (1999d) 'The Evolution of Modern Demography and the Debate on Sustainable Development', *Antipode*, Radical Journal of Geography, vol. 31, no. 3.

Mac Laughlin, J. (1999e) 'The New Intelligentsia and the Reconstruction of the Irish Nation', *The Irish Review*, vol 24, pp. 53–66.

Mac Laughlin, J. (1999f) '"Pestilence on their Backs, Famine in their Stomachs": The Racial Construction of Irishness and the Irish in

Victorian Britain', in Graham, C. and Kirkland, R. (eds) *Cultural Theory and Ireland* (London: Macmillan).

Mac Laughlin, J. and Agnew, J. (1986) 'Hegemony and the Regional Question: The Political Geography of Regional Industrial Policy in Northern Ireland', *Annals of the Association of American Geographers*, vol. 76, no. 2.

Magdoff, H. (1978) *Imperialism: From the Colonial Age to the Present* (New York: Norton).

Margadant, T. (1979) *French Peasants in Revolt* (Princeton: Princeton University Press).

Marx, K. (1950) 'The Class Struggles in France 1848–1850', in Marx, K. and Engels, F., *Selected Works* (London: Lawrence and Wishart).

Marx, K. (1962) *The Poverty of Philosophy* (Moscow: Foreign Languages Press).

Marx, K. and Engels, F. (1974) *The German Ideology* (London: Lawrence and Wishart).

Marx, K. and Engels, F. (1976) *On Colonialism* (London: Lawrence and Wishart).

Marx, K. and Engels, F. (1987) *On Colonialism* (London: Lawrence and Wishart).

Maurice, J. (1886) *Letters from Donegal* (London: Duffy).

Medhurst, K. (1982) *The Basques* (London: Minority Rights Report).

Meinig, D. (1986) *The Shaping of America* (New Haven: Yale).

Migdal, J. (1974) *Peasants, Politics and Revolution* (Princeton: Princeton University Press).

Mill, J. (1946) *Considerations on Representative Government* (London: Routledge).

Miller, K. (1985) *Emigrants and Exiles* (New York: Oxford).

Mills, C. Wright (1963) *Power, Politics and People* (New York: Oxford University Press).

Mitchell, F. (1976) *The Irish Landscape* (London: Collins).

Moore, Barrington (1966) *Social Origins of Dictatorship and Democracy* (Boston: Beacon).

Morgan, E. (1975) *American Slavery, American Freedom* (New York: Norton).

Munter, R. (1967) *History of the Irish Newspaper* (Cambridge: Cambridge University Press).

Murphy, T. (1912) *The Literature Crusade in Ireland* (Limerick: Catholic Truth Society).

Nairn, T. (1977) *The Break-up of Britain* (London: New Left Books).

Newman, J. (1851) *Lecture on the Present Condition of Catholics in England* (London: Edwards).

O'Ceallaigh, D. (1994) *Reconsiderations of Irish History and Culture* (Dublin: Leirmheas).

O'Danacher, C. (1978) *Ireland's Vernacular Architecture* (Cork: Mercier Press).

O'Driscoll, R. (1971) *Theatre and Nationalism in Twentieth Century Ireland* (London: Routledge).

O'Faolain, S. (1980) *King of the Beggars* (Dublin: Poolbeg).

O'Farrell, P. (1975) *England and Ireland since 1800* (Oxford: Oxford University Press).

O'Gallchobair, P. (1975) *History of Landlordism in Donegal* (Ballyshannon: Donegal Democrat).

O'Giolláin, D. (2000) *Locating Ireland* (Cork: Cork University Press).

O'Grada, C. (1973) 'Seasonal Migration and Post-Famine Adjustment in the West of Ireland', *Studia Hibernia*, vol. xxxiii.

O'Neill, K. (1993) 'Looking at the Pictures: Art and Artfulness in Colonial Ireland', in Dalsimer, A. (ed.) *Visualising Ireland* (New York: Faber).

O'Riordan, M. (1905) *Catholicity and Progress in Ireland* (London: Kegan Paul).

O'Shea, J. (1983) *Priests and People in Post-Famine Tipperary* (Dublin: Wolfhound Press).

O'Tuathail, G. (1996) *Critical Geopolitics* (London: Routledge).

Patterson, H. (1980) *Class Conflict and Sectarianism* (Belfast: Blackstaff).

Payne, S. (1974) *Basque Nationalism* (New York: Norton).

Peet, R. (1985) 'Social Origins of Environmental Determinism', *Annals of the Association of American Geographers*, vol. 75, no. 1.

Peet, R. (1986) 'The Destruction of Regional Cultures', in Johnston, R. and Taylor, P. (eds) *A World in Crisis* (London: Blackwell).

Petition of Soldiers (1655) (Dublin: Ms., National Library).

Phelan, M. (1913) 'A Gaelicized or Socialized Ireland – Which?', *The Catholic Bulletin*.

Pike, F. (1997) *The United States and Latin America: Myths and Stereotypes of Civilization and Nature* (New York: Norton).

Poliakov, L. (1974) *The Aryan Myth* (London: Chatto and Windus).

Pollard, H. (1923) *The Secret Societies of Ireland* (London: Phillip Allan).

Quinn, D. (1966) *The Elizabethans in Ireland* (Cornell: Cornell University Press).

Quinn, D. (1967) 'Ireland and Sixteenth Century European Expansion', in Williams, D. (ed.) *Historical Studies* (London: Bowes and Bowes).

Quinn, Q. (1976) 'Renaissance Influences in English Colonisation', *Transactions of the Royal Historical Society*, vol. 26.

Rahnema, A. (1994) *Pioneers of Islamic Revival* (London: Zed Press).

Ratzel, F. (1898) 'The Territorial Growth of States', *Scottish Geographical Magazine*, vol. 12.

Reclus, E. (1876) *Nouvelle Geographie Universelle* (Paris: Hachette).

Regan, C. (1980) 'Economic Development in Ireland', *Antipode*, vol. 11, no. 2.

Rehfisch, F. (1975) *Gypsies, Tinkers and Other Travellers* (London: Academic Press).

Renan, E. (1882) *Qu'est ce que une nation?* (Paris: Pleiade).

Richards, D. (1994) *Masks of Difference* (Cambridge: Cambridge University Press).

Rietbergen, P. (1998) *Europe: A Cultural History* (London: Routledge).

Rowse, A.L. (1957) 'Tudor Expansion: Transition from Medieval to Modern History', *William and Mary Quarterly*, vol. xiv.

Rowse, A.L. (1973) *The Expansion of Elizabethan England* (London: Cardinal).

Rude, G. (1964) *The Crowd in History* (New York: Wiley).

Rude, G. (1980) *Ideology and Popular Protest* (New York: Pantheon).

Russell, B. (1965) *Freedom versus Organisation* (London: Allen and Unwin).

Said, E. (1991) *Orientalism* (Harmondsworth: Pelican).

Said, E. (1994) *Culture and Imperialism* (London: Verso).

Santayana, G. (1905) *The Life of Reason* (London: Constable).

Scott, J. (1976) *The Moral Economy of the Peasant* (New Haven: Yale).

Semple, E. (1911) *Influences of Geographic Environment* (London: Constable).

Seton-Watson, H. (1977) *Nations and States* (London: Methuen).

Sheehy, J. (1980) *The Rediscovery of Ireland's Past* (London: Thames and Hudson).

Slater, E. and McDonough, T. (1994) 'Bulwark of Landlordism and Capitalism: Dynamics of Feudalism in Nineteenth Century Ireland', *Research in Political Economy*, vol. 14.

Smith, A.D. (1971) *Theories of Nationalism* (London: Duckworth).

Smith, A.D. (1972) *The Wealth of Nations* (Harmondsworth: Penguin).

Smith, A.D. (1979) *The Newspaper: An International History* (London: Thames and Hudson).

Smith, A.D. (1981) *The Ethnic Revival* (Cambridge: Cambridge University Press).

Smith, A.D. (1984) 'Ethnic Myths and Ethnic Revivals', *European Journal of Sociology*, vol. 22, pp. 283–305.

Smith, A.D. (1986) *The Ethnic Origin of Nations* (London: Blackwell).

Smith, A.D. (1996a) 'Chosen Peoples', in Hutchinson, J. and Smith, A.D. (eds) *Ethnicity* (Oxford: Oxford University Press).

Smith, A.D. (1996b) 'Nationalism and the Historians', in Balakrishnan, G. and Anderson, B. (eds) *Mapping and the Nation* (London: Verso).

Smyth, W.J. (1988) 'Society and Settlement in Seventeenth Century Ireland – the Relevance of "The 1659 Census"', in Smyth, W.J. and Whelan, K. (eds) *Common Ground* (Cork: Cork University Press).

Smyth, W.J. (1992) 'Making the Documents of Conquest Speak', in Gulliver, P. and Silverman, M. (eds) *Approaching the Past: Historical Anthropology through Irish Case Studies* (New York: Columbia University Press).

Smyth, W.J. (1997) 'A Plurality of Irelands', in Graham, B. (ed.) *In Search of Ireland* (London: Routledge).

Snyder, L. (1954) *The Meaning of Nationalism* (New Brunswick: Rutgers).

Soboul, A. (1964) *The Parisian Sans Culottes and the French Revolution, 1893–94* (Oxford: Clarendon).

Spenser, E. (1596) *View of the Present State of Ireland* (London: Lawrence Finn).

Springhall. J. (1986) 'Up Guards and At Them', in Mackenzie, J. (ed.) *Imperialism and Popular Culture* (Manchester: Manchester University Press).

Stalin, J. (1953) *Marxism and the National Question* (Moscow: Progress Press).

Stewart, A.T.Q. (1967) *The Narrow Ground* (London: Faber).

Stoddart, R. (1986) *On Geography and its History* (Oxford: Blackwell).

Stoler, A. (1995) *Race and the Education of Desire* (Durham: Duke University Press).

Strauss, E. (1951) *Irish Nationalism and British Democracy* (London: F.G. James).

Suny, R.G. (1994) *Revenge of the Past: Nationalism, Revolution and the Collapse of the Soviet Union* (Stanford: Stanford University Press).

Taylor, P. (1993) *Political Geography: World Economy, Nation-state and Locality* (Harlow: Longman).

Thackery, W. (1887) *The Irish Sketchbook* (London: Smith, Elder and Co.).

Thompson, E.P. (1968) *The Making of the English Working Class* (Harmondsworth: Pelican).

Thompson, E.P. (1971) 'The Moral Economy of the English Crowd in the Eighteenth Century', *Past and Present*, no. 50.

Thompson, E.P. (1975) *Whigs and Hunters* (New York: Pantheon).

Thompson, E.P. (1978) *The Poverty of Theory* (New York: Monthly Review Press).

Tilly, C. (ed.) (1975) *The Formation of National States in Europe* (Princeton: Princeton University Press).

Tilly, C. (1978) *From Mobilization to Revolution* (Reading: Archon).

Tukes, J.H. (1889) *Donegal: Suggestions for Improvement of Congested Districts and Extension of Railways, Fisheries etc.* (Dublin: Hodges and Figgis).

Vaughan, W. (1977) 'Landlord and Tenant Relations in Ireland between the Famine and the Land War', in Cullen, L. and Smout, T., *Comparative Aspects of Scottish and Irish Economic and Social History* (Edinburgh: John Donald).

Vaughan, W. (1984) *Sin, Sheep and Scotsmen* (Belfast: Appletree).

Viroli, M. (1997) *For Love of Country* (Oxford: Oxford University Press).

Wallerstein, I. (1974) *The Modern World System I* (New York: Academic Press).

Warner, M. (1983) *Joan of Arc* (Harmondsworth: Penguin).

Weber, E. (1972) *Europe since 1715* (New York: Norton).

Weber, E. (1977) *Peasants into Frenchmen* (California: Stanford University Press).

Weber, M. (1978) *Economy and Society* (Berkeley: University of California Press).

Whelan, K. (1983) 'Catholic Parish, Catholic Church and Village Development in Ireland', *Irish Geography*, vol. 16.

Whelan, K. (1985) 'The Catholic Church in Co. Tipperary, 1700–1900', in Nolan, W. (ed.) *Tipperary: History and Society* (Dublin: Geography Publications).

Whelan, K. (1996) *Tree of Liberty* (Cork: Cork University Press).

Whelan, K. (1998) *Fellowship of Freedom* (Cork: Cork University Press).

Williams, C. (ed.) (1982) *National Separatism* (Cardiff: University of Wales Press).

Williams, C. (1984a) 'Minority Groups in the Modern State', in Pacione, M. (ed.) *Progress in Human Geography* (London: Croom Helm).

Williams, C. (1984b) 'Ideology in the Interpretation of Minority Cultures', *Political Geography Quarterly*, vol. 3, no. 2.

Williams, C. and Smith, A. (1983) 'The National Construction of Social Space', *Progress in Human Geography*, vol. 7.

Williams, G. (1985) *When Was Wales* (Harmondsworth: Pelican).

Williams, R. (1980) *Problems in Materialism and Culture* (London: Verso).

Williams, R. (1981) *Culture* (London: Fontana).

Wilson, W. (1976) *Folklore and Nationalism in Modern Finland* (Bloomington: Indiana University Press).

Wolf, E. (1973) *Peasant Wars of the Twentieth Century* (New York: Norton).

Wolf, E. (1985) *Europe's People Without a History* (London: Allison and Busby).

Index